ACCA

PAPER P2

CORPORATE REPORTING
(INTERNATIONAL)

P R A C T I C E & R E V I S I O N K I T

In this January 2010 edition

- We discuss the **best strategies** for revising and taking your ACCA exams

- We show you how to be **well prepared** for your exam

- We give you **lots of great guidance** on tackling questions

- We show you how you can **build your own exams**

- We provide you with **three** mock exams including the **December 2009 exam**

- We provide the **ACCA examiner's answers** as well as our own to the June and December 2009 exams as an additional revision aid

Our **i-Pass** product also supports this paper.

FOR EXAMS IN 2010

First edition 2007
Fifth edition January 2010

ISBN 9780 7517 8060 4
(previous ISBN 9780 7517 6667 7)

e-ISBN 9780 7517 8254 7

British Library Cataloguing-in-Publication Data
A catalogue record for this book
is available from the British Library

Published by

BPP Learning Media Ltd
BPP House, Aldine Place
London W12 8AA

www.bpp.com/learningmedia

Printed in the United Kingdom

We are grateful to the Association of Chartered Certified
Accountants for permission to reproduce past
examination questions. The suggested answers have
been prepared by BPP Learning Media Ltd, except where
otherwise stated.

Your learning materials, published by BPP Learning
Media Ltd, are printed on paper sourced from
sustainable, managed forests.

ii

Contents

	Page
Finding questions	
Question index	iv
Topic index	viii
Using your BPP Practice and Revision Kit	ix
Passing P2	
Revising P2	x
Passing the P2 exam	xi
Exam information	xiii
Exam update	xvi
Useful websites	xxi
Planning your question practice	
BPP's question plan	xxii
Build your own exams	xxv
Questions and answers	
Questions	3
Answers	87
Exam practice	
Mock exam 1	
• Questions	267
• Plan of attack	277
• Answers	278
Mock exam 2	
• Questions	291
• Plan of attack	301
• Answers	304
Mock exam 3 (December 2009)	
• Questions	317
• Plan of attack	327
• Answers	329
ACCA examiner's answers	
• June 2009	347
• December 2009	359
Mathematical tables	371
Review form & free prize draw	

Question index

The headings in this checklist/index indicate the main topics of questions, but questions often cover several different topics.

Questions set under the old syllabus *Advanced Corporate Reporting* paper are included because their style and content are similar to those which appear in the P2 exam. The questions have been amended to reflect the current exam format.

	Marks	Time allocation Mins	Page number Question	Page number Answer
Part A: Regulatory and ethical framework				
Financial reporting framework				
1 Conceptual framework (12/07)	25	45	3	87
2 Accounting standards and disclosure (12/08)	25	45	3	89
Environmental and social reporting				
3 Glowball (ACR, Pilot paper)	25	45	3	92
Part B: Accounting standards				
Non-current assets				
4 Prochain (ACR, 6/06)	25	45	5	94
5 Johan (12/08)	25	45	6	96
Employee benefits				
6 Preparation question: Defined benefit scheme	–	–	7	99
7 Macaljoy (12/07)	25	45	9	100
8 Savage (ACR, 12/05)	25	45	10	104
9 Smith (6/09)	25	45	11	105
Income taxes				
10 Cohort (ACR, 6/02)	25	45	12	108
11 Panel (ACR, 12/05)	25	45	13	109
12 Kesare (Pilot paper)	25	45	14	112
Financial instruments				
13 Preparation question: Financial instruments	–	–	15	114
14 Ambush (ACR, 12/05)	25	45	16	114
15 Wader (ACR, 6/07)	25	45	16	117
16 Sirus (6/08)	25	45	17	120
17 Aron (6/09)	25	45	19	123
Share-based payment				
18 Vident (ACR, 6/05)	25	45	20	128
19 Leigh (ACR, 6/07)	25	45	21	130
Events after reporting period, provisions and contingencies				
20 Ryder (ACR, 12/05)	25	45	22	133
21 Electron (Pilot paper)	25	45	23	135

		Marks	Time allocation Mins	Page number Question	Answer

Related parties

		Marks	Time allocation Mins	Page number Question	Answer
22	Egin Group (ACR, 6/06)	25	45	24	138
23	Engina (ACR, Pilot paper)	25	45	25	140

Leases

		Marks	Time allocation Mins	Page number Question	Answer
24	Preparation question: Leases	–	–	26	142

Part C: Group financial statements

Revision of basic groups

		Marks	Time allocation Mins	Page number Question	Answer
25	Marrgrett (12/08)	25	45	27	143
26	Preparation question: Associate	–	–	28	146

Complex groups

		Marks	Time allocation Mins	Page number Question	Answer
27	Preparation question: 'D'-shaped group	–	–	29	148
28	X Group	30	54	30	151
29	Glove (ACR, 6/07, amended)	25	45	31	154
30	Case study question: Rod	50	90	33	159
31	Case study question: Exotic	50	90	35	165

Changes in group structures

		Marks	Time allocation Mins	Page number Question	Answer
32	Preparation question: Part disposal	–	–	37	170
33	Ejoy (ACR, 6/06, amended)	25	45	39	172
34	Case study question: Bravado (6/09)	50	90	40	176
35	Case study question: Base Group	50	90	42	182
36	Case study question: Beth (12/07, amended)	50	90	45	187

Foreign transactions and entities

		Marks	Time allocation Mins	Page number Question	Answer
37	Preparation question: Foreign operation	–	–	47	193
38	Memo (ACR, 6/04, amended)	32	58	49	195
39	Case study question: Ribby (6/08, amended)	50	90	51	199

Group statements of cash flows

		Marks	Time allocation Mins	Page number Question	Answer
40	Preparation question: Consolidated statement of cash flows	–	–	53	206
41	Portal (ACR, Pilot Paper, amended)	25	45	56	207
42	Case study question: Andash	50	90	58	210
43	Case study question: Squire	50	90	61	215
44	Case study question: Zambeze (Pilot paper, amended)	50	90	63	219
45	Case study question: Warrburt (12/08)	50	90	66	223

Part D: Performance reporting

Performance reporting

		Marks	Time allocation Mins	Page number Question	Answer
46	Mineral (ACR, 12/01)	25	45	70	227
47	Value relevance (ACR, 12/02)	25	45	71	230
48	Rockby and Bye (ACR, 6/04, amended)	19	35	72	232
49	Ashlee (ACR, 6/05)	25	45	73	234
50	Enterprise (ACR, 6/04, amended)	25	45	74	236
51	Carpart (6/09)	25	45	75	239
52	Tyre (ACR, 6/06)	25	45	76	242
53	Ghorse (12/07)	25	45	77	244

		Time allocation	Page number	
	Marks	Mins	Question	Answer
Current developments and implications of changes				
54 Handrew (ACR, 6/05)	25	45	78	247
55 Fair values (ACR, 6/07)	25	45	80	250
56 Implementing IFRS (6/08)	25	45	80	253
Specialised entities				
57 IFRS and SMEs (ACR, 6/06, amended)	25	45	80	255
58 Seejoy (ACR, 12/06)	25	45	81	258
59 Norman (6/08)	25	45	82	260

Mock exam 1

60   Jay (ACR 6/05, amended)
61   Router (ACR, 6/07)
62   Gear Software (ACR 6/03)
63   Autol (ACR 12/02)

Mock exam 2

64   Lateral (ACR 12/05, amended)
65   Barking (ACR 12/03)
66   Gow (ACR 12/06, amended)
67   Jones and Cousin (ACR 12/06)

Mock exam 3 (December 2009)

68   Grange
69   Key
70   Burley
71   Financial instruments and complexity

Planning your question practice

Our guidance from page xxii shows you how to organise your question practice, either by attempting questions from each syllabus area or **by building your own exams** – tackling questions as a series of practice exams.

ACCA examiner's answers

The ACCA examiner's answers to questions marked '**Pilot paper**', '**12/07**', '**6/08**' or '**12/08**' can be found on the BPP website at the following link:

www.bpp.com/acca/examiner-solutions

Additional question guidance

Additional guidance to certain questions can be found on the BPP website at the following link:

www.bpp.com/acca/extra-question-guidance

Using your BPP Learning Media products

This Kit gives you the question practice and guidance you need in the exam. Our other products can also help you pass:

- **Learning to Learn Accountancy** gives further valuable advice on revision
- **Passcards** provide you with clear topic summaries and exam tips
- **Success CDs** help you revise on the move
- **i-Pass CDs** offer tests of knowledge against the clock

You can purchase these products by visiting www.bpp.com/mybpp.

You can view demonstrations of i-Learn and i-Pass products by visiting www.bpp.com/acca/study-materials/#ilearn. Scroll down the page until you find the sections for i-Learn and i-Pass and click on the appropriate 'View demo' button.

Topic index

Listed below are the key Paper P2 syllabus topics and the numbers of the questions in this Kit covering those topics.

If you need to concentrate your practice and revision on certain topics or if you want to attempt all available questions that refer to a particular subject, you will find this index useful.

Syllabus topic	Question numbers
Associates	26
Consolidated statement of financial position	30, 31
Consolidated statement of comprehensive income	38
Consolidated statement of cash flows	40 – 44
Corporate citizenship	46
Disposals	32 – 35
Employee benefits	6 – 9
Environmental issues	3
Ethics	42 – 45
Financial instruments	13 – 17
Foreign currency	37 – 39
IAS 1 (revised)	Throughout
Impairment	45, 55
International issues	54 – 56
IFRS 2	18, 19
IFRS 3	25 – 45
Joint ventures	33
Measurement of performance	50
Multi-company structure	27 – 31
Non-current assets	4, 5
Provisions	20, 21
Related party transactions	22, 23
Reporting performance	50
Revenue recognition	5, 51, 52
Share-based payment	18, 19
Taxation	10 – 12

Using your BPP Practice and Revision Kit

Tackling revision and the exam

You can significantly improve your chances of passing by tackling revision and the exam in the right ways. Our advice is based on feedback from ACCA examiners.

- We look at the dos and don'ts of revising for, and taking, ACCA exams
- We focus on Paper P2; we discuss revising the syllabus, what to do (and what not to do) in the exam, how to approach different types of question and ways of obtaining easy marks

Selecting questions

We provide signposts to help you plan your revision.

- A full **question index**
- A **topic index** listing all the questions that cover key topics, so that you can locate the questions that provide practice on these topics, and see the different ways in which they might be examined
- **BPP's question plan** highlighting the most important questions and explaining why you should attempt them
- **Build your own exams**, showing how you can practise questions in a series of exams

Making the most of question practice

At BPP Learning Media we realise that you need more than just questions and model answers to get the most from your question practice.

- Our **Top tips** included for certain questions provide essential advice on tackling questions, presenting answers and the key points that answers need to include
- We show you how you can pick up **Easy marks** on some questions, as we know that picking up all readily available marks often can make the difference between passing and failing
- We include **marking guides** to show you what the examiner rewards
- We include **examiners' comments** to show you where students struggled or performed well in the actual exam
- We refer to the **2009 BPP Study Text** (for exams in December 2009 and June 2010) for detailed coverage of the topics covered in questions
- In a bank at the end of this Kit we include the **examiner's answers** to the June and December 2009 papers. Used in conjunction with our answers they provide an indication of all possible points that could be made, issues that could be covered and approaches to adopt.

Attempting mock exams

There are three mock exams that provide practice at coping with the pressures of the exam day. We strongly recommend that you attempt them under exam conditions. **Mock exams 1 and 2** reflect the question styles and syllabus coverage of the exam; **Mock exam 3** is the December 2009 paper.

Revising P2

BPP Learning Media is committed to giving you the best possible support in your quest for exam success. With this in mind, we have produced **guidance** on how to revise and techniques you can apply to **improve your chances of passing** the exam. This guidance can be found on the BPP Learning Media web site at the following link:

www.bpp.co/acca/examtips/Revising-for-ACCA-exams.doc

A paper copy of this guidance is available by emailing learningmedia@bpp.com

Topics to revise

P2 – or its old syllabus equivalent – has the reputation of being a difficult paper. However its pass rate is usually quite high. Although the examiner, Graham Holt, sets challenging questions, the styles of question he uses are now familiar because he has been the examiner for many years. He has also provided a great deal of feedback in his examiner's reports and in the very detailed published marking schemes, many of which are included in this Kit.

Graham Holt has warned very strongly against question-spotting and trying to predict the topics that will be included in the exam. He has on occasions examined the same topic in two successive sittings. He regards few areas as off-limits for questions, and nearly all of the major areas of the syllabus can and have been tested.

That said, exams over the years have shown that the following areas of the syllabus are very important, and your revision therefore needs to cover them particularly well.

- **Group accounts.** You should not omit any aspect of group accounts, as they come up every sitting. We would advise against question spotting, but if a statement of cash flows, say, has not come up for a few sittings, it might be a good bet. Group accounts will always be examined as part of the 50 mark case study question, in which you may also expect a question on some aspect of **ethics**

- **Emerging issues.** The impact of a change in accounting standards on the financial statements is often examined.

- **Share based payment** usually comes up as part of a question.

- **Financial instruments** was the subject of a *Student Accountant* article, so is ripe for examination.

- **Developments in financial reporting**, for example, the new IFRS for Small and Medium-sized Entities.

Question practice

Question practice under timed conditions is essential, so that you can get used to the pressures of answering exam questions in **limited time** and practise not only the key techniques but allocating your time between different requirements in each question. Our list of recommended questions includes compulsory Section A and optional Section B questions; it's particularly important to do all the Section A case-study-style questions in full as a case study involving group accounts will always come up.

Passing the P2 exam

What to expect on the paper

Of course you cannot know in advance what questions are going to come up, but you can have a fair idea of what kind of questions.

Question 1

This will always be a case study, with half or a little more than half on group accounts. It will often involve high speed number crunching. Easy marks, it cannot be said too often, will always be available for basic consolidation techniques. You cannot pass the groups part on these alone, but it can give you a foothold. Question 1 usually has a bit of a twist, for example financial instruments or pensions. This question will also contain an element of written explanation and a question on ethics or corporate social accounting. For example, the June 2009 paper had a business combination achieved in stages; then you were asked to explain whether a loan to a director was ethical.

Questions 2 and 3

These are very often – although not always - multi-standard, mini-case-studies, involving you in giving advice to the directors on accounting treatment, possibly where the directors have followed the wrong treatment. Being multi-standard, you may be able to answer parts, but not all of a question, so it makes sense to look through the paper to select a question where you can answer most of it. If Part (a) is on an area you are not confident about, do not dismiss the question out of hand.

The examiner is testing whether you can identify the issues. Even if you don't get the accounting treatment exactly right, you will still gain some credit for showing that you have seen what the problem is about. So do not be afraid to have a stab at something, even if you are not sure of the details.

Question 4

This question is generally on developments in financial reporting. It is usually general in nature, rather than linked to a specific accounting standard. It may cover an aspect of reporting financial performance – for example the Management Commentary. It may also cover performance measures, small company reporting, EBITDA or the environment. In December 2008 Paper, Question 4 asked about the importance of disclosure in accounting standards and whether it is always a good thing.

While you certainly cannot bluff your way through Question 4, if you know your material it is a good way of earning marks without high speed number crunching.

Question 4 may now include a computational aspect illustrating the topic you have just discussed.

Exam technique for P2

Do not be needlessly intimidated

There is no shortcut to passing this exam. It looks very difficult indeed, and many students wonder if they will ever pass. But most students generally do. Why is this?

Easy marks

All the questions are demanding, but there are many easy marks to be gained. Suppose, for example, you had a consolidated statement of cash flows with a disposal, a pension complication and a financial instruments calculation. There will be easy marks available simply for the basic cash flow aspects, setting out the proforma, setting up your workings, presenting your work neatly. If you recognise, as you should, that the disposal needs to be taken into account, of course you will get marks for that, even if you make a mistake in the arithmetic. If you get the pension bit right, so much the better, but you could pass the question comfortably while omitting this altogether. If you're short of time, this is what you should do.

Be ruthless in ignoring the complications

Look at the question. Within reason, if there are complications – often only worth a few marks – that you know you will not have time or knowledge to do, cross them out. It will make you feel better. Than tackle the bits you can do. This is how people pass a seemingly impossible paper.

Be ruthless in allocating your time

At BPP, we have seen how very intelligent students do two almost perfect questions, one averagely good and one sketchy. The first eight to ten marks are the easiest to get. Then you have to push it up to what you think is fifteen (thirty for the case study question), to get yourself a pass.

Do your best question either first or second, and the compulsory question either first or second. The compulsory question, being on groups, will always have some easy marks available for consolidation techniques.

Exam information

Format of the exam

		Number of marks
Section A:	1 compulsory case study	50
Section B:	Choice of 2 from 3 questions (25 marks each)	50
		100

Section A will consist of one scenario based question worth 50 marks. It will deal with the preparation of consolidated financial statements including group statements of cash flow and with issues in financial reporting.

Students will be required to answer two out of three questions in Section B, which will normally comprise two questions which will be scenario or case-study based and one question which will be an essay. Section B could deal with any aspects of the syllabus.

Additional information

The Study Guide provides more detailed guidance on the syllabus.

December 2009

Section A

1   Consolidated statement of financial position with changes in group structure

Section B

2   Impairment: discussion and calculation
3   Revenue recognition; recognition of assets; joint control
4   Complexity in financial instruments

The December 2009 paper is Mock Exam 3 in this Kit.

June 2009

Section A	*Question in this Kit*
1 Business combination achieved in stages; ethics	34

Section B	
2 Financial instruments: fair value, convertible bonds, derecognition, foreign subsidiary's debt, interest on employee loan	17
3 Revenue recognition, assets	51
4 Employee benefits: problems of current treatments	9

Examiner's comments. The structure of the paper was similar to previous diets with the exception that a computational element was introduced in question 4. This was the first sitting where the technical aspects of IFRS 3 (Revised) *Business combinations* were examined in Question 1. It seemed as though many candidates were not adequately prepared for the question even though several articles had appeared in the student accountant. The results overall were disappointing. The main reasons for this appeared to be lack of a thorough understanding of IFRS 3 (Revised), poor time management and difficulty in applying knowledge to questions. In addition, candidates often spent too much time on Question 1 with the result that the other two questions on the paper were poorly answered either through lack of time or knowledge Time management is extremely important and the examiner repeatedly refers to this weakness in approach by candidates. Candidates often did not answer all parts of a question. Current issues are another weakness.

December 2008

Section A   *Question in this Kit*

1   Group statement of cash flows with adjustments and interpretation; ethics   45

Section B

2   Changes to accounting for business combinations   25
3   Tangibles, intangibles and revenue recognition   5
4   Accounting standards and disclosure   2

The December 2008 paper is Mock Exam 3 in this Kit.

> **Examiner's comments.** The paper was generally well answered and the pass rate was pleasing. However candidates must learn to apply their knowledge and not simply reiterate definitions.
>
> The approach to the examination seems to be improving with little evidence of time pressure although some candidates are still failing to produce answers to all parts of the paper and appear to be spending too much time on question 1. Also candidates are often not using the information in the question to develop their answers even when the question requires the information to be used. There is a minimum amount of information required in each question in order to gain a pass standard and candidates do sometimes not appreciate this.

June 2008

Section A   *Question in this Kit*

1   Groups with a foreign subsidiary, other adjustments and the remainder on ethical issues   39

Section B

2   Segment reporting and revenue recognition in a specialised industry   59
3   Retirement benefits and financial instruments   16
4   Transition to IFRS   56

> The examiner was fairly satisfied with candidates' performance, but it was uneven. The case study question in Section A was well answered but some of the questions in Section B were quite poorly answered. Students seem to have difficulty applying standards to the scenarios given in the questions. They often clearly have the knowledge but they are unable to use this knowledge in answering the question. Also this exam was unusual in as much as many candidates did not answer the essay question, which is normally question 4 in the paper. This was surprising as the question dealt with the implementation of International Financial Reporting Standards, which is very topical. Greater technical knowledge is needed for success in this examination, together with the ability to apply that knowledge. Also time management is a problem to some candidates as they spend too much time on question 1, which results in quite short answers to the remaining questions, which limits the amount of marks available on these questions.

December 2007

Section A   *Question in this Kit*

1   Piecemeal acquisition; factored receivables; environmental provision and report; ethical
     and social altitudes   36

Section B

2   Retirement benefits; provisions   7
3   Discontinued operations; deferred tax; impairment; lease   33
4   Conceptual framework   1

Generally candidates performed quite well. Some spent too much time on question 1 with the result that the remaining questions were not given sufficient time allocation. Additionally some candidates did not write in sufficient detail on the discursive parts of the paper and others wrote too much in question 1 on the computational part. This part of the paper is designed to test candidates' computational skills and brief explanations are often useful to the marker but a detailed discussion of the relevant standard is not normally required. Candidates need to develop skill at discursive elements, as this comprises a significant part of the paper.

Candidates should where possible make sure that they show all workings and start each question on a new page. Time management is critical and candidates should not spend a disproportionate amount of time on a single question. When the time allocated to a question is over, candidates should move on and start a new question, leaving sufficient space to come back and finish the question if time allows.

Pilot paper

Section A   *Question in this Kit*

1   Statement of cash flows; criteria for consolidation; ethical behaviour   44

Section B

2   Environmental provision, leasing; EABSD; share-based payment   21
3   Deferred tax with pension scheme and financial instruments   12
4   Adoption of IFRS; proposals on business combinations   –

Exam update

Examinable documents

The following documents are examinable for the June and December 2010 sittings.

Knowledge of new examinable regulations issued by 30 September will be required in examination sessions being held in the following calendar year. Documents may be examinable even if the effective date is in the future.

The documents listed as being examinable are the latest that were issued prior to 30 September 2009 and will be examinable in June and December 2010 examination sessions.

The study guide offers more detailed guidance on the depth and level at which the examinable documents will be examined. The study guide should be read in conjunction with the examinable documents list.

Title

International Accounting Standards (IASs)/International Financial Reporting Standards (IFRSs)

IAS 1	Presentation of financial statements
IAS 2	Inventories
IAS 7	Statement of cash flows
IAS 8	Accounting policies, changes in accounting estimates and errors
IAS 10	Events after the reporting period
IAS 11	Construction contracts
IAS 12	Income taxes
IAS 16	Property, plant and equipment
IAS 17	Leases
IAS 18	Revenue
IAS 19	Employee benefits
IAS 20	Accounting for government grants and disclosure of government assistance
IAS 21	The effects of changes in foreign exchange rates
IAS 23	Borrowing costs
IAS 24	Related party disclosures
IAS 27	Consolidated and separate financial statements
IAS 28	Investments in associates
IAS 29	Financial reporting in hyperinflationary economies
IAS 31	Interests in joint ventures
IAS 32	Financial Instruments: presentation
IAS 33	Earnings per share
IAS 34	Interim financial reporting
IAS 36	Impairment of assets
IAS 37	Provisions, contingent liabilities and contingent assets
IAS 38	Intangible assets
IAS 39	Financial Instruments: recognition and measurement
IAS 40	Investment property
IAS 41	Agriculture
IFRS 1	First-time adoption of international financial reporting standards
IFRS 2	Share-based payment
IFRS 3	Business combinations (revised Jan 2008)
IFRS 5	Non-current assets held for sale and discontinued operations
IFRS 7	Financial instruments: disclosures
IFRS 8	Operating segments
IFRS	For Small and Medium-sized Entities

Title

Other Statements

Framework for the Preparation and Presentation of Financial Statements

Interpretations of the International Financial Reporting Interpretations Committee (IFRIC)

SIC-12	Consolidation – special purpose entities
SIC-13	Jointly controlled entities – non monetary contributions by venturers
SIC-15	Operating leases – incentives
SIC-21	Income taxes – recovery of revalued non-depreciable assets
SIC-27	Evaluating the substance of transactions in the legal form of a lease
SIC-32	Intangible assets – website costs
IFRIC 1	Changes in existing decommissioning, restoration and similar liabilities
IFRIC 4	Determining whether an arrangement contains a lease
IFRIC 5	Rights to interests from decommissioning restoration and environmental rehabilitation funds
IFRIC 7	Applying the restatement approach under IAS 29 Financial reporting in hyperinflationary economies
IFRIC 9	Reassessment of embedded derivatives
IFRIC 10	Interim financial reporting and impairment
IFRIC 11	IFRS 2: group and treasury share transactions
IFRIC 12	Service concession arrangements
IFRIC 13	Customer loyalty programmes
IFRIC 16	Hedges of a net investment in a foreign operation.
IFRIC 17	Distribution of non-cash assets to owners

EDs, Discussion Papers and Other Documents

ED	Simplifying earnings per share: proposed amendments to IAS 37
ED	Improvements to IFRS 5
ED	Discount rate for employee benefits: proposed amendments to IAS 19
ED	An improved conceptual framework for financial reporting Chapters 1 and 2
ED	Management commentary
ED	Fair value measurements
ED	Preliminary views on amendments to IAS 19 Employee benefits
DP	Credit risk in liability measurement
DP	Leases
DP	Revenue recognition in contracts with customers
DP	Preliminary view on financial statement presentation
ED	Classification of rights issues: proposed amendments to IAS 32
ED	Financial instruments: classification and measurements: draft amendments to other IFRS and guidance
ED	Derecognition: proposed amendments to IAS 39 and IFRS 7
ED	Income Tax

Current issues: IFRS for Small and Medium-Sized Entities

Overview

The *IFRS for Small and Medium-Sized Entities* (IFRS for SMEs) was published in July 2009, and therefore falls to be examinable in 2010. It is only 230 pages, and has simplifications that reflect the needs of users of SMEs' financial statements and cost-benefit considerations. It is designed to facilitate financial reporting by small and medium-sized entities in a number of ways:

(a)   It provides significantly less guidance than full IFRS.

(b)   Many of the principles for recognising and measuring assets, liabilities, income and expenses in full IFRSs are simplified.

(c)   Where full IFRSs allow accounting policy choices, the IFRS for SMEs allows only the easier option.

(d)   Topics not relevant to SMEs are omitted.

(e)   Significantly fewer disclosures are required.

(f)   The standard has been written in clear language that can easily be translated.

Scope

The IFRS is suitable for all entities except those whose securities are publicly traded and financial institutions such as banks and insurance companies. It is the first set of international accounting requirements developed specifically for small and medium-sized entities (SMEs). Although it has been prepared on a similar basis to IFRS, it is a stand-alone product and will be updated on its own timescale.

The IFRS will be revised only once every three years. It is hoped that this will further reduce the reporting burden for SMEs.

There are no quantitative thresholds for qualification as a SME; instead, the scope of the IFRS is determined by a test of public accountability. As with full iFRS, it is up to legislative and regulatory authorities and standard setters in individual jurisdictions to decide who is permitted or required to use the IFRS for SMEs.

Effective date

The IFRS for SMEs does not contain an effective date; this is determined in each jurisdiction.

Accounting policies

For situations where the IFRS for SMEs does not provide specific guidance, it provides a hierarchy for determining a suitable accounting policy. An SME must consider, in descending order:

•   The guidance in the IFRS for SMEs on similar and related issues.

•   The definitions, recognition criteria and measurement concepts in Section 2 *Concepts and Pervasive Principles* of the standard.

The entity also has the option of considering the requirements and guidance in full IFRS dealing with similar topics. However, it is under no obligation to do this, or to consider the pronouncements of other standard setters.

Overlap with full IFRS

In the following areas, the recognition and measurement guidance in the IFRS for SMEs is like that in the full IFRS.

•   Provisions and contingencies
•   Hyperinflation accounting
•   Events after the end of the reporting period

Omitted topics

The IFRS for SMEs does not address the following topics that are covered in full IFRS.

- Earnings per share
- Interim financial reporting
- Segment reporting
- Classification for non-current assets (or disposal groups) as held for sale

Examples of options in full IFRS not included in the IFRS for SMEs

- Revaluation model for intangible assets and property, plant and equipment

- Proportionate consolidation for investments in jointly-controlled entities

- Financial instrument options, including available-for-sale, held to maturity and fair value options

- Choice between cost and fair value models for investment property (measurement depends on the circumstances)

- Options for government grants

Principal recognition and measurement simplifications

(a) **Financial instruments**

Financial instruments meeting specified criteria are measured at cost or amortised cost. All others are measured at fair value through profit or loss. The procedure for derecognition has been simplified, as have hedge accounting requirements.

(b) **Goodwill and other indefinite-life intangibles**

These are always amortised over their estimated useful life (or ten years if it cannot be estimated).

(c) **Investments in associates and joint ventures**

These can be measured at cost, but fair value must be used if there is a published price quotation.

(d) **Research and development costs and borrowing costs** must be expensed.

(e) **Property, plant and equipment and intangibles**

There is no need to review residual value, useful life and depreciation method unless there is an indication that they have changed since the most recent reporting date.

(f) **Defined benefit plans**

All actuarial gains and losses are to be recognised immediately (in profit or loss or other comprehensive income). All past service costs are to be recognised immediately in profit or loss. To measure the defined benefit obligation, the projected unit credit method must be used.

(g) **Income tax**

Follow the ED *Income tax,* which simplifies IAS 12.

(h) **Available-for-sale assets**

There is no separate available-for-sale classification; holding an asset or group of assets for sale is an indicator of impairment.

(i) **Biological assets**

SMEs are to use the cost-depreciation-impairment model unless the fair value is readily determinable, in which case the fair value through profit or loss model is required.

(j) **Equity-settled share-based payment**

If observable market prices are not available to measure the fair value of the equity-settled share-based payment, the directors' best estimate is used.

Likely effect

Because there is no supporting guidance in the IFRS for SMEs, it is likely that differences will arise from full IFRS, even where the principles are the same. Most of the exemptions in the IFRS for SMEs are on grounds of cost or undue effort. However, despite the practical advantages of a simpler reporting framework, there will be costs involved for those moving to IFRS – even a simplified IFRS – for the first time.

Important !

Please check the following link for updates on documents and other matters relating to P2 (International):

www.bpp.com/acca-p2-updates-int

Useful websites

The websites below provide additional sources of information of relevance to your studies for *Corporate Reporting*.

- ACCA   www.accaglobal.com
- BPP   www.bpp.com
- IASB   www.iasb.org
- Financial Times   www.ft.com
- Accountancy Foundation   www.accountancyfoundation.com
- International Federation of Accountants (IFAC)   www.ifac.org

Planning your question practice

We have already stressed that question practice should be right at the centre of your revision. Whilst you will spend some time looking at your notes and Paper P2 Passcards, you should spend the majority of your revision time practising questions.

We recommend two ways in which you can practise questions.

- Use **BPP's question plan** to work systematically through the syllabus and attempt key and other questions on a section-by-section basis

- **Build your own exams** – attempt questions as a series of practice exams

These ways are suggestions and simply following them is no guarantee of success. You or your college may prefer an alternative but equally valid approach.

BPP's question plan

The BPP plan below requires you to devote a **minimum of 50 hours** to revision of Paper P2. Any time you can spend over and above this should only increase your chances of success.

Step 1   **Review your notes** and the chapter summaries in the Paper P2 **Passcards** for each section of the syllabus.

Step 2   **Answer the key questions** for that section. These questions have boxes round the question number in the table below and you should answer them in full. Even if you are short of time you must attempt these questions if you want to pass the exam. You should complete your answers without referring to our solutions.

Step 3   **Attempt the other questions** in that section. For some questions we have suggested that you prepare **answer plans or do the calculations** rather than full solutions. Planning an answer means that you should spend about 40% of the time allowance for the questions brainstorming the question and drawing up a list of points to be included in the answer.

Step 4   Attempt **Mock exams 1, 2 and 3** under strict exam conditions.

Syllabus section	2009 Passcards chapters	Questions in this Kit	Comments	Done ☑
Conceptual framework	2	1	Learn our answer. Covers most aspects of this topic that are likely to come up.	☐
Environmental, social and cultural issues	3	3	Comes up regularly. This question covers most topics you're likely to need.	☐
Non-current assets	4	5	Johan. A recent question that requires you to think clearly about the issues. Do in full.	☐
Taxation	6	12	A demanding question from the pilot paper. Answer in full.	☐
Employee benefits	5	7	Accounting for employee benefits. Do in full. Make sure that you understand how the calculation 'works'.	☐
Leasing contracts	10	24	Leasing will come up as part of a longer question.	☐
Financial instruments	7	16	Sirus. Do in full. Very topical.	☐
Mixed bag	A11	21	Electron. Typical 'mixed tag' question from the Pilot paper.	☐
Measurement of performance	18	46	Mineral. Useful question. Answer plan.	☐
Reporting financial performance	18	48	Rockby and Bye. Redo if necessary to make sure you have this topic well sorted for the exam.	☐
Share-based payment	16	18	Vident. A full question on a favourite topic.	☐
Related party disclosures	8	32	Egin Group. Useful question. Prepare an answer plan and make sure you remember the key learning points for exam purposes.	☐
Associates and joint ventures	12	26	Revision question to remind you of IAS 28 and 31.	☐
Complex groups	13	30	Rod. A high priority question. Make sure you review your answer thoroughly. Identify areas where you require remedial action.	☐ ☐
		31	Multi-company case study question. Do in full.	☐
Changes in group structures	14	34	Bravado. Good, recent question.	☐
		35	Base group – case study questions testing changes in group structure. Do in full.	☐
		36	Beth – recent case study with step acquisition.	
Foreign currency transaction	16	38	Memo. A useful question. Have a good stab at it.	☐
		39	Ribby – a case study question with FX. Do in full.	

Syllabus section	2009 Passcards chapters	Questions in this Kit	Comments	Done ✓
Statements of cash flows	17	42	Andash: a case study question with a group statement of cash flows. Do in full.	☐
		45	Warrburt. Statements of cash flows can yield sure marks. Do and redo till you can complete one quickly and accurately in an exam.	☐
			This case is a study question. Do in full.	
		44	A case study question from the Pilot paper. Do in full.	
Current events	19	54	Useful coverage of range of issues. Do in full.	☐

BPP LEARNING MEDIA

Build your own exams

Having revised your notes and the BPP Passcards, you can attempt the questions in the Kit as a series of practice exams. You can organise the questions in the following ways.

- Either you can attempt complete past exam papers; recent papers are listed below:

	December 07 Question in Kit	June 08 Question in kit	December 08 Question in kit	June 09 Question in kit
Section A				
1	36	39	45	34
Section B				
2	7	59	25	17
3	3	16	5	51
4	1	56	2	9

- Or you can make up practice exams, either yourself or using the suggestions we have listed below.

	Practice exams						
	1	2	3	4	5	6	7
Section A							
1	30	31	35	42	43	44	39
Section B							
2	10	11	14	15	18	21	59
3	8	19	22	23	52	53	16
4	47	30	54	55	55	56	56

Whichever practice exams you use, you must attempt **Mock exams 1, 2 and 3** at the end of your revision.

Questions

ACCA examiner's answers

Remember that you can access the ACCA examiner's solutions to questions marked **'Pilot paper'** or **'12/07'** on the BPP website using the following link:

www.bpp.com/acca/examiner-solutions

Additional question guidance

Remember that you can find additional guidance to certain questions on the BPP website using the following link:

www.bpp.com/acca/extra-question-guidance

REGULATORY AND ETHICAL FRAMEWORK

Questions 1 to 3 cover Regulatory and Ethical Framework, the subject of Part A of the BPP Study Text for Paper P2.

BPP Note. **Statement of financial position** is the revised IAS 1 term for **balance sheet**.

1 Conceptual framework
45 mins

`12/07`

The International Accounting Standards Board (IASB) has begun a joint project to revisit its conceptual framework for financial accounting and reporting. The goals of the project are to build on the existing frameworks and converge them into a common framework.

Required

(a) Discuss why there is a need to develop an agreed international conceptual framework and the extent to which an agreed international conceptual framework can be used to resolve practical accounting issues.

(13 marks)

(b) Discuss the key issues which will need to be addressed in determining the basic components of an internationally agreed conceptual framework.

(10 marks)

Appropriateness and quality of discussion.

(2 marks)

(Total = 25 marks)

2 Accounting standards and disclosure
45 mins

`12/08`

Whilst acknowledging the importance of high quality corporate reporting, the recommendations to improve it are sometimes questioned on the basis that the marketplace for capital can determine the nature and quality of corporate reporting. It could be argued that additional accounting and disclosure standards would only distort a market mechanism that already works well and would add costs to the reporting mechanism, with no apparent benefit. It could be said that accounting standards create costly, inefficient, and unnecessary regulation. It could be argued that increased disclosure reduces risks and offers a degree of protection to users. However, increased disclosure has several costs to the preparer of financial statements.

Required

(a) Explain why accounting standards are needed to help the market mechanism work effectively for the benefit of preparers and users of corporate reports.

(9 marks)

(b) Discuss the relative costs to the preparer and benefits to the users of financial statements of increased disclosure of information in financial statements.

(14 marks)

Quality of discussion and reasoning.

(2 marks)

(Total = 25 marks)

3 Glowball
45 mins

`ACR, Pilot paper`

The directors of Glowball, a public limited company, had discussed the study by the Institute of Environmental Management which indicated that over 35% of the world's largest 250 corporations are voluntarily releasing green reports to the public to promote corporate environmental performance and to attract customers and investors. They have heard that their main competitors are applying the 'Global Reporting Initiative' (GRI) in an effort to develop a worldwide format for corporate environmental reporting. However, the directors are unsure as to what this initiative actually means. Additionally they require advice as to the nature of any legislation or standards relating to environmental reporting, as they are worried that any environmental report produced by the company may not be of sufficient quality and may detract and not enhance their image if the report does not comply with recognised standards. Glowball has a reputation for ensuring the preservation of the environment in its business activities.

Further the directors have collected information in respect of a series of events which they consider to be important and worthy of note in the environmental report but are not sure as to how they would be incorporated in the environmental report or whether they should be included in the financial statements.

The events are as follows.

(a) Glowball is a company that pipes gas from offshore gas installations to major consumers. The company purchased its main competitor during the year and found that there were environmental liabilities arising out of the restoration of many miles of farmland that had been affected by the laying of a pipeline. There was no legal obligation to carry out the work but the company felt that there would be a cost of around $150 million if the farmland was to be restored.

(b) Most of the offshore gas installations are governed by operating licenses which specify limits to the substances which can be discharged to the air and water. These limits vary according to local legislation and tests are carried out by the regulatory authorities. During the year the company was prosecuted for infringements of an environmental law in the USA when toxic gas escaped into the atmosphere. In 20X2 the company was prosecuted five times and in 20X1 eleven times for infringement of the law. The final amount of the fine/costs to be imposed by the courts has not been determined but is expected to be around $5 million. The escape occurred over the seas and it was considered that there was little threat to human life.

(c) The company produced statistics that measure their improvement in the handling of emissions of gases which may have an impact on the environment. The statistics deal with:

(i) Measurement of the release of gases with the potential to form acid rain. The emissions have been reduced by 84% over five years due to the closure of old plants.

(ii) Measurement of emissions of substances potentially hazardous to human health. The emissions are down by 51% on 20W8 levels.

(iii) Measurement of emissions to water that removes dissolved oxygen and substances that may have an adverse effect on aquatic life. Accurate measurement of these emissions is not possible but the company is planning to spend $70 million on research in this area.

(d) The company tries to reduce the environmental impacts associated with the siting and construction of its gas installations. This is done in the way that minimises the impact on wild life and human beings. Additionally when the installations are at the end of their life, they are dismantled and are not sunk into the sea. The current provision for the decommissioning of these installations is $215 million and there are still decommissioning costs of $407 million to be provided as the company's policy is to build up the required provision over the life of the installation.

Required

Prepare a report suitable for presentation to the directors of Glowball in which you discuss the following elements:

(a) Current reporting requirements and guidelines relating to environmental reporting. **(10 marks)**

(b) The nature of any disclosure which would be required in an environmental report and/or the financial statements for the events (a)-(d) above. **(15 marks)**

(The mark allocation includes four marks for the style and layout of the report.) **(Total = 25 marks)**

ACCOUNTING STANDARDS

Questions 4 to 24 cover Accounting Standards, the subject of Part B of the BPP Study Text for Paper P2.

BPP Note. **Statement of financial position** is the revised IAS 1 term for **balance sheet**.

4 Prochain

45 mins

ACR, 6/06

Prochain, a public limited company, operates in the fashion industry and has a financial year end of 31 May 20X6. The company sells its products in department stores throughout the world. Prochain insists on creating its own selling areas within the department stores which are called 'model areas'. Prochain is allocated space in the department store where it can display and market its fashion goods. The company feels that this helps to promote its merchandise. Prochain pays for all the costs of the 'model areas' including design, decoration and construction costs. The areas are used for approximately two years after which the company has to dismantle the 'model areas'. The costs of dismantling the 'model areas' are normally 20% of the original construction cost and the elements of the area are worthless when dismantled. The current accounting practice followed by Prochain is to charge the full cost of the 'model areas' against profit or loss in the year when the area is dismantled. The accumulated cost of the 'model areas' shown in the statement of financial position at 31 May 20X6 is $20 million. The company has estimated that the average age of the 'model areas' is eight months at 31 May 20X6. **(7 marks)**

Prochain acquired 100% of a sports goods and clothing manufacturer, Badex, a private limited company, on 1 June 20X5. Prochain intends to develop its own brand of sports clothing which it will sell in the department stores. The shareholders of Badex valued the company at $125 million based upon profit forecasts which assumed significant growth in the demand for the 'Badex' brand name. Prochain had taken a more conservative view of the value of the company and estimated the fair value to be in the region of $108 million to $112 million of which $20 million relates to the brand name 'Badex'. Prochain is only prepared to pay the full purchase price if profits from the sale of 'Badex' clothing and sports goods reach the forecast levels. The agreed purchase price was $100 million plus a further payment of $25 million in two years on 31 May 20X7. This further payment will comprise a guaranteed payment of $10 million with no performance conditions and a further payment of $15 million if the actual profits during this two year period from the sale of Badex clothing and goods exceed the forecast profit. The forecast profit on Badex goods and clothing over the two year period is $16 million and the actual profits in the year to 31 May 20X6 were $4 million. Prochain did not feel at any time since acquisition that the actual profits would meet the forecast profit levels. **(8 marks)**

After the acquisition of Badex, Prochain started developing its own sports clothing brand 'Pro'. The expenditure in the period to 31 May 20X6 was as follows:

Period from	Expenditure type	$m
1 June 20X5 – 31 August 20X5	Research as to the extent of the market	3
1 September 20X5 – 30 November 20X5	Prototype clothing and goods design	4
1 December 20X5 – 31 January 20X6	Employee costs in refinement of products	2
1 February 20X6 – 30 April 20X6	Development work undertaken to finalise design of product	5
1 May 20X6 – 31 May 20X6	Production and launch of products	6
		20

The costs of the production and launch of the products include the cost of upgrading the existing machinery ($3 million), market research costs ($2 million) and staff training costs ($1 million). Currently an intangible asset of $20 million is shown in the financial statements for the year ended 31 May 20X6. **(6 marks)**

Prochain owns a number of prestigious apartments which it leases to famous persons who are under a contract of employment to promote its fashion clothing. The apartments are let at below the market rate. The lease terms are short and are normally for six months. The leases terminate when the contracts for promoting the clothing terminate. Prochain wishes to account for the apartments as investment properties with the difference between the market rate and actual rental charged to be recognised as an employee benefit expense. **(4 marks)**

Assume a discount rate of 5·5% where necessary.

Required

Discuss how the above items should be dealt with in the financial statements of Prochain for the year ended 31 May 20X6 under International Financial Reporting Standards.

(Total = 25 marks)

5 Johan

45 mins

`12/08`

Johan, a public limited company, operates in the telecommunications industry. The industry is capital intensive with heavy investment in licences and network infrastructure. Competition in the sector is fierce and technological advances are a characteristic of the industry. Johan has responded to these factors by offering incentives to customers and, in an attempt to acquire and retain them, Johan purchased a telecom licence on 1 December 20X6 for $120 million. The licence has a term of six years and cannot be used until the network assets and infrastructure are ready for use. The related network assets and infrastructure became ready for use on 1 December 20X7. Johan could not operate in the country without the licence and is not permitted to sell the licence. Johan expects its subscriber base to grow over the period of the licence but is disappointed with its market share for the year to 30 November 20X8. The licence agreement does not deal with the renewal of the licence but there is an expectation that the regulator will grant a single renewal for the same period of time as long as certain criteria regarding network build quality and service quality are met. Johan has no experience of the charge that will be made by the regulator for the renewal but other licences have been renewed at a nominal cost. The licence is currently stated at its original cost of $120 million in the statement of financial position under non-current assets.

Johan is considering extending its network and has carried out a feasibility study during the year to 30 November 20X8. The design and planning department of Johan identified five possible geographical areas for the extension of its network. The internal costs of this study were $150,000 and the external costs were $100,000 during the year to 30 November 20X8. Following the feasibility study, Johan chose a geographical area where it was going to install a base station for the telephone network. The location of the base station was dependent upon getting planning permission. A further independent study has been carried out by third party consultants in an attempt to provide a preferred location in the area, as there is a need for the optimal operation of the network in terms of signal quality and coverage. Johan proposes to build a base station on the recommended site on which planning permission has been obtained. The third party consultants have charged $50,000 for the study. Additionally Johan has paid $300,000 as a single payment together with $60,000 a month to the government of the region for access to the land upon which the base station will be situated. The contract with the government is for a period of 12 years and commenced on 1 November 20X8. There is no right of renewal of the contract and legal title to the land remains with the government.

Johan purchases telephone handsets from a manufacturer for $200 each, and sells the handsets direct to customers for $150 if they purchase call credit (call card) in advance on what is called a prepaid phone. The costs of selling the handset are estimated at $1 per set. The customers using a prepaid phone pay $21 for each call card at the purchase date. Call cards expire six months from the date of first sale. There is an average unused call credit of $3 per card after six months and the card is activated when sold.

Johan also sells handsets to dealers for $150 and invoices the dealers for those handsets. The dealer can return the handset up to a service contract being signed by a customer. When the customer signs a service contract, the customer receives the handset free of charge. Johan allows the dealer a commission of $280 on the connection of a customer and the transaction with the dealer is settled net by a payment of $130 by Johan to the dealer being the cost of the handset to the dealer ($150) deducted from the commission ($280). The handset cannot be sold separately by the dealer and the service contract lasts for a 12 month period. Dealers do not sell prepaid phones, and Johan receives monthly revenue from the service contract.

The chief operating officer, a non-accountant, has asked for an explanation of the accounting principles and practices which should be used to account for the above events.

Required

Discuss the principles and practices which should be used in the financial year to 30 November 20X8 to account for:

(a) The licences **(8 marks)**
(b) The costs incurred in extending the network **(7 marks)**
(c) The purchase of handsets and the recognition of revenue from customers and dealers **(8 marks)**

Appropriateness and quality of discussion. **(2 marks)**

(Total = 25 marks)

6 Preparation question: Defined benefit scheme

BPP Note. In this question, proformas are given to you to help you get used to setting out your answer. You may wish to transfer them to a separate sheet, or alternatively to use a separate sheet for your workings.

Brutus Co operates a defined benefit pension plan for its employees conditional on a minimum employment period of 6 years. The present value of the future benefit obligations and the fair value of its plan assets on 1 January 20X1 were $110 million and $150 million respectively.

In the financial statements for the year ended 31.12.X0, there were unrecognised actuarial gains of $43 million. (Brutus Co's accounting policy is to use the 10% corridor approach to recognition of actuarial gains and losses).

The pension plan received contributions of $7m and paid pensions to former employees of $10m during the year.

Extracts from the most recent actuary's report show the following:

Present value of pension plan obligation at 31 December 20X1	$116m
Market value of plan assets at 31 December 20X1	$140m
Present cost of pensions earned in the period	$11m
Yield on high quality corporate bonds at 1 January 20X1	10%
Long term expected return on scheme assets for the period	12%

On 1 January 20X1, the rules of the pension plan were changed to improve benefits for plan members. The actuary has advised that this will cost $20 million in total, $12 million of which relates to employees who have already completed their minimum service period. The remaining benefits relate to employees who have worked for the company for an average period of two years.

The average remaining working life of plan members at 31.12.X1 is 7 years. This tends to remain static as people leave and join.

Required

Produce the extracts for the financial statements for the year ended 31 December 20X1.

Assume contributions and benefits were paid on 31 December.

DEFINED BENEFIT SCHEME PROFORMA

NOTE TO STATEMENT OF COMPREHENSIVE INCOME

Defined benefit expense recognised in profit or loss

$'m

Current service cost
Interest cost
Expected return on plan assets
Net actuarial (gains)/losses recognised
Past service cost – vested benefits
Past service cost – non-vested benefits
_____
_____

STATEMENT OF FINANCIAL POSITION NOTES

Net pension liability recognised in the statement of financial position

	31 December 20X1 $'m	31 December 20X0 $'m
Present value of pension obligation		
Fair value of plan assets	_____	_____
Unrecognised actuarial gains		
Unrecognised past service cost	_____	_____
	_____	_____

Changes in the present value of the defined benefit obligation

	$'m
Opening defined benefit obligation	
	_____
	_____

Changes in the fair value of plan assets

	$'m
Opening fair value of plan assets	
	_____
	_____

Working

Recognised/unrecognised actuarial gains and losses

	$'m
	_____
	_____

7 Macaljoy

45 mins

12/07

Macaljoy, a public limited company, is a leading support services company which focuses on the building industry. The company would like advice on how to treat certain items under IAS 19 *Employee benefits* and IAS 37 *Provisions, contingent liabilities and contingent assets*. The company operates the Macaljoy (2006) Pension Plan which commenced on 1 November 2006 and the Macaljoy (1990) Pension Plan, which was closed to new entrants from 31 October 2006, but which was open to future service accrual for the employees already in the scheme. The assets of the schemes are held separately from those of the company in funds under the control of trustees. The following information relates to the two schemes.

Macaljoy (1990) Pension Plan

The terms of the plan are as follows.

(i) Employees contribute 6% of their salaries to the plan.

(ii) Macaljoy contributes, currently, the same amount to the plan for the benefit of the employees.

(iii) On retirement, employees are guaranteed a pension which is based upon the number of years service with the company and their final salary.

The following details relate to the plan in the year to 31 October 2007:

	$m
Present value of obligation at 1 November 2006	200
Present value of obligation at 31 October 2007	240
Fair value of plan assets at 1 November 2006	190
Fair value of plan assets at 31 October 2007	225
Current service cost	20
Pension benefits paid	19
Total contributions paid to the scheme for year to 31 October 2007	17

Actuarial gains and losses are recognised in 'other comprehensive income'.

Macaljoy (2006) Pension Plan

Under the terms of the plan, Macaljoy does not guarantee any return on the contributions paid into the fund. The company's legal and constructive obligation is limited to the amount that is contributed to the fund. The following details relate to this scheme:

	$m
Fair value of plan assets at 31 October 2007	21
Contributions paid by company for year to 31 October 2007	10
Contributions paid by employees for year to 31 October 2007	10

The discount rates and expected return on plan assets for the two plans are:

	1 November 2006	31 October 2007
Discount rate	5%	6%
Expected return on plan assets	7%	8%

The company would like advice on how to treat the two pension plans, for the year ended 31 October 2007, together with an explanation of the differences between a defined contribution plan and a defined benefit plan.

Questions 9

Warranties

Additionally the company manufactures and sells building equipment on which it gives a standard one year warranty to all customers. The company has extended the warranty to two years for certain major customers and has insured against the cost of the second year of the warranty. The warranty has been extended at nil cost to the customer. The claims made under the extended warranty are made in the first instance against Macaljoy and then Macaljoy in turn makes a counter claim against the insurance company. Past experience has shown that 80% of the building equipment will not be subject to warranty claims in the first year, 15% will have minor defects and 5% will require major repair. Macaljoy estimates that in the second year of the warranty, 20% of the items sold will have minor defects and 10% will require major repair.

In the year to 31 October 2007, the following information is relevant.

	Standard warranty (units)	Extended warranty (units)	Selling price per unit (both)($)
Sales	2,000	5,000	1,000

	Major repair $	Minor defect $
Cost of repair (average)	500	100

Assume that sales of equipment are on 31 October 2007 and any warranty claims are made on 31 October in the year of the claim. Assume a risk adjusted discount rate of 4%.

Required

Draft a report suitable for presentation to the directors of Macaljoy which:

(a) (i) Discusses the nature of and differences between a defined contribution plan and a defined benefit plan with specific reference to the company's two schemes. **(7 marks)**

   (ii) Shows the accounting treatment for the two Macaljoy pension plans for the year ended 31 October 2007 under IAS 19 *Employee benefits*. **(7 marks)**

(b) (i) Discusses the principles involved in accounting for claims made under the above warranty provision. **(6 marks)**

   (ii) Shows the accounting treatment for the above warranty provision under IAS 37 *Provisions, contingent liabilities and contingent assets* for the year ended 31 October 2007. **(3 marks)**

Appropriateness of the format and presentation of the report and communication of advice. **(2 marks)**

(Total = 25 marks)

8 Savage

45 mins

ACR, 12/05

Savage, a public limited company, operates a funded defined benefit plan for its employees. The plan provides a pension of 1% of the final salary for each year of service. The cost for the year is determined using the projected unit credit method. This reflects service rendered to the dates of valuation of the plan and incorporates actuarial assumptions primarily regarding discount rates, which are based on the market yields of high quality corporate bonds. The expected average remaining working lives of employees is twelve years.

The directors have provided the following information about the defined benefit plan for the current year (year ended 31 October 20X5).

(a) The actuarial cost of providing benefits in respect of employees' service for the year to 31 October 20X5 was $40 million. This is the present value of the pension benefits earned by the employees in the year.

(b) The pension benefits paid to former employees in the year were $42 million.

(c) Savage should have paid contributions to the fund of $28 million. Because of cash flow problems $8 million of this amount had not been paid at the financial year end of 31 October 20X5.

(d) The present value of the obligation to provide benefits to current and former employees was $3,000 million at 31 October 20X4 and $3,375 million at 31 October 20X5.

(e)   The fair value of the plan assets was $2,900 million at 31 October 20X4 and $3,170 million (including the contributions owed by Savage) at 31 October 20X5. The actuarial gains recognised at 31 October 20X4 were $336 million.

With effect from 1 November 20X4, the company had amended the plan so that the employees were now provided with an increased pension entitlement. The benefits became vested immediately and the actuaries computed that the present value of the cost of these benefits at 1 November 20X4 was $125 million. The discount rates and expected rates of return on the plan assets were as follows from the following dates:

	31 October 20X4	31 October 20X5
Discount rate	6%	7%
Expected rate of return on plan assets	8%	9%

The company has recognised actuarial gains and losses in profit or loss up to 31 October 20X4 but now wishes to recognise such gains and losses outside profit or loss in 'other comprehensive income'.

Required

(a)   Show the amounts which will be recognised in the statement of financial position, in profit or loss and in 'other comprehensive income' of Savage for the year ended 31 October 20X5 under IAS 19 *Employee benefits*, and the movement in the asset and liability in the statement of financial position. (Your calculations should show the changes in the present value of the obligation and the fair value of the plan assets during the year. Ignore any deferred taxation effects and assume that pension benefits and the contributions paid were settled at 31 October 20X5.)   **(21 marks)**

(b)   Explain how the non-payment of contributions and the change in the pension benefits should be treated in the financial statements of Savage for the year ended 31 October 20X5.   **(4 marks)**

(Total = 25 marks)

9 Smith   45 mins

6/09

(a)   Accounting for defined benefit pension schemes is a complex area of great importance. In some cases, the net pension liability even exceeds the market capitalisation of the company. The financial statements of a company must provide investors, analysts and companies with clear, reliable and comparable information on a company's pension obligations, discount rates and expected returns on plan assets.

Required

(i)   Discuss the current requirements of IAS 19 *Employee benefits* as regards the accounting for actuarial gains and losses, setting out the main criticisms of the approach taken and the advantages of immediate recognition of such gains and losses.   **(11 marks)**

(ii)   Discuss the implications of the current accounting practices in IAS 19 for dealing with the setting of discount rates for pension obligations and the expected returns on plan assets.   **(6 marks)**

Professional marks will be awarded in part (a) for clarity and quality of discussion.   **(2 marks)**

(b)   Smith, a public limited company and Brown a public limited company utilise IAS 19 *Employee benefits* to account for their pension plans. The following information refers to the company pension plans for the year to 30 April 20X9.

(i)   At 1 May 20X8, plan assets of both companies were fair valued at $200 million and both had net unrecognised actuarial gains of $6 million.

(ii)   At 30 April 20X9, the fair value of the plan assets of Smith was $219 million and that of Brown was $276 million.

(iii)   The contributions received were $70 million and benefits paid were $26 million for both companies. These amounts were paid and received on 1 November 20X8.

(iv)   The expected return on plan assets was 7% at 1 May 20X8 and 8% on 30 April 20X9.

(v)   The present value of the defined benefit obligation was less than the fair value of the plan assets at both 1 May 20X8 and 30 April 20X9.

(vi)   Actuarial losses on the obligation for the year were negligible for both companies.

(vii)   Both companies use the corridor approach to recognise actuarial gains and losses.

Required

Show how the use of the expected return on assets can cause comparison issues for potential investors using the above scenario for illustration.   **(6 marks)**

(Total = 25 marks)

10 Cohort

45 mins

ACR, 6/02

is a private limited company and has two 100% owned subsidiaries, Legion and Air, both themselves private limited companies. Cohort acquired Air on 1 January 20X2 for $5 million when the fair value of the net assets was $4 million, and the tax base of the net assets was $3.5 million. The acquisition of Air and Legion was part of a business strategy whereby Cohort would build up the 'value' of the group over a three year period and then list its existing share capital on the stock exchange.

(a)   The following details relate to the acquisition of Air, which manufactures electronic goods.

(i)   Part of the purchase price has been allocated to intangible assets because it relates to the acquisition of a database of key customers from Air. The recognition and measurement criteria for an intangible asset under IFRS 3 *Business combinations*/IAS 38 *Intangible assets* do not appear to have been met but the directors feel that the intangible asset of $0.5 million will be allowed for tax purposes and have computed the tax provision accordingly. However, the tax authorities could possibly challenge this opinion.

(ii)   Air has sold goods worth $3 million to Cohort since acquisition and made a profit of $1 million on the transaction. The inventory of these goods recorded in Cohort's statement of financial position at the year end of 31 May 20X2 was $1.8 million.

(iii)   The balance on the retained earnings of Air at acquisition was $2 million. The directors of Cohort have decided that, during the three years to the date that they intend to list the shares of the company, they will realise earnings through future dividend payments from the subsidiary amounting to $500,000 per year. Tax is payable on any remittance or dividends and no dividends have been declared for the current year.   **(13 marks)**

(b)   Legion was acquired on 1 June 20X1 and is a company which undertakes various projects ranging from debt factoring to investing in property and commodities. The following details relate to Legion for the year ending 31 May 20X2.

(i)   Legion has a portfolio of readily marketable government securities which are held as current assets. These investments are stated at market value in the statement of financial position with any gain or loss taken to the income statement. These gains and losses are taxed when the investments are sold. Currently the accumulated unrealised gains are $4 million.

(ii)   Legion has calculated that it requires a specific allowance of $2 million against loans in its portfolio. Tax relief is available when the specific loan is written off.

(iii)   When Cohort acquired Legion it had unused tax losses brought forward. At 1 June 20X1, it appeared that Legion would have sufficient taxable profit to realise the deferred tax asset created by these losses but subsequent events have proven that the future taxable profit will not be sufficient to realise all of the unused tax loss.

The current tax rate for Cohort is 30% and for public companies is 35%.   **(12 marks)**

Required

Write a note suitable for presentation to the partner of an accounting firm setting out the deferred tax implications of the above information for the Cohort Group of companies.

(Total = 25 marks)

11 Panel

The directors of Panel, a public limited company, are reviewing the procedures for the calculation of the deferred tax liability for their company. They are quite surprised at the impact on the liability caused by changes in accounting standards such as IFRS 1 *First time adoption of International Financial Reporting Standards* and IFRS 2 *Share-based payment*. Panel is adopting International Financial Reporting Standards for the first time as at 31 October 20X5 and the directors are unsure how the deferred tax provision will be calculated in its financial statements ended on that date including the opening provision at 1 November 20X3.

Required

(a) (i) Explain how changes in accounting standards are likely to have an impact on the deferred tax liability under IAS 12 *Income taxes*. **(5 marks)**

   (ii) Describe the basis for the calculation of the deferred taxation liability on first time adoption of IFRS including the provision in the opening IFRS statement of financial position. **(4 marks)**

Additionally the directors wish to know how the provision for deferred taxation would be calculated in the following situations under IAS 12 *Income taxes*:

(i) On 1 November 20X3, the company had granted ten million share options worth $40 million subject to a two year vesting period. Local tax law allows a tax deduction at the exercise date of the intrinsic value of the options. The intrinsic value of the ten million share options at 31 October 20X4 was $16 million and at 31 October 20X5 was $46 million. The increase in the share price in the year to 31 October 20X5 could not be foreseen at 31 October 20X4. The options were exercised at 31 October 20X5. The directors are unsure how to account for deferred taxation on this transaction for the years ended 31 October 20X4 and 31 October 20X5.

(ii) Panel is leasing plant under a finance lease over a five year period. The asset was recorded at the present value of the minimum lease payments of $12 million at the inception of the lease which was 1 November 20X4. The asset is depreciated on a straight line basis over the five years and has no residual value. The annual lease payments are $3 million payable in arrears on 31 October and the effective interest rate is 8% per annum. The directors have not leased an asset under a finance lease before and are unsure as to its treatment for deferred taxation. The company can claim a tax deduction for the annual rental payment as the finance lease does not qualify for tax relief.

(iii) A wholly owned overseas subsidiary, Pins, a limited liability company, sold goods costing $7 million to Panel on 1 September 20X5, and these goods had not been sold by Panel before the year end. Panel had paid $9 million for these goods. The directors do not understand how this transaction should be dealt with in the financial statements of the subsidiary and the group for taxation purposes. Pins pays tax locally at 30%.

(iv) Nails, a limited liability company, is a wholly owned subsidiary of Panel, and is a cash generating unit in its own right. The value of the property, plant and equipment of Nails at 31 October 20X5 was $6 million and purchased goodwill was $1 million before any impairment loss. The company had no other assets or liabilities. An impairment loss of $1·8 million had occurred at 31 October 20X5. The tax base of the property, plant and equipment of Nails was $4 million as at 31 October 20X5. The directors wish to know how the impairment loss will affect the deferred tax liability for the year. Impairment losses are not an allowable expense for taxation purposes.

Assume a tax rate of 30%.

Required

(b) Discuss, with suitable computations, how the situations (i) to (iv) above will impact on the accounting for deferred tax under IAS 12 *Income taxes* in the group financial statements of Panel. **(16 marks)**

   (The situations in (i) to (iv) above carry equal marks) **(Total = 25 marks)**

12 Kesare

Pilot paper

The following statement of financial position relates to Kesare Group, a public limited company, at 30 June 20X6.

	$'000
Assets	
Non current assets:	
Property, plant and equipment	10,000
Goodwill	6,000
Other intangible assets	5,000
Financial assets (cost)	9,000
	30,000
Current assets	
Trade receivables	7,000
Other receivables	4,600
Cash and cash equivalents	6,700
	18,300
Total assets	48,300
Equity and liabilities	
Equity	
Share capital	9,000
Other reserves	4,500
Retained earnings	9,130
Total equity	22,630
Non-current liabilities	
Long term borrowings	10,000
Deferred tax liability	3,600
Employee benefit liability	4,000
Total non-current liabilities	17,600
Current liabilities	
Current tax liability	3,070
Trade and other payables	5,000
Total current liabilities	8,070
Total liabilities	25,670
Total equity and liabilities	48,300

The following information is relevant to the above statement of financial position:

(i) The financial assets are classified as 'available for sale' but are shown in the above statement of financial position at their cost on 1 July 20X5. The market value of the assets is $10.5 million on 30 June 20X6. Taxation is payable on the sale of the assets.

(ii) The stated interest rate for the long term borrowing is 8 per cent. The loan of $10 million represents a convertible bond which has a liability component of $9.6 million and an equity component of $0.4 million. The bond was issued on 30 June 20X6.

(iii) The defined benefit plan had a rule change on 1 July 20X5. Kesare estimate that of the past service costs of $1 million, 40 per cent relates to vested benefits and 60 per cent relates to benefits that will vest over the next five years from that date. The past service costs have not been accounted for.

(iv) The tax bases of the assets and liabilities are the same as their carrying amounts in the statement of financial position at 30 June 20X6 except for the following:

(1)

	$'000
Property, plant and equipment	2,400
Trade receivables	7,500
Other receivables	5,000
Employee benefits	5,000

(2) Other intangible assets were development costs which were all allowed for tax purposes when the cost was incurred in 20X5.

(3) Trade and other payables includes an accrual for compensation to be paid to employees. This amounts to $1 million and is allowed for taxation when paid.

(v) Goodwill is not allowable for tax purposes in this jurisdiction.

(vi) Assume taxation is payable at 30%.

Required

(a) Discuss the conceptual basis for the recognition of deferred taxation using the temporary difference approach to deferred taxation.   **(7 marks)**

(b) Calculate the deferred tax liability at 30 June 20X6 after any necessary adjustments to the financial statements showing how the deferred tax liability would be dealt with in the financial statements. (Assume that any adjustments do not affect current tax. Candidates should briefly discuss the adjustments required to calculate deferred tax liability.)   **(18 marks)**

(Total = 25 marks)

Two marks will be awarded for the quality of the discussion of the conceptual basis of deferred taxation in (a).

13 Preparation question: Financial instruments

(a) Graben Co purchases a bond for $441,014 on 1 January 20X1. It will be redeemed on 31 December 20X4 for $600,000. The bond will be held to maturity and carries no coupon.

Required

Calculate the valuation of the bond for the statement of financial position as at 31 December 20X1 and the finance income for 20X1 shown in the income statement.

Compound sum of $1: $(1 + r)^n$

Year	2%	4%	6%	8%	10%	12%	14%
1	1.0200	1.0400	1.0600	1.0800	1.1000	1.1200	1.1400
2	1.0404	1.0816	1.1236	1.1664	1.2100	1.2544	1.2996
3	1.0612	1.1249	1.1910	1.2597	1.3310	1.4049	1.4815
4	1.0824	1.1699	1.2625	1.3605	1.4641	1.5735	1.6890
5	1.1041	1.2167	1.3382	1.4693	1.6105	1.7623	1.9254

(b) Baldie Co issues 4,000 convertible bonds on 1 January 20X2 at par. The bond is redeemable 3 years later at its par value of $500 per bond, which is its nominal value.

The bonds pay interest annually in arrears at an interest rate (based on nominal value) of 5%. Each bond can be converted at the maturity date into 30 $1 shares.

The prevailing market interest rate for three year bonds that have no right of conversion is 9%.

Required

Show the statement of financial position valuation at 1 January 20X2.

Cumulative 3 year annuity factors:

5% 2.723
9% 2.531

14 Ambush

Ambush, a public limited company, is assessing the impact of implementing IAS 39 *Financial instruments: recognition and measurement.* The directors realise that significant changes may occur in their accounting treatment of financial instruments and they understand that on initial recognition only certain financial assets or liabilities can be designated as one to be measured at fair value through profit or loss. There are certain issues that they wish to have explained and these are set out below.

Required

(a) Outline in a report to the directors of Ambush the following information

  (i)   How financial assets and liabilities are measured and classified, briefly setting out the accounting method used for each category. (Hedging relationships can be ignored.) **(10 marks)**

  (ii) Why the 'fair value option' was initially introduced and why it caused such concern. **(5 marks)**

(b) Ambush loaned $200,000 to Bromwich on 1 December 2003. The effective and stated interest rate for this loan was 8 per cent. Interest is payable by Bromwich at the end of each year and the loan is repayable on 30 November 2007. At 30 November 2005, the directors of Ambush have heard that Bromwich is in financial difficulties and is undergoing a financial reorganisation. The directors feel that it is likely that they will only receive $100,000 on 30 November 2007 and no future interest payment. Interest for the year ended 30 November 2005 had been received. The financial year end of Ambush is 30 November 2005.

  Required

  (i)   Outline the requirements of IAS 39 as regards the impairment of financial assets. **(6 marks)**

  (ii) Explain the accounting treatment under IAS 39 of the loan to Bromwich in the financial statements of Ambush for the year ended 30 November 2005. **(4 marks)**

  (Total = 25 marks)

Note. You need not consider the requirements of IFRS 1 *First-time adoption of International Financial Reporting Standards* in answering this question.

15 Wader

Wader, a public limited company, is assessing the nature of its provisions for the year ended 31 May 20X7. The following information is relevant.

(a) The impairment of trade receivables has been calculated using a formulaic approach which is based on a specific percentage of the portfolio of trade receivables. The general provision approach has been used by the company at 31 May 20X7. At 31 May 20X7, one of the credit customers, Tray, has come to an arrangement with Wader whereby the amount outstanding of $4 million from Tray will be paid on 31 May 20X8 together with a penalty of $100,000. The total amount of trade receivables outstanding at 31 May 20X7 was $11 million including the amount owed by Tray. The following is the analysis of the trade receivables.

	Balance $m	Cash expected $m	Due date
Tray	4	4.1	31 May 20X8
Milk	2	2.0	31 July 20X7
Other receivables	5	4.6	On average 31 July 20X7
	11	10.7	

Wader has made an allowance of $520,000 against trade receivables which represents the difference between the cash expected to be received and the balance outstanding plus a 2% general allowance. Milk has a similar credit risk to the 'other receivables'. **(7 marks)**

(b)   Wader is assessing the valuation of its inventory. It has a significant quantity of a product and needs to evaluate its value for the purposes of the statement of financial position. Sales of the product are high, but it incurs high production costs. The reason for its success is that a sales commission of 20% of the list selling price is paid to the salesforce. The following details relate to this product.

	$ per unit
List price – normal selling price	50
Allocation of customer discounts on selling price	2.5
Warehouse overheads until estimated sale date	4
Basic salaries of sales team	2
Cost of product	35

The product is collected from the warehouses of Wader by the customer.   **(4 marks)**

(c)   Wader is reviewing the accounting treatment of its buildings. The company uses the 'revaluation model' for its buildings. The buildings had originally cost $10 million on 1 June 20X5 and had a useful economic life of 20 years. They are being depreciated on a straight line basis to a nil residual value. The buildings were revalued downwards on 31 May 20X6 to $8 million which was the buildings' recoverable amount. At 31 May 20X7 the value of the buildings had risen to $11 million which is to be included in the financial statements. The company is unsure how to treat the above events.   **(7 marks)**

(d)   Wader has decided to close one of its overseas branches. A board meeting was held on 30 April 20X7 when a detailed formal plan was presented to the board. The plan was formalised and accepted at that meeting. Letters were sent out to customers, suppliers and workers on 15 May 20X7 and meetings were held prior to the year end to determine the issues involved in the closure. The plan is to be implemented in June 20X7. The company wish to provide $8 million for the restructuring, but are unsure as to whether this is permissible. Additionally, there was an issue raised at one of the meetings. The operations of the branch are to be moved to another country from June 20X7, but the operating lease on the present buildings of the branch is non-cancellable and runs for another two years, until 31 May 20X9. The annual rent of the buildings is $150,000 payable in arrears on 31 May and the lessor has offered to take a single payment of $270,000 on 31 May 20X8 to settle the outstanding amount owing and terminate the lease on that date. Wader has additionally obtained permission to sublet the building at a rental of $100,000 per year, payable in advance on 1 June. The company needs advice on how to treat the above under IAS 37 *Provisions, contingent liabilities and contingent assets*.   **(7 marks)**

Required

Discuss the accounting treatments of the above items in the financial statements for the year ended 31 May 20X7.

Note: a discount rate of 5% should be used where necessary. Candidates should show suitable calculations where necessary.

(Total = 25 marks)

16 Sirus   **45 mins**

6/08

Sirus is a large national public limited company (plc). The directors' service agreements require each director to purchase 'B' ordinary shares on becoming a director and this capital is returned to the director on leaving the company. Any decision to pay a dividend on the 'B' shares must be approved in a general meeting by a majority of all of the shareholders in the company. Directors are the only holders of 'B' shares.

Sirus would like advice on how to account under International Financial Reporting Standards (IFRSs) for the following events in its financial statements for the year ended 30 April 20X8.

(a)   The capital subscribed to Sirus by the directors and shareholders is shown as follows in the statement of financial position as at 30 April 20X8:

Equity	$m
Ordinary 'A' shares	100
Ordinary 'B' shares	20
Retained earnings	30
Total equity	150

On 30 April 20X8 the directors had recommended that $3 million of the profits should be paid to the holders of the ordinary 'B' shares, in addition to the $10 million paid to directors under their employment contracts. The payment of $3 million had not been approved in a general meeting. The directors would like advice as to whether the capital subscribed by the directors (the ordinary 'B' shares) is equity or a liability and how to treat the payments out of profits to them. **(6 marks)**

(b)   When a director retires, amounts become payable to the director as a form of retirement benefit as an annuity. These amounts are not based on salaries paid to the director under an employment contract. Sirus has contractual or constructive obligations to make payments to former directors as at 30 April 20X8 as follows.

(i)   Certain former directors are paid a fixed annual amount for a fixed term beginning on the first anniversary of the director's retirement. If the director dies, an amount representing the present value of the future payment is paid to the director's estate.

(ii)   In the case of other former directors, they are paid a fixed annual amount which ceases on death.

The rights to the annuities are determined by the length of service of the former directors and are set out in the former directors' service contracts. **(6 marks)**

(c)   On 1 May 20X7 Sirus acquired another company, Marne plc. The directors of Marne, who were the only shareholders, were offered an increased profit share in the enlarged business for a period of two years after the date of acquisition as an incentive to accept the purchase offer. After this period, normal remuneration levels will be resumed. Sirus estimated that this would cost them $5 million at 30 April 20X8, and a further $6 million at 30 April 20X9. These amounts will be paid in cash shortly after the respective year ends.

(5 marks)

(d)   Sirus raised a loan with a bank of $2 million on 1 May 20X7. The market interest rate of 8% per annum is to be paid annually in arrears and the principal is to be repaid in 10 years time. The terms of the loan allow Sirus to redeem the loan after seven years by paying the interest to be charged over the seven year period, plus a penalty of $200,000 and the principal of $2 million. The effective interest rate of the repayment option is 9.1%. The directors of Sirus are currently restructuring the funding of the company and are in initial discussions with the bank about the possibility of repaying the loan within the next financial year. Sirus is uncertain about the accounting treatment for the current loan agreement and whether the loan can be shown as a current liability because of the discussions with the bank. **(6 marks)**

Appropriateness of the format and presentation of the report and quality of discussion   **(2 marks)**

Required

Draft a report to the directors of Sirus which discusses the principles and nature of the accounting treatment of the above elements under International Financial Reporting Standards in the financial statements for the year ended 30 April 20X8.

(Total = 25 marks)

17 Aron

The directors of Aron, a public limited company, are worried about the challenging market conditions which the company is facing. The markets are volatile and illiquid. The central government is injecting liquidity into the economy. The directors are concerned about the significant shift towards the use of fair values in financial statements. IAS 39 *Financial instruments: recognition and measurement* defines fair value and requires the initial measurement of financial instruments to be at fair value. The directors are uncertain of the relevance of fair value measurements in these current market conditions.

Required

(a)   Briefly discuss how the fair value of financial instruments is determined, commenting on the relevance of fair value measurements for financial instruments where markets are volatile and illiquid.   **(4 marks)**

(b)   Further they would like advice on accounting for the following transactions within the financial statements for the year ended 31 May 20X8.

   (i)   Aron issued one million convertible bonds on 1 June 20X5. The bonds had a term of three years and were issued with a total fair value of $100 million which is also the par value. Interest is paid annually in arrears at a rate of 6% per annum and bonds, without the conversion option, attracted an interest rate of 9% per annum on 1 June 20X5. The company incurred issue costs of $1 million. If the investor did not convert to shares they would have been redeemed at par. At maturity all of the bonds were converted into 25 million ordinary shares of $1 of Aron. No bonds could be converted before that date. The directors are uncertain how the bonds should have been accounted for up to the date of the conversion on 31 May 20X8 and have been told that the impact of the issue costs is to increase the effective interest rate to 9.38%.   **(6 marks)**

   (ii) Aron held 3% holding of the shares in Smart, a public limited company, The investment was classified as available-for-sale and at 31 May 20X8 was fair valued at $5 million. The cumulative gain recognised in equity relating to the available-for-sale investment was $400,000. On the same day, the whole of the share capital of Smart was acquired by Given, a public limited company, and as a result, Aron received shares in Given with a fair value of $5.5 million in exchange for its holding in Smart. The company wishes to know how the exchange of shares in Smart for the shares in Given should be accounted for in its financial records.   **(4 marks)**

   (iii) The functional and presentation currency of Aron is the dollar ($). Aron has a wholly owned foreign subsidiary, Gao, whose functional currency is the zloti. Gao owns a debt instrument which is held for trading. In Gao's financial statements for the year ended 31 May 20X7, the debt instrument was carried at its fair value of 10 million zloti.

   At 31 May 20X8, the fair value of the debt instrument had increased to 12 million zloty. The exchange rates were:

	Zloti to $1
31 May 20X7	3
31 May 20X8	2
Average rate for year to 31 May 20X8	2.5

   The company wishes to know how to account for this instrument in Gao's entity financial statements and the consolidated financial statements of the group.   **(5 marks)**

   (iv) Aron granted interest free loans to its employees on 1 June 20X7 of $10 million. The loans will be paid back on 31 May 20X9 as a single payment by the employees. The market rate of interest for a two year loan on both of the above dates is 6% per annum. The company is unsure how to account for the loan but wishes to classify the loans as 'loans and receivables' under IAS 39 *Financial instruments: recognition and measurement*.   **(4 marks)**

Required

Discuss, with relevant computations, how the above financial instruments should be accounted for in the financial statements for the year ended 31 May 20X8.

Note. The mark allocation is shown against each of the transactions above.

Note. The following discount and annuity factors may be of use.

	Discount factors			Annuity factors		
	6%	9%	9.38%	6%	9%	9.38%
1 year	0.9434	0.9174	0.9142	0.9434	0.9174	0.9174
2 years	0.8900	0.8417	0.8358	1.8334	1.7591	1.7500
3 years	0.8396	0.7722	0.7642	2.6730	2.5313	2.5142

Professional marks will be awarded for clarity and quality of discussion. **(2 marks)**

(Total = 25 marks)

18 Vident

45 mins

ACR, 6/05

The directors of Vident, a public limited company, are reviewing the impact of IFRS 2 *Share-based payment* on the financial statements for the year ended 31 May 20X5 as they will adopt the IFRS. However, the directors of Vident are unhappy about having to apply the standard and have put forward the following arguments as to why they should not recognise an expense for share-based payments.

(i)   They feel that share options have no cost to their company and, therefore, there should be no expense charged in profit and loss.

(ii)   They do not feel that the expense arising from share options under IFRS 2 actually meets the definition of an expense under the *Framework* document.

(iii)   The directors are worried about the dual impact of the IFRS on earnings per share, as an expense is shown in the income statement and the impact of share options is recognised in the diluted earnings per share calculation.

(iv)   They feel that accounting for share-based payment may have an adverse effect on their company and may discourage it from introducing new share option plans.

The following share option schemes were in existence at 31 May 20X5:

Director's name	Grant date	Options granted	Fair value of options at grant date $	Exercise price $	Performance conditions	Vesting date	Exercise date
J. Van Heflin	1 June 20X3	20,000	5	4·50	A	6/20X5	6/20X6
R. Ashworth	1 June 20X4	50,000	6	6	B	6/20X7	6/20X8

The price of the company's shares at 31 May 20X5 is $12 per share and at 31 May 20X4 was $12·50 per share.

The performance conditions which apply to the exercise of executive share options are as follows:

Performance Condition A

The share options do not vest if the growth in the company's earnings per share (EPS) for the year is less than 4%.

The rate of growth of EPS was 4·5% (20X3), 4·1% (20X4), 4·2% (20X5). The directors must still work for the company on the vesting date.

Performance Condition B

The share options do not vest until the share price has increased from its value of $12·50 at the grant date (1 June 20X4) to above $13·50. The director must still work for the company on the vesting date.

No directors have left the company since the issue of the share options and none are expected to leave before June 20X7. The shares vest and can be exercised on the first day of the due month.

The directors are uncertain about the deferred tax implications of adopting IFRS 2. Vident operates in a country where a tax allowance will not arise until the options are exercised and the tax allowance will be based on the option's intrinsic value at the exercise date.

Assume a tax rate of 30%.

Required

Draft a report to the directors of Vident setting out:

(a) The reasons why share-based payments should be recognised in financial statements and why the directors' arguments are unacceptable **(9 marks)**

(b) A discussion (with suitable calculations) as to how the directors' share options would be accounted for in the financial statements for the year ended 31 May 20X5 including the adjustment to opening balances **(9 marks)**

(c) The deferred tax implications (with suitable calculations) for the company which arise from the recognition of a remuneration expense for the directors' share options **(7 marks)**

(Total = 25 marks)

19 Leigh

45 mins

ACR, 6/07

(a) Leigh, a public limited company, purchased the whole of the share capital of Hash, a limited company, on 1 June 20X6. The whole of the share capital of Hash was formerly owned by the five directors of Hash and under the terms of the purchase agreement, the five directors were to receive a total of three million ordinary shares of $1 of Leigh on 1 June 20X6 (market value $6 million) and a further 5,000 shares per director on 31 May 20X7, if they were still employed by Leigh on that date. All of the directors were still employed by Leigh at 31 May 20X7.

Leigh granted and issued fully paid shares to its own employees on 31 May 20X7. Normally share options issued to employees would vest over a three year period, but these shares were given as a bonus because of the company's exceptional performance over the period. The shares in Leigh had a market value of $3 million (one million ordinary shares of $1 at $3 per share) on 31 May 20X7 and an average fair value of $2.5 million (one million ordinary shares of $1 at $2.50 per share) for the year ended 31 May 20X7. It is expected that Leigh's share price will rise to $6 per share over the next three years. **(10 marks)**

(b) On 31 May 20X7, Leigh purchased property, plant and equipment for $4 million. The supplier has agreed to accept payment for the property, plant and equipment either in cash or in shares. The supplier can either choose 1.5 million shares of the company to be issued in six months time or to receive a cash payment in three months time equivalent to the market value of 1.3 million shares. It is estimated that the share price will be $3.50 in three months time and $4 in six months time.

Additionally, at 31 May 20X7, one of the directors recently appointed to the board has been granted the right to choose either 50,000 shares of Leigh or receive a cash payment equal to the current value of 40,000 shares at the settlement date. This right has been granted because of the performance of the director during the year and is unconditional at 31 May 20X7. The settlement date is 1 July 20X8 and the company estimates the fair value of the share alternative is $2.50 per share at 31 May 20X7. The share price of Leigh at 31 May 20X7 is $3 per share, and if the director chooses the share alternative, they must be kept for a period of four years. **(9 marks)**

(c) Leigh acquired 30% of the ordinary share capital of Handy, a public limited company, on 1 April 20X6. The purchase consideration was one million ordinary shares of Leigh which had a market value of $2.50 per share at that date and the fair value of the net assets of Handy was $9 million. The retained earnings of Handy were $4 million and other reserves of Handy were $3 million at that date. Leigh appointed two directors to the Board of Handy, and it intends to hold the investment for a significant period of time. Leigh exerts significant influence over Handy. The summarised statement of financial position of Handy at 31 May 20X7 is as follows.

	$m
Share capital of $1	2
Other reserves	3
Retained earnings	5
	10
Net assets	10

There had been no new issues of shares by Handy since the acquisition by Leigh and the estimated recoverable amount of the net assets of Handy at 31 May 20X7 was $11 million. **(6 marks)**

Required

Discuss with suitable computations how the above share-based transactions should be accounted for in the financial statements of Leigh for the year ended 31 May 20X7.

(Total = 25 marks)

20 Ryder

45 mins

ACR, 12/05

Ryder, a public limited company, is reviewing certain events which have occurred since its year end of 31 October 2005. The financial statements were authorised on 12 December 2005. The following events are relevant to the financial statements for the year ended 31 October 2005:

(a) Ryder disposed of a wholly owned subsidiary, Krup, a public limited company, on 10 December 2005 and made a loss of $9 million on the transaction in the group financial statements. As at 31 October 2005, Ryder had no intention of selling the subsidiary which was material to the group. The directors of Ryder have stated that there were no significant events which have occurred since 31 October 2005 which could have resulted in a reduction in the value of Krup. The carrying value of the net assets and purchased goodwill of Krup at 31 October 2005 were $20 million and $12 million respectively. Krup had made a loss of $2 million in the period 1 November 2005 to 10 December 2005. **(6 marks)**

(b) Ryder acquired a wholly owned subsidiary, Metalic, a public limited company, on 21 January 2004. The consideration payable in respect of the acquisition of Metalic was 2 million ordinary shares of $1 of Ryder plus a further 300,000 ordinary shares if the profit of Metalic exceeded $6 million for the year ended 31 October 2005. The profit for the year of Metalic was $7 million and the ordinary shares were issued on 12 November 2005. The annual profits of Metalic had averaged $7 million over the last few years and, therefore, Ryder had included an estimate of the contingent consideration in the cost of the acquisition at 21 January 2004. The fair value used for the ordinary shares of Ryder at this date including the contingent consideration was $10 per share. The fair value of the ordinary shares on 12 November 2005 was $11 per share. Ryder also made a one for four bonus issue on 13 November 2005 which was applicable to the contingent shares issued. The directors are unsure of the impact of the above on earnings per share and the accounting for the acquisition. **(8 marks)**

(c) The company acquired a property on 1 November 2004 which it intended to sell. The property was obtained as a result of a default on a loan agreement by a third party and was valued at $20 million on that date for accounting purposes which exactly offset the defaulted loan. The property is in a state of disrepair and Ryder intends to complete the repairs before it sells the property. The repairs were completed on 30 November 2005. The property was sold after costs for $27 million on 9 December 2005. The property was classified as 'held for sale' at the year end under IFRS 5 *Non-current assets held for sale and discontinued operations* but shown at the net sale proceeds of $27 million. Property is depreciated at 5% per annum on the straight-line basis and no depreciation has been charged in the year. **(6 marks)**

(d)   The company granted share appreciation rights (SARs) to its employees on 1 November 2003 based on ten million shares. The SARs provide employees at the date the rights are exercised with the right to receive cash equal to the appreciation in the company's share price since the grant date. The rights vested on 31 October 2005 and payment was made on schedule on 1 December 2005. The fair value of the SARs per share at 31 October 2004 was $6, at 31 October 2005 was $8 and at 1 December 2005 was $9. The company has recognised a liability for the SARs as at 31 October 2004 based upon IFRS 2 *Share-based payment* but the liability was stated at the same amount at 31 October 2005.   **(5 marks)**

Required

Discuss the accounting treatment of the above events in the financial statements of the Ryder Group for the year ended 31 October 2005, taking into account the implications of events occurring after the end of the reporting period.

(The mark allocations are set out after each paragraph above.)   **(Total = 25 marks)**

21 Electron   **45 mins**

Pilot paper

Electron, a public limited company, operates in the energy sector. The company has grown significantly over the last few years and is currently preparing its financial statements for the year ended 30 June 20X6.

Electron buys and sells oil and currently has a number of oil trading contracts. The contracts to purchase oil are treated as non-current assets and amortised over the contracts' durations. On acceptance of a contract to sell oil, fifty per cent of the contract price is recognised immediately with the balance being recognised over the remaining life of the contract. The contracts always result in the delivery of the commodity.   **(4 marks)**

Electron has recently constructed an ecologically efficient power station. A condition of being granted the operating licence by the government is that the power station be dismantled at the end of its life which is estimated to be 20 years. The power station cost $100 million and began production on 1 July 20X5. Depreciation is charged on the power station using the straight line method. Electron has estimated at 30 June 20X6 that it will cost $15 million (net present value) to restore the site to its original condition using a discount rate of five per cent. Ninety-five per cent of these costs relate to the removal of the power station and five per cent relates to the damage caused through generating energy.   **(7 marks)**

Electron has leased another power station, which was relatively inefficient, to a rival company on 30 June 20X6. The beneficial and legal ownership remains with Electron and in the event of one of Electron's power stations being unable to produce energy, Electron can terminate the agreement. The leased power station is being treated as an operating lease with the net present value of the income of $40 million being recognised in profit or loss. The fair value of the power station is $70 million at 30 June 20X6. A deposit of $10 million was received on 30 June 20X6 and it is included in the net present value calculation.   **(5 marks)**

The company has a good relationship with its shareholders and employees. It has adopted a strategy of gradually increasing its dividend payments over the years. On 1 August 20X6, the board proposed a dividend of 5c per share for the year ended 30 June 20X6. The shareholders will approve the dividend along with the financial statements at the general meeting on 1 September 20X6 and the dividend will be paid on 14 September 20X6. The directors feel that the dividend should be accrued in the financial statements for the year ended 30 June 20X6 as a 'valid expectation' has been created.   **(3 marks)**

The company granted share options to its employees on 1 July 20X5. The fair value of the options at that date was $3 million. The options vest on 30 June 20X8. The employees have to be employed at the end of the three year period for the options to vest and the following estimates have been made:

Estimated percentage of employees leaving during vesting period at:

Grant date 1 July 20X5	5%
30 June 20X6	6% **(4 marks)**
Effective communication to the directors	**(2 marks)**

Draft a report suitable for presentation to the directors of Electron which discusses the accounting treatment of the above transactions in the financial statements for the year ended 30 June 20X6, including relevant calculations.

(Total = 25 marks)

22 Egin Group

45 mins

ACR, 6/06

On 1 June 20X5, Egin, a public limited company, was formed out of the reorganisation of a group of companies with foreign operations. The directors require advice on the disclosure of related party information but are reluctant to disclose information as they feel that such transactions are a normal feature of business and need not be disclosed.

Under the new group structure, Egin owns 80% of Briars, 60% of Doye, and 30% of Eye. Egin exercises significant influence over Eye. The directors of Egin are also directors of Briars and Doye but only one director of Egin sits on the management board of Eye. The management board of Eye comprises five directors. Originally the group comprised five companies but the fifth company, Tang, which was a 70% subsidiary of Egin, was sold on 31 January 20X6. There were no transactions between Tang and the Egin Group during the year to 31 May 20X6. 30% of the shares of Egin are owned by another company, Atomic, which exerts significant influence over Egin. The remaining 40% of the shares of Doye are owned by Spade.

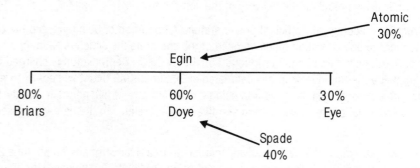

During the current financial year to 31 May 20X6, Doye has sold a significant amount of plant and equipment to Spade at the normal selling price for such items. The directors of Egin have proposed that where related party relationships are determined and sales are at normal selling price, any disclosures will state that prices charged to related parties are made on an arm's length basis.

The directors are unsure how to treat certain transactions relating to their foreign subsidiary, Briars. Egin purchased 80% of the ordinary share capital of Briars on 1 June 20X5 for 50 million euros when its net assets were fair valued at 45 million euros. At 31 May 20X6, it is established that goodwill is impaired by 3 million euros. Additionally, at the date of acquisition, Egin had made an interest free loan to Briars of $10 million. The loan is to be repaid on 31 May 20X7. An equivalent loan would normally carry an interest rate of 6% taking into account Briars' credit rating.

The exchange rates were as follows:

	Euros to $
1 June 20X5	2
31 May 20X6	2·5
Average rate for year	2·3

Financial liabilities of the group are normally measured at amortised cost.

One of the directors of Briars who is not on the management board of Egin owns the whole of the share capital of a company, Blue, that sells goods at market price to Briars. The director is in charge of the production at Briars and also acts as a consultant to the management board of the group.

(a)　(i)　Discuss why it is important to disclose related party transactions, explaining the criteria which determine a related party relationship.　**(5 marks)**

　　(ii)　Describe the nature of any related party relationships and transactions which exists:

　　　　(1)　within the Egin Group including Tang　**(5 marks)**
　　　　(2)　between Spade and the Egin Group　**(3 marks)**
　　　　(3)　between Atomic and the Egin Group　**(3 marks)**

　　　　commenting on whether transactions should be described as being at 'arm's length'.

(b)　Describe with suitable calculations how the goodwill arising on the acquisition of Briars will be dealt with in the group financial statements and how the loan to Briars should be treated in the financial statements of Briars for the year ended 31 May 20X6.　**(9 marks)**

(Total = 25 marks)

23 Engina

45 mins

ACR, Pilot paper

Engina, a foreign company, has approached a partner in your firm to assist in obtaining a local Stock Exchange listing for the company. Engina is registered in a country where transactions between related parties are considered to be normal but where such transactions are not disclosed. The directors of Engina are reluctant to disclose the nature of their related party transactions as they feel that although they are a normal feature of business in their part of the world, it could cause significant problems politically and culturally to disclose such transactions.

The partner in your firm has requested a list of all transactions with parties connected with the company and the directors of Engina have produced the following summary:

(a)　Every month, Engina sells $50,000 of goods per month to Mr Satay, the financial director. The financial director has set up a small retailing business for his son and the goods are purchased at cost price for him. The annual turnover of Engina is $300 million. Additionally Mr Satay has purchased his company car from the company for $45,000 (market value $80,000). The director, Mr Satay, earns a salary of $500,000 a year, and has a personal fortune of many millions of pounds.

(b)　A hotel property had been sold to a brother of Mr Soy, the Managing Director of Engina, for $4 million (net of selling cost of $0.2 million). The market value of the property was $4.3 million but in the foreign country, property prices were falling rapidly. The carrying value of the hotel was $5 million and its value in use was $3.6 million. There was an over supply of hotel accommodation due to government subsidies in an attempt to encourage hotel development and the tourist industry.

(c)　Mr Satay owns several companies and the structure of the group is as follows.

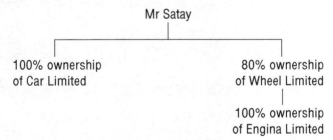

Engina earns 60% of its profits from transactions with Car and 40% of its profits from transactions from Wheel. All the above companies are incorporated in the same country.

Required

Write a report to the directors of Engina setting out the reasons why it is important to disclose related party transactions and the nature of any disclosure required for the above transactions under IAS 24 *Related party disclosures.*　**(25 marks)**

The mark allocation will be as follows:

	Mark
Style/layout of report	4
Reasons	8
Transaction (a)	4
(b)	5
(c)	4
	25

24 Preparation question: Leases

Sugar Co leased a machine from Spice Co. The terms of the lease are as follows:

Inception of lease	1 January 20X1
Lease term	4 years at $78,864 per annum payable in arrears
Present value of minimum lease payments	$250,000
Useful life of asset	4 years

Required

(a) Calculate the interest rate implicit in the lease, using the table below.

This table shows the present value of $1 per annum, receivable or payable at the end of each year for n years.

Years (n)	Interest rates		
	6%	8%	10%
1	0.943	0.926	0.909
2	1.833	1.783	1.736
3	2.673	2.577	2.487
4	3.465	3.312	3.170
5	4.212	3.993	3.791

(b) Prepare the extracts from the financial statements of Sugar Co for the year ended 31 December 20X1. Notes to the accounts are not required.

GROUP FINANCIAL STATEMENTS

Questions 25 to 45 cover Group Financial Statements, the subject of Part C of the BPP Study Text for Paper P2.

Note. All these questions have been revised to take account of the changes to IFRS 3 *Business contributions*.

25 Marrgrett

45 mins

`12/08`

Marrgrett, a public limited company, is currently planning to acquire and sell interests in other entities and has asked for advice on the impact of IFRS 3 (Revised) *Business combinations* and IAS 27 (Revised) *Consolidated and separate financial statements*. The company is particularly concerned about the impact on earnings, net assets and goodwill at the acquisition date and any ongoing earnings impact that the new standards may have.

The company is considering purchasing additional shares in an associate, Josey, a public limited company. The holding will increase from 30% stake to 70% stake by offering the shareholders of Josey cash and shares in Marrgrett. Marrgrett anticipates that it will pay $5 million in transaction costs to lawyers and bankers. Josey had previously been the subject of a management buyout. In order that the current management shareholders may remain in the business, Marrgrett is going to offer them share options in Josey subject to them remaining in employment for two years after the acquisition. Additionally, Marrgrett will offer the same shareholders, shares in the holding company which are contingent upon a certain level of profitability being achieved by Josey. Each shareholder will receive shares of the holding company up to a value of $50,000, if Josey achieves a pre-determined rate of return on capital employed for the next two years.

Josey has several marketing-related intangible assets that are used primarily in marketing or promotion of its products. These include trade names, internet domain names and non-competition agreements. These are not currently recognised in Josey's financial statements.

Marrgrett does not wish to measure the non-controlling interest in subsidiaries on the basis of the proportionate interest in the identifiable net assets, but wishes to use the 'full goodwill' method on the transaction. Marrgrett is unsure as to whether this method is mandatory, or what the effects are of recognising 'full goodwill'. Additionally the company is unsure as to whether the nature of the consideration would affect the calculation of goodwill.

To finance the acquisition of Josey, Marrgrett intends to dispose of a partial interest in two subsidiaries. Marrgrett will retain control of the first subsidiary but will sell the controlling interest in the second subsidiary which will become an associate. Because of its plans to change the overall structure of the business, Marrgrett wishes to recognise a re-organisation provision at the date of the business combination.

Required

Discuss the principles and the nature of the accounting treatment of the above plans under International Financial Reporting Standards setting out any impact that IFRS 3 (Revised) *Business combinations* and IAS 27 (Revised) *Consolidated and separate financial statements* might have on the earnings and net assets of the group.

Note: this requirement includes 2 professional marks for the quality of the discussion.

(25 marks)

26 Preparation question: Associate

The statements of financial position of J Co and its investee companies, P Co and S Co, at 31 December 20X5 are shown below.

STATEMENTS OF FINANCIAL POSITION AS AT 31 DECEMBER 20X5

	J Co $'000	P Co $'000	S Co $'000
Assets			
Non-current assets			
Freehold property	1,950	1,250	500
Plant and equipment	795	375	285
Investments	1,500	–	–
	4,245	1,625	785
Current assets			
Inventories	575	300	265
Trade receivables	330	290	370
Cash	50	120	20
	955	710	655
	5,200	2,335	1,440
Equity and liabilities			
Equity			
Share capital ($1 ordinary shares)	2,000	1,000	750
Retained earnings	1,460	885	390
	3,460	1,885	1,140
Non-current liabilities			
12% debentures	500	100	–
Current liabilities			
Bank overdraft	560		
Trade payables	680	350	300
	1,240	350	300
	5,200	2,335	1,440

Additional information

(a)   J Co acquired 600,000 ordinary shares in P Co on 1 January 20X0 for $1,000,000 when the accumulated retained earnings of P Co were $200,000.

(b)   At the date of acquisition of P Co, the fair value of its freehold property was considered to be $400,000 greater than its value in P Co's statement of financial position. P Co had acquired the property ten years earlier and the buildings element (comprising 50% of the total value) is depreciated on cost over 50 years.

(c)   J Co acquired 225,000 ordinary shares in S Co on 1 January 20X4 for $500,000 when the retained profits of S Co were $150,000.

(d)   P Co manufactures a component used by J Co only. Transfers are made by P Co at cost plus 25%. J Co held $100,000 of these components in inventories at 31 December 20X5.

(e)   It is the policy of J Co to review goodwill for impairment annually. The goodwill in P Co was written off in full some years ago. An impairment test conducted at the year end revealed impairment losses on the investment in S Co of $92,000.

(f)   It is the group's policy to value the non-controlling interest at acquisition at fair value. The market price of the shares of the non-controlling shareholders just before the acquisition was $1.65.

Required

Prepare, in a format suitable for inclusion in the annual report of the J Group, the consolidated statement of financial position at 31 December 20X5.

27 Preparation question: 'D'-shaped group

> **BPP note**. In this question, a proforma is given to you for Part (a) to help you get used to setting out your answer. You may wish to transfer it to a separate sheet or to use a separate sheet for workings.

Below are the statements of financial position of three companies as at 31 December 20X9.

	Bauble Co $'000	Jewel Co $'000	Gem Co $'000
Non-current assets			
Property, plant and equipment	720	60	70
Investments in group companies	185	100	–
	905	160	70
Current assets	175	95	90
	1,080	255	160
Equity			
Share capital – $1 ordinary shares	400	100	50
Retained earnings	560	90	65
	960	190	115
Current liabilities	120	65	45
	1,080	255	160

You are also given the following information:

(a) Bauble Co acquired 60% of the share capital of Jewel Co on 1 January 20X2 and 10% of Gem on 1 January 20X3. The cost of the combinations were $142,000 and $43,000 respectively. Jewel Co acquired 70% of the share capital of Gem Co on 1 January 20X3.

(b) The retained earnings balances of Jewel Co and Gem Co were:

	1 January 20X2 $'000	1 January 20X3 $'000
Jewel Co	45	60
Gem Co	30	40

(c) No impairment loss adjustments have been necessary to date.

(d) It is the group's policy to value the non-controlling interest at acquisition at its proportionate share of the fair value of the subsidiary's identifiable net assets.

Required

(a) Prepare the consolidated statement of financial position for Bauble Co and its subsidiaries as at 31 December 20X9.

(b) Calculate the total goodwill arising on acquisition if Bauble Co had acquired its investments in Jewel and Gem on 1 January 20X3 at a cost of $142,000 and $43,000 respectively and Jewel Co had acquired its investment in Gem Co on 1 January 20X2.

(a)   BAUBLE – CONSOLIDATED STATEMENT OF FINANCIAL POSITION AS AT 31 DECEMBER 20X9

	$'000
Non-current assets	
Property, plant and equipment	
Goodwill	_____
	_____
Current assets	_____
	_____
Equity attributable to owners of the parent	
Share capital – $1 ordinary shares	
Retained earnings	_____
	_____
Non-controlling interest	_____
	_____
Current liabilities	_____
	_____

28 X Group   54 mins

X, a public limited company, acquired 100 million ordinary shares of $1 in Y, a public limited company on 1 April 20X6 when the retained earnings were $120 million. Y acquired 45 million ordinary shares of $1 in Z, a public limited company, on 1 April 20X4 when the retained earnings were $10 million. On 1 April 20X4 there were no material differences between the book values and the fair values of Z. On 1 April 20X6, the retained earnings of Z were $20 million.

Y acquired 30% of the ordinary shares of W, a limited company, on 1 April 20X6 for $50 million when the retained earnings of W were $7 million. Y is in a position to exercise significant influence over W and there were no material differences between the book values and the fair values of W at that date.

There had been no share issues since 1 April 20X4 by any of the group companies. The following statements of financial position relate to the group companies as at 31 March 20X9.

	X	Y	Z	W
	$m	$m	$m	$m
Property, plant and equipment	900	100	30	40
Intangible assets		30		
Investment in Y	320			
Investment in Z		90		
Investment in W		50		
Net current assets	640	360	75	73
	1,860	630	105	113
Share capital	360	150	50	80
Share premium	250	120	10	6
Retained earnings	1,050	210	30	17
	1,660	480	90	103
Non-current liabilities	200	150	15	10
	1,860	630	105	113

(i)   The following fair value table sets out the book values of certain assets and liabilities of the group companies together with any accounting policy adjustments to ensure consistent group policies at 1 April 20X6.

	Book value		Accounting policy adj.		Fair value adj.		Value after adjustments	
	$m	$m	$m	$m	$m	$m	$m	$m
	Y	Z	Y	Z	Y	Z	Y	Z
Property, plant and equipment	90	20			30	10	120	30
Intangible non-current assets	30		(30)				–	
Inventory	20	12	2		(8)	(5)	14	7
Allowance for receivables	(15)				(9)		(24)	

These values had not been incorporated into the financial records. The group companies have consistent accounting policies at 31 March 20X9, apart from the non-current intangible assets in Y's books.

(ii)   During the year ended 31 March 20X9, Z had sold goods to X and Y. At 31 March 20X9, there were $44 million of these goods in the inventory of X and $16 million in the inventory of Y. Z had made a profit of 25% on selling price on the goods.

(iii) On 1 June 20X7, an amount of $36 million was received by Y from an arbitration award against Q. This receipt was secured as a result of an action against Q prior to Y's acquisition by X but was not included in the assets of Y at 1 April 20X6.

(iv) The group writes goodwill off immediately to reserves. However it has decided to bring its accounting policies into line with IFRSs and not local accounting policies. Thus goodwill will be capitalised under IFRS 3 *Business combinations*. At 31 March 20X6, property, plant and equipment had a remaining useful life of 10 years.

(v)   It is the group's policy to value the non-controlling interest at its proportionate share of the fair value of the subsidiary's identifiable net assets.

Required

(a)   Prepare a consolidated statement of financial position as at 31 March 20X9 for the X group.   **(25 marks)**

(b)   Explain how the change in accounting policy as regards goodwill should be dealt with in the financial statements of the X group under International Financial Reporting Standards.   **(5 marks)**

All calculations should be rounded to the nearest million dollars.   **(Total = 30 marks)**

29 Glove

45 mins

ACR, 6/07, amended

The following draft statements of financial position relate to Glove, Body and Fit, all public limited companies, as at 31 May 20X7.

	Glove $m	Body $m	Fit $m
Assets			
Non-current assets			
Property, plant and equipment	260	20	26
Investment in Body	60		
Investment in Fit		30	
Available for sale investments	10		
Current assets	65	29	20
Total assets	395	79	46
Ordinary shares	150	40	20
Other reserves	30	5	8
Retained earnings	135	25	10
Total equity	315	70	38
Non-current liabilities	45	2	3
Current liabilities	35	7	5
Total liabilities	80	9	8
Total equity and liabilities	395	79	46

The following information is relevant to the preparation of the group financial statements.

(a)   Glove acquired 80% of the ordinary shares of Body on 1 June 20X5 when Body's other reserves were $4 million and retained earnings were $10 million. The fair value of the net assets of Body was $60 million at 1 June 20X5. Body acquired 70% of the ordinary shares of Fit on 1 June 20X5 when the other reserves of Fit were $8 million and retained earnings were $6 million. The fair value of the net assets of Fit at that date was $39 million. The excess of the fair value over the net assets of Body and Fit is due to an increase in the value of non-depreciable land of the companies. There have been no issues of ordinary shares in the group since 1 June 20X5.

(b)   Body owns several trade names which are highly regarded in the market place. Body has invested a significant amount in marketing these trade names and has expensed the costs. None of the trade names has been acquired externally and, therefore, the costs have not been capitalised in the statement of financial position of Body. On the acquisition of Body by Glove, a firm of valuation experts valued the trade names at $5 million and this valuation had been taken into account by Glove when offering $60 million for the investment in Body. The valuation of the trade names is not included in the fair value of the net assets of Body above. Group policy is to amortise intangible assets over ten years.

(c)   On 1 June 20X5, Glove introduced a new defined benefit retirement plan. At 1 June 20X5, there were no unrecognised actuarial gains and losses. The following information relates to the retirement plan.

	31 May 20X6	31 May 20X7
	$m	$m
Unrecognised actuarial losses to date	3	5
Present value of obligation	20	26
Fair value of plan assets	16	20

The expected average remaining working lives of the employees in the plan is ten years at 31 May 20X6 and 31 May 20X7. Glove wishes to defer actuarial gains and losses by using the 'corridor' approach. The defined benefit liability is included in non-current liabilities.

(d)   Glove has issued 30,000 convertible bonds with a three year term repayable at par. The bonds were issued at par with a face value of $1,000 per bond. Interest is payable annually in arrears at a nominal interest rate of 6%. Each bond can be converted at any time up to maturity into 300 shares of Glove. The bonds were issued on 1 June 20X6 when the market interest rate for similar debt without the conversion option was 8% per annum. Glove does not wish to account for the bonds at fair value through profit or loss. The interest has been paid and accounted for in the financial statements. The bonds have been included in non-current liabilities at their face value of $30 million and no bonds were converted in the current financial year.

(e)   On 31 May 20X7, Glove acquired plant with a fair value of $6 million. In exchange for the plant, the supplier received land, which was currently not in use, from Glove. The land had a carrying value of $4 million and an open market value of $7 million. In the financial statements at 31 May 20X7, Glove had made a transfer of $4 million from land to plant in respect of this transaction.

(f)   Goodwill has been tested for impairment at 31 May 20X6 and 31 May 20X7 and no impairment loss occurred.

(g)   It is the group's policy to value the non-controlling interest at acquisition at its proportionate share of the fair value of the subsidiary's identifiable net assets.

(h)   Ignore any taxation effects.

Required

Prepare the consolidated statement of financial position of the Glove Group at 31 May 20X7 in accordance with International Financial Reporting Standards (IFRS).

(25 marks)

30 Case study question: Rod

90 mins

The following draft statements of financial position relate to Rod, a public limited company, Reel, a public limited company, and Line, a public limited company, as at 30 November 20X3.

	Rod $m	Reel $m	Line $m
Non-current assets			
Property, plant and equipment	1,230	505	256
Investment in Reel	640		
Investment in Line	160	100	
	2,030	605	256
Current assets			
Inventory	300	135	65
Trade receivables	240	105	49
Cash at bank and in hand	90	50	80
	630	290	194
Total assets	2,660	895	450
Equity			
Share capital	1,500	500	200
Share premium account	300	100	50
Revaluation surplus			70
Retained earnings	625	200	60
	2,425	800	380
Non-current liabilities	135	25	20
Current liabilities	100	70	50
Total equity and liabilities	2,660	895	450

The following information is relevant to the preparation of the group financial statements.

(a) Rod had acquired eighty per cent of the ordinary share capital of Reel on 1 December 20X0 when the retained earnings were $100 million. The fair value of the net assets of Reel was $710 million at 1 December 20X0. Any fair value adjustment related to net current assets and these net current assets had been realised by 30 November 20X3. There had been no new issues of shares in the group since the current group structure was created.

(b) Rod and Reel had acquired their holdings in Line on the same date as part of an attempt to mask the true ownership of Line. Rod acquired forty per cent and Reel acquired twenty-five per cent of the ordinary share capital of Line on 1 December 20X1. The retained earnings of Line on that date were $50 million and those of Reel were $150 million. There was no revaluation surplus in the books of Line on 1 December 20X1. The fair values of the net assets of Line at December 20X1 were not materially different from their carrying values.

(c) The group operates in the pharmaceutical industry and incurs a significant amount of expenditure on the development of products. These costs were formerly written off to the income statement as incurred but then reinstated when the related products were brought into commercial use. The reinstated costs are shown as 'development inventories'. The costs do not meet the criteria in IAS 38 *Intangible assets* for classification as intangibles and it is unlikely that the net cash inflows from these products will be in excess of the development costs. In the current year, Reel has included $20 million of these costs in inventory. Of these costs $5 million relates to expenditure on a product written off in periods prior to 1 December 20X0. Commercial sales of this product had commenced during the current period. The accountant now wishes to ensure that the financial statements comply strictly with IAS/IFRS as regards this matter.

(d) Reel had purchased a significant amount of new production equipment during the year. The cost before trade discount of this equipment was $50 million. The trade discount of $6 million was taken to the income statement. Depreciation is charged on the straight line basis over a six year period.

(e) The policy of the group is now to state property, plant and equipment at depreciated historical cost. The group changed from the revaluation model to the cost model under IAS 16 *Property, plant and equipment* in the year ended 30 November 20X3 and restated all of its assets to historical cost in that year except for the property, plant and equipment of Line which had been revalued by the directors of Line 1 December 20X2. The values were incorporated in the financial records creating revaluation surplus of $70 million. The property, plant and equipment of Line were originally purchased on December 20X1 at a cost of $300 million. The assets are depreciated over six years on the straight line basis. The group does not make an annual transfer from revaluation reserves to retained earnings in respect of the excess depreciation charged on revalued property, plant and equipment. There were no additions or disposals of the property, plant and equipment of Line for the two years ended 30 November 20X3.

(f)   It is the group's policy to value the non-controlling interest at acquisition at its proportionate share of the subsidiary's identifiable net assets.

(g)   During the year the directors of Rod decided to form a defined benefit pension scheme for the employees of the parent and contributed cash to it of $100 million. The following details relate to the scheme at 30 November 20X3.

	$m
Present value of obligation	130
Fair value of plan assets	125
Current service cost	110
Interest cost – scheme liabilities	20
Expected return on pension scheme assets	10

The only entry in the financial statements made to date is in respect of the cash contribution which has been included in Rod's trade receivables. The directors have been uncertain as how to deal with the above pension scheme in the consolidated financial statements because of the significance of the potential increase in the charge to the income statement relating to the pension scheme. They wish to recognise immediately any actuarial gain in profit or loss.

Required

(a)   Show how the defined benefit pension scheme should be dealt with in the consolidated financial statements.
(5 marks)

(b)   Prepare a consolidated statement of financial position of the Rod Group for the year ended 30 November 20X3 in accordance with the standards of the International Accounting Standards Board.   **(22 marks)**

(c)   You are now advising the financial director of Rod about certain aspects of the financial statements for the year ended 30 November 20X4. The director has summarised these points as follows.

    (i)   **Restructuring of the group.** A formal announcement for a restructuring of the group was made after the year end on 5 December 20X4. A provision has not been made in the financial statements as a public issue of shares is being planned and the company does not wish to lower the reported profits. Prior to the year end, the company has sold certain plant and issued redundancy notices to some employees in anticipation of the formal commencement of the restructuring. The company prepared a formal plan for the restructuring which was approved by the board and communicated to the trade union representatives prior to the year end. The directors estimate the cost of the restructuring to be $60 million, and it could take up to two years to complete the restructuring. The estimated cost of restructuring includes $10 million for retraining and relocating existing employees, and the directors feel that costs of $20 million (of which $5 million is relocation expenses) will have been incurred by the time the financial statements are approved.   **(7 marks)**

    (ii)   **Fine for illegal receipt of a state subsidy.** The company was fined on 10 October 20X4 for the receipt of state subsidies that were contrary to a supra-national trade agreement. The subsidies were used to offset trading losses in previous years. Rod has to repay to the government $300 million plus interest of $160 million. The total repayment has been treated as an intangible asset which is being amortised over twenty years with a full year's charge in the current year.   **(5 marks)**

The financial director wishes to prepare a report for submission to the Board of Directors which discusses the above accounting treatment of the key points in the financial statements.

(d)   Rod spends many millions of pounds on research in innovative areas. Often the research and development expenditure does not provide a revenue stream for many years. The company has gained a significant expertise in this field and is frustrated by the fact that the value which is being created is not shown in the statement of financial position, but the cost of the innovation is charged to profit or loss. The knowledge gained by the company is not reported in the financial statements.

Advise the directors on the current problems of reporting financial performance in the case of a 'knowledge led' company such as Rod. **(8 marks)**

(e) In many organisations, bonus payments related to annual profits form a significant part of the total remuneration of all senior managers, not just the top few managers. The directors of Rod feel that the chief internal auditor makes a significant contribution to the company's profitability, and should therefore receive a bonus based on profit.

Advise the directors as to whether this is appropriate. **(3 marks)**

(Total = 50 marks)

31 Case study question: Exotic   90 mins

The Exotic Group carries on business as a distributor of warehouse equipment and importer of fruit into the country. Exotic was incorporated in 20X1 to distribute warehouse equipment. It diversified its activities during 20X3 to include the import and distribution of fruit, and expanded its operations by the acquisition of shares in Melon in 20X5 and in Kiwi in 20X7.

Accounts for all companies are made up to 31 December.

The draft income statements for Exotic, Melon and Kiwi for the year ended 31 December 20X9 are as follows.

	Exotic	Melon	Kiwi
	$'000	$'000	$'000
Revenue	45,600	24,700	22,800
Cost of sales	18,050	5,463	5,320
Gross profit	27,550	19,237	17,480
Distribution costs	(3,325)	(2,137)	(1,900)
Administrative expenses	(3,475)	(950)	(1,900)
Finance costs	(325)	–	–
Profit before tax	20,425	16,150	13,680
Income tax expense	8,300	5,390	4,241
Profit for the year	12,125	10,760	9,439
Dividends paid and declared for the period	9,500	–	–

The draft statements of financial position as at 31 December 20X9 are as follows.

	Exotic	Melon	Kiwi
	$'000	$'000	$'000
Non-current assets			
Property, plant and equipment (NBV)	35,483	24,273	13,063
Investments			
Shares in Melon	6,650		
Shares in Kiwi		3,800	
	42,133	28,073	13,063
Current assets	1,568	9,025	8,883
	43,701	37,098	21,946
Equity			
$1 ordinary shares	8,000	3,000	2,000
Retained earnings	22,638	24,075	19,898
	30,638	27,075	21,898
Current liabilities	13,063	10,023	48
	43,701	37,098	21,946

The following information is available relating to Exotic, Melon and Kiwi.

(a) On 1 January 20X5 Exotic acquired 2,700,000 $1 ordinary shares in Melon for $6,650,000 at which date there was a credit balance on the retained earnings of Melon of $1,425,000. No shares have been issued by Melon since Exotic acquired its interest.

(b) On 1 January 20X7 Melon acquired 1,600,000 $1 ordinary shares in Kiwi for $3,800,000 at which date there was a credit balance on the retained earnings of Kiwi of $950,000. No shares have been issued by Kiwi since Melon acquired its interest.

(c) During 20X9, Kiwi had made intragroup sales to Melon of $480,000 making a profit of 25% on cost and $75,000 of these goods were in inventories at 31 December 20X9.

(d) During 20X9, Melon had made intragroup sales to Exotic of $260,000 making a profit of 33$\frac{1}{3}$% on cost and $60,000 of these goods were in inventories at 31 December 20X9.

(e) On 1 November 20X9 Exotic sold warehouse equipment to Melon for $240,000 from inventories. Melon has included this equipment in its property, plant and equipment. The equipment had been purchased on credit by Exotic for $200,000 in October 20X9 and this amount is included in its current liabilities as at 31 December 20X9.

(f) Melon charges depreciation on its warehouse equipment at 20% on cost. It is company policy to charge a full year's depreciation in the year of acquisition to be included in the cost of sales.

(g) An impairment test conducted at the year end did not reveal any impairment losses.

(h) It is the group's policy to value the non-controlling interest at fair value at the date of acquisition. The fair value of the non-controlling interests in Melon on 1 January 20X5 was $500,000. The fair value of the 28% non-controlling interest in Kiwi on 1 January 20X7 was $900,000.

Required

Prepare for the Exotic Group:

(a) A consolidated income statement for the year ended 31 December 20X9 **(16 marks)**

(b) A consolidated statement of financial position as at that date **(12 marks)**

(c) The following year, Exotic acquired the whole of the share capital of Zest Software, a public limited company and merged Zest Software with its existing business. The directors feel that the goodwill ($10 million) arising on the purchase has an indefinite economic life. Additionally, Exotic acquired a 50% interest in a joint venture which gives rise to a net asset of $2 million. The net asset is comprised of negative goodwill ($1 million) arising on the acquisition of the interest in the joint venture and deducted from the interest in the net assets ($3 million). Exotic is proposing to net the $2 million against a loan made by the joint venture to Exotic of $5 million, and show the resultant balance in non-current liabilities. The equity method of accounting has been used to account for the interest in the joint venture. It is proposed to treat negative goodwill in the same manner as the goodwill on the purchase of Zest Software and leave it in the statement of financial position indefinitely. **(11 marks)**

(d) Advise the directors of Exotic on the issues relating to the reporting of environmental information in financial statements and the current reporting requirements in the UK. **(11 marks)**

(Total = 50 marks)

32 Preparation question: Part disposal

BPP note. In this question, proformas are given to you to help you get used to setting out your answer. You may wish to transfer them to a separate sheet or to use a separate sheet for your workings.

Angel Co bought 70% of the share capital of Shane Co for $120,000 on 1 January 20X6. At that date Shane Co's retained earnings stood at $10,000.

The statements of financial position at 31 December 20X8, summarised income statements to that date and movement on retained earnings are given below:

	Angle Co $'000	Shane Co $'000
STATEMENTS OF FINANCIAL POSITION		
Non-current assets		
Property, plant and equipment	200	80
Investment in Shane Co	120	–
	320	80
Current assets	890	140
	1,210	220
Equity		
Share capital – $1 ordinary shares	500	100
Retained reserves	400	90
	900	190
Current liabilities	310	30
	1,210	220
SUMMARISED STATEMENTS OF COMPREHENSIVE INCOME		
Profit before interest and tax	100	20
Income tax expense	(40)	(8)
Profit for the year	60	12
Other comprehensive income, net of tax	10	6
Total comprehensive income for the year	70	18
MOVEMENT IN RETAINED RESERVES		
Balance at 31 December 20X7	330	72
Total comprehensive income for the year	70	18
Balance at 31 December 20X8	400	90

Angel Co sells one half of its holding in Shane Co for $120,000 on 30 June 20X8. At that date, the fair value of the 35% holding in Shane was slightly more at $130,000 due to a share price rise. The remaining holding is to be dealt with as an associate. This does not represent a discontinued operation.

No entries have been made in the accounts for the above transaction.

Assume that profits accrue evenly throughout the year.

It is the group's policy to value the non-controlling interest at acquisition fair value. The fair value of the non-controlling interest on 1 January 20X6 was $51m.

Required

Prepare the consolidated statement of financial position, statement of comprehensive income and a reconciliation of movement in retained reserves for the year ended 31 December 20X8.

Ignore income taxes on the disposal. No impairment losses have been necessary to date.

PART DISPOSAL PROFORMA

ANGEL GROUP
CONSOLIDATED STATEMENT OF FINANCIAL POSITION
AS AT 31 DECEMBER 20X8

$'000

Non-current assets
Property, plant and equipment
Investment in Shane

Current assets

Equity attributable to owners of the parent
Share capital
Retained earnings

Current liabilities

CONSOLIDATED STATEMENT OF COMPREHENSIVE INCOME
FOR THE YEAR ENDED 31 DECEMBER 20X8

$'000

Profit before interest and tax
Profit on disposal of shares in subsidiary
Share of profit of associate
Profit before tax
Income tax expense
Profit for the year
Other comprehensive income net of tax
Share of other comprehensive income of associate
Other comprehensive income for the year
Total comprehensive income for the year

Profit attributable to:
 Owners of the parent
 Non-controlling interests

Total comprehensive income attributable to
    Owners of the parent
    Non-controlling interests

CONSOLIDATED RECONCILIATION OF MOVEMENT IN RETAINED RESERVES

$'000

Balance at 31 December 20X7
Total comprehensive income for the year
Balance at 31 December 20X8

33 Ejoy

ACR, 6/06, amended

Ejoy, a public limited company, has acquired two subsidiaries. The details of the acquisitions are as follows:

Company	Date of acquisition	Ordinary share capital of $1 $m	Reserves at acquisition $m	Fair value of net assets at acquisition $m	Cost of investment $m	Ordinary share capital of $1 acquired $m
Zbay	1 June 20X4	200	170	600	520	160
Tbay	1 December 20X5	120	80	310	216	72

Any fair value adjustments relate to non-depreciable land. The draft income statements for the year ended 31 May 20X6 are:

	Ejoy $m	Zbay $m	Tbay $m
Revenue	2,500	1,500	800
Cost of sales	(1,800)	(1,200)	(600)
Gross profit	700	300	200
Other income	70	10	–
Distribution costs	(130)	(120)	(70)
Administrative expenses	(100)	(90)	(60)
Finance costs	(50)	(40)	(20)
Profit before tax	490	60	50
Income tax expense	(200)	(26)	(20)
Profit for the year	290	34	30
Profit for year 31 May 20X5	190	20	15

The following information is relevant to the preparation of the group financial statements.

(a) Tbay was acquired exclusively with a view to sale and at 31 May 20X6 meets the criteria of being a disposal group. The fair value of Tbay at 31 May 20X6 is $300 million and the estimated selling costs of the shareholding in Tbay are $5 million.

(b) Ejoy entered into a joint venture with another company on 31 May 20X6. The joint venture is a limited company and Ejoy has contributed assets at fair value of $20 million (carrying value $14 million). Each party will hold five million ordinary shares of $1 in the joint venture. The gain on the disposal of the assets ($6 million) to the joint venture has been included in 'other income'.

(c) On acquisition, the financial statements of Tbay included a large cash balance. Immediately after acquisition Tbay paid a dividend of $40 million. The receipt of the dividend is included in other income in the income statement of Ejoy. Since the acquisition of Zbay and Tbay, there have been no further dividend payments by these companies.

(d) Zbay has a loan asset which was carried at $60 million at 1 June 20X5. The loan's effective interest rate is six per cent. On 1 June 20X5 the company felt that because of the borrower's financial problems, it would receive $20 million in approximately two years time, on 31 May 20X7. At 31 May 20X6, the company still expects to receive the same amount on the same date. The loan asset is classified as 'loans and receivables'.

(e) On 1 June 20X5, Ejoy purchased a five year bond with a principal amount of $50 million and a fixed interest rate of five per cent which was the current market rate. The bond is classified as an 'available for sale' financial asset. Because of the size of the investment, Ejoy has entered into a floating interest rate swap. Ejoy has designated the swap as a fair value hedge of the bond. At 31 May 20X6, market interest rates were six per cent. As a result, the fair value of the bond has decreased to $48·3 million. Ejoy has received $0·5 million in net interest payments on the swap at 31 May 20X6 and the fair value hedge has been 100% effective in the period, and you should assume any gain/loss on the hedge is the same as the loss/gain on the bond. No entries have been made in the income statement to account for the bond or the hedge.

(f) No impairment of the goodwill arising on the acquisition of Zbay had occurred at 1 June 20X5. The recoverable amount of Zbay was $630 million and the value in use of Tbay was $290 million at 31 May 20X6. Impairment losses on goodwill are charged to cost of sales.

(g)   Assume that profits accrue evenly throughout the year and ignore any taxation effects.

(h)   It is the group's policy to value the non-controlling interest at its proportionate share of the fair value of the subsidiary's identifiable net assets.

Required

Prepare a consolidated income statement for the Ejoy Group for the year ended 31 May 20X6 in accordance with International Financial Reporting Standards.

(25 marks)

34 Case study question: Bravado   90 mins

Bravado, a public limited company, has acquired two subsidiaries and an associate. The draft statements of financial position are as follows at 31 May 20X9.

	Bravado $m	Message $m	Mixted $m
Assets			
Non-current assets			
Property, plant and equipment	265	230	161
Investments in subsidiaries:			
Message	300		
Mixted	128		
Investment in associate: Clarity	20		
Available-for-sale financial assets	51	6	5
	764	236	166
Current assets			
Inventories	135	55	73
Trade receivables	91	45	32
Cash and cash equivalents	102	100	8
	328	200	113
	1,092	436	279
Total assets			
Equity and liabilities			
Share capital	520	220	100
Retained earnings	240	150	80
Other components of equity	12	4	7
Total equity	772	374	187
Non-current liabilities:			
Long-term borrowings	120	15	5
Deferred tax	25	9	3
Total non-current liabilities	145	24	8
Current liabilities			
Trade and other payables	115	30	60
Current tax payable	60	8	24
Total current liabilities	175	38	84
Total liabilities	320	62	92
Total equity and liabilities	1,092	436	279

The following information is relevant to the preparation of the group financial statements.

(a)   On 1 June 20X8, Bravado acquired 80% of the equity interests of Message, a private entity. The purchase consideration comprised cash of $300 million. The fair value of the identifiable net assets of Message was $400 million, including any related deferred tax liability arising on acquisition. The owners of Message had to dispose of the entity for tax purposes by a specified date, and therefore sold the entity to the first company to bid for it, which was Bravado. An independent valuer has stated that the fair value of the non-controlling interest in Message was $86 million on 1 June 20X8. Bravado does not wish to measure the non-controlling interest in subsidiaries on the basis of the proportionate interest in the identifiable net assets, but wishes to use the 'full goodwill' method. The retained earnings of Message were $136 million and other components of equity were $4 million at the date of acquisition. There had been no new issue of capital by Message since the date of acquisition and the excess of the fair value of the net assets is due to an increase in the value of non-depreciable land.

(b)   On 1 June 20X7, Bravado acquired 6% of the ordinary shares of Mixted. Bravado had treated this investment as available-for-sale in the financial statements to 31 May 20X8, but had restated the investment at cost on Mixted becoming a subsidiary. On 1 June 20X8, Bravado acquired a further 64% of the ordinary shares of Mixted and gained control of the company. The consideration for the acquisitions was as follows.

	Holding	Consideration
		$m
1 June 20X7	6%	10
1 June 20X8	64%	118
	70%	128

Under the purchase agreement of 1 June 20X8, Bravado is required to pay the former shareholders 30% of the profits of Mixted on 31 May 20Y0 for each of the financial years to 31 May 20X9 and 31 May 20Y0. The fair value of this arrangement was estimated at $12 million at 1 June 20X8 and at 31 May 20X9 this value had not changed. This amount has not been included in the financial statements.

At 1 June 20X8, the fair value of the equity interest in Mixted held by Bravado before the business combination was $15 million, and the fair value of the non-controlling interest in Mixted was $53 million. The fair value of the identifiable net assets at 1 June 20X8 of Mixted was $170 million (excluding deferred tax assets and liabilities), and the retained earnings and other components of equity were $55 million and $7 million respectively. There had been no new issue of share capital by Mixted since the date of acquisition and the excess of the fair value of the net assets is due to an increase in the value of property, plant and equipment (PPE).

The fair value of the PPE was provisional pending receipt of the final valuations for these assets. These valuations were received on 1 December 20X8 and they resulted in a further increase of $6 million in the fair value of the net assets at the date of acquisition. This increase does not affect the fair value of the non-controlling interest. PPE is depreciated on the straight-line basis over seven years. The tax base of the identifiable net assets of Mixted was $166 million at 1 June 20X8. The tax rate of Mixted is 30%.

(c)   Bravado acquired a 10% interest in Clarity, a public limited company, on 1 June 20X7 for $8 million. The investment was accounted for as an available-for-sale investment and at 31 May 20X8, its value was $9 million. On 1 June 20X8, Bravado acquired an additional 15% interest in Clarity for $11 million and achieved significant influence. Clarity made profits after dividends of $6 million and $10 million for the years to 31 May 20X8 and 31 May 20X9.

(d)   On 1 June 20X7, Bravado purchased an equity instrument of 11 million dinars which was its fair value. The instrument was classified as available-for-sale. The relevant exchange rates and fair values were as follows:

	$ to dinars	Fair value of instrument – dinars
1 June 20X7	4.5	11
31 May 20X8	5.1	10
31 May 20X9	4.8	7

Bravado has not recorded any change in the value of the instrument since 31 May 20X8. The reduction in fair value as at 31 May 20X9 is deemed to be as a result of impairment.

(e)   Bravado manufactures equipment for the retail industry. The inventory is currently valued at cost. There is a market for the part completed product at each stage of production. The cost structure of the equipment is as follows.

	Cost per unit	Selling price per unit
	$	$
Production process: 1st stage	1,000	1,050
Conversion costs: 2nd stage	500	
Finished product	1,500	1,700

The selling costs are $10 per unit, and Bravado has 100,000 units at the first stage of production and 200,000 units of the finished product at 31 May 20X9. Shortly before the year end, a competitor released a new model onto the market which caused the equipment manufactured by Bravado to become less attractive to customers. The result was a reduction in the selling price to $1,450 of the finished product and $950 for 1st stage product.

(f)   The directors have included a loan to a director of Bravado in cash and cash equivalents of $1 million. The loan has no specific repayment date on it but is repayable on demand. The directors feel that there is no problem with this accounting entry as there is a choice of accounting policy within International Financial Reporting Standards (IFRS) and that showing the loan as cash is their choice of accounting policy as there is no IFRS which says that this policy cannot be utilised.

(g)   There is no impairment of goodwill arising on the acquisitions.

Required

(a)   Prepare a consolidated statement of financial position as at 31 May 20X9 for the Bravado Group. **(35 marks)**

(b)   Calculate and explain the impact on the calculation of goodwill if the non-controlling interest was calculated on a proportionate basis for Message and Mixted. **(8 marks)**

(c)   Discuss the view of the directors that there is no problem with showing a loan to a director as cash and cash equivalents, taking into account their ethical and other responsibilities as directors of the company. **(5 marks)**

Professional marks will be awarded in part (c) for clarity and expression of your discussion. **(2 marks)**

(Total = 50 marks)

35 Case study question: Base Group   90 mins

(a)   Base, a public limited company, acquired two subsidiaries, Zero and Black, both public limited companies, on 1 June 20X1. The details of the acquisitions at that date are as follows.

Subsidiary	Ordinary Share capital of $1 $m	Reserves $m	Fair value of net assets at acquisition $m	Cost of Investment $m	Ordinary share capital acquired $m
Zero	350	250	770	600	250
Black	200	150	400	270	120

The draft income statements for the year ended 31 May 20X3 are:

	Base $m	Zero $m	Black $m
Revenue	3,000	2,300	600
Cost of sales	(2,000)	(1,600)	(300)
Gross profit	1,000	700	300
Distribution costs	(240)	(230)	(120)
Administrative expenses	(200)	(220)	(80)
Finance cost: interest expense	(20)	(10)	(12)
Investment income receivable (including intragroup dividends paid May 20X3)	100	–	–
Profit before tax	640	240	88
Income tax expense	(130)	(80)	(36)
Profit for the year	510	160	52
Reserves 1 June 20X2	1,400	400	190

The following information is relevant to the preparation of the group financial statements.

(i)   On 1 December 20X2, Base sold 50 million $1 ordinary shares in Zero for $155 million. The only accounting entry made by Base was to record the receipt of the cash consideration in the cash account and in a suspense account.

(ii)   The fair value of Base's investment in Zero on 1 December 20X2 (just after the disposal) was $650m. The fair value of Base's investment in Black on 1 March 20X3 (just after the disposal) was $240m.

(iii)   On 1 March 20X3, Base sold 40 million $1 ordinary shares in Black for $2.65 per share. Only the cash receipt has been recorded in the cash account and a suspense account.

(iv)   Black had sold $150 million of goods to Base on 30 April 20X3. There was no opening inventory of intragroup goods but the closing inventories of these goods in Base's financial statements was $90 million. The profit on these goods was 30% on selling price.

(v)   Base has implemented in full IAS 19 *Employee benefits* in its financial statements. The directors have included the following amounts in the figure for cost of sales.

	$m
Current service cost	5
Actuarial deficit on obligation	4
Interest cost	3
Actuarial gain on assets	(2)
Charged to cost of sales	10

The accounting policy in respect of these accounts is recognition in profit or loss using the 10% corridor approach. The fair value of the plan assets at 31 May 20X2 was $48 million and the present value of the defined benefit obligation was $54 million at that date. The net cumulative unrecognised actuarial loss at 31 May 20X2 was $3 million and the expected remaining working lives of the employees was ten years.

(vi)   Base issued on 1 June 20X2 a redeemable debt instrument at a cost of $20 million. The debt is repayable in four years at $24.7 million. Base has included the redeemable debt in its statement of financial position at $20 million. The effective interest cost on the bond is 5.4%.

(vii)   Base had carried out work for a group of companies (Drum Group) during the financial year to 31 May 20X2. Base had accepted one million share options of the Drum Group in full settlement of the debt owed to them. At 1 June 20X2 these share options were valued at $3 million which was the value of the outstanding debt. The following table gives the prices of these shares and the fair value of the option.

	Share price	Fair value of option
31 May 20X2	$13	$3
31 May 20X3	$10	$1

The options had not been exercised during the year and remained at $3 million in the statement of financial position of Base. The options can be exercised at any time after 31 May 20X5 for $8·50 per share.

(viii) Base had paid a dividend of $50 million in the year and Zero had paid a dividend of $70 million in May 20X3.

(ix)   The post acquisition profit or loss effect of the fair value adjustments has been incorporated into the subsidiaries' records. Goodwill is reviewed for impairment annually. At 1 June 20X2 the group had recognised impairment losses of $10 million relating to Zero and $10m relating to Black. No further impairment losses were necessary during the year ending 31 May 20X3.

(x)   In regard to Zero, the group has opted to value the non-controlling interest on acquisition at its proportionate share of the subsidiary's identifiable net assets. In regard to Black it has opted to measure the non-controlling interest at fair value. The fair value of the non-controlling interest of Black on 1 June 20X1 was $180m.

(xi)   Ignore the tax implications of any capital gains made by the Group and assume profits accrue evenly throughout the year.

Required

Prepare a consolidated income statement for the Base Group for the year ended 31 May 20X3 in accordance with International Accounting Standards/International Financial Reporting Standards.

Show separately any required adjustment to the parent's equity in the group statement of financial position on the disposal of shares in subsidiaries. **(30 marks)**

(b)   A small but material part of the revenue of the group results mainly from the sale of software under licences which provide customers with the right to use these products. Base has stated that it follows emerging best practice in terms of its revenue recognition policy which it regards as US GAAP. It has stated that the International Accounting Standards Board has been slow in revising its current standards and the company has therefore adopted the US standard SAB 101 *Revenue Recognition in Financial Statements*. The group policy is as follows.

(i)   If services are essential to the functioning of the software (for example setting up the software) and the payment terms are linked, the revenue for both software and services is recognised on acceptance of the contract.

(ii)   Fees from the development of customised software, where service support is incidental to its functioning, are recognised at the completion of the contract.

Required

Discuss whether this policy is acceptable. (No knowledge of US GAAP is required.) **(5 marks)**

(c)   The directors of the Base group feel that their financial statements do not address a broad enough range of users' needs. They have reviewed the published financial statements and have realised that there is very little information about the corporate environmental governance. Base discloses the following environmental information in the financial statements.

(i)   The highest radiation dosage to a member of the public
(ii)   Total acid gas emissions and global warming potential

Contribution to clean air through emissions savings

Required

(i)   Explain the factors which provide encouragement to companies to disclose social and environmental information in their financial statements, briefly discussing whether the content of such disclosure should be at the company's discretion. **(9 marks)**

(ii)   Describe how the current disclosure by the Base Group of 'corporate environmental governance' could be extended and improved. **(6 marks)**

(Total = 50 marks)

Beth, a public limited company, has produced the following draft statements of financial position as at 30 November 20X7. Lose and Gain are both public limited companies:

	Beth $m	Lose $m	Gain $m
Assets			
Non current assets			
Property, plant and equipment	1,700	200	300
Intangible assets	300		
Investment in Lose	200		
Investment in Gain	180		
	2,380	200	300
Current assets			
Inventories	800	100	150
Trade receivables	600	60	80
Cash	500	40	20
	1,900	200	250
Total assets	4,280	400	550
Share capital of $1	1,500	100	200
Other reserves	300		
Retained earnings	400	200	300
Total equity	2,200	300	500
Non-current liabilities	700		
Current liabilities	1,380	100	50
Total liabilities	2,080	100	50
Total equity and liabilities	4,280	400	550

The following information is relevant to the preparation of the group financial statements of the Beth Group.

(i)

Date of acquisition	Holding acquired %	Retained earnings at acquisition $m	Purchase consideration $m
Lose: 1 December 20X5	20	80	40
1 December 20X6	60	150	160
Gain: 1 December 20X6	30	260	180

Lose and Gain have not issued any share capital since the acquisition of the shareholdings by Beth. The fair values of the net assets of Lose and Gain were the same as their carrying amounts at the date of the acquisitions.

Beth did not have significant influence over Lose at any time before gaining control of Lose, but does have significant influence over Gain. There has been no impairment of goodwill on the acquisition of Lose since its acquisition, but the recoverable amount of the net assets of Gain has been deemed to be $610 million at 30 November 20X7.

It is the group's policy to value its non-controlling interests at fair value. The fair value of the non-controlling interest in Lose at 1 December 20X6 was $53.33m.

The fair value of the 20% holding in Lose on 30th November 20X6 was also $53.33m.

(ii) Lose entered into an operating lease for a building on 1 December 20X6. The building was converted into office space during the year at a cost to Lose of $10 million. The operating lease is for a period of six years, at the end of which the building must be returned to the lessor in its original condition. Lose thinks that it would cost $2 million to convert the building back to its original condition at prices at 30 November 20X7. The entries that had been made in the financial statements of Lose were the charge for operating lease rentals ($4 million per annum) and the improvements to the building. Both items had been charged to the income statement. The improvements were completed during the financial year.

(iii) On 1 October 20X7, Beth sold inventory costing $18 million to Gain for $28 million. At 30 November 20X7, the inventory was still held by Gain. The inventory was sold to a third party on 15 December 20X7 for $35 million.

(iv) Beth had contracted to purchase an item of plant and equipment for 12 million euros on the following terms:

Payable on signing contract (1 September 20X7)	50%
Payable on delivery and installation (11 December 20X7)	50%

The amount payable on signing the contract (the deposit) was paid on the due date and is refundable. The following exchange rates are relevant:

20X7	Euros to 1 dollar
1 September	0·75
30 November	0·85
11 December	0·79

The deposit is included in trade receivables at the rate of exchange on 1 September 20X7. A full year's charge for depreciation of property, plant and equipment is made in the year of acquisition using the straight line method over six years.

(v) Beth sold some trade receivables which arose during November 20X7 to a factoring company on 30 November 20X7. The trade receivables sold are unlikely to default in payment based on past experience but they are long dated with payment not due until 1 June 20X8. Beth has given the factor a guarantee that it will reimburse any amounts not received by the factor. Beth received $45 million from the factor being 90% of the trade receivables sold. The trade receivables are not included in the statement of financial position of Beth and the balance not received from the factor (10% of the trade receivables factored) of $5 million has been written off against retained earnings.

(vi) Beth granted 200 share options to each of its 10,000 employees on 1 December 20X6. The shares vest if the employees work for the Group for the next two years. On 1 December 20X6, Beth estimated that there would be 1,000 eligible employees leaving in each year up to the vesting date. At 30 November 20X7, 600 eligible employees had left the company. The estimate of the number of employees leaving in the year to 30 November 20X8 was 500 at 30 November 20X7. The fair value of each share option at the grant date (1 December 20X6) was $10. The share options have not been accounted for in the financial statements.

(vii) The Beth Group operates in the oil industry and contamination of land occurs including the pollution of seas and rivers. The Group only cleans up the contamination if it is a legal requirement in the country where it operates. The following information has been produced for Beth by a group of environmental consultants for the year ended 30 November 20X7:

Cost to clean up contamination $m	Law existing in country
5	No
7	To come into force in December 20X7
4	Yes

The directors of Beth have a widely publicised environmental attitude which shows little regard for the effects on the environment of their business. The Group does not currently produce a separate environmental report and no provision for environmental costs has been made in the financial statements. Any provisions would be shown as non-current liabilities. Beth is likely to operate in these countries for several years.

Other information

Beth is currently suffering a degree of stagnation in its business development. Its domestic and international markets are being maintained but it is not attracting new customers. Its share price has not increased whilst that of its competitors has seen a rise of between 10% and 20%. Additionally it has recently received a significant amount of adverse publicity because of its poor environmental record and is to be investigated by regulators in several countries. Although Beth is a leading supplier of oil products, it has never felt the need to promote socially responsible policies and practices or make positive contributions to society because it has always maintained its market share. It is renowned for poor customer support, bearing little regard for the customs and cultures in the communities where it does business. It had recently made a decision not to pay the amounts owing to certain small and medium entities (SMEs) as the directors feel that SMEs do not have sufficient resources to challenge the non-payment in a court of law. The management of the company is quite authoritarian and tends not to value employees' ideas and contributions.

Required

(a)   Prepare the consolidated statement of financial position of the Beth Group as at 30 November 20X7 in accordance with International Financial Reporting Standards. **(35 marks)**

(b)   Describe to the Beth Group the possible advantages of producing a separate environmental report.

(8 marks)

(c)   Discuss the ethical and social responsibilities of the Beth Group and whether a change in the ethical and social attitudes of the management could improve business performance. **(7 marks)**

Note. Requirement (c) includes 2 professional marks for development of the discussion of the ethical and social responsibilities of the Beth Group.

(Total = 50 marks)

37 Preparation question: Foreign operation

BPP Note. In this question the proformas are given to you to help you get used to setting out your answer. You may wish to transfer them to a separate sheet, or alternatively use a separate sheet for your workings only.

Standard Co acquired 80% of Odense SA for $520,000 on 1 January 20X4 when the retained reserves of Odense were 2,100,000 Danish Krone.

An impairment test conducted at the year end revealed impairment losses of 168,000 Danish Krone relating to Odense's recognised goodwill. No impairment losses had previously been recognised.

The translation differences in the consolidated financial statements at 31 December 20X5 relating to the translation of the financial statements of Odense (excluding goodwill) were $27,000. Retained reserves of Odense in Odense's separate financial statements in the post-acquisition period to 31 December 20X5 as translated amounted to $138,000. The dividends charged to retained earnings in 20X6 were paid on 31 December 20X6.

It is the group's policy to value the non-controlling interest at acquisition at its proportionate share of the fair value of the subsidiary's net assets.

Exchange rates were as follows:

	Kr to $1
1 January 20X4	9.4
31 December 20X5	8.8
31 December 20X6	8.1
Average 20X6	8.4

Required

Prepare the consolidated statement of financial position, statement of comprehensive income and statement of changes in equity extract for retained earnings of the Standard Group for the year ended 31 December 20X6.

Set out your answer below, using a separate sheet for workings.

STATEMENTS OF FINANCIAL POSITION AT 31 DECEMBER 20X6

	Standard $'000	Odense Kr'000	Rate	Odense $'000	Consol $'000
Property, plant and equipment	1,285	4,400	8.1	543	
Investment in Odense	520	–		–	
Goodwill	–	–		–	
	1,805	4,400		543	
Current assets	410	2,000	8.1	247	
	2,215	6,400		790	
Share capital	500	1,000	9.4	106	
Retained reserves	1,115				
Pre-acquisition		2,100	9.4	224	
Post-acquisition			Bal	324	
	–	–			
	1,615	5,300		654	
Non-controlling interest					
Loans	200	300	8.1	37	
Current liabilities	400	800	8.1	99	
	600	1,100		136	
	2,215	6,400		790	

STATEMENT OF COMPREHENSIVE INCOME FOR YEAR ENDED 31 DECEMBER 20X6

	Standard $'000	Odense Kr'000	Rate	Odense $'000	Consol $'000
Revenue	1,125	5,200	8.4	619	
Cost of sales	(410)	(2,300)	8.4	(274)	
Gross profit	715	2,900		345	
Other expenses	(180)	(910)	8.4	(108)	
Impairment loss	–	–		–	
Dividend from Odense	40				
Profit before tax	575	1,990		237	
Income tax expense	(180)	(640)	8.4	(76)	
Profit for the year	395	1,350		161	
Other comprehensive income for the year					
Exchange differences on translation of foreign operation	–	–			
Total comprehensive income for the year	395	1,350			
Profit attributable to:					
Owners of the parent					
Non-controlling interest					
Total comprehensive income attributable to:					
Owners of the parent					
Non-controlling interest					

STATEMENTS OF CHANGES IN EQUITY FOR THE YEAR (EXTRACT FOR RETAINED RESERVES)

	Standard $'000	Odense Kr'000
Balance at 1 January 20X6	915	3,355
Dividends paid	(195)	(405)
Total comprehensive income for the year	395	1,350
Balance at 31 December 20X6	1,115	4,300

CONSOLIDATED STATEMENT OF CHANGES IN EQUITY FOR YEAR ENDED 31 DECEMBER 20X6 (EXTRACTS)

	Retained Earnings $'000
Balance at 1 January 20X6	1,065
Dividends paid	
Total comprehensive income for the year	
Balance at 31 December 20X6	

38 Memo

58 mins

ACR, 6/04, amended

Memo, a public limited company, owns 75% of the ordinary share capital of Random, a public limited company which is situated in a foreign country. Memo acquired Random on 1 May 20X3 for 120 million crowns (CR) when the retained profits of Random were 80 million crowns. Random has not revalued its assets or issued any share capital since its acquisition by Memo. The following financial statements relate to Memo and Random:

STATEMENTS OF FINANCIAL POSITION AT 30 APRIL 20X4

	Memo $m	Random CRm
Property, plant and equipment	297	146
Investment in Random	48	–
Loan to Random	5	–
Current assets	355	102
	705	248
Equity		
Ordinary shares of $1/1CR	60	32
Share premium account	50	20
Retained earnings	360	95
	470	147
Non current liabilities	30	41
Current liabilities	205	60
	705	248

INCOME STATEMENTS FOR YEAR ENDED 30 APRIL 20X4

	Memo $	Random CRm
Revenue	200	142
Cost of sales	(120)	(96)
Gross profit	80	46
Distribution and administrative expenses	(30)	(20)
Profit from operations	50	26
Interest receivable	4	–
Interest payable	–	(2)
Profit before taxation	54	24
Income tax expense	(20)	(9)
Profit after taxation	34	15

The following information is relevant to the preparation of the consolidated financial statements of Memo.

(a) Goodwill is reviewed for impairment annually. At 30 April 20X4, the impairment loss on recognised goodwill was CR4.2m.

(b) During the financial year Random has purchased raw materials from Memo and denominated the purchase in crowns in its financial records. The details of the transaction are set out below:

	Date of transaction	Purchase price	Profit percentage on selling price
		$m	
Raw materials	1 February 20X4	6	20%

At the year end, half of the raw materials purchased were still in the inventory of Random. The intragroup transactions have not been eliminated from the financial statements and the goods were recorded by Random at the exchange rate ruling on 1 February 20X4. A payment of $6 million was made to Memo when the exchange rate was 2·2 crowns to $1. Any exchange gain or loss arising on the transaction is still held in the current liabilities of Random.

(c) Memo had made an interest free loan to Random of $5 million on 1 May 20X3. The loan was repaid on 30 May 20X4. Random had included the loan in non-current liabilities and had recorded it at the exchange rate at 1 May 20X3.

(d) The fair value of the net assets of Random at the date of acquisition is to be assumed to be the same as the carrying value.

(e) The functional currency of Random is the Crown.

(f) The following exchange rates are relevant to the financial statements:

	Crowns to $
30 April/1 May 20X3	2·5
1 November 20X3	2·6
1 February 20X4	2
30 April 20X4	2·1
Average rate for year to 30 April 20X4	2

(g) Memo has paid a dividend of $8 million during the financial year and this is not included in the income statement.

It is the group's policy to value the non-controlling interest at acquisition at its proportionate share of the fair value of the subsidiary's identifiable net assets.

Required

Prepare a consolidated statement of comprehensive income for the year ended 30 April 20X4 and a consolidated statement of financial position at that date in accordance with International Financial Reporting Standards.

(Candidates should round their calculations to the nearest $100,000.) **(32 marks)**

6/08, amended

The following draft statements of financial position relate to Ribby, Hall, and Zian, all public limited companies, as at 31 May 20X8.

	Ribby $m	Hall $m	Zian Dinars m
Assets			
Non-current assets:			
Property, plant and equipment	250	120	360
Investment in Hall	98	–	–
Investment in Zian	30	–	–
Financial assets	10	5	148
Current assets	22	17	120
Total assets	410	142	628
Equity			
Ordinary shares	60	40	209
Other components of equity	30	10	–
Retained earnings	120	80	307
Total equity	210	130	516
Non-current liabilities	90	5	40
Current liabilities	110	7	72
Total equity and liabilities	410	142	628

The following information needs to be taken account of in the preparation of the group financial statements of Ribby.

(a) Ribby acquired 70% of the ordinary shares of Hall on 1 June 20X6 when Hall's other components of equity were $10 million and retained earnings were $60 million. The fair value of the net assets of Hall was $120 million at the date of acquisition. Ribby acquired 60% of the ordinary shares of Zian for 330 million dinars on 1 June 20X6 when Zian's retained earnings were 220 million dinars. The fair value of the net assets of Zian on 1 June 20X6 was 495 million dinars. The excess of the fair value over the net assets of Hall and Zian is due to an increase in the value of non-depreciable land. There have been no issues of ordinary shares since acquisition and goodwill on acquisition is not impaired for either Hall or Zian.

(b) Zian is located in a foreign country and imports its raw materials at a price which is normally denominated in dollars. The product is sold locally at selling prices denominated in dinars, and determined by local competition. All selling and operating expenses are incurred locally and paid in dinars. Distribution of profits is determined by the parent company, Ribby. Zian has financed part of its operations through a $4 million loan from Hall which was raised on 1 June 20X7. This is included in the financial assets of Hall and the non-current liabilities of Zian. Zian's management have a considerable degree of authority and autonomy in carrying out the operations of Zian and other than the loan from Hall, are not dependent upon group companies for finance.

(c) Ribby has a building which it purchased on 1 June 20X7 for 40 million dinars and which is located overseas. The building is carried at cost and has been depreciated on the straight-line basis over its useful life of 20 years. At 31 May 20X8, as a result of an impairment review, the recoverable amount of the building was estimated to be 36 million dinars.

(d) Ribby has a long-term loan of $10 million which is owed to a third party bank. At 31 May 20X8, Ribby decided that it would repay the loan early on 1 July 20X8 and formally agreed this repayment with the bank prior to the year end. The agreement sets out that there will be an early repayment penalty of $1 million.

(e) The directors of Ribby announced on 1 June 20X7 that a bonus of $6 million would be paid to the employees of Ribby if they achieved a certain target production level by 31 May 20X8. The bonus is to be paid partly in cash and partly in share options. Half of the bonus will be paid in cash on 30 November 20X8 whether or not the employees are still working for Ribby. The other half will be given in share options on the same date, provided that the employee is still in service on 30 November 20X8. The exercise price and number of options will be fixed by management on 30 November 20X8. The target production was met and management expect 10% of employees to leave between 31 May 20X8 and 30 November 20X8. No entry has been made in the financial statements of Ribby.

(f)   Ribby operates a defined benefit pension plan that provides a pension of 1·2% of the final salary for each year of service, subject to a minimum of four years service. On 1 June 20X7, Ribby improved the pension entitlement so that employees receive 1·4% of their final salary for each year of service. This improvement applied to all prior years service of the employees. As a result, the present value of the defined benefit obligation on 1 June 20X7 increased by $4 million as follows:

	$m
Employees with more than four years service	3
Employees with less than four years service (average service of two years)	1
	4

Ribby had not accounted for the improvement in the pension plan.

(g)   Ribby is considering selling its subsidiary, Hall. Just prior to the year end, Hall sold inventory to Ribby at a price of $6 million. The carrying value of the inventory in the financial records of Hall was $2 million. The cash was received before the year end, and as a result the bank overdraft of Hall was virtually eliminated at 31 May 20X8. After the year end the transaction was reversed, and it was agreed that this type of transaction would be carried out again when the interim financial statements were produced for Hall, if the company had not been sold by that date.

(h)   The following exchange rates are relevant to the preparation of the group financial statements:

	Dinars to $
1 June 20X6	11
1 June 20X7	10
31 May 20X8	12
Average for year to 31 May 20X8	10.5

(i)   It is the group's policy to value the non-controlling interest at acquisition at fair value. The fair value of the non-controlling interest in Hall on 1 June 20X6 was $42m. The fair value of the NCI in Zian on 1 June 20X6 was 220 dinars.

Required

(a)   Discuss and apply the principles set out in IAS 21 *The effects of changes in foreign exchange rates* in order to determine the functional currency of Zian.   **(8 marks)**

(b)   Prepare a consolidated statement of financial position of the Ribby Group at 31 May 20X8 in accordance with International Financial Reporting Standards.   **(35 marks)**

(c)   Discuss how the manipulation of financial statements by company accountants is inconsistent with their responsibilities as members of the accounting profession, setting out the distinguishing features of a profession and the privileges that society gives to a profession. (Your answer should include reference to the above scenario.)   **(7 marks)**

Note: requirement (c) includes 2 marks for the quality of the discussion.

(Total = 50 marks)

	$m	$m
Share capital		100
Retained earnings		320
		420
Current liabilities (including taxation $25 million)		130
		550

The loss on the sale of the subsidiary in the group accounts comprised:

		$m
Sale proceeds:	ordinary shares	300
	cash	75
		375
Net assets sold (80% of 420)		(336)
Goodwill		(64)
Loss on sale		(25)

The accountant was unsure as to how to deal with the above disposal and has simply included the above loss in the statement of cash flows without any further adjustments.

(b) During the year, Portal has transferred several of its items of property, plant and equipment to a newly created company, Site, which is owned jointly with another company.

The following information related to the accounting for the investment in Site:

		$m
Purchase cost:	property, plant and equipment transferred	200
	cash	25
		225
Dividend received		(10)
Profit for year on joint venture after tax		55
Revaluation of property, plant and equipment		30
Closing balance per statement of financial position – Site		300

The statement of cash flows showed the cost of purchasing a stake in Site of $225 million. Site is accounted for using the equity accounting approach rather than by proportional consolidation.

(c) The taxation amount in the statement of cash flows is the difference between the opening and closing balances on the taxation account. The charge for taxation in the income statement is $171.

(d) Included in the cash flow figure for the disposal of property, plant and equipment is the sale and leaseback, on an operating basis, of certain land and buildings. The sale proceeds of the land and buildings were $1,000 million in the form of an 8% loan note receivable by Portal in 20X2. The total profit on the sale of tangible non-current assets, including the land and buildings, was $120 million.

(e) The non-controlling interest figure in the statement comprised the difference between the opening and closing statement of financial position totals. The profit attributable to the non-controlling interest for the year was $75 million.

(f) The cash generated from operations is the profit before taxation adjusted for the statement of financial position movement in inventory, trade receivables and current liabilities and the depreciation charge for the year. The interest receivable credited to the income statement was $27 million and the interest payable was $19 million.

(g) It is the group's policy to value the non-controlling interest at its proportionate share of the fair value of the subsidiary's identifiable net assets.

Required

(a) Prepare a revised group statement of cash flows for Portal, taking into account notes (a) to (f) above, and using the format set out in the question. **(18 marks)**

(b) Prepare a brief presentation on the usefulness and information content of group statements of cash flows generally and specifically on the group statement of cash flows of Portal. **(7 marks)**

(Total = 25 marks)

42 Cash study question: Andash

90 mins

(a)   The following draft group financial statements relate to Andash, a public limited company.

ANDASH
DRAFT GROUP STATEMENTS OF FINANCIAL POSITION AS AT

	20X6 $m	20X5 $m
Assets		
Non-current assets		
Property, plant and equipment	5,170	4,110
Goodwill	120	130
Investment in associate	60	–
	5,350	4,240
Current assets		
Inventories	2,650	2,300
Trade receivables	2,400	1,500
Cash and cash equivalents	140	300
	5,190	4,100
Total assets	10,540	8,340
Equity and liabilities		
Equity attributable to owners of parent		
Share capital	400	370
Other reserves	120	80
Retained earnings	1,250	1,100
	1,770	1,550
Non-controlling interest	200	180
Total equity	1,970	1,730
Non-current liabilities		
Long term borrowings	3,100	2,700
Deferred tax	400	300
Total non-current liabilities	3,500	3,000
Current liabilities		
Trade payables	4,700	2,800
Interest payable	70	40
Current tax payable	300	770
Total current liabilities	5,070	3,610
Total liabilities	8,570	6,610
Total equity and liabilities	10,540	8,340

ANDASH
DRAFT GROUP INCOME STATEMENT FOR THE YEAR ENDED 31 OCTOBER 20X6

	$m
Revenue	17,500
Cost of sales	(14,600)
Gross profit	2,900
Distribution costs	(1,870)
Administrative expenses	(490)
Finance costs – interest payable	(148)
Gain on disposal of subsidiary	8
Profit before tax	400
Income tax expense	(160)
Profit for the year	240
Profit attributable to owners of parent	200
Profit attributable to non-controlling interest	40
	240

ANDASH

DRAFT STATEMENT OF CHANGES IN EQUITY OF THE PARENT FOR THE YEAR ENDED 31 OCTOBER 20X6

	Share capital $m	Other reserves $m	Retained earnings $m	Total $m
Balance at 31 October 20X5	370	80	1,100	1,550
Profit for period			200	200
Dividends			(50)	(50)
Issue of share capital	30	30		60
Share options issued		10		10
Balance at 31 October 20X6	400	120	1,250	1,770

The following information relates to the draft group financial statements of Andash.

(i)   There had been no disposal of property, plant and equipment during the year. The depreciation for the period included in cost of sales was $260 million. Andash had issued share options on 31 October 20X6 as consideration for the purchase of plant. The value of the plant purchased was $9 million at 31 October 20X6 and the share options issued had a market value of $10 million. The market value had been used to account for the plant and share options.

(ii)   Andash had acquired 25 per cent of Joma on 1 November 20X5. The purchase consideration was 25 million ordinary shares of Andash valued at $50 million and cash of $10 million. Andash has significant influence over Joma. The investment is stated at cost in the draft group statement of financial position. The reserves of Joma at the date of acquisition were $20 million and at 31 October 20X6 were $32 million. Joma had sold inventory in the period to Andash at a selling price of $16 million. The cost of the inventory was $8 million and the inventory was still held by Andash at 31 October 20X6. there was no goodwill arising on the acquisition of Joma.

(iii)   Andash owns 60% of a subsidiary Broiler, a public limited company. The goodwill arising on acquisition was $90 million. The carrying value of Broiler's identifiable net assets (excluding goodwill arising on acquisition) in the group consolidated financial statements is $240 million at 31 October 20X6. The recoverable amount of Broiler is expected to be $260 million and no impairment loss has been recorded up to 31 October 20X5.

(iv)   On 30 April 20X6 a wholly owned subsidiary, Chang was disposed of Chang prepared interim financial statements on that date which are as follows:

	$m
Property, plant and equipment	10
Inventories	8
Trade receivables	4
Cash and cash equivalents	5
	27

	$m
Share capital	10
Retained earnings	4
Trade payables	6
Current tax payable	7
	27

The consolidated carrying values of the assets and liabilities at that date were the same as above. The group received cash proceeds of $32 million and the carrying amount of goodwill was $10 million.

(Ignore the taxation effects of any adjustments required to the group financial statements and round all calculations to the nearest $million.)

BPP note: Assume no dividend was paid by Joma during the period.

(v)   It is the group's policy to value the non-controlling interest at its proportionate share of the fair value of the subsidiary's identifiable net assets.

Prepare a group statement of cash flows using the indirect method for the Andash Group for the year ended 31 October 20X6 in accordance with IAS 7 *Statement of cash flows* after making any necessary adjustments required to the draft group financial statements of Andash as a result of the information above.

(Candidates are not required to produce the adjusted group financial statements of Andash.)   **(25 marks)**

(b)   Andash manufactures mining equipment and extracts natural gas. You are advising the directors on matters relating to the year ended 31 October 20X7.

The directors are uncertain about the role of the IASB's *Framework for the Preparation and Presentation of Financial Statements* (the *Framework*) in corporate reporting. Their view is that accounting is based on the transactions carried out by the company and these transactions are allocated to the company's accounting periods by using the matching and prudence concepts. The argument put forward by the directors is that the *Framework* does not take into account the business and legal constraints within which companies operate. Further they have given two situations which have arisen in the current financial statements where they feel that the current accounting practice is inconsistent with the *Framework*.

Situation 1

Andash has recently constructed a natural gas extraction facility and commenced production one year ago (1 November 20X6). There is an operating licence given to the company by the government which requires the removal of the facility and rectification of the damage caused by extraction of natural gas at the end of its life, which is estimated at 20 years. Depreciation is charged on the straight line basis. The cost of the construction of the facility was $200 million and the net present value at 1 November 20X6 of the future costs to be incurred in order to return the extraction site to its original condition are estimated at $50 million (using a discount rate of 5% per annum). 80 per cent of these costs relate to the removal of the facility and 20% relate to the rectification of the damage caused through the extraction of the natural gas. The auditors have told the company that a provision for decommissioning has to be set up.

Situation 2

Andash purchased a building on 1 November 20X6 for $10 million. The building qualified for a grant of $2 million which has been treated as a deferred credit in the financial statements. The tax allowances are reduced by the amount of the grant. There are additional temporary differences of $40 million in respect of deferred tax liabilities at the year end. Also the company has sold extraction equipment which carries a five year warranty. The directors have made a provision for the warranty of $4 million at 31 October 20X7 which is deductible for tax when costs are incurred under the warranty. In addition to the warranty provision the company has unused tax losses of $70 million. The directors of the company are unsure as to whether a deferred tax liability is required.

(Assume that the depreciation of the building is straight line over ten years, and tax allowances of 25% on the reducing balance basis can be claimed on the building. Tax is payable at 30%.)

Required

(i)   Explain the importance of the *Framework* to the reporting of corporate performance and whether it takes into account the business and legal constraints placed upon companies.   **(6 marks)**

(ii)   Explain with reasons and suitable extracts/computations the accounting treatment of the above two situations in the financial statements for the year ended 31 October 20X7.   **(14 marks)**

(iii)   Discuss whether the treatment of the items in the situations above appears consistent with the *Framework*.   **(5 marks)**

(Total = 50 marks)

	$m
Property, plant and equipment	70
Inventories and work in progress	90
	160

The purchase consideration was $100 million in cash and $25 million (discounted value) deferred consideration which is payable on 1 July 20X6. The difference between the discounted value of the deferred consideration ($25 million) and the amount payable ($29 million) is included in 'finance costs'. Zambeze wants to set up a provision for reconstruction costs of $10 million retrospectively on the acquisition of Damp. This provision has not yet been set up.

(b)   There had been no disposals of property, plant and equipment during the year. Depreciation for the period charged in cost of sales was $60 million.

(c)   Current liabilities comprised the following items:

	20X6	20X5
	$m	$m
Trade payables	1,341	1,200
Interest payable	50	45
Taxation	190	185
	1,581	1,430

(d)   Non-current liabilities comprised the following:

	20X6	20X5
	$m	$m
Deferred consideration – purchase of Damp	29	–
Liability for the purchase of property, plant and equipment	144	–
Loans repayable	621	555
Deferred tax liability	30	25
Retirement benefit liability	26	20
	850	600

(e)   The retirement benefit liability comprised the following:

	$m
Movement in year	
Liability at 1 July 20X5	20
Current and past service costs charged to profit or loss	13
Contributions paid to retirement benefit scheme	(7)
Liability 30 June 20X6	26

There was no actuarial gain or loss in the year.

(f)   Goodwill was impairment tested on 30 June 20X6 and any impairment was included in the financial statements for the year ended 30 June 20X6.

(g)   The Finance Director has set up a company, River, through which Zambeze conducts its investment activities. Zambeze has paid $400 million to River during the year and this has been included in dividends paid. The money was invested in a specified portfolio of investments. Ninety five per cent of the profits and one hundred per cent of the losses in the specified portfolio of investments are transferred to Zambeze. An investment manager has charge of the company's investments and owns all of the share capital of River. An agreement between the investment manager and Zambeze sets out the operating guidelines and prohibits the investment manager from obtaining access to the investments for the manager's benefit. An annual transfer of the profit/loss will occur on 30 June annually and the capital will be returned in four years time. The transfer of $400 million cash occurred on 1 January 20X6 but no transfer of profit/loss has yet occurred. The statement of financial position of River at 30 June 20X6 is as follows:

RIVER: STATEMENT OF FINANCIAL POSITION AT 30 JUNE 20X6

	$m
Investment at fair value through profit or loss	390
	390
Share capital	400
Retained earnings	(10)
	390

(h) It is the group's policy to value the non-controlling interest at its proportionate share of the fair value of the subsidiary's identifiable net assets.

Required

(a) Prepare a group statement of cash flows for the Zambeze Group for the year ended 30 June 20X6 using the indirect method. **(35 marks)**

(b) Discuss the issues which would determine whether River should be consolidated by Zambeze in the group financial statements. **(9 marks)**

(c) Discuss briefly the importance of ethical behaviour in the preparation of financial statements and whether the creation of River could constitute unethical practice by the finance director of Zambeze. **(6 marks)**

(Total = 50 marks)

Two marks are available for the quality of the discussion of the issues regarding the consolidation of River and the importance of ethical behaviour.

45 Case study question: Warrburt   90 mins

12/08

Note: This question has been amended in accordance with issues raised with the examiner.

The following draft group financial statements relate to Warrburt, a public limited company:

WARRBURT GROUP: STATEMENT OF FINANCIAL POSITION AS AT 30 NOVEMBER 20X8

	30 Nov 20X8 $m	30 Nov 20X7 $m
Assets		
Non-current assets		
Property, plant and equipment	350	360
Goodwill	80	100
Other intangible assets	228	240
Investment in associate	100	–
Available-for-sale financial assets	142	150
	900	850
Current assets		
Inventories	135	198
Trade receivables	92	163
Cash and cash equivalents	288	323
	515	684
Total assets	1,415	1,534
Equity and liabilities		

Equity attributable to owners of the parent: to last million		
Share capital	650	595
Retained earnings	367	454
Other components of equity	25	20
	1,042	1,069
Non-controlling interest	70	53
Total equity	1,112	1,122
Non-current liabilities		
Long-term borrowing	20	64
Deferred tax	28	26
Long-tem provisions	100	96
Total non-current liabilities	148	186
Current liabilities:		
Trade payables	115	180
Current tax payable	35	42
Short-term provisions	5	4
Total current liabilities	155	226
Total liabilities	303	412
Total equity and liabilities	1,415	1,534

WARRBURT GROUP: STATEMENT OF COMPREHENSIVE INCOME FOR THE YEAR ENDED 30 NOVEMBER 20X8

	$m
Revenue	910
Cost of sales	(886)
Gross profit	24
Other income	31
Distribution costs	(40)
Administrative expenses	(35)
Finance costs	(9)
Share of profit of associate	6
Loss before tax	(23)
Income tax expense	(29)
Loss for the year from continuing operations	(52)
Loss for the year	(52)
Other comprehensive income for the year (after tax)	
Available-for-sale financial assets (AFS)	27
Re-classification of gains on available-for-sale financial assets to profit or loss	(24)
Gains on property revaluation	2
Actuarial losses on defined benefit plan	(4)
Other comprehensive income for the year (after tax)	1
Total comprehensive income for the year	(51)
Profit/loss attributable to:	
Owners of the parent	(74)
Non-controlling interest	22
	(52)
Total comprehensive income attributable to:	
Owners of the parent	(73)
Non-controlling interest	22
	(51)

WARRBURT GROUP: STATEMENT OF CHANGES IN EQUITY FOR THE YEAR ENDED 30 NOVEMBER 20X8

	Share capital $m	Retained earnings $m	AFS financial assets $m	Revaluation surplus $m	Total $m	Non-controlling interest $m	Total equity $m
Balance at 1 December 20X7	595	454	16	4	1,069	53	1,122
Share capital issued	55				55		55
Dividends		(9)			(9)	(5)	(14)
Total comprehensive income for the year		(78)	3	2	(73)	22	(51)
Balance at 30 November 20X8	650	367	19	6	1,042	70	1,112

NOTE TO STATEMENT OF CHANGES IN EQUITY:

	$m
Profit/loss attributable to owners of parent	(74)
Actuarial losses on defined benefit plan	(4)
Total comprehensive income for year – retained earnings	(78)

The following information relates to the financial statements of Warrburt.

(i)   Warrburt holds available-for-sale (AFS) financial assets which are owned by the holding company. The following schedule relates to those assets.

	$m
Balance 1 December 20X7	150
Less sales of AFS financial assets at carrying value	(38)
Add gain on revaluation of AFS financial assets	30
	142

The sale proceeds of the AFS financial assets were $45 million. Profit on the sale of AFS financial assets is shown as 'other income' in the financial statements. Deferred tax of $3 million arising on the revaluation gain above has been taken into account in 'other comprehensive income' for the year. The profit held in equity on the AFS financial assets that were sold of $24 million, has been transferred to profit or loss.

(ii)   The retirement benefit liability is shown as a long-term provision in the statement of financial position and comprises the following:

	$m
Liability at 1 December 20X7	96
Expense for period	10
Contributions to scheme (paid)	(10)
Actuarial losses	4
Liability at 30 November 20X8	100

Warrburt recognises actuarial gains and losses in the statement of comprehensive income in the period in which they occur. The benefits paid in the period by the trustees of the scheme were $3 million. There is no tax impact with regards to the retirement benefit liability.

(iii)   The property, plant and equipment (PPE) in the statement of financial position comprises the following:

	$m
Carrying value at 1 December 20X7	360
Additions at cost	78
Gains on property revaluation	4
Disposals	(56)
Depreciation	(36)
Carrying value at 30 November 20X8	350

Plant and machinery with a carrying value of $1 million had been destroyed by fire in the year. The asset was replaced by the insurance company with new plant and machinery which was valued at $3 million. The machines were acquired directly by the insurance company and no cash payment was made to Warrburt.

The company included the net gain on this transaction in 'additions at cost' and as a deduction from administrative expenses.

The disposal proceeds were $63 million. The gain on disposal is included in administrative expenses. Deferred tax of $2 million has been deducted in arriving at the 'gains on property revaluation' figure in 'other comprehensive income'.

The remaining additions of PPE comprised imported plant and equipment from an overseas supplier on 30 June 20X8. The cost of the PPE was 380 million dinars with 280 million dinars being paid on 31 October 20X8 and the balance to be paid on 31 December 20X8.

The rates of exchange were as follows:

	Dinars to $1
30 June 20X8	5
31 October 20X8	4·9
30 November 20X8	4·8

Exchange gains and losses are included in administrative expenses.

(iv)   Warrburt purchased a 25% interest in an associate for cash on 1 December 20X7. The net assets of the associate at the date of acquisition were $300 million. The associate made a profit after tax of $24 million and paid a dividend of $8 million out of these profits in the year ended 30 November 20X8. Assume a tax rate of 25%.

(v)   An impairment test had been carried out at 30 November 20X8, on goodwill and other intangible assets. The result showed that goodwill was impaired by $20 million and other intangible assets by $12 million.

(vi)   The short term provisions relate to finance costs which are payable within six months.

Warrburt's directors are concerned about the results for the year in the statement of comprehensive income and the subsequent effect on the statement of cash flows. They have suggested that the proceeds of the sale of property, plant and equipment and the sale of available-for-sale financial assets should be included in 'cash generated from operations'. The directors are afraid of an adverse market reaction to their results and of the importance of meeting targets in order to ensure job security, and feel that the adjustments for the proceeds would enhance the 'cash health' of the business.

Required

(a)   Prepare a group statement of cash flows for Warrburt for the year ended 30 November 20X8 in accordance with IAS 7 *Statement of cash flows*, using the indirect method.   **(35 marks)**

(b)   Discuss the key issues which the statement of cash flows highlights regarding the cash flow of the company.   **(10 marks)**

(c)   Discuss the ethical responsibility of the company accountant in ensuring that manipulation of the statement of cash flows, such as that suggested by the directors, does not occur.   **(5 marks)**

Note: requirements (b) and (c) include 2 professional marks in total for the quality of the discussion.

(Total = 50 marks)

PERFORMANCE REPORTING

Questions 46 to 59 cover Performance Reporting, the subject of Part D of the BPP Study Text for Paper P2.

BPP Note. **Statement of financial position** is the revised IAS 1 term for **balance sheet**.

46 Mineral

45 mins

`ACR, 12/01`

Mineral, a public limited company, has prepared its financial statements for the year ended 31 October 20X3. The following information relates to those financial statements.

	20X3	20X2
	$m	$m
Group revenue	250	201
Gross profit	45	35
Profit before interest and tax	10	9
Profit before tax	12	8
Profit for the year	5	4
Non-current assets	42	36
Current assets	55	43
Current liabilities	25	24
Non-current liabilities – long-term loans	13	9
Equity	59	46

The company expects to achieve growth in retained earnings of about 20% in the year to 31 October 20X4. Thereafter retained earnings are expected to accelerate to produce growth of between 20% and 25%. The growth will be generated by the introduction of new products and business efficiencies in manufacturing and in the company's infrastructure.

Mineral manufactures products from aluminium and other metals and is one of the largest producers in the world. Production for 20X3 increased by 18% through the acquisition of a competitor company, increased production at three of its plants and through the regeneration of old plants. There has been a recent growth in the consumption of its products because of the substitution of aluminium for heavier metals in motor vehicle manufacture. Cost reductions continued as a business focus in 20X3 and Mineral has implemented a cost reduction programme to be achieved by 20X6. Targets for each operation have been set.

Mineral's directors feel that its pricing strategy will help it compensate for increased competition in the sector. The company recently reduced the price of its products to the motor vehicle industry. This strategy is expected to increase demand and the usage of aluminium in the industry. However, in spite of the environmental benefits, certain car manufacturers have formed a cartel to prevent the increased usage of aluminium in car production.

In the period 20X3 to 20X5, Mineral expects to spend around $40 million on research and development and investment in non-current assets. The focus of the investments will be on enlarging the production capabilities. An important research and development project will be the joint project with a global car manufacturer to develop a new aluminium alloy car body.

In January 20X3, Mineral commenced a programme of acquisition of its own ordinary shares for cancellation. At 31 October 20X3, Mineral had purchased and cancelled five million ordinary shares of $1. In addition a subsidiary of Mineral had $4 million of convertible redeemable loan notes outstanding. The loan notes mature on 15 June 20X6 and are convertible into ordinary shares at the option of the holder. The competitive environment requires Mineral to provide medium and long term financing to its customers in connection with the sale of its products. Generally the financing is placed with third party lenders but due to the higher risks associated with such financing, the amount of the financing expected to be provided by Mineral itself is likely to increase.

The directors of Mineral have attempted to minimise the financial risk to which the group is exposed. The company operates in the global market place with the inherent financial risk that this entails. The management have performed a sensitivity analysis assuming a 10% adverse movement in foreign exchange rates and interest rates applied to hedging contracts and other exposures. The analysis indicated that such market movement would not have a material effect on the company's financial position.

Mineral has a reputation for responsible corporate behaviour and sees the work force as the key factor in the profitable growth of the business. During the year the company made progress towards the aim of linking environmental performance with financial performance by reporting the relationship between the eco-productivity index for basic production, and water and energy costs used in basic production. A feature of this index is that it can be segregated at site and divisional level and can be used in the internal management decision-making process.

The directors of Mineral are increasingly seeing their shareholder base widen with the result that investors are more demanding and sophisticated. As a result, the directors are uncertain as to the nature of the information which would provide clear and credible explanations of corporate activity. They wish their annual report to meet market expectations. They have heard that many companies deal with three key elements of corporate activity, namely reporting business performance, the analysis of the financial position, and the nature of corporate citizenship, and have asked your firm's advice in drawing up the annual report.

Required

Draft a report to the directors of Mineral setting out the nature of information which could be disclosed in annual reports in order that there might be better assessment of the performance of the company.

Candidates should use the information in the question and produce their report under the headings:

(a)	Reporting business performance	**(10 marks)**
(b)	Analysis of financial position	**(6 marks)**
(c)	The nature of corporate citizenship	**(5 marks)**

Marks will be awarded for the presentation and style of the report. **(4 marks)**

(Total = 25 marks)

47 Value relevance

45 mins

ACR, 12/02

The 'value relevance' of published financial statements is increasingly being called into question. Financial statements have been said to no longer have the same relevance to investors as they had in the past. Investment analysts are developing their own global investment performance standards which increasingly do not use historical cost as a basis for evaluating a company. The traditional accounting ratio analysis is outdated with a new range of performance measures now being used by analysts.

Companies themselves are under pressure to report information which is more transparent and which includes many non-financial disclosures. At the same time the move towards global accounting standards has become more important to companies wishing to raise capital in foreign markets. Corporate reporting is changing in order to meet the investors' needs. However, earnings are still the critical 'number' in both the company and the analyst's eyes.

In order to meet the increasing information needs of investors, standard setters are requiring the use of prospective information and current values more and more with the traditional historical cost accounts and related ratios seemingly becoming less and less important.

Required

(a) Discuss the importance of published financial statements as a source of information for the investor, giving examples of the changing nature of the performance measures being utilised by investors. **(11 marks)**

(b) Discuss how financial reporting is changing to meet the information requirements of investors and why the emphasis on the 'earnings' figure is potentially problematic. **(8 marks)**

(c) Discuss whether the intended use of fair values will reduce the importance of historical cost information.
(6 marks)

(Total = 25 marks)

48 Rockby and Bye

Rockby, a public limited company, has committed itself before its year-end of 31 March 20X4 to a plan of action to sell a subsidiary, Bye. The sale is expected to be completed on 1 July 20X4 and the financial statements of the group were signed on 15 May 20X4. The subsidiary, Bye, a public limited company, had net assets at the year end of $5 million and the book value of related goodwill is $1 million. Bye has made a loss of $500,000 from 1 April 20X4 to 15 May 20X4 and is expected to make a further loss up to the date of sale of $600,000. Rockby was, at 15 May 20X4, negotiating the consideration for the sale of Bye but no contract has been signed or public announcement made as of that date.

Rockby expected to receive $4·5 million for the company after selling costs. The value-in-use of Bye at 15 May 20X4 was estimated at $3·9 million.

Further, the non-current assets of Rockby include the following items of plant and head office land and buildings.

(i)   **Property, plant and equipment held for use in operating leases**. At 31 March 20X4 the company has at carrying value $10 million of plant which has recently been leased out on operating leases. These leases have now expired. The company is undecided as to whether to sell the plant or lease it to customers under finance leases. The fair value less selling costs of the plant is $9 million and the value-in-use is estimated at $12 million.

Plant with a carrying value of $5 million at 31 March 20X4 has ceased to be used because of a downturn in the economy. The company had decided at 31 March 20X4 to maintain the plant in workable condition in case of a change in economic conditions. Rockby subsequently sold the plant by auction on 14 May 20X4 for $3 million net of costs.

(ii) The Board of Rockby approved the relocation of the head office site on 1 March 20X3. The head office land and buildings were renovated and upgraded in the year to 31 March 20X3 with a view to selling the site. During the improvements, subsidence was found in the foundations of the main building. The work to correct the subsidence and the renovations were completed on 1 June 20X3. As at 31 March 20X3 the renovations had cost $2·3 million and the cost of correcting the subsidence was $1 million. The carrying value of the head office land and buildings was $5 million at 31 March 20X3 before accounting for the renovation. Rockby moved its head office to the new site in June 20X3, and at the same time, the old head office property was offered for sale at a price of $10 million.

However, the market for commercial property had deteriorated significantly and as at 31 March 20X4, a buyer for the property had not been found. At that time the company did not wish to reduce the price and hoped that market conditions would improve. On 20 April 20X4, a bid of $8·3 million was received for the property and eventually it was sold (net of costs) for $7·5 million on 1 June 20X4. The carrying value of the head office land and buildings was $7 million at 31 March 20X4.

Non-current assets are shown in the financial statements at historical cost.

Required

(a)   Discuss the way in which the sale of the subsidiary, Bye, would be dealt with in the group financial statements of Rockby at 31 March 20X4.   **(7 marks)**

(b)   Discuss whether the following non-current assets should be classed as 'held for sale'.

(i)   The items of plant in the group financial statements at 31 March 20X4;   **(7 marks)**

(ii)   The head office land and buildings in the group financial statements at 31 March 20X3 and 31 March 20X4.   **(5 marks)**

(Total = 19 marks)

49 Ashlee

Ashlee, a public limited company, is preparing its group financial statements for the year ended 31 March 20X5. The company applies newly issued IFRSs at the earliest opportunity. The group comprises three companies, Ashlee, the holding company, and its 100% owned subsidiaries Pilot and Gibson, both public limited companies. The group financial statements at first appeared to indicate that the group was solvent and in a good financial position. However, after the year end, but prior to the approval of the financial statements, mistakes have been found which affect the financial position of the group to the extent that loan covenant agreements have been breached.

As a result the loan creditors require Ashlee to cut its costs, reduce its operations and reorganise its activities. Therefore, redundancies are planned and the subsidiary, Pilot, is to be reorganised. The carrying value of Pilot's net assets, including allocated goodwill, was $85 million at 31 March 20X5, before taking account of reorganisation costs. The directors of Ashlee wish to include $4 million of reorganisation costs in the financial statements of Pilot for the year ended 31 March 20X5. The directors of Ashlee have prepared cash flow projections which indicate that the net present value of future net cash flows from Pilot is expected to be $84 million if the reorganisation takes place and $82 million if the reorganisation does not take place.

Ashlee had already decided prior to the year end to sell the other subsidiary, Gibson. Gibson will be sold after the financial statements have been signed. The contract for the sale of Gibson was being negotiated at the time of the preparation of the financial statements and it is expected that Gibson will be sold in June 20X5.

The carrying amounts of Gibson and Pilot, including allocated goodwill, were as follows at the year end.

	Gibson	Pilot
	$m	$m
Goodwill	30	5
Property, plant and equipment: cost	120	55
valuation	180	
Inventories	100	20
Trade receivables	40	10
Trade payables	(20)	(5)
	450	85

The fair value of the net assets of Gibson at the year end was $415 million and the estimated costs of selling the company were $5 million.

Part of the business activity of Ashlee is to buy and sell property. The directors of Ashlee had signed a contract on 1 March 20X5 to sell two of its development properties which are carried at the lower of cost and net realisable value under IAS 2 *Inventories*. The sale was agreed at a figure of $40 million (carrying value $30 million). A receivable of $40 million and profit of $10 million were recognised in the financial statements for the year ended 31 March 20X5. The sale of the properties was completed on 1 May 20X5 when the legal title passed. The policy used in the prior year was to recognise revenue when the sale of such properties had been completed.

Additionally, Ashlee had purchased, on 1 April 20X4, 150,000 shares of a public limited company, Race, at a price of $20 per share. Ashlee had incurred transaction costs of $100,000 to acquire the shares. The company is unsure how to classify this investment in the financial statements for the year ended 31 March 20X5. The quoted price of the shares at 31 March 20X5 was $25 per share. The shares purchased represent approximately 1% of the issued share capital of Race and are not classified as 'held for trading'.

There is no goodwill arising in the group financial statements other than that set out above.

Required

Discuss the implications, with suitable computations, of the above events for the group financial statements of Ashlee for the year ended 31 March 20X5.

(25 marks)

LEARNING MEDIA

50 Enterprise

ACR, 6/04, amended

Enterprise, a public limited company, has four business segments which are reported separately in its internal accounts. The segments are vehicle leasing, vehicle sales, property letting, and insurance. Each business segment constituted a 100% owned subsidiary of the group except for the vehicle leasing and sales segments which comprised two subsidiaries each. The results of these segments for the year ended 30 April 20X4 before taking account of the information below are as follows.

SEGMENT INFORMATION AS AT 30 APRIL 20X4 BEFORE THE SALE OF CARP

		Revenue		Segment results (profit/(loss))	Segment assets	Segment liabilities
		External	Internal			
		$m	$m	$m	$m	$m
Vehicle leasing:	Carp	40	2	9	39	17
	Far	5	3	(1)	8	3
Vehicle sales:	Fish	30	5	(8)	35	12
	Near	25	0	(4)	12	4
Property letting		60	65	15	96	32
Insurance		40	4	(4)	58	47
		200	79	7	248	115

There were no significant intragroup balances in the segment assets and liabilities. Carp and Far, both public limited companies, formed the leasing segment and Carp was 80% and Far is 100% owned by Enterprise. Carp had been originally formed by the Enterprise Group. Enterprise decided to sell Carp and the sale was completed on 30 April 20X4. On the same date the group acquired a radio station. The fair values of the assets and liabilities of the radio station were respectively $30 million and $13 million. The purpose of the purchase of the radio station was to use it as a medium for advertising the group's services and products. The radio station is to be included within the 'Insurance' segment as it is principally this product that it will advertise.

The remainder of the share capital of Carp is owned by a director of Carp who is not a director of Enterprise. During the current financial year this director had leased a number of vehicles from Carp for his family members. The lease payments were agreed at a discount of 20% to the market rate.

The group operates a defined benefit pension scheme for its employees. During the year, the directors of Enterprise sold a property to the pension fund and entered into a leaseback agreement for the same property. The directors and some employees constitute the board of the pension fund and the fund is managed by a merchant bank. Before the sale of Carp, the group had a defined benefit obligation with a net present value of $40 million and plan assets with a fair value of $25 million and unrecognised actuarial gains of $12 million. The sale of the subsidiary had reduced the net present value of the obligation at 30 April 20X4 to $30 million. No transfer of assets was made to the purchasing company's pension scheme.

Fish and Near, public limited companies, constitute the vehicle sales segment. They were wholly acquired on 1 May 20X1 from Motors, a public limited company, for $30 million when the fair value of their net assets was $22 million. At 30 April 20X2, when the carrying value of the net assets of Fish and Near were respectively $20 million and $5 million, an impairment review was carried out because of the impact of a new tax law on the goodwill and an impairment loss recognised. However, the actual net cash flows for the years 20X3 and 20X4 were higher than forecast, because of the pessimistic nature of the original forecasts and a change in economic conditions. The group revised the calculation of the recoverable amount of the segment based on a revision of all future cash flows from 1 May 20X4. The recoverable amount of Fish and Near at the respective dates is set out below:

	Recoverable amount at 30 April 20X2 (original cash flows)	Recoverable amount at 30 April 20X4 (revised cash flows)
	$m	$m
Fish	16	29
Near	8	10

The depreciated historical cost of Fish and Near's net assets at 30 April 20X4 was $26 million and $8 million. The assets had not previously been revalued.

The tax law is still in place at 30 April 20X4.

Required

(a) Discuss by specific reference to the information above:

    (i)   Which segments of Enterprise would constitute a 'reportable' segment under IFRS 8 *Operating segments* as at 30 April 20X4, after the sale of Carp and the purchase of the radio station. **(7 marks)**

    (ii)   Which parties would be deemed to be related parties under IAS 24 *Related party disclosures* for disclosure purposes in the financial statements of Carp and Enterprise as at 30 April 20X4. **(5 marks)**

(b) Calculate the financial effect of the sale of Carp on the pension scheme, showing the gain or loss resulting from the curtailment of the pension obligation and the net pension liability after the sale of Carp. **(6 marks)**

(c) Describe with suitable calculations, the nature of any impairment reviews that would have been carried out on the net assets of Fish and Near at 30 April 20X2 and 30 April 20X4. **(7 marks)**

(Total = 25 marks)

51 Carpart

45 mins

6/09

Carpart, a public limited company, is a vehicle part manufacturer, and sells vehicles purchased from the manufacturer. Carpart has entered into supply arrangements for the supply of car seats to two local companies, Vehiclex and Autoseat.

(a) **Vehiclex**

This contract will last for five years and Carpart will manufacture seats to a certain specification which will require the construction of machinery for the purpose. The price of each car seat has been agreed so that it includes an amount to cover the cost of constructing the machinery but there is no commitment to a minimum order of seats to guarantee the recovery of the costs of constructing the machinery. Carpart retains the ownership of the machinery and wishes to recognise part of the revenue from the contract in its current financial statements to cover the cost of the machinery which will be constructed over the next year.

(4 marks)

(b) **Autoseat**

Autoseat is purchasing car seats from Carpart. The contract is to last for three years and Carpart is to design, develop and manufacture the car seats. Carpart will construct machinery for this purpose but the machinery is so specific that it cannot be used on other contracts. Carpart maintains the machinery but the know-how has been granted royalty free to Autoseat. The price of each car seat includes a fixed price to cover the cost of the machinery. If Autoseat decides not to purchase a minimum number of seats to cover the cost of the machinery, then Autoseat has to repay Carpart for the cost of the machinery, including any interest incurred.

Autoseat can purchase the machinery at any time in order to safeguard against the cessation of production by Carpart. The purchase price would be the cost of the machinery not yet recovered by Carpart. The machinery has a life of three years and the seats are only sold to Autoseat who sets the levels of production for a period. Autoseat can perform a pre-delivery inspection on each seat and can reject defective seats.

(9 marks)

(c) **Vehicle sales**

Carpart sells vehicles on a contract for their market price (approximately $20,000 each) at a mark-up of 25% on cost. The expected life of each vehicle is five years. After four years, the car is repurchased by Carpart at 20% of its original selling price. This price is expected to be significantly less than its fair value. The car must be maintained and serviced by the customer in accordance with certain guidelines and must be in good condition if Carpart is to repurchase the vehicle.

The same vehicles are also sold with an option that can be exercised by the buyer two years after sale. Under this option, the customer has the right to ask Carpart to repurchase the vehicle for 70% of its original purchase price. It is thought that the buyers will exercise the option. At the end of two years, the fair value of the vehicle is expected to be 55% of the original purchase price. If the option is not exercised, then the buyer keeps the vehicle.

Carpart also uses some of its vehicles for demonstration purposes. These vehicles are normally used for this purpose for an eighteen-month period. After this period, the vehicles are sold at a reduced price based upon their condition and mileage. **(10 marks)**

Professional marks will be awarded for clarity and quality of discussion. **(2 marks)**

Required

Discuss how the above transactions would be accounted for under International Financial Reporting Standards in the financial statements of Carpart.

Note. The mark allocation is shown against each of the arrangements above.

(Total = 25 marks)

52 Tyre

45 mins

ACR, 6/06

Tyre, a public limited company, operates in the vehicle retailing sector. The company is currently preparing its financial statements for the year ended 31 May 20X6 and has asked for advice on how to deal with the following items.

(a) Tyre requires customers to pay a deposit of 20% of the purchase price when placing an order for a vehicle. If the customer cancels the order, the deposit is not refundable and Tyre retains it. If the order cannot be fulfilled by Tyre, the company repays the full amount of the deposit to the customer. The balance of the purchase price becomes payable on the delivery of the vehicle when the title to the goods passes. Tyre proposes to recognise the revenue from the deposits immediately and the balance of the purchase price when the goods are delivered to the customer. The cost of sales for the vehicle is recognised when the balance of the purchase price is paid. Additionally, Tyre had sold a fleet of cars to Hub and gave Hub a discount of 30% of the retail price on the transaction. The discount given is normal for this type of transaction. Tyre has given Hub a buyback option which entitles Hub to require Tyre to repurchase the vehicles after three years for 40% of the purchase price. The normal economic life of the vehicles is five years and the buyback option is expected to be exercised. **(8 marks)**

(b) The property of the former administrative centre of Tyre is owned by the company. Tyre had decided in the year that the property was surplus to requirements and demolished the building on 10 June 20X6. After demolition, the company will have to carry out remedial environmental work, which is a legal requirement resulting from the demolition. It was intended that the land would be sold after the remedial work had been carried out. However, land prices are currently increasing in value and, therefore, the company has decided that it will not sell the land immediately. Tyre uses the 'cost model' in IAS 16 *Property, plant and equipment* and has owned the property for many years. **(7 marks)**

(c) Tyre has entered into two new long lease property agreements for two major retail outlets. Annual rentals are paid under these agreements. Tyre has had to pay a premium to enter into these agreements because of the outlets' location. Tyre feels that the premiums paid are justifiable because of the increase in revenue that will occur because of the outlets' location. Tyre has analysed the leases and has decided that one is a finance lease and one is an operating lease but the company is unsure as to how to treat this premium. **(5 marks)**

(d) Tyre recently undertook a sales campaign whereby customers can obtain free car accessories, by presenting a coupon, which has been included in an advertisement in a national newspaper, on the purchase of a vehicle. The offer is valid for a limited time period from 1 January 20X6 until 31 July 20X6. The management are unsure as to how to treat this offer in the financial statements for the year ended 31 May 20X6. **(5 marks)**

Required

Advise the directors of Tyre on how to treat the above items in the financial statements for the year ended 31 May 20X6.

(The mark allocation is shown against each of the above items.)   **(Total = 25 marks)**

53 Ghorse   **45 mins**

12/07

Ghorse, a public limited company, operates in the fashion sector and had undertaken a group re-organisation during the current financial year to 31 October 20X7. As a result the following events occurred.

(a)   Ghorse identified two manufacturing units, Cee and Gee, which it had decided to dispose of in a single transaction. These units comprised non-current assets only. One of the units, Cee, had been impaired prior to the financial year end on 30 September 20X7 and it had been written down to its recoverable amount of $35 million. The criteria in IFRS 5 *Non-current assets held for sale and discontinued operations*, for classification as held for sale had been met for Cee and Gee at 30 September 20X7. The following information related to the assets of the cash generating units at 30 September 20X7:

	Depreciated historical cost	Fair value less cost to sell and recoverable amount	Carrying value under IFRS
	$m	$m	$m
Cee	50	35	35
Gee	70	90	70
	120	125	105

The fair value less costs to sell had risen at the year end to $40 million for Cee and $95 million for Gee. The increase in the fair value less costs to sell had not been taken into account by Ghorse.   **(7 marks)**

(b)   As a consequence of the re-organisation, and a change in government legislation, the tax authorities have allowed a revaluation of the non-current assets of the holding company for tax purposes to market value at 31 October 20X7. There has been no change in the carrying values of the non-current assets in the financial statements. The tax base and the carrying values after the revaluation are as follows:

	Carrying amount at 31 October 20X7	Tax base at 31 October 20X7 after revaluation	Tax base at 31 October 20X7 before revaluation
	$m	$m	$m
Property	50	65	48
Vehicles	30	35	28

Other taxable temporary differences amounted to $5 million at 31 October 20X7. Assume income tax is paid at 30%. The deferred tax provision at 31 October 20X7 had been calculated using the tax values before revaluation.   **(6 marks)**

(c)   A subsidiary company had purchased computerised equipment for $4 million on 31 October 20X6 to improve the manufacturing process. Whilst re-organising the group, Ghorse had discovered that the manufacturer of the computerised equipment was now selling the same system for $2·5 million. The projected cash flows from the equipment are:

		Cash flows
		$
Year ended 31 October	20X8	1.3
	20X9	2.2
	20Y0	2.3

The residual value of the equipment is assumed to be zero. The company uses a discount rate of 10%. The directors think that the fair value less costs to sell of the equipment is $2 million. The directors of Ghorse propose to write down the non-current asset to the new selling price of $2·5 million. The company's policy is to depreciate its computer equipment by 25% per annum on the straight line basis. **(5 marks)**

(d) The manufacturing property of the group, other than the head office, was held on an operating lease over eight years. On re-organisation on 31 October 20X7, the lease has been renegotiated and is held for twelve years at a rent of $5 million per annum paid in arrears. The fair value of the property is $35 million and its remaining economic life is thirteen years. The lease relates to the buildings and not the land. The factor to be used for an annuity at 10% for 12 years is 6·8137. **(5 marks)**

The directors are worried about the impact that the above changes will have on the value of its non-current assets and its key performance indicator which is 'Return on Capital Employed' (ROCE). ROCE is defined as operating profit before interest and tax divided by share capital, other reserves and retained earnings. The directors have calculated ROCE as $30 million divided by $220 million, ie 13·6% before any adjustments required by the above.

Formation of opinion on impact on ROCE. **(2 marks)**

Required

Discuss the accounting treatment of the above transactions and the impact that the resulting adjustments to the financial statements would have on ROCE.

Note. Your answer should include appropriate calculations where necessary and a discussion of the accounting principles involved.

(Total = 25 marks)

54 Handrew

45 mins

ACR, 6/05

Handrew, a public limited company, is adopting International Financial Reporting Standards (IFRS) in its financial statements for the year ended 31 May 20X5. The directors of the company are worried about the effect of the move to IFRS on their financial performance and the views of analysts. The directors have highlighted some 'headline' differences between IFRS and their current local equivalent standards and require a report on the impact of a move to IFRS on the key financial ratios for the current period.

Differences between local Generally Accepted Accounting Practice (GAAP) and IFRS

Leases

Local GAAP does not require property leases to be separated into land and building components. Long-term property leases are accounted for as operating leases in the financial statements of Handrew under local GAAP. Under the terms of the contract, the title to the land does not pass to Handrew but the title to the building passes to the company.

The company has produced a schedule of future minimum operating lease rentals and allocated these rentals between land and buildings based on their relative fair value at the start of the lease period. The operating leases commenced on 1 June 20X4 when the value of the land was $270 million and the building was $90 million. Annual operating lease rentals paid in arrears commencing on 31 May 20X5 are land $30 million and buildings $10 million. These amounts are payable for the first five years of the lease term after which the payments diminish. The minimum lease term is 40 years.

The net present value of the future minimum operating lease payments as at 1 June 20X4 was land $198 million and buildings $86 million. The interest rate used for discounting cash flows is 6%. Buildings are depreciated on a straight line basis over 20 years and at the end of this period, the building's economic life will be over. The lessor intends to redevelop the land at some stage in the future. Assume that the tax allowances on buildings are given to the lessee on the same basis as the depreciation charge based on the net present value at the start of the lease, and that operating lease payments are fully allowable for taxation.

Answers

ACCA examiner's answers

Remember that you can access the ACCA examiner's solutions to questions marked **'Pilot paper'**, **'12/07'**, **'6/08' or '12/08'** on the BPP website using the following link:

www.bpp.com/acca/examiner-solutions

Additional question guidance

Remember that you can find additional guidance to certain questions on the BPP website using the following link:

www.bpp.com/acca/extra-question-guidance

1 Conceptual framework

Marking scheme

		Marks
(a)	Subjective	13
(b)	Up to 2 marks per key issue	10
	(i) Objectives	
	(ii) Qualitative characteristics	
	(iii) Definitions	
	(iv) Recognition and de-recognition	
	(v) Measurement	
	(vi) Reporting entity	
	(vii) Presentation and disclosure	
	Appropriateness and quality of discussion	2
	Maximum	25

(a)   **The need for a conceptual framework**

The financial reporting process is concerned with providing information that is useful in the business and economic decision-making process. Therefore a conceptual framework will form the theoretical basis for determining which events should be accounted for, how they should be measured and how they should be communicated to the user.

Although it is theoretical in nature, a conceptual framework for financial reporting has highly practical final aims.

The **danger of not having a conceptual framework** is demonstrated in the way some countries' standards have developed over recent years; standards tend to be produced in a **haphazard and fire-fighting approach**. Where an agreed framework exists, the standard-setting body act as an architect or designer, rather than a fire-fighter, building accounting rules on the foundation of sound, agreed basic principles.

The lack of a conceptual framework also means that fundamental principles are tackled more than once in different standards, thereby producing contradictions and inconsistencies in basic concepts, such as those of prudence and matching. This leads to ambiguity and it affects the true and fair concept of financial reporting.

Another problem with the lack of a full conceptual framework has become apparent in the USA. The large number of highly detailed standards produced by the Financial Accounting Standards Board (FASB) has created a financial reporting environment governed by specific rules rather than general principles. FASB has 'concept statements' but a full conceptual framework would be better.

A conceptual framework can also bolster standard setters against political pressure from various 'lobby groups' and interested parties. Such pressure would only prevail if it was acceptable under the conceptual framework.

Can it resolve practical accounting issues?

A framework cannot provide all the answers for standard setters. It can provide **basic principles** which can be used when deciding between alternatives, and can narrow the range of alternatives that can be considered. In the UK, the *Statement of Principles* has provided **definitions that have formed the basis of definitions in accounting standards,** as has the IASB's framework in areas such as financial instruments and provisions. A framework can also provide guidance in the absence of an accounting standard. For example, there is no IFRS dealing specifically with off balance sheet finance, so the IASB *Framework* must form the basis for decisions.

However, a conceptual framework is **unlikely**, on past form, to **provide all** the **answers to practical accounting problems**. There are a number of reasons for this:

(i)   Financial statements are intended for a variety of users, and it is not certain that a single conceptual framework can be devised which will suit all users.

(ii)   Given the diversity of user requirements, there may be a need for a variety of accounting standards, each produced for a different purpose (and with different concepts as a basis).

(iii)   It is not clear that a conceptual framework makes the task of preparing and then implementing standards any easier than without a framework.

The IASB's recent Discussion Paper on the conceptual framework has been criticised by the UK Accounting Standards Board at least partly on grounds of practical utility – it is thought to be **too theoretical,** and also for focusing on **some users (decision makers) at the expense of others (shareholders).** Perhaps it is not possible to satisfy all users.

(b)   **Key issues in determining the basic components of an internationally agreed conceptual framework**

(i)   **Objectives.** There needs to be agreement on the principal users of financial statements. Are the statements produced for shareholders or for other users, and is decision usefulness the main purpose or is it stewardship? The UK Accounting Standards Board has expressed concern that the IASB Discussion Paper on the conceptual framework does not resolve these matters.

(ii)   **Qualitative characteristics.** Consensus needs to be reached on the qualitative characteristics of financial statements. The IASB Discussion Paper proposes the following:

(1)   **Relevance**: predictive value, confirmatory value, timeliness

(2)   **Faithful representation**: data must be verifiable, neutral and complete (replacing 'reliability')

(3)   **Comparability (including consistency)**

(4)   **Understandability**: for users who have a reasonable knowledge of business and economic activities and financial accounting

(5)   **Constraints of financial reporting**

Materiality (all material information included; not cluttered with immaterial information)

Benefits and costs (the benefits of financial information should justify the costs).

The ASB is not happy that 'reliability' may be replaced by 'faithful representation', but there was in any case a conflict or trade-off between reliability and relevance. For example, historical cost is more reliable, but fair values are more relevant.

- IAS 1 (revised) *Presentation of financial statements* requires disclosure of facts material to a proper understanding of financial statements.
- IAS 37 *Provisions, contingent liabilities and contingent assets* requires provisions for environmental damage to be recognised.

National and legal requirements

In the UK, the Companies Act 2006 requires disclosure of environmental matters in the Expanded Business Review. which will replace the Operating and Financial Review in 2008. Other countries require environmental reporting under national law.

Voluntary disclosure: sustainability

Most environmental disclosure is voluntary, although lists of companies in particular are under a great deal of pressure to make such disclosures. There have been a number of **initiatives** in the past (CERES, Friends of the Earth Charter) but the most important of these is the **Global Reporting Initiative (GRI)**.

The GRI is an international not-for-profit organisation, with many stakeholders. Its aim is to develop **Sustainability Reporting Guidelines** for voluntary use. These guidelines cover a number of areas (economic, environmental and social), and the latest guidelines were published in 2006. The GRI specified key performance indicators for each area. For environmental reporting the indicators are: materials; energy; water; biodiversity; emissions; energy and waste; products and services; compliance, transport.

Comments on 'environmental events'

(a)   Of relevance to the farmland restoration is IAS 37 *Provisions, contingent liabilities and contingent assets.* Provisions for environmental liabilities should be recognised where there is a **legal or constructive obligation** to rectify environmental damage or perform restorative work. The mere existence of the restorative work does not give rise to an obligation and there is no legal obligation. However, it could be argued that there is a constructive obligation arising from the company's approach in previous years, which may have given rise to an **expectation** that the work would be carried out. If this is the case, a provision of $150m would be required in the financial statements. In addition, this provision and specific examples of restoration of land could be included in the environmental report.

(b)   The treatment of the **fine** is straightforward: it is an obligation to transfer economic benefits. An estimate of the fine should be made and a **provision** set up in the financial statements for $5m. This should be mentioned in the environmental report. The report might also **put the fines in context** by stating how many tests have been carried out and how many times the company has passed the tests. The directors may feel that it would do the company's reputation no harm to point out the fact that the number of prosecutions has been falling from year to year.

(c)   These statistics are good news and need to be covered in the environmental report. However, the emphasis should be on **accurate factual reporting** rather than boasting. It might be useful to provide target levels for comparison, or an industry average if available. The emissions statistics should be split into three categories:

- Acidity to air and water
- Hazardous substances
- Harmful emissions to water

As regards the aquatic emissions, the $70m planned expenditure on **research** should **be mentioned in the environmental report**. It shows a commitment to benefiting the environment. However, **IAS 37 would not permit a provision** to be made for this amount, since an obligation does not exist and the **expenditure is avoidable**. Nor does it qualify as development expenditure under IAS 38.

(d)   The environmental report should mention the steps the company is taking to minimise the harmful impact on the environment in the way it sites and constructs its gas installations. The report should also explain the policy of dismantling the installations rather than sinking them at the end of their useful life.

Currently the company builds up a provision for decommissioning costs over the life of the installation. However, IAS 37 does not allow this. Instead, the **full amount must be provided** as soon as there is an **obligation** arising as a result of **past events**, the **settlement** of which is **expected** to result in an **outflow of**

resources. The obligation exists right at the beginning of the installation's life, and so the full $407m must be provided for. A corresponding asset is created.

4 Prochain

Text reference. This topic is covered in Chapters 4 and 1 of your text.

Top tips. This question was a case study that dealt with the accounting issues for an entity engaged in the fashion industry. The areas examined were fundamental areas of the syllabus: non-current assets, intangible assets, determination of the purchase consideration for the subsidiary, and research and development expenditure. Tricky bits to get right were:

(a)   A provision for dismantling the 'model areas' would need to be set up and discounted back to the present.
(b)   Contingent consideration that is not probable would not be included in the cost of acquisition.
(c)   Investment properties do not include properties owned and occupied by the entity.

 When discussing the development expenditure, the criteria for capitalisation may be remembered using the mnemonic PIRATE.

Easy marks. Stating the obvious – that the model areas are items of property, plant and equipment and need to be depreciated will earn you easy marks, as will mentioning the basic distinction between research and development expenditure and listing the criteria when talking about the brand.

Examiner's comment. Generally, candidates answered the question quite well, obtaining a pass mark, although accounting for the non-current assets did confuse some candidates.

Marking scheme

	Marks
Model areas	7
Purchase of Badex	8
Research and Development	6
Apartments	4
Maximum/Available	25

Model areas

IAS 16 *Property, plant and equipment* is the relevant standard here. The model areas are held for use in the supply of goods and are used in more than one accounting period. The company should recognise the costs of setting up the model areas as **tangible non-current assets** and should **depreciate** the costs over their useful lives. **Subsequent measurement should be based on cost**. In theory the company could measure the model areas at fair value if the revaluation model of IAS 16 was followed, but it would be difficult to measure their fair value reliably.

IAS 16 states that the initial cost of an asset **should include** the initial estimate of the **costs of dismantling and removing the item and restoring the site** where the entity has an obligation to do so. A **present obligation appears to exist**, as defined by IAS 37 *Provisions, contingent liabilities and contingent assets* and therefore the entity should also **recognise a provision** for that amount. The provision should be **discounted to its present value** and the unwinding of the discount recognised in profit or loss.

At 31 May 20X6, the entity should recognise a non-current asset of $15.7 million (cost of $23.6 million (W) less accumulated depreciation of $7.9 million (W)) and a provision of $3.73 million (W).

Working

	$m
Cost of model areas	20.0
Plus provision $(20 \times 20\% \times \dfrac{1}{1.055^2} \ (= 0.898)$	3.6
Cost on initial recognition	23.6
Less accumulated depreciation $(23.6 \times 8/24)$	(7.9)
Net book value at 31 May 20X6	15.7
Provision: on initial recognition $(20 \times 20\% \times 0.898)$	3.6
Plus unwinding of discount $(3.6 \times 5.5\% \times 8/12)$	0.13
Provision at 31 May 20X6	3.73

Purchase of Badex

IFRS 3 *Business Combinations* states that the consideration transferred in a business combination shall be measured at **fair value at the acquisition date**.

The **$100 million cash paid** on the acquisition date, 1 June 20X5 is **recognised as purchase consideration**. The **$25 million payable on 31 May 20X7** (two years after acquisition) should be **split** into the **$10 million deferred consideration** which should be **discounted to its present value** by two years ($10m x $1/1.055^2$ = $8.98m) and the **contingent consideration** of $15 million. The contingent consideration should be measured at its **acquisition-date fair value**. Here, as the profit forecast targets are unlikely to be met, **the fair value would be significantly less than $15 million** but as the percentage chance of the targets being met and other relevant information are not given, it is not possible to establish a fair value.

Prochain should also recognise a corresponding **financial liability for the deferred and contingent consideration** (rather than equity) as they meet the definition of a financial liability in IAS 32 *Financial Instruments: Presentation*. This is because Prochain has a **contractual obligation to deliver cash** on 31 May 20X7 providing the conditions of the contingent consideration are met. At the year end 31 May 20X6, any **changes in the contingent consideration** as a result of changes in expectations of the targets being met will be recognised in **profit or loss** (rather than adjusting goodwill).

Under IFRS 3, any associated **transaction costs** should be **expensed to profit or loss**.

A further issue concerns the valuation and treatment of the 'Badex' brand name. IAS 38 *Intangible Assets* prohibits the recognition of internally generated brands and therefore the brand will not **be recognised in Badex's individual statement of financial position** prior to the acquisition. However, **IFRS 3 requires intangible assets** of an acquiree to be **recognised in a business combination if they meet the identifiability criteria** in IAS 38. For an intangible to be identifiable, the asset must be separable or it must arise from contractual or legal rights. Here, these **criteria appear to have been met** as the brand could be sold separately from the entity. Therefore, the 'Badex' brand should be **recognised as an intangible asset at $20m in the consolidated statement of financial position**.

Development of own brand

IAS 38 *Intangible assets* divides a development project into a research phase and a development phase. In the research phase of a project, an entity cannot yet demonstrate that the expenditure will generate probable future economic benefits. Therefore expenditure on **research** must be **recognised as an expense when it occurs**.

Development expenditure is capitalised when an entity demonstrates **all** the following.

(a)   The **technical feasibility** of completing the project

(b)   Its **intention to complete** the asset and use or sell it

(c)   Its **ability to use or sell** the asset

(d)   That the asset will generate **probable future economic benefits**

(e)   The availability of **adequate technical, financial and other resources** to complete the development and to use or sell it

(f)   Its ability to **reliably measure** the expenditure attributable to the asset.

Assuming that all these criteria are met, the cost of the development should comprise **all directly attributable costs** necessary to **create the asset** and to make it **capable of operating in the manner intended by management**.

Directly attributable costs **do not include selling or administrative costs,** or **training costs** or market research. The **cost of upgrading** existing machinery can be recognised as **property, plant and equipment**. Therefore the expenditure on the project should be treated as follows:

	Expense (income statement)	Recognised in statement of financial position Intangible Assets	Recognised in statement of financial position Property, plant and equipment
	$m	$m	$m
Research	3		
Prototype design		4	
Employee costs		2	
Development work		5	
Upgrading machinery			3
Market research	2		
Training	1		
	6	11	3

Prochain should **recognise $11 million** as an intangible asset.

Apartments

The apartments are leased to persons who are under contract to the company. Therefore they **cannot be classified as investment property.** IAS 40 *Investment property* specifically states that **property occupied by employees** is not investment property. The apartments must be treated as **property, plant and equipment,** carried at cost or fair value and depreciated over their useful lives.

Although the rent is below the market rate the difference between the actual rent and the market rate is simply **income foregone** (or an opportunity cost). In order to recognise the difference as an employee benefit cost it would also be necessary to **gross up rental income** to the market rate. The financial statements would **not present fairly** the financial performance of the company. Therefore the company **cannot recognise the difference** as an employee benefit cost.

5 Johan

Text reference. Intangibles and PPE are covered in Chapter 4 of the Study Text, and leasing in Chapter 10. Revenue recognition is covered in Chapter 1. This could also be viewed as a specialised industry question, as covered in Chapter 20 of the text.

Top tips. Although this question is set in a specialised industry, it draws on principles relating to intangibles, tangibles, leases and revenue recognition that are applicable in most industries. It is important to consider basic points, such as: does the licence meet the definition of an intangible asset, and how are such assets carried in the SOFP? In Part (c), a hint is given in the question that the prepaid phones and the service contracts should be treated differently: if you treat them both the same, you must have got one of them wrong.

Easy marks. These are available for identifying which standards apply and outlining the principles applicable, and you will gain these marks whether or not you come to the correct conclusion about the accounting treatment.

Examiner's comment. The question was not well answered with candidates failing to recognise the key accounting principles required. The main areas where candidates had problems was determining when the intangible asset should be recognised, determining the amortisation period for the asset, recognising that there was a lease and not a contingent liability, allocating the lease premium, determining when the revenue should be recognised on the sale of the handsets on the agency agreement and recognising the write down of inventory. Candidates did not appear to be able to draft answers where the main purpose of the question is to advise clients. Candidates seemed to be able to produce definitions but not to apply them.

		Marks
Intangible assets:	Licence	2
	Amortisation	2
	Impairment	2
	Renewal	2
		8
Tangible fixed assets:	Cost	1
	Feasibility study	1
	Location and condition	1
	Capitalised costs	1
Leases:	Operating lease	2
	Prepayment	1
		7
Inventory		2
IAS 18 Revenue recognition:	Recognition	2
	Agency	2
	Separability	2
		8
Discussion		2
	Available	25

(a) **Licences**

The relevant standard here is IAS 38 *Intangible assets*. An intangible asset may be **recognised if it meets the identifiability criteria** in IAS 38, if it is probable that future economic benefits attributable to the asset will flow to the entity and if its fair value can be **measured reliably**. For an intangible asset to be identifiable the asset must be separable or it must arise from contractual or other legal rights. It appears that these **criteria have been met**. The licence has been acquired separately, and its value can be measured reliably at $120 million (cost). It is also expected that future economic benefits will flow to Johan. Therefore **the licence will be recognised as an intangible asset at cost.**

Regarding **subsequent valuation,** IAS 38 has two models: the **cost model** and the **revaluation model**. The revaluation model can only be used if intangible assets are traded in an active market. As Johan cannot sell the licence, this is not the case here, so Johan **cannot use the revaluation model.**

Under the **cost model,** intangible assets must be carried at **cost less amortisation and impairment losses.** The depreciable amount of an asset is cost less residual value; since the licence has no residual value, the depreciable amount is the cost. However, an impairment review should have been undertaken at 30 November 20X7, before amortisation commenced, and the licence written down, if necessary to its recoverable amount.

The **depreciable amount** must be **allocated over the useful life of the licence on a systematic basis.** The basis of allocation should reflect the **pattern of consumption** of the asset's benefit, unless this cannot be reliably determined, in which case the straight line basis would be used. The **straight line basis is appropriate**, in any case, for this licence, because the economic benefit is Johan's ability to earn income from the licence which accrues on a time basis and is not affected by wear and tear as some assets would be.

The **amortisation starts on the day that the network is available for use,** that is 1 December 20X7. Although the licence runs for six years from the date of purchase, 1 December 20X6, economic benefits cannot flow to the entity before the network assets and infrastructure are ready for use.

Other licences have been renewed at a nominal cost. It could therefore be argued that the licence should be amortised over two periods totalling eleven years: a period of five years from 1 December 20X7 to the renewal date, followed by six years from the renewal date. However, Johan does not know for certain what charge the regulator will make on renewal, so it would be more **appropriate to amortise the licence over a five year period,** that is $24 million per annum.

For the purposes of any **impairment review**, the licence and network assets should be classified as a single cash generating unit. They cannot be used separately from one another. There are **indications that the licence may be impaired:** disappointing market share, fierce competition and difficulty in retaining customers. Therefore the cash generating unit (licence and network assets) **must be tested for impairment.**

(b) **Costs incurred in extending the network**

The applicable standards here are IAS 16 *Property, plant and equipment,* and IAS 17 *Leases.*

IAS 16 states that the **cost** of an item of property, plant and equipment should be **recognised when two conditions** have been fulfilled:

It is probable that future economic benefits associated with the item will flow to the entity.

The cost of the item can be measured reliably.

The cost, according to IAS 16, includes **directly attributable costs of bringing the asset to the location and condition necessary for it to be capable of operating in a manner intended by management**. Examples of such directly attributable costs are site preparation costs and installation and assembly costs.

Applying the first criterion (probability of economic benefits) would **exclude the costs of the feasibility study**, both internal and external, because by definition, the economic benefits of a feasibility study are uncertain. These costs, $250,000 in total, should be **expensed as incurred.**

Applying the IAS 16 definition of directly attributable costs, the selection of the base station site is critical for the optimal operation of the network, and is part of the process of bringing the network assets to the location and condition necessary for operation. The **$50,000 paid to third party consultants** to find a suitable site is part of the cost of constructing the network, and **may thus be capitalised.**

The other costs – a payment of $300,000 followed by $60,000 a month for twelve years – is a **lease**, and is governed by IAS 17. IAS 17 defines a lease as an agreement whereby the lessor conveys to the lessee, in return for a payment or series of payments, the right to use an asset for an agreed period of time.

The question arises as to whether the payments are to be treated as **a finance lease or as an operating lease**. IAS 17 defines a finance lease as a lease that transfers substantially all the risks and rewards incidental to ownership of the leased asset to the lessee. An operating lease is a lease other than a finance lease.

In the case of the contract with the government for access to the land, there is **no transfer of ownership**. The term of the lease is **not for the major part of the asset's life**, because the land has an indefinite economic life. The lease **cannot therefore be said to transfer substantially all the risks and rewards of ownership** to Johan. Accordingly, the contract should be treated as an operating lease. The initial payment of $300,000 should be treated as a prepayment in the statement of financial position, and charged to profit or loss for the year on a straight line basis over the life of the contract. The monthly payments of $60,000 should be expensed. No value will be shown for the lease contract in the statement of financial position.

(c) **Purchase of handsets and revenue recognition**

The applicable standards in this case are IAS 2 *Inventories* and IAS 18 *Revenue.*

Inventory of handsets

IAS 2 states that inventories must be valued at the lower of cost and net realisable value. The handsets cost $200, and the net realisable value is selling price of $150 less costs to sell of $1, which is $149. All handsets in inventory – whether they are to be sold to prepaid customers or dealers – must be written down to $149 per handset.

Call cards and prepaid phones

Under IAS 18, revenue is recognised by reference to the stage of completion of the transaction at the reporting date. In the case of the call cards, revenue is generated by the provision of services, not the sale of the card itself, and accordingly revenue should be recognised as the services are provided. The $21 received per call card should therefore be treated as deferred revenue at the point of sale. Of this, $18 per card should be recognised over the six month period from the date of the sale. The $3 of unused credit – an average figure may be used rather than the figure for each card – should be recognised when the card expires, that is when Johan has no further obligation to the customer.

Sales to dealers

Johan bears the risk of loss in value of the handset, as the dealer may return any handsets before a service contract is signed with a customer. In addition, Johan sets the price of the handset. Therefore the **dealer, in this case, is acting as an agent for the sale of the handset and service contract.** The handset cannot be sold separately from the service contract, so the two transactions must be taken together because the commercial effect of either transaction cannot be understood in isolation. Johan earns revenue from the service contract with the final customer, not from the sale of the handset to the dealer.

IAS 18 does not deal directly with agency, but implies that revenue for an agent is not the amounts collected on behalf of the principal, but the commission earned for collecting them. From Johan's point of view **revenue is not earned when the handsets are sold to the dealer, so revenue should not be recognised at this point**. Instead the net payment of $130 (commission paid to the agent less cost of the handset) should be recognised as a customer acquisition cost, which may qualify as an intangible asset under IAS 38. If it is so recognised, it will be amortised over the twelve month contract. **Revenue from the service contract will be recognised as the service is rendered.**

6 Preparation question: Defined benefit scheme

Note to the statement of comprehensive income

Defined benefit expense recognised in profit or loss

	$m
Current service cost	11
Interest cost (10% × (110 + 20))	13
Expected return on plan assets (12% × 150)	(18)
Recognised actuarial gains (Working)	(4)
Past service cost – vested benefits	12
Past service cost – non-vested benefits $\left(\dfrac{20-12}{4} = \dfrac{8}{4} \right)$	2
	16

Statement of financial position notes

Net defined benefit liability recognised in the statement of financial position

	31 December 20X1 $m	31 December 20X0 $m
Present value of pension obligation	116	110
Fair value of plan assets	(140)	(150)
	(24)	(40)
Unrecognised actuarial gains/(losses) (Working)	42	43
Unrecognised past service costs (8 – 8/4)	(6)	–
	12	3

Changes in the present value of the defined benefit obligation

	$m
Opening defined benefit obligation	110
Interest cost (10% × (110 + 20))	13
Current service cost	11
Benefits paid	(10)
Past service cost	20
Actuarial gain (balancing figure)	(28)
Closing defined benefit obligation	116

Changes in the fair value of plan assets

	$m
Opening fair value of plan assets	150
Expected return on plan assets (12% × 150)	18
Contributions	7
Benefits paid	(10)
Actuarial loss (balancing figure)	(25)
Closing fair value of plan assets	140

Working

Recognised/Unrecognised actuarial gains and losses

	$m	$m
Corridor limits, greater of:		
10% of pension obligation b/d (10% × 110)	11	
10% of plan assets b/d (10% × 150)	15	
⇒ Corridor limit	15	
Unrecognised gains b/d		43
Gain recognised in profit or loss [(43 − 15)/7]		(4)
Gain on obligation in the year		28
Loss on assets in the year		(25)
Unrecognised gains c/d		42

7 Macaljoy

Text reference. Pensions are covered in Chapter 5; provisions in Chapter 9.

Top tips. Part (a)(i) is very straightforward, but make sure you relate your answer to the pension schemes of Macaljoy. Similarly in Part (b)(i), you need to write specifically about warranty provisions, as well as more generally about provisions.

Easy marks. Two marks are available for presentation and communication, and would be silly marks to lose. Plus there are marks for straightforward bookwork that you can get even if you don't get all the calculations right.

Examiner's comments. The question was quite well answered and candidates often produced good quality answers. The examiner was surprised to see that several candidates confused defined benefit and defined contribution schemes. Also at this level, it is important that candidates have an in depth knowledge of the differences between the two schemes rather than just a general view of the differences. Professional marks were awarded for the structure of the report and consideration of certain factors, that is:

(a) The intended purpose of the document
(b) Its intended users and their needs
(c) The appropriate type of document
(d) Logical and appropriate structure/format
(e) Nature of background information and technical language
(f) Detail required
(g) Clear, concise and precise presentation

				Marks
(a)	Pensions	(i)	Explanation	7
		(ii)	Calculation	7
(b)	Provisions	(i)	Explanation	6
			Calculation	3
Structure of report				2
Maximum				25

To: The Directors
       Macaljoy

Date: 1 November 2007

Subject: **Pension plans and warranty claims**

The purpose of this report is to explain the difference between defined benefit and defined contribution pension plans, and to show the accounting treatment of Macaljoy's pension schemes. It also discusses the principles of accounting for warranty claims and shows the accounting treatment of Macaljoy's warranty claims.

(a)   (i)   **Defined contribution plans and defined benefit plans**

With **defined contribution** plans, the employer (and possibly, as here, current employees too) pay regular contributions into the plan of a given or 'defined' amount each year. The contributions are invested, and the size of the post-employment benefits paid to former employees depends on how well or how badly the plan's investments perform. If the investments perform well, the plan will be able to afford higher benefits than if the investments performed less well.

The 2006 scheme is a defined contribution plan. The employer's liability is limited to the contributions paid.

With **defined benefit** plans, the size of the post-employment benefits is determined in advance, ie the benefits are 'defined'. The employer (and possibly, as here, current employees too) pay contributions into the plan, and the contributions are invested. The size of the contributions is set at an amount that is expected to earn enough investment returns to meet the obligation to pay the post-employment benefits. If, however, it becomes apparent that the assets in the fund are insufficient, the employer will be required to make additional contributions into the plan to make up the expected shortfall. On the other hand, if the fund's assets appear to be larger than they need to be, and in excess of what is required to pay the post-employment benefits, the employer may be allowed to take a 'contribution holiday' (ie stop paying in contributions for a while).

The **main difference** between the two types of plans lies in **who bears the risk**: if the employer bears the risk, even in a small way by guaranteeing or specifying the return, the plan is a defined benefit plan. A defined contribution scheme must give a benefit formula based solely on the amount of the contributions.

A defined benefit scheme may be created even if there is no legal obligation, if an employer has a practice of guaranteeing the benefits payable.

The 1990 scheme is a defined benefit scheme. Macaljoy, the employer, guarantees a pension based on the service lives of the employees in the scheme. The company's liability is not limited to the amount of the contributions. This means that the employer bears the investment risk: if the return on the investment is not sufficient to meet the liabilities, the company will need to make good the difference.

(ii) **Accounting treatment: 2006 scheme**

No assets or liabilities will be recognised for this defined contribution scheme. The **contributions** paid by the company of $10m will be **charged to profit or loss**. The contributions paid by the employees will be part of the wages and salaries cost.

Accounting treatment: 1990 scheme

The accounting treatment is as follows:

AMOUNTS RECOGNISED IN THE STATEMENT OF FINANCIAL POSITION

	31 October 2007 $m	1 November 2006 $m
Present value of obligation	240	200
Fair value of plan assets	(225)	(190)
Liability	15	10

EXPENSE RECOGNISED IN PROFIT OR LOSS
FOR THE YEAR ENDED 31 OCTOBER 2007

	$m
Current service cost	20.0
Interest cost: 5% × 200	10.0
Expected return on plan assets: 7% × 190	(13.3)
Net expense	16.7

AMOUNT RECOGNISED IN OTHER COMPREHENSIVE INCOME
FOR THE YEAR ENDED 31 OCTOBER 2007

	$m
Actuarial loss on obligation	(29.0)
Actuarial gain on plan assets	23.7
Net actuarial loss	(5.3)

CHANGE IN THE PRESENT VALUE OF THE OBLIGATION

	$m
Present value of obligation at 1 November 2006	200
Interest cost	10
Current service cost	20
Benefits paid	(19)
Actuarial loss on obligation	29
Present value of obligation at 31 October 2007	240

CHANGE IN THE FAIR VALUE OF PLAN ASSETS

	$m
Fair value of plan assets at 1 November 2006	190.0
Expected return on plan assets	13.3
Contributions	17.0
Benefits paid	(19.0)
Actuarial gain on plan assets	23.7
Fair value of plan assts at 31 October 2007	225.0

(b) **Warranty provisions**

(i) **Principles**

Under IAS 37 *Provisions, contingent liabilities and contingent assets*, provisions must be recognised in the following circumstances.

(1) There is a **legal** or **constructive obligation** to transfer benefits as a result of past events.
(2) It is probably that **an outflow of economic resources** will be required to **settle** the **obligation.**
(3) A **reasonable estimate** of the amount required to settle the obligation can be made.

If the company can **avoid expenditure by its future action, no provision** should be recognised. A legal or constructive obligation is one created by an **obligating event.** Constructive obligations arise when an entity is committed to certain expenditures because of a pattern of behaviour which the public would expect to continue.

IAS 37 states that the amount recognised should be the **best estimate of the expenditure required to settle the obligation at the end of the reporting period.** The estimate should **take the various possible outcomes into account** and should be the **amount that an entity would rationally pay** to settle the obligation at the reporting date or to transfer it to a third party. In the case of warranties, the provision will be made at a probability weighted expected value, taking into account the risks and uncertainties surrounding the underlying events.

The amount of the provision should be **discounted to present value** if the time value of money is material using a **risk adjusted rate.** If some or all of the expenditure is expected to be **reimbursed** by a third party, the reimbursement should be **recognised as a separate asset,** but only if it is virtually certain that the reimbursement will be received.

(ii) **Accounting treatment**

In Macaljoy's case, the past event giving rise to the obligation is the sale of the product with a warranty. A provision for the warranty will be made as follows:

Year 1: $280,000
Year 2: $350,000

If material, the provisions may be discounted:

Year 1: $269,000
Year 2: $323,000

Calculations are shown below.

Macaljoy may be able to **recognise the asset and income from the insurance claim,** but only if the insurance company has validated the claim and **receipt is virtually certain.** In general contingent assets are not recognised, but disclosed if an inflow of economic benefits is probable.

Calculations

Year 1: warranty

	Expected value $'000	Discounted expected value (4%) $'000
80% × Nil	0	
15% × 7,000 × $100	105	
5% × 7,000 × $500	175	
	280	$280,000/1.04 = $269,000*

Year 2: extended warranty

	Expected value $'000	Discounted expected value (4%) $'000
70% × Nil	0	
20% × 5,000 × $100	100	
10% × 5,000 × $500	250	
	350	$350,000/(1.04)² = $323,000*

*Note. These figures are rounded

8 Savage

(a)   AMOUNTS RECOGNISED IN THE STATEMENT OF FINANCIAL POSITION

	31 October 20X5 $m	31 October 20X4 $m
Present value of obligation	3,375	3,000
Less: fair value of plan assets (3,170 – 8)	(3,162)	(2,900)
Liability	213	100

EXPENSE RECOGNISED IN PROFIT OR LOSS FOR YEAR ENDED 31 OCTOBER 20X5

	$m
Current service cost	40
Interest cost	188
Expected return on assets	(232)
Past service cost	125
	121

AMOUNT RECOGNISED IN OTHER COMPREHENSIVE INCOME
FOR YEAR ENDED 31 OCTOBER 20X5

	$m
Actuarial loss on obligation	64
Actuarial gain on plan assets	(52)
Net actuarial loss recognised	(12)

CHANGES IN THE PRESENT VALUE OF THE OBLIGATION

	$m
Present value of obligation at 1 November 20X4	3,000
Past service cost	125
Interest cost (6% × 3,125)	188
Current service cost	40
Benefits paid	(42)
Actuarial loss on obligation (balancing figure)	64
Present value of obligation at 31 October 20X5	3,375

Note: the past service costs of $125 million are recognised immediately because the benefits vest on 1 November 20X4. They are also included in opening scheme liabilities for the purpose of calculating interest.

CHANGES IN THE FAIR VALUE OF PLAN ASSETS

	$m
Fair value of plan assets at 1 November 20X4	2,900
Expected return on plan assets (8% × 2,900)	232
Contributions	20
Benefits paid	(42)
Actuarial gain on plan assets (balancing figure)	52
Fair value of plan assets at 31 October 20X4 (3,170 – 8)	3,162

(b)   At 31 October 20X5, contributions of $8 million remain unpaid. IAS 19 *Employee benefits* states that **plan assets do not include unpaid contributions**. However, contributions payable of $8 million should be disclosed in the notes to the accounts of Savage at 31 October 20X5. This amount is payable to the Trustees.

IAS 19 also states that where there are changes to a defined benefit plan, **past service costs** should be **recognised immediately if the benefits have already vested**. The benefits vested on 1 November 20X4 and therefore past service costs of $125 million should be recognised in profit or loss for the year ended 31 October 20X5.

9 Smith

Text reference. Employee benefits are covered in Chapter 5.

Top tips. In Part (a)(i) of this question you had to discuss the current requirements of IAS 19 *Employee benefits* as regards accounting for actuarial gains and losses whilst setting out the main criticisms of the approach taken and the advantages of immediate recognition of such gains and losses. Part (a)(ii) required the discussion of the implications of the current accounting practices in IAS 19 for dealing with the setting of discount rates for pension obligations and the expected returns on plan assets. You also need knowledge of the criticisms levelled at the standard. The immediate recognition of gains has advantages to an entity. In Part (c) you had to use the numbers given in the question scenario to show how the use of the expected return on assets could cause comparison issues for potential investors. It is not untypical to have to apply the rules of accounting to a scenario. The two companies had the same opening fair value of assets, same contributions in the year and the same benefits paid but different fair values of asserts at the year end. Despite very different performance, the amount shown as expected return on plan assets in the statement of comprehensive income was identical for both companies and the actuarial gains and losses were not to be recognised in the current period.

Easy marks. These are available in Part (a) for knowledge of the rules of IAS 19. The examiner said 'a knowledge of the principles would produce at least a pass standard answer'. And even if you didn't spot that the expected return on plan assets was the same for both companies you would get marks for the straightforward calculation.

Examiner's comment. Most candidates did the calculations satisfactorily but were weak on discussions, with some just defining the nature of defined contribution and defined benefit schemes.

Marking scheme

		Marks
(a)	Subjective	17
	Professional marks	2
		19
(b)	Calculation	3
	Discussion	3
		6
		25

(a) (i) **Actuarial gains and losses**

An entity's defined benefit pension scheme can be a significant net asset or liability. The size of some schemes, together with the complexity of the accounting, has meant that IAS 19 *Employee benefits* has **come in for criticism**.

One area that is particularly problematic is the **treatment of actuarial gains and losses**. It has been said that the IAS 19 treatment does not provide clear, full and understandable information to users. Specifically, IAS 19 gives a number of options for recognition of actuarial gains and losses, including the option to delay such recognition. This can mean that the figure in the statement of financial position (and profit or loss for the year) is misleading.

Currently the treatment of actuarial gains and losses is to recognise them:

(ii) In **profit or loss** either in the **period in which they occur** or **deferred** on a systematic basis

(iii) In **other comprehensive income** in the period in which they occur.

In the former case, IAS 19 requires (**as a minimum**) that the following actuarial gains and losses are recognised in profit or loss for the period:

$$\frac{\text{Net actuarial gains or losses brought forward outside 10\% corridor}}{\text{Average remaining working lives of participating employees}}$$

The '10% corridor' limit is defined as the *higher of:*

(1) 10% brought forward present value of benefit obligations
(2) 10% brought forward fair value of plan assets.

The **main problems with the deferred recognition** model (ii) are:

(1) It is **inconsistent** the treatment of other assets and liabilities.

(2) It means that the employer is **not matching** the cost of providing post-employment benefits (as represented by the changes in plan assets and benefit obligations) to the periods in which those changes take place.

(3) The accounting is **complex** and requires complex records to be kept.

(4) The statement of financial position figure could be **misleading**, for example, the plan may be in surplus and a liability shown in the financial statements or the plan may be in deficit with an asset shown.

A discussion paper issued in March 2008 proposed eliminating deferred recognition, and requiring immediate recognition in all cases. It still gives options as to where items should be recognised (profit or loss for the year or other comprehensive income).

Immediate recognition has the following **advantages**:

(1) By eliminating the options it **improves consistency** and comparability between accounting periods between different entities.

(2) It gives a more **faithful representation** of the entity's financial position. A surplus in the pension plan will result in an asset being recognised and a deficit in a liability being recognised.

(3) The financial statements are **easier to understand** and more transparent than if deferred recognition is used.

(4) The income and expense recognised in profit or loss (or in other comprehensive income) **correspond** to changes in the fair value of the plan assets or the defined benefit obligation.

(5) It is **consistent with the IASB *Framework***, which requires that 'the effects of transactions and other events are recognised when they occur … and recorded … and reported in the financial statements of the periods to which they relate.

(6)   It is **consistent with IAS 8** Accounting policies, changes in accounting estimates and errors (changes in estimates must be included in the period in which the assets and liabilities change as a result) **and IAS 37** Provisions, contingent liabilities and contingent assets (changes in long term liabilities must be recognised in the period in which they occur).

(iv)   **Discount rate**

Currently under IAS 19, the **discount rate** used to discount pension obligations should be determined by reference to **market yields** (at the year end) on high quality fixed-rate corporate bonds. In the absence of a 'deep' market in such bonds, the yields on comparable government bonds should be used as reference instead. The maturity of the corporate bonds that are used to determine a discount rate should have a term to maturity that is consistent with the expected maturity of the post-employment benefit obligations, although a single weighted average discount rate is sufficient.

The techniques used to quantify pension liabilities rely on a number of assumptions, including the return that is expected to be made on assets in the time before the benefit will be paid. As was noted in the March 2008 Discussion Paper, this may not be appropriate because it does not reflect the present economic burden of the liability. The proposal in the Discussion Paper was that the liability should be **quantified** for financial reporting purposes **at an assessment of the cost of settling the benefit**, which will typically **reflect all future cash flows**. Information about the riskiness of the liability would be conveyed by disclosure rather than by adjusting the liability. Accordingly **the cash flows should be discounted at the risk-free rate**. However, in October 2009, the IASB decided not to proceed with this amendment, and the position remains problematic.

Return on plan assets

The **return on plan assets** is interest, dividends and other revenue derived from the plan assets, together with realised and unrealised gains or losses on the plan assets, less any cost of administering the plan and loss any tax payable by the plan itself. The expected return on the plan assets is a component element in the income statement (in profit or loss), not the actual returns. The **difference between the expected return and the actual return** is an **actuarial gain or loss**, and may be recognised in a number of different ways (see part (i)). The **inconsistency** in treatment and the **mismatch** if the return is recognised in the year and an actuarial loss deferred, makes this part of accounting for employee benefits **problematic** too.

(b)   **Smith and Brown: expected return on plan assets**

Some of the problems of inconsistency and lack of comparability outlined in Part (a) can be seen by comparing two companies, Smith and Brown, with **very different investment performance**.

The expected and actual returns on plan assets for the two companies was as follows:

	Smith $m	Brown $m
Fair value of plan assets at 1 May 20X8	200.0	200.0
Contributions received	70.0	70.0
Benefits paid	(26.0)	(26.0)
Expected return on plan assets: $(200 \times 7\%) + ((70 - 26) \times 6/12 \times 7\%)$	15.5	15.5
	259.5	259.5
Actuarial (loss)/gain	(40.5)	16.5
Fair value of plan assets at 30 April 20X9	219.0	276.0
Unrecognised actuarial gain at 1 May 20X8	6.0	6.0
Actuarial (loss)/gain in the year	(40.5)	16.5
Unrecognised actuarial (loss)/ gain	34.5	22.5

Both companies use the **corridor approach** to recognising actuarial gains and losses. This is based on opening plan assets, liabilities, gains and losses. 10% of the plan assets is $200m × 10% = $20m. (This would be used as the question says it is more than the present value of the defined benefit obligation.) The unrecognised actuarial at 1 May 20X8 of $6m are therefore below the corridor limit and would not be recognised in the year.

The **performance of Smith** (as shown by the fair value of the plan assets at the end of the year) has been **poor compared to that of Brown**. However, this is **not reflected in the amounts recognised** in profit or loss for the current year. The expected return on plan assets is identical for both companies, and the actuarial loss for Smith, and gain for Brown, is not recognised in the year. The real return on the plan assets, as opposed to the expected return, is not recognised in the year, because most of it shows up as an actuarial gain or loss.

The result of the above is that **comparison is difficult**. Two companies with different performances are showing the same result. This could be **misleading for investors**, especially as IAS 19 is complex and may not be understood.

10 Cohort

Text reference. Taxation is in Chapter 6 of the text.

Top tips. This question required a knowledge of deferred tax (IAS 12). The question focused on the key areas of the Standard and required an understanding of those areas. It did not require detailed computational knowledge but the ability to take a brief outline scenario and advise the client accordingly. Rote knowledge would be of little use in this situation.

Examiner's comment. Some candidates scored quite well on the question but again guessing at the answer was a fruitless exercise. The key areas were intragroup profit in inventory, unremitted earnings of subsidiaries, revaluation of securities, general provisions and tax losses. Basically an appreciation was required of how to deal with each of these areas but unfortunately most candidates struggled to deal with the issues involved.

		Marks
Air	– acquisition	5
	– intangible asset	3
	– intra group profit	3
	– unremitted earnings	3
Legion	– long term investments	4
	– loan provision	4
	– deferred tax asset	4
	Available	26
	Maximum	25

Acquisition of the subsidiaries – general

Fair value adjustments have been made for consolidation purposes in both cases and these will **affect the deferred tax charge for the year**. This is because the deferred tax position is viewed **from the perspective of the group** as a whole. For example, it may be possible to recognise deferred tax assets which previously could not be recognised by individual companies, because there are now sufficient tax profits available within the group to utilise unused tax losses. Therefore a **provision** should be made for **temporary differences between fair values of the identifiable net assets acquired and their carrying values** ($4 million less $3.5 million in respect of Air). **No provision should be made for the temporary difference** of $1 million **arising on goodwill** recognised as a result of the combination with Air.

Future listing

Cohort plans to seek a listing in three years time. Therefore it will become a **public company** and will be subject to a **higher rate of tax**. IAS 12 states that deferred tax should be measured at the **average tax rates expected to apply in the periods in which the timing differences are expected to reverse**, based on current enacted tax rates and laws. This means that Cohort may be paying tax at the higher rate when some of its timing differences reverse and this should be taken into account in the calculation.

Acquisition of Air

(a)   The directors have calculated the tax provision on the assumption that the intangible asset of $0.5 million will be allowed for tax purposes. However, this is not certain and the directors **may eventually have to pay the additional tax**. If the directors cannot be persuaded to adjust their calculations **a liability for the additional tax should be recognised.**

(b)   The intra-group transaction has resulted in an **unrealised profit** of $0.6 million in the group accounts and this will be **eliminated on consolidation**. The tax charge in the group income statement includes the tax on this profit, for which **the group will not become liable to tax until the following period. From the perspective of the group, there is a temporary difference**. Because the temporary difference arises in the financial statements of Cohort, **deferred tax should be provided** on this difference (an asset) using the rate of tax payable by Cohort.

(c)   **Deferred tax should be recognised on the unremitted earnings of subsidiaries** unless the parent is able to **control the timing of dividend payments** and it is **unlikely that dividends will be paid for the foreseeable future**. Cohort controls the dividend policy of Air and this means that there would normally be no need to make a provision in respect of unremitted profits. However, the profits of Air **will be distributed** to Cohort over the next few years and **tax will be payable** on the dividends received. Therefore a **deferred tax liability should be shown.**

Acquisition of Legion

(a)   A **temporary difference arises** where non-monetary assets are **revalued upwards** and the **tax treatment of the surplus is different from the accounting treatment**. In this case, the revaluation surplus has been **recognised in profit or loss** for the current period, rather than in equity but no corresponding adjustment has been made to the tax base of the investments because the gains will be taxed in future periods. Therefore the company **should recognise a deferred tax liability on the temporary difference of $4 million**.

(b)   A temporary difference arises when the provision for the loss on the loan portfolio is first recognised. The general allowance is expected to increase and therefore it is unlikely that the temporary difference will reverse in the near future. However, a **deferred tax liability should still be recognised**. The temporary difference gives rise to a **deferred tax asset**. IAS 12 states that **deferred tax assets should not be recognised unless it is probable that taxable profits will be available** against which the taxable profits can be utilised. **This is affected by the situation in point (c) below**.

(c)   In theory, unused tax losses give rise to a deferred tax asset. However, IAS 12 states that **deferred tax assets should only be recognised to the extent that they are regarded as recoverable**. They should be regarded as recoverable to the extent that on the basis of all the evidence available it is **probable that there will be suitable taxable profits against which the losses can be recovered**. The future taxable profit of Legion **will not be sufficient to realise all the unused tax loss. Therefore the deferred tax asset is reduced to the amount that is expected to be recovered**.

This reduction in the deferred tax asset implies that it was **overstated at 1 June 20X1**, when it was acquired by the group. As these are the first post-acquisition financial statements, **goodwill should also be adjusted**.

11 Panel

Text reference. Tax is covered in Chapter 6 of the text.

Top tips. This is a single topic question, which is a departure from the examiner's usual mixed standard question. The IFRS 1 aspects are likely to become less frequent over time.

Easy marks. Part (b) (iii) and (iv) are easier than (i) and (ii), though they carry the same number of marks.

(a)   (i)   **The impact of changes in accounting standards**

IAS 12 *Income taxes* is based on the idea that all **changes in assets and liabilities** have unavoidable **tax consequences**. Where the recognition criteria in IFRS are different from those in tax law, the **carrying amount of an asset or liability in the financial statements is different from the amount at which it is stated for tax purposes (its 'tax base')**. These differences are known as **'temporary differences'**. The practical effect of these differences is that a transaction or event occurs in a different accounting period from its tax consequences. For example, income from interest receivable is recognised in the financial statements in one accounting period but it is only taxable when it is actually received in the following accounting period.

IAS 12 requires a company to make **full provision** for the tax effects of temporary differences. Where a change in an accounting standard results in a change to the carrying value of an asset or liability in the financial statements, the **amount of the temporary difference** between the carrying value and the tax base **also changes**. Therefore the amount of the deferred tax liability is affected.

    (ii)   **Calculation of deferred tax on first time adoption of IFRS**

IFRS 1 *First time adoption of International Financial Reporting Standards* requires a company to **prepare an opening IFRS statement of financial position** and to **apply IAS 12 to temporary differences** between the carrying amounts of assets and liabilities and their tax bases at that date. Panel prepares its opening IFRS statement of financial position sheet **at 1 November 20X3**. The carrying values of its assets and liabilities are **measured in accordance with IFRS 1** and **other applicable IFRSs** in force at 31 October 20X5. The deferred tax provision is based on **tax rates that have been enacted or substantially enacted by the end of the reporting period**. Any **adjustments** to the deferred tax liability under previous GAAP are **recognised directly in equity (retained earnings)**.

(b)   (i)   **Share options**

Under IFRS 2 *Share based payment* the company **recognises an expense** for the employee services received in return for the share options granted over the vesting period. The related tax deduction **does not arise until the share options are exercised**. Therefore a **deferred tax asset arises**, based on the difference between the intrinsic value of the options and their carrying amount (normally zero).

At 31 October 20X4 the tax benefit is as follows:

	$m
Carrying amount of share based payment	–
Less: tax base of share based payment (16 ÷ 2)	(8)
Temporary difference	(8)

The **deferred tax asset is $2.4 million** (30% × 8). This is recognised at 31 October 20X4 provided that taxable profit is available against which it can be utilised. Because the tax effect of the remuneration expense is greater than the tax benefit, the tax benefit is **recognised in profit or loss.** (The tax effect of the remuneration expense is 30% × $40 million ÷ 2 = $6 million.)

At 31 October 20X5 there is **no longer a deferred tax asset** because the options have been exercised. The **tax benefit receivable is $13.8 million** (30% × $46 million). Therefore the deferred tax asset of $2.4 million is no longer required.

    (ii)   **Leased plant**

An asset leased under a finance lease is **recognised as an asset** owned by the company and the **related obligation** to pay lease rentals is **recognised as a liability**. Each instalment payable is treated partly as interest and partly as repayment of the liability. The **carrying amount** of the plant for accounting purposes is the **net present value of the lease payments less depreciation**.

A **temporary difference** effectively arises between the value of the plant for accounting purposes and the equivalent of the outstanding obligations, as the annual rental payments quality for the relief. The tax base of the asset is the amount deductable for tax in future, which is zero. The tax base of the liability is the carrying amount less any future tax deductible amounts, which will give a **tax base of zero.**

Therefore at 31 October 20X5 a **net temporary difference** will be as follows:

	$m	$m
Carrying value in financial statements:		
Asset:		
Net present value of future lease payments at inception of lease	12	
Less depreciation (12 ÷ 5)	(2.4)	
		9.60
Less finance lease liability		
Liability at inception of lease	12.00	
Interest (8% × 12)	0.96	
Lease rental	(3.00)	
		(9.96)
		0.36
Less tax base		(0.00)
Temporary difference		0.36

A **deferred tax asset of $108,000** (30% × 360,000) arises.

(iii) **Intra-group sale**

Pins has **made a profit of $2 million** on its sale to Panel. Tax is **payable on the profits of individual companies**. Pins is liable for tax on this profit in the current year and will have provided for the related tax in its individual financial statements. However, **from the viewpoint of the group** the profit **will not be realised until the following year**, when the goods are sold to a third party and must be **eliminated** from the consolidated financial statements. Because the group **pays tax before the profit is realised** there is a **temporary difference of $2 million** and a **deferred tax asset of $600,000** (30% × $2 million).

(iv) **Impairment loss**

The impairment loss in the financial statements of Nails **reduces the carrying value** of property, plant and equipment, but is **not allowable for tax**. Therefore the **tax base** of the property, plant and equipment **is different from its carrying value** and there is a **temporary difference**.

Under IAS 36 *Impairment of assets* the impairment loss is allocated first to goodwill and then to other assets:

	Goodwill	Property, plant and equipment	Total
	$m	$m	$m
Carrying value at 31 October 20X5	1	6.0	7.0
Impairment loss	(1)	(0.8)	(1.8)
	–	5.2	5.2

IAS 12 states that **no deferred tax should be recognised on goodwill** and therefore **only the impairment loss relating to the property, plant and equipment affects the deferred tax position.**

The effect of the impairment loss is as follows:

	Before impairment	After impairment	Difference
	$m	$m	$m
Carrying value	6	5.2	
Tax base	(4)	(4)	
Temporary difference	2	1.2	0.8
Tax liability (30%)	0.6	0.36	0.24

Therefore the impairment loss reduces deferred the tax liability by $240,000.

12 Kesare

Marking scheme

		Marks
(a)	Quality of discussion	2
	Framework	1
	Temporary difference	2
	Liability	1
	Weakness	1
		7
(b)	Adjustments: Available for sale assets	2
	Convertible bond	2
	Defined benefit plan	2
	Property, plant and equipment	1
	Deferred tax: Goodwill	1
	Other intangibles	1
	Financial assets	1
	Trade receivables	1
	Other receivables	1
	Long-term borrowings	1

		Marks
	Employee benefits	1
	Trade payables	1
	Calculation	3
	Maximum	18
	Available	25
	Professional communication	2

(a) IAS 12 *Income taxes* is based on the idea that **all changes in assets and liabilities** have **unavoidable tax consequences.** Where the recognition criteria in IFRS are different from those in tax law, **the carrying amount of an asset or liability in the financial statements is different from its tax base** (the amount at which it is stated for tax purposes). These differences are known as **temporary differences.** The practical effect of these differences is that a transaction or event occurs in a different accounting period from its tax consequences. For example, depreciation is recognised in the financial statements in different accounting periods from capital allowances.

IAS 12 requires a company to make **full provision** for the tax effects of temporary differences. Both **deferred tax assets**, and **deferred tax liabilities** can arise in this way.

It may be argued that deferred tax assets and liabilities **do not meet the definition of assets and liabilities** in the IASB *Framework.* Under the *Framework* an asset is the right to receive economic benefits as a result of past events, and a liability is an obligation to transfer economic benefits, again as a result of past events.

Under IAS 12, the tax effect of transactions are recognised in the same period as the transactions themselves, but in practice, tax is paid in accordance with tax legislation when it becomes a legal liability. There is a **conceptual weakness** or inconsistency, in that only one liability, that is tax, is being provided for, and not other costs, such as overhead costs.

(b)

	$'000	Adjustments to financial statements $'000	Tax base $'000	Temporary difference $'000
Property, plant and equipment	10,000		2,400	7,600
Goodwill	6,000		6,000	
Other intangible assets	5,000		0	5,000
Financial assets (cost)	9,000	1,500	9,000	1,500
Total non-current assets	30,000			
Trade receivables	7,000		7,500	(500)
Other receivables	4,600		5,000	(400)
Cash and cash-equivalents	6,700		6,700	–
Total current assets	18,300			
Total assets	48,300			
Share capital	(9,000)			
Other reserves	(4,500)	1,500		
		400		
Retained earnings	9,130	(520)		
Total equity	(22,630)			
Long term borrowings	(10,000)	(400)	(10,000)	400
Deferred tax liability	(3,600)		(3,600)	–
Employee benefits	(4,000)	520	(5,000)	480
Current tax liability	(3,070)		(3,070)	–
Trade and other payables	(5,000)		(4,000)	(1,000)
Total liabilities	(25,670)			13,080

	$'000
Deferred tax liability	
Liability b/fwd	3,600
Charge (bal fig)	324
Deferred tax liability c/fwd 14,980 × 30%	4,494
Deferred tax asset – c/fwd 1,900 × 30%	(570)
Net deferred tax liability 13,080 × 30%	3,924

Notes on adjustments

(i) The financial assets are shown at cost. However, per IAS 39, since they are classified as 'available for sale', they should instead be valued at fair value, with the increase ($10,500 – $9,000 = $1,500) going to equity.

(ii) IAS 32 states that convertible bonds must be split into debt and equity components. This involves reducing debt and increasing equity by $400.

(iii) The defined benefit plan needs to be adjusted to reflect the change. The liability must be increased by 40% × $1m + (60% × $1m ÷ 5) = $520,000. The same amount is charged to retained earnings.

(iv) The development costs have already been allowed for tax, so the tax base is nil. No deferred tax is recognised on goodwill.

(v) The accrual for compensation is to be allowed when paid, ie in a later period. The tax base relating to trade and other payables should be reduced by $1m.

13 Preparation question: Financial instruments

(a)   INCOME STATEMENT

$

Finance income
   (441,014 × (W1) 8%)   35,281

STATEMENT OF FINANCIAL POSITION

Non-current assets
   Financial asset (441,014 + 35,281)   476,295

Working: Effective interest rate

$$\frac{600,000}{441,014} = 1.3605$$

∴ from tables interest rate is 8%

(b)   **Compound instrument**

Presentation

	$
Non-current liabilities	
Financial liability component of convertible bond (Working)	1,797,467
Equity	
Equity component of convertible bond (2,000,000 – (Working) 1,797,467)	202,533

Working

$

Fair value of equivalent non-convertible debt
Present value of principal payable at end of 3 years   1,544,367

$$(4,000 \times \$500 = \$2m \times \frac{1}{(1.09)^3})$$

Present value of interest annuity payable annually in arrears
for 3 years [(5% × $2m) × 2.531]   253,100
                                                                      1,797,467

14 Ambush

Text reference. Financial instruments are covered in Chapter 7 of your text.

Top tips. A whole question on IAS 39 may appear daunting, but in fact this question is quite fair.

Easy marks. These are available for the discursive aspects, which are most of the question.

Examiner's comment. The first part of the question was well answered but candidates' answers on the fair value option and impairment were of poorer quality. Candidates often set out the requirement for the impairment of non current assets rather than financial instruments. There are some similarities but the conditions are different. The problems of the fair value option are well documented and some candidates answered this part of the question very well. However many candidates offered little in the way of logical argument as to why it has caused concern. Overall however the question was well answered.

To: Directors of Ambush

From:

Subject: IAS 39 *Financial instruments: Recognition and measurement*

Date: December 20X5

As requested, this report outlines the way in which financial instruments are measured and classified and explains why the fair value option was initially introduced.

(a)   (i)   **How financial assets and liabilities are measured and classified**

IAS 39 states that all financial assets and liabilities should be **measured at fair value when they are first recognised.** This is normally their cost (the fair value of the consideration given or received). Fair value **includes transaction costs** unless the instrument is **classified as 'at fair value through profit or loss'**, in which case transaction costs are **recognised in profit or loss for the year**.

The way in which an instrument is measured subsequently **depends on its classification**. There are **four categories**:

- Financial assets and liabilities at fair value through profit or loss
- Held to maturity investments
- Loans and receivables
- Available-for-sale financial assets

Financial assets and liabilities **at fair value through profit or loss** includes all items **held for trading** and all **derivative financial instruments**. Until recently it was possible to designate any financial asset or liability as 'at fair value through profit or loss'. However, as a result of the problems explained below **IAS 39 has now been amended to restrict the use of 'the fair value option'.** Unless this classification is required it can now only be used if it **results in more relevant information**, because either:

(1)   It **eliminates or significantly reduces inconsistencies** that would otherwise arise from measuring assets or liabilities or recognising the gains and losses on them on different bases; or

(2)   A group of financial assets, financial liabilities or both is **managed** and its **performance is evaluated** on a **fair value basis**, in accordance with a documented risk management or investment strategy.

Held to maturity investments have **fixed or determinable payments** and **fixed maturity.** The company must have the **positive intention and ability** to **hold them to maturity.** There are a number of detailed conditions that must be met before an instrument can be classified in this way. Equity instruments cannot be held to maturity investments.

Loans and receivables have **fixed or determinable payments** and are **not quoted in an active market.**

Available for sale financial assets are all **items that do not fall into the other categories.** Financial instruments not required to be classified as at fair value through profit or loss can be designated as available for sale.

IAS 39 **restricts reclassifications** between categories. Instruments cannot be reclassified into or out of 'at fair value through profit or loss'. There are penalties if held to maturity investments are reclassified or sold; a company cannot use this category again for two years.

Most financial assets are measured at fair value. Exceptions are **held to maturity investments** and **loans and receivables**, which are measured at **amortised cost**, using the **effective interest rate method**. This involves adjusting the cost of an instrument to reflect interest and repayments. The interest is allocated to accounting periods so as to achieve a **constant rate on the carrying amount** over the term of the instrument. Investments in **unquoted equity instruments** for which there is no reliable market value are measured at **cost**.

Financial **liabilities at fair value through profit or loss** are measured at **fair value. Other financial liabilities** are measured at **amortised cost.**

The way in which **gains and losses on remeasurement** are treated also depends upon the classification of the instruments. Gains and losses relating to instruments at **fair value through profit or loss** are **recognised in profit or loss**, even if they are unrealised. Gains and losses relating to changes in the fair value of **available for sale financial assets** are **recognised in equity** and **reclassified from equity to profit on loss as a reclassification adjustment** when the asset is sold. Changes in **amortised cost** are recognised in **profit or loss.**

(ii) **Financial instruments held at fair value**

The main advantage of holding financial instruments of fair value is that **fair value provides more relevant information** than historic cost. Fair value also has **specific advantages**. It eliminates the burden of **separating embedded derivatives** and it **eliminates volatility** in the income statement where matched positions of financial assets and financial liabilities are not measured consistently.

However, in practice fair value has **disadvantages**. It can be **used inappropriately**. For example:

- Companies could apply fair value to financial instruments whose fair value is **not verifiable**. Because the valuation is **subjective**, they would then have scope to **manipulate profit or loss**.
- Use of fair values **could increase volatility** in the income statement if the option were applied **selectively**.
- If **financial liabilities were held at fair value**, a company might recognise gains and losses as a result of **changes in its own creditworthiness**.

For those reasons, IAS 39 **restricts use of fair value to certain financial instruments and not others.**

(b) (i) **Impairment of financial assets**

IAS 39 states that **at each reporting date**, an entity should **assess** whether there is any **objective evidence that a financial asset or group of assets is impaired. Indications** of impairment include **significant financial difficulty** of the issuer; the probability that the borrower will **enter bankruptcy**; a **default** in interest or principal payments; or (for available for sale financial assets) a significant and prolonged **decline in fair value** below cost.

Where there is objective evidence of impairment, the entity should **determine the amount** of any impairment loss, which should be **recognised immediately in profit or loss**. Only losses relating to **past events** can be recognised. **Two conditions** must be met before an impairment loss is recognised:

- There is **objective evidence** of impairment as a result of one or more events that **occurred after the initial recognition** of the asset; and
- The **impact on the estimated future cash flows** of the asset can be **reliably estimated.**

For financial assets **carried at amortised cost** (held to maturity investments and loans and receivables) the impairment loss is the **difference** between the asset's **carrying amount** and its **recoverable amount**. The asset's recoverable amount is the **present value of estimated future cash flows**, discounted at the financial instrument's **original** effective interest rate.

For financial assets **carried at cost** because their fair value cannot be reliably measured, the impairment loss is the **difference** between the asset's **carrying amount** and the **present value of estimated future cash flows**, discounted at the **current market rate of return for a similar financial instrument.**

For **available for sale** financial assets, the impairment loss is the **difference** between the **acquisition cost** (net of any principal repayment and amortisation) and **current fair value** (for equity instruments) or **recoverable amount** (for debt instruments).

Assets at **fair value through profit or loss** are **not subject to impairment testing**, because changes in fair value are automatically recognised immediately in profit or loss.

		Marks
(a)	Definition of financial liability and equity	3
	Principle in IAS 32	1
	Discussion	2
(b)	IAS 19	1
	Financial liability	2
	Provision	1
	Build up over service period	1
	Recalculate annually	1
(c)	Purchase method	1
	Cost of business combinations	1
	Future payment	1
	Remuneration versus cost of acquisition	2
(d)	Not exercised	2
	Expected exercise	1
	IAS 39	1
	Current v non-current	2
Communication in report		2
	Maximum	25

Report

To: The Directors, Sirus
From: Accountant
Date: 15 June 20X8

Accounting treatment of items in the financial statements

(a) Directors' ordinary 'B' shares

The capital of Sirus must be shown **either as a liability or as equity**. The criteria for distinguishing between financial liabilities and equity are found in IAS 32 *Financial instruments: presentation.* Equity and liabilities must be classified **according to their substance, not just their legal form,**

A **financial liability** is defined as any liability that is:

(i) A contractual obligation:

– To deliver cash or another financial asset to another entity, or

– To exchange financial instruments with another entity under conditions that are potentially unfavourable; or

(ii) a contract that will or may be settled in the entity's own equity instruments.

An **equity instrument** is any contract that evidences a **residual interest** in the assets of an entity after deducting all of its liabilities

The **ordinary 'B' shares,** the capital subscribed by the directors must, according to the directors' service agreements, be returned to any director on leaving the company. There is thus a **contractual obligation** to deliver cash. The redemption **is not discretionary,** and Sirus has no right to avoid it. The mandatory nature of the repayment makes this capital a **liability** (if it were discretionary, it would be equity). On initial recognition, that is when the 'B' shares are purchased, the financial liability must be stated at the **present value of the amount due on redemption,** discounted over the life of the service contract. In subsequent periods, the financial liability may be carried at fair value through profit or loss, or at amortised cost under IAS 39.

In contrast, the **payment of $3 million** to holders of 'B' shares, is discretionary in that it must be approved in a general meeting by a majority of all shareholders. This approval may be refused, and so it would not be correct to show the $3 million as a liability in the statement of financial position at 30 April 20X8. Instead, it should be recognised when approved. The dividend when recognised will be treated as **interest expense**. This is because IAS 32 (para 35-36) requires the treatment of dividends to follow the treatment of the instrument, ie because the instrument is treated as a liability, the dividends are treated as an expense.

(b) **Directors' retirement benefits**

These are unfunded defined benefit plans, which are likely to be governed by IAS 19 *Employee benefits,* but IAS 32 and 39 on financial instruments, and IAS 37 *Provisions, contingent liabilities and contingent assets* also apply.

Sirus has contractual or constructive obligations to make payments to former directors. The treatment and applicable standard depends on the obligation.

(i) **Fixed annuity with payment to director's estate on death**. This **meets the definition of a financial liability under IAS 32**, because there is a contractual obligation to deliver cash or a financial asset. The firm does not have the option to withhold the payment. The rights to these annuities are earned over the directors' period of service, so it follows that the costs should also be recognised over this service period.

(ii) **Fixed annuity ceasing on death**

The timing of the death is clearly uncertain, which means that the annuities have a **contingent element** with a mortality risk to be calculated by an actuary. It meets the definition of an insurance contract, which is outside the scope of IAS 39, as are employers' obligations under IAS 19. However, insofar as there is a constructive obligation, these annuities fall within the scope of IAS 37, because these are liabilities of uncertain timing or amount. The amount of the obligation should be measured in a manner similar to a warranty provision: that is the **probability of the future cash outflow** of the present obligation should be measured for the class of all such obligations. An estimate of the costs should include any liability for post retirement payments that directors have earned so far. The liability should **be built up over the service period** and will in practice be calculated on an actuarial basis as under IAS 19 *Employee benefits.* If the effect is material, the liability will be discounted. It should be **re-calculated every year** to take account of directors joining or leaving, or any other changes.

(c) **Acquisition of Marne**

An increased profit share is payable to the directors of Marne if the purchase offer is accepted. The question arises of whether this additional payment constitutes **remuneration or consideration** for the business acquired. Because the payment is for two years only, after which time remuneration falls back to normal levels, the payment should be seen as part of the **purchase consideration.**

The second issue is the treatment of this consideration. IFRS 3 (revised January 2008) *Business combinations* requires that an acquirer must be identified for all business combinations. In this case Sirus is the acquirer. The cost of the combination must be measured as the sum of the fair values, at the date of exchange, of assets given or liabilities assumed in exchange for control.

IFRS 3 recognises that, by entering into an acquisition, the acquirer becomes obliged to make additional payments. Not recognising that obligation means that the consideration recognised at the acquisition date is not fairly stated.

The revised IFRS 3 **requires recognition of contingent consideration, measured at fair value, at the acquisition date.** This is, arguably, consistent with how other forms of consideration are fair valued.

The acquirer may be required to pay contingent consideration in the form of equity or of a debt instrument or cash. In this case, it is in the form of cash, or increased remuneration.

Accordingly, the **cost of the combination must include the full $11m,** measured at net present value at 1 May 20X7. The payment of $5 million would be discounted for one year and the payment of $6 million for two years.

(d)   **Repayment of bank loan**

The bank loan is to be repaid in ten years' time, but the terms of the loan state that Syrus can pay it off in seven years. The issue arises as to **whether the early repayment option is likely to be exercised.**

If, when the loan was taken out on 1 May 20X7 the option **of early repayment was not expected to be exercised,** then at 30 April 20X8 the normal terms apply. The loan would be stated at $2 million in the statement of financial position, and the effective interest would be 8% × $2 million = $160,000, the interest paid.

If at 1 May 20X7 it was expected that the **early repayment option would be exercised**, then the **effective interest rate would be 9.1%,** and the effective interest 9.1% × $2 million = $182,000. The cash paid would still be $160,000, and the difference of $22,000 would be added to the carrying amount of the financial liability in the statement of financial position, giving $2,022,000.

IAS 39 *Financial instruments: recognition and measurement* requires that the carrying amount of a financial asset or liability should be adjusted to reflect actual cash flows or revised estimates of cash flows. This means that, even if it was thought at the outset that early repayment would not take place, if **expectations then change, the carrying amount must be revised** to reflect future estimated cash flows using the effective interest rate.

The directors of Sirus are currently in discussion with the bank regarding repayment in the next financial year. However, these discussions do not create a legal obligation to repay the loan in twelve months, and Sirus has an unconditional right to defer settlement for longer than twelve months. Accordingly, **it would not be correct to show the loan as a current liability on the basis of the discussions with the bank.**

I hope that this report is helpful to you.

Signed, Accountant

17 Aron

Text reference. Financial instruments are covered in Chapter 7 of the BPP Study Text.

Top tips. Part (a) required a brief discussion of how the fair value of financial instruments is determined with a comment on the relevance of fair value measurements for financial instruments where markets are volatile and illiquid. Part (b) required you to discuss the accounting for four different financial instruments. The financial instruments ranged from a convertible bond to transfer of shares to a debt instrument in a foreign subsidiary to interest free loans. Bear in mind that you need to discuss the treatment and not just show the accounting entries. And while you may not have come across the specific treatment of interest-free loans before, you can apply the principles of IAS 39 (what is fair value in this case?) and the *Framework*.

Easy marks. These are available for the discussion in Part (a) and the convertible bond.

Examiner's comment. This was the best answered question on the paper. Part (a) was quite well answered although the answers were quite narrow and many candidates simply described the classification of financial instruments in loans and receivables, available for sale etc. In Part (b) many candidates simply showed the accounting entries without any discussion. If the accounting entries were incorrect then it was difficult to award significant marks for the attempt. The treatment of the convertible bond was quite well done except for the treatment of the issue costs and the conversion of the bond. This part of the question often gained good marks. Again the treatment of the transfer of shares and interest free loans was well done but the exchange and fair value gains were often combined and not separated in the case of the debt instrument of the foreign subsidiary.

			Marks
(a)	Fair value – subjective		4
(b)	Convertible bond:	explanation	2
		calculation	4
	Shares in Smart:	explanation	2
		calculation	2
	Foreign subsidiary:	explanation of principles	2
		accounting treatment	3
	Interest free loan:	explanation of principles	2
		accounting treatment	2
	Quality of explanations		2
		Available/Maximum	25

(a) **Fair value**

The **fair value** of an asset is the amount for which an asset could be exchanged, or a liability settled, between knowledgeable, willing parties in an arm's length transaction. The fair value is normally the transaction price or quoted market prices. If market prices are not reliable, the fair value may be **estimated** using a valuation technique, for example, by discounting cash flows or a pricing model such as Black Scholes.

There is an element of **subjectivity** in fair valuing, arising from the fact that the methods all involve estimation. Different methods will therefore result in different values, but if the market is efficient, these differences should not be material.

The IASB believes that fair value is the **most appropriate measure** for most financial instruments. In a 2008 Discussion Paper it stated that, long-term, it was the **only** appropriate measure. Fair value can be said to be more **relevant** than historical cost because it is based on current market values rather than a value that is, in some cases, many years out of date. Fair values for an entity's assets, it can be argued, give a closer approximation to the value of the entity as a whole.

However, while it is more relevant, fair value, being based on estimates, may be less **reliable.** There is more scope for manipulation. Particular difficulties arise where quoted prices are unavailable. If this is the case – and it frequently is – there is more reliance on estimates.

Not all markets are liquid and transparent. Where a market is **illiquid**, it is particularly difficult to apply fair value measurement, because the information will not be available. In addition, not all markets are stable; some are volatile. Fair valuing gives a measurement at a particular point in time, but in a **volatile** market this measure may not apply long term. It needs to be considered whether an asset is to be actively traded or held for the long term.

Disclosure is important in helping to deal with some of the problems of fair value, particularly as it provides an indicator of a company's risk profile.

(b) (i) **Convertible bond**

Some financial instruments contain both a liability and an equity element. In such cases, IAS 32 requires the component parts of the instrument to be **classified separately**, according to the substance of the contractual arrangement and the definitions of a financial liability and an equity instrument.

One of the most common types of compound instrument, as here, is **convertible debt**. This creates a primary financial liability of the issuer and grants an option to the holder of the instrument to convert it into an equity instrument (usually ordinary shares) of the issuer. This is the economic equivalent of the issue of conventional debt plus a warrant to acquire shares in the future.

Although in theory there are several possible ways of calculating the split, the following method is recommended:

(1)   Calculate the value for the liability component.
(2)   Deduct this from the instrument as a whole to leave a residual value for the equity component.

The reasoning behind this approach is that an entity's equity is its residual interest in its assets amount after deducting all its liabilities.

The **sum of the carrying amounts** assigned to liability and equity will always be equal to the carrying amount that would be ascribed to the instrument **as a whole**.

The **equity component is not re-measured.** However, the **liability component** is measured at amortised cost using an **effective interest rate** (here 9.38%).

It is important to note that the issue costs (here $1million) are allocated in proportion to the value of the liability and equity components when the initial split is calculated.

Step 1   Calculate liability element

A 9% discount rate is used, which is the market rate for similar bonds without the conversion rights:

Present value of interest at end of:	
Year 1 (31 May 20X6) ($100m × 6%) × 0.9174	5,505
Year 2 (31 May 20X7) ($100m × 6%) × 0.8417	5,050
Year 3 (31 May 20X8) ($100m × ($100m × 6%)) × 0.7722	81,852
Total liability component	92,407
Total equity element	7,593
Proceeds of issue	100,000

Step 2   Allocate issue costs

	Liability $'000	Equity $'000	Total $'000
Proceeds	92,407	7,593	100,000
Issue cost	(924)	(76)	(1,000)
	91,483	7,517	99,000

The double entry is:

		$'000	$'000			$'000	$'000
DEBIT	Cash	100,000		CREDIT	Cash		1,000
CREDIT	Liability		92,407	DEBIT	Liability	924	
CREDIT	Equity		7,593	DEBIT	Equity	76	

Step 3   Re-measure liability using effective interest rate

	$'000
Cash – 1.6.20X5 (net of issue costs per Step 2)	91,483
Effective interest to 31.5.20X6 (9.38% × 91,483)	8,581
Coupon paid (6% × $100m)	(6,000)
At 31.5.20X6	94,064
Effective interest to 31.5.20X7 (9.38% × 94,064)	8,823
Coupon paid (6% × $100m)	(6,000)
At 31.5.20X7	96,887
Effective interest to 31.5.20X8 (9.38% × 96,887)	9,088
Coupon paid (6% × $100m)	(6,000)
At 31.5.20X8	100,000*

Step 4 Conversion of bond

On conversion of the bond on 31 May 20X8, Aron will issue 25 million ordinary shares. The consideration for these shares will be the original equity component (net of its share of issue costs) together with the balance on the liability.

	$'000
Share capital – 25 million at $1	25,000
Share premium	82,517
Equity and liability components (100,000 + 7,593 – 76)	107,517

(ii) Shares in Smart

The issue here is whether the shares in Smart should be **derecognised**. Derecognition is the removal of a previously recognised financial instrument from an entity's statement of financial position.

An entity should derecognise a **financial asset** when:

(a) The **contractual rights** to the cash flows from the financial asset **expire**, or

(b) The entity **transfers substantially all the risks and rewards of ownership** of the financial asset to another party.

In this case, Aron no longer retains any risks and rewards of ownership. Accordingly the financial asset shares in Smart should be derecognised. At the same time Aron needs to recognise a new financial asset, namely the shares in Given, and this must be recognised at fair value. Additionally, the cumulative gain recognised in equity relating to the available-for-sale investment ($400,000) must be reclassified to profit or loss for the year

There will be a gain to profit or loss for the year, calculated as follows:

	$m
Proceeds	5.5
Carrying amount of shares in Smart	5.0
Gain on derecognition	0.5
Gain reclassified from equity	0.4
Gain to profit or loss for the year	0.9

The total gain on disposal is thus $900,000.

The double entry (including the recognition of the shares in Given) is as follows:

DEBIT	Shares in Given	$5.5m	
CREDIT	Shares in Smart		$5m
CREDIT	Gain on sale		$0.5m
DEBIT	Other comprehensive income	$0.4m	
CREDIT	Gain on sale		$0.4m

(iii) Foreign subsidiary

Two International Accounting Standards apply to this transaction:

(1) The debt instrument in the foreign subsidiary's financial statements is dealt with under IAS 39 *Financial instruments: recognition and measurement.*

(2) The translation of the financial statements of the foreign subsidiary is governed by IAS 21 *The effects of changes in foreign exchange rates.*

Under IAS 21, **all exchange differences resulting from translation are recognised in other comprehensive income until the subsidiary is disposed of**. This includes exchange differences that arise on financial instruments carried at fair value through profit or loss and financial assets classified as available-for-sale. It is important to distinguish gains that result from increases in fair value from gains that result from changes in exchange rates.

The debt instrument owned by Gao is held for trading, and will therefore be carried at **fair value through profit or loss** in Gao's financial statements. At 31 May 20X8, there will be a gain in the financial statements of Gao 12m – 10m = 2 million zloti. In accordance with IAS 39, this will be credited to profit or loss for the year in Gao's statement of comprehensive income.

In the consolidated financial statements, the carrying value of the debt at 1 June 20X7 would be calculated using the exchange rate at that date as: 10 million zloti ÷ 3 = $3.3m. By 31 May 20X8, the carrying value will have increased to: 12 million zloti ÷ 2 = $6m. **Part of the increase** in value of $6m - $ 3.3m = $2.7m is attributable to a **change in the exchange rate**, and **part** of it to an **increase in fair value**. Only the latter can be recognised in profit or loss for the year.

Aaron will use the average rate for the year of 2.5 to translate the statement of comprehensive income, giving a gain of 2 million zloti ÷ 2.5 = $800,000 to be taken to profit or loss for the year. The remaining part of the increase in value, $2.7m - $0.8m = $1.9m will be **classified in other comprehensive income** until Gao is disposed of.

The accounting is as follows:

	$m
Balance at 1 June 20X7	3.3
Increase in year	2.7
Balance at 31 May 20X8	6.0

DEBIT	Debt instrument	$2.7m	
CREDIT	Profit or loss		$0.8m
CREDIT	Equity		$1.9m

(iv) **Interest free loans**

IAS 39 requires financial assets to be measured on initial recognition at **fair value** plus transaction costs. Usually the fair value of the consideration given represents the fair value of the asset. However, this is not necessarily the case with an interest-free loan. An interest free loan to an employee is not costless to the employer, and the **face value may not be the same as the fair value.**

To arrive at the fair value of the loan, Aaron needs to consider **other market transactions** in the same instrument. The market rate of interest for a two year loan on the date of issue (1 June 20X7) and the date of repayment (31 May 20X9) is 6% pa, and this is rate should be used in valuing the instrument. The **fair value** may be estimated as the **present value of future receipts using the market interest rate**. There will be a difference between the face value and the fair value of the instrument, calculated as follows:

	$m
Face value of loan at 1 June 20X7	10.0
Fair value of loan at 1 June 20X7: 10 × 0.8900	8.9
Difference	1.1

The **difference** of $1.1m is the extra cost to the employer of not charging a market rate of interest. It will be treated as **employee compensation** under IAS 19 *Employee benefits*. This employee compensation must be charged over the two year period to the statement of comprehensive income, through profit or loss for the year.

Aron wishes to classify the loan under IAS 39 as 'loans and receivables'. It must therefore be measured at 31 May 20X8 at **amortised cost** using the effective interest method. The **effective interest rate** is 6%, so the value of the loan in the statement of financial position is: $8.9m × 1.06 = $9.43m. Interest will be credited to profit or loss for the year of: $8.9 × 6% = $53m.

The **double entry** is as follows:

At 1 June 20X7

DEBIT	Loan	$8.9m	
DEBIT	Employee compensation	$1.1m	
CREDIT	Cash		$10m

At 31 May 20X8

DEBIT	Loan	$0.53m	
CREDIT	Profit or loss - interest		$0.53m

18 Vident

Marking scheme

		Marks
(a)	Discussion	9
(b)	Computation and discussion	9
(c)	Computation and discussion	7
	Available/Maximum	25

REPORT

To: Directors of Vident

Subject: IFRS 2 Share based payment

From:

Date: 20X5

As requested, this report explains why share based payments should be recognised in the financial statements. It also explains how the directors' share options should be accounted for in the financial statements for the year ended 31 May 20X5.

(a) **Why share based payments should be recognised in the financial statements**

IFRS 2 *Share based payment* applies to **all share option schemes granted after 7 November 2002**. The directors have put forward several arguments for not recognising the expense of remunerating directors in this way.

Share options have no cost to the company

When shares are **issued for cash** or in a business acquisition, **an accounting entry is needed** to **recognise the receipt of cash** (or other resources) as consideration for the issue. Share options (the right to receive shares in future) **are also issued in consideration for resources**: services rendered by directors or employees. These resources are **consumed by the company** and it would be **inconsistent not to recognise an expense**.

Share issues do not meet the definition of an expense in the IASB Framework

The *Framework* defines an expense as a **decrease in economic benefits** in the form of **outflows of assets** or **incurrences of liabilities**. It is not immediately obvious that employee services meet the definition of an asset and therefore **it can be argued that consumption of those services does not meet the definition of an expense**. However, share options **are issued for consideration in the form of employee services** so that **arguably there is an asset**, although it is **consumed at the same time that it is received**. Therefore the recognition of an expense relating to share based payment is **consistent with the *Framework***.

20 Ryder

(a)   **Disposal of subsidiary**

The issue here is the value of the subsidiary at 31 October 20X5. The directors have stated that there has been no significant event since the year end which could have resulted in a reduction in its value. This, taken together with the loss on disposal, indicates that the subsidiary had **suffered an impairment at 31 October 20X5.** IAS 10 requires the sale to be treated as an **adjusting event** after the reporting period as it provides **evidence of a condition that existed at the end of the reporting period.**

The assets of Krup should be **written down to their recoverable amount**. In this case this is the eventual sale proceeds. Therefore the value of the net assets and purchased goodwill of Krup should be **reduced by $11 million** (the loss on disposal of $9 million plus the loss of $2 million that occurred between 1 November 2005 and the date of sale). IAS 36 *Impairment of assets* states that an impairment loss should be allocated to goodwill first and therefore the **purchased goodwill of $12 million is reduced to $1 million.** The impairment loss of $11 million is **recognised in profit or loss.**

Because there was no intention to sell the subsidiary at 31 October 20X5, **IFRS 5 *Non current assets held for sale and discontinued operations* does not apply**. The disposal is **disclosed** in the notes to the financial statements in accordance with IAS 10.

(b)   **Issue of shares at fair value**

IFRS 3 *Business combinations* (revised January 2008) recognises that, by entering into an acquisition, the acquirer becomes obliged to make additional payments. The revised IFRS 3 **requires recognition of contingent consideration, measured at fair value, at the acquisition date.**

The treatment of **post-acquisition changes** in the fair value of the contingent consideration **depends on the circumstances.**

(i)   If the change is due to **additional information** that affects the position at the acquisition date, **goodwill should be re-measured, as a retrospective adjustment**. The additional information must come to light **within the measurement period,** a maximum of one year after acquisition.

(ii)   If the change is **due to events which took place after the acquisition date,** for example meeting earnings target, an **equity instrument is not re-measured.** Other instruments are re-measured, with changes to total comprehensive income.

Ryder has **correctly included** an estimate of the amount of consideration in the cost of the acquisition on 21 January 20X4. This would have been based on the fair value of the ordinary shares at that date of $10 per share, giving a total of 300,000 × $10 = $3,000,000:

DEBIT Investment $3,000,000
CREDIT Equity $3,000,000

As the consideration is in the form of shares, and the change is due to an event which took place after the acquisition date (the rise in share price), **the consideration is not remeasured.**

The value of the contingent shares should be included in a **separate category of equity** in the statement of financial position at 31 October 20X5. They should be transferred to share capital and share premium after the actual issue of the shares on 12 November 20X5.

The other matter is whether the share issue and the bonus issue affect the calculation of earnings per share for the year ended 31 October 20X5. IAS 33 *Earnings per share* states that contingently issuable shares should be included in the calculation of basic earnings per share only from the date that all conditions are met. As the conditions were met at 31 October 20X5, the shares should be included in the calculation from that date, even though the shares were not issued until after the year end. In the case of diluted earnings per share, IAS 33 requires contingently issue shares to be included from the beginning of the period in which all conditions are met, ie from 1 September 20X4. IAS 33 also states that if there is a bonus share issue after the year end but before the financial statements are authorised for issue, the bonus shares should be included in the calculation (and in the calculation of earnings per share for all previous periods presented).

Both IAS 10 and IAS 33 require **disclosure of all material share transactions** or potential share transactions entered into after the reporting period end, excluding the bonus issue. Therefore **details of the issue of the contingent shares should be disclosed** in the notes to the financial statements.

(c)   **Property**

The property appears to have been **incorrectly classified** as 'held for sale'. Although the company had always intended to sell the property, IFRS 5 states that in order to qualify as 'held for sale' an asset must be **available for immediate sale in its present condition**. Because **repairs were needed** before the property could be sold and these were **not completed until after the reporting period end**, this was clearly **not the case at 31 October 20X5**.

In addition, even if the property had been correctly classified, it has been **valued incorrectly**. IFRS 5 requires assets held for sale to be valued at **the lower of their carrying amount or fair value less costs to sell.** The property **should have been valued at its carrying amount of $20 million**, not at the eventual sale proceeds of $27 million.

The property **must be included within property, plant and equipment** and must be **depreciated**. Therefore its **carrying amount at 31 October 20X5 is $19 million** ($20 million less depreciation of $1 million). The **gain of $7 million** that the company has previously recognised **should be reversed**.

Although the property cannot be classified as 'held for sale' in the financial statements for the year ended 31 October 2005, it **will qualify for the classification after the end of the reporting period**. Therefore details of the sale should be **disclosed** in the notes to the financial statements.

(d)   **Share appreciation rights**

The granting of share appreciation rights is a **cash settled share based payment transaction** as defined by IFRS 2 *Share based payment*. IFRS 2 requires these to be **measured at the fair value of the liability** to pay cash. The liability should be **re-measured at each reporting date and at the date of settlement**. Any **changes in fair value** should be **recognised in profit or loss** (the income statement) for the period.

However, the company has **not remeasured the liability since 31 October 20X4**. Because IFRS 2 requires the expense and the related liability to be recognised over the two-year vesting period, the rights should be measured as follows:

	$m
At 31 October 20X4: ($6 × 10 million × ½)	30
At 31 October 20X5 ($8 × 10 million)	80
At 1 December 20X5 (settlement date) ($9 × 10 million)	90

Therefore at 31 October 20X5 the liability **should be re-measured to $80 million** and an **expense of $50 million** should be recognised in profit or loss for the year.

The additional expense of $10 million resulting from the remeasurement at the settlement date is not included in the financial statements for the year ended 31 October 20X5, but is recognised the following year.

21 Electron

Text reference. Environmental provisions are covered in Chapter 9; share schemes in Chapter 8.

Top tips. This is a multi-standard question on environmental provisions, leases, proposed dividend and a share option scheme. The good thing about this kind of question is that, even if you don't know all the standards tested, you can get marks for the ones you do know. The question on the power station is similar to one you will have already met in this kit, and you have come across longer, more complicated questions on share-based payment, a favourite topic with this examiner.

Easy marks. The proposed dividend is straightforward, as is the explanation (if not the calculations) for the provision. The treatment of share options provides 4 easy marks for nothing much in the way of complications.

Marking scheme

	Marks
Oil contracts	4
Power station	7
Operating leases	5
Proposed dividend	3
Share options	4
Effective communication	2
Available/Maximum	25

REPORT

To: The Directors, Electron
From: Accountant
Date: July 20X6

Accounting treatment of transactions

The purpose of this report is to explain the accounting treatment required for the following items.

- Oil trading contracts
- Power station
- Operating lease
- Proposed dividend
- Share options

Oil trading contracts

The first point to note is that the contracts always result in the delivery of the commodity. They are therefore correctly treated as normal sale and purchase contracts, **not financial instruments.**

The adoption of a policy of **deferring recognising revenue and costs is appropriate** in general terms because of the duration of the contracts. Over the life of the contracts, costs and revenues are equally matched. However, there is a mismatch between costs and revenues in the early stages of the contracts.

In the first year of the contract, 50% of revenues are recognised immediately. However, costs, in the form of amortisation, are recognised evenly over the duration of the contract. This means that **in the first year, a higher proportion of the revenue is matched against a smaller proportion of the costs.** It could also be argued that revenue is inflated in the first year.

While there is no detailed guidance on accounting for this kind of contract, IAS 18 *Revenue* and the IASB *Framework* give general guidance. IAS 18 states that revenue and expenses that relate to the same transaction or event should be recognised simultaneously, and the *Framework* says that the 'measurement and display of the financial effect of like transactions must be carried out in a consistent way'.

It would be advisable, therefore, to match revenue and costs, and to **recognise revenue evenly** over the duration of the contract.

Power station

IAS 37 *Provisions, contingent liabilities and contingent assets* states that a provision should be recognised if:

- There is a present obligation as a result of a past transaction or event and
- It is probable that an outflow of resources embodying economic benefits will be required to settle the obligation
- A reliable estimate can be made of the amount of the obligation

In this case, the obligating event is the **installation of the power station**. The **operating licence** has created a **legal obligation** to incur the cost of removal, the expenditure is **probable,** and a **reasonable estimate** of the amount can be made.

Because Electron cannot operate its power station without incurring an obligation to pay for removal, **the expenditure also enables it to acquire economic benefits** (income from the energy generated). Therefore Electron correctly **recognises an asset** as well as a provision, and **depreciates this asset over its useful life of 20 years.**

Electron should recognise a provision for the cost of removing the power station, but should not include the cost of rectifying the damage caused by the generation of electricity until the power is generated. In this case the cost of rectifying the damage would be 5% of the total discounted provision.

The accounting treatment is as follows:

STATEMENT OF FINANCIAL POSITION AT 30 JUNE 20X6 (EXTRACTS)

	$m
Property, plant and equipment	
Power station	100.0
Decommissioning costs (W)	13.6
	113.6
Depreciation (113.6 ÷ 20)	(5.7)
	107.9
Provisions	
Provision for decommissioning at 1 July 20X5	13.6
Plus unwinding of discount (13.6 × 5%)	0.7
	14.3
Provision for damage (0.7(W)÷20)	0.1
	14.4

STATEMENT OF COMPREHENSVIE INCOME FOR THE YEAR ENDED 30 JUNE 20X6 (EXTRACTS)

	$m
Depreciation	5.7
Provision for damage	0.1
Unwinding of discount (finance cost)	0.7

Working

	$m
Provision for removal costs at 1 July 20X5 (95% × (15 ÷ 1.05))	13.6
Provision for damage caused by extraction at 30 June 20X6 (5% (15 ÷ 1.05))	0.7

Operating lease

One issue here is the **substance** of the lease agreement. IAS 17 *Leases* classifies leases as either finance leases or operating leases. A finance lease **transfers substantially all the risks and rewards of ownership to the lessee**, while an operating lease does not. The company **retains legal ownership of the equipment** and also **retains the benefits of ownership** (the equipment remains available for use in its operating activities). In addition, the **present value of the minimum lease payments is only 57.1% of the fair value of the leased assets** ($40 million ÷ $70 million). For a lease to be a finance lease, the present value of the minimum lease payments should be **substantially all** the fair value of the leased assets. Therefore the lease **appears to be correctly classified as an operating lease**.

A further issue is the **treatment of the fee received**. The company has recognised the whole of the net present value of the future income from the lease in profit or loss for the year to 30 June 20X6, despite the fact that only a deposit of $10 million has been received. In addition, the date of inception of the lease is 30 June 20X6, so **the term of the lease does not actually fall within the current period.** IAS 17 states that **income from operating leases should be recognised on a straight line basis over the lease term** unless another basis is more appropriate. IAS 18 *Revenue* and SIC 27 *Evaluating the substance of transactions involving the legal form of a lease* also apply here. Neither of these allows revenue to be recognised **before an entity has performed under the contract** and therefore **no revenue should be recognised** in relation to the operating leases for the current period.

Proposed dividend

The dividend was **proposed after the end of the reporting period** and therefore IAS 10 *Events after the reporting period* applies. This **prohibits the recognition of proposed dividends** unless these are declared before the end of the reporting period. The directors **did not have an obligation** to pay the dividend **at 31 October 20X5** and therefore there **cannot be a liability**. The directors seem to be arguing that their past record creates a constructive obligation as defined by IAS 37 *Provisions, contingent liabilities and contingent assets*. A constructive obligation may exist as a result of the proposal of the dividend, but this had **not arisen at the end of the reporting period**.

Although the proposed dividend is not recognised it was **approved before the financial statements were authorised for issue** and should be **disclosed** in the notes to the financial statements.

Share options

The share options granted on 1 July 20X5 are **equity-settled transactions**, and are governed by IFRS 2 *Share based payment*. The aim of this standard is to recognise the cost of share based payment to employees over the period in which the services are rendered. The options are generally **charged to the income statement** on the basis of their **fair value at the grant date**. If the equity instruments are traded on an active market, market prices must be used. Otherwise an option pricing model would be used.

The conditions attached to the shares state that the share options will vest in three years' time provided that the employees remain in employment with the company. Often there are other conditions such as growth in share price, but here **employment is the only condition**.

The **treatment** is as follows:

- Determine the fair value of the options at grant date.
- Charge this fair value to the income statement equally over the three year vesting period, making adjustments at each accounting date to reflect the best estimate of the number of options that will eventually vest. This will depend on the estimated percentage of employees leaving during the vesting period.

For the year ended 30 June 20X6, the charge to the income statement is $3m × 94% × 1/3 = $940,000. Shareholders' equity will be increased by an amount equal to this income statement charge.

22 Egin Group

Text reference. Related parties are covered in Chapter 10 of the text.

Top tips. This question dealt with the importance of the disclosure of related party transactions and the criteria determining a related party. Additionally, it required candidates to identify related parties, and to account for goodwill and a loan made to one of the related parties which was an foreign subsidiary. Don't forget, from your group accounting knowledge, that goodwill relating to the foreign subsidiary is treated as a foreign currency asset and translated at the closing rate of exchange.

Easy marks. Part (a) should earn you five very easy marks, as it is basic knowledge. Part (b) is application, but very straightforward. This leaves only nine marks for the more difficult aspects.

Examiner's comment. The importance of related parties and their criteria was quite well answered, although candidates often quoted specific examples rather than the criteria for establishing related parties. The identification of related party relationships was well answered, but the accounting for the goodwill of the foreign subsidiary (and the loan made to it) were poorly answered.

Marking scheme

			Marks
(a)	(i)	Reasons and explanation	5
	(ii)	Egin	5
		Spade	3
		Atomic	3
(b)		Goodwill	5
		Loan	5
		Available	26
		Maximum	25

(a) (i) **Why it is important to disclose related party transactions**

The directors of Egin are correct to say that related party transactions are a normal feature of business. However, where a company **controls** or can exercise **significant influence** over another the **financial performance and position of both companies can be affected**. For example, one group company can sell goods to another at artificially low prices. Even where there are no actual transactions between group companies, **a parent normally influences the way in which a subsidiary operates**. For example, a parent may instruct a subsidiary not to trade with particular customers or suppliers or not to undertake particular activities.

In the absence of other information, users of the financial statements **assume that a company pursues its interests independently** and undertakes transactions on an **arm's length basis** on terms that could have been obtained in a transaction with a third party. Knowledge of related party relationships and transactions affects the way in which users assess a company's operations and the risks and opportunities that it faces. Therefore **details of an entity's controlling party and transactions with related parties should be disclosed.** Even if the company's transactions and operations have not been affected by a related party relationship, **disclosure puts users on notice that they may be affected in future.**

IAS 24 *Related party disclosures* states that a party is related to another if:

(1) – the party **controls**, is **controlled** by, or is under **common control** with the entity or
     – has an interest in the entity that gives it **significant influence** over the entity or
     – has **joint control** over the entity

(2)   the party is an **associate** of the entity or a **joint venture**

(3)   the party is a member of the **key management personnel** of the entity or its parent

(4)   the party is a **close family member** of anyone referred to in (a) or (c) above

(5)   the party is **controlled, jointly controlled** or **significantly influenced** by any individual in (c) or (d) above

Control is the **power to govern the financial and operating policies of an entity** so as to obtain benefits from its activities. Significant influence is the **power to participate** in the financial and operating policy decisions of the entity but is not control over those policies. Significant influence may be gained by share ownership, statute or agreement.

(ii)   **Nature of related party relationships**

Within the Egin Group

Briars and Doye are related parties of Egin because they are **controlled** by Egin. **Eye is also a related party of Egin** because Egin has **significant influence** over it. **Briars and Doye** are also **related parties of each other** because they are under **common control**.

Briars and Doye may not be related parties of Eye, as there is only one director in common and IAS 24 states that entities are not necessarily related simply because they have a director in common. A related party relationship probably exists if this director **actually exercises control** or **significant influence** over the policies of the companies in practice.

Although Tang was sold several months before the year end it was a **related party of Egin, Briars and Doye until then**. Therefore the related party relationship between Tang and the Egin group **should be disclosed** even though there were no transactions between them during the period.

Blue is a related party of Briars as a **director of Briars controls it**. Because the director is not on the management board of Egin it is **not clear whether Blue is also a related party of Egin group**. This would depend on whether the director is considered key management personnel at a group level. The director's services as a consultant to the group may mean that a related party relationship exists.

Between Spade and the Egin Group

Spade is a related party of Doye because it holds **significant voting power** in Doye. This means that the **sale** of plant and equipment **to Spade must be disclosed**. **Egin is not necessarily a related party of Spade** simply because both have an investment in Doye. A related party relationship will only exist if one party **exercises influence** over another **in practice.**

The directors have proposed that disclosures should state that prices charged to related parties are set on an **arm's length basis**. Because the transaction took place **between related parties** by definition it **cannot have taken place on an arm's length basis** and this description would be **misleading**. Doye sold plant and equipment to Spade at **normal selling prices** and this is the information that should be disclosed.

Between Atomic and the Egin Group

Atomic is a related party of Egin because it can exercise **significant influence** over it. It is **also a related party of Briars and Doye** because **Egin controls Briars and Doye**. It is **unlikely that Eye is a related party of Atomic** because Eye is an associate of an associate. Atomic would have to be able to **exercise significant influence in practice** for a related party relationship to exist.

(b)   **Goodwill arising on the acquisition of Briars**

IAS 21 *The effect of changes in foreign exchange rates* states that goodwill arising on the acquisition of a foreign subsidiary should be expressed in the functional currency of the foreign operation and **retranslated at the closing rate at each year-end**. Goodwill is calculated and translated as follows:

	Euros m	Rate	$m
Consideration transferred	50	⎫	25.0
Non-controlling interests (45 × 20%)	9	2	4.5
Less fair value of identifiable net assets at acquisition	(45)	⎬	(22.5)
Goodwill at acquisition	14	⎭	7.0
Impairment	(3)	2.5	(1.2)
Exchange loss (balancing figure)			(1.4)
At 31 May 20X6	11	2.5	4.4

Alternative working

	Euros m	Rate	$m
Consideration transferred	50	2	25.0
Less fair value of identifiable net assets acquired (80% × 45)	(36)	2	(18.0)
Goodwill at acquisition	14		7.0
Impairment	(3)	2.5	(1.2)
Exchange loss (balancing figure)			(1.4)
At 31 May 20X6	11	2.5	4.4

Goodwill is measured at **$4.4 million** in the statement of financial position. An impairment loss of **$1.2 million** is **recognised in profit or loss** and an **exchange loss of $1.4 million** is **recognised in other comprehensive income** (and taken to the translation reserve in equity).

Loan to Briars

The loan is a **financial liability measured at amortised cost**. The loan is measured at **fair value** on initial recognition. Fair value is the amount for which the liability could be settled between **knowledgeable, willing parties on an arm's length basis**. This would normally be the actual transaction price. However, Egin and Briars are **related parties** and the transaction **has not taken place on normal commercial terms**.

IAS 39 *Financial instruments: Recognition and measurement* states that it is necessary to **establish what the transaction price would have been** in an arm's length exchange motivated by normal business considerations. The amount that will eventually be repaid to Egin is $10 million and the normal commercial rate of interest is 6%. Therefore the fair value of the loan is its **discounted present value**, which is **retranslated at the closing rate** at each year-end.

Therefore the loan is measured at the following amounts in the statement of financial position:

	$'000	Rate	Euros000
At 1/6/20X5 ($10 \times \frac{1}{1.06^2}$)	8,900	2	17,800
Interest (unwinding of discount) (8,900 × 6%)	534	2.3	1,228
Exchange loss			4,557
At 31/5/20X6 ($10 \times \frac{1}{1.06}$)	9,434	2.5	23,585

The **unwinding of the discount** is recognised as a **finance cost** in profit or loss for the year and the **exchange loss** is also **recognised in profit or loss**.

Note. it would also be possible to calculate the finance cost for the year ended 31 May 20X6 at the closing rate. This would increase the exchange loss and the total expense recognised in profit and loss would be the same.

23 Engina

Text reference. Related parties are covered in Chapter 10.

Top tips. A good test of your ability to apply IAS 24 to a practical scenario.

	Marks
Style of letter/report	4
Reasons	8
Goods to directors	4
Property	5
Group	4
Maximum	25

REPORT

To: The Directors
          Engina Co
          Zenda
          Ruritania

From: Ann Accountant

Date: 12 May 20X3

Related Party Transactions

The purpose of this report is to explain why it is necessary to **disclose related party transactions**. We appreciate that you may regard such disclosure as politically and culturally **sensitive**. However, there are **sound reasons why International Financial Reporting Standards require such disclosures**. It should be emphasised that related party transactions are a **normal part of business** life, and the disclosures are required to give a **fuller picture** to the users of accounts, rather than because they are problematic.

Prior to the issue of IAS 24, disclosures in respect of related parties were concerned with directors and their relationship with the group. The **IASB extends this definition and also the required disclosures**. This reflects the objective of the IASB to provide **useful data for investors**, not merely for companies to report on stewardship activities.

Unless investors know that transactions with related parties have not been carried out at **'arm's length'** between independent parties, they may fail to ascertain the **true financial position**.

Related party transactions typically take place on **terms which are significantly different** from those undertaken on normal commercial terms.

IAS 24 requires all material related party transactions to be disclosed.

It should be noted that related party transactions are not necessarily fraudulent or intended to deceive. Without proper disclosures, investors may be disadvantaged – IAS 24 seeks to remedy this.

Sale of goods to the director

(a)   **Disclosure** of related party transactions is only necessary when the transactions are material. For the purposes of IAS 24, however, transactions are material when their disclosure might reasonably be **expected to influence decisions made by users of the financial statements, irrespective of their amount**.

(b)   The **materiality** of a related party transaction with an individual, for example a director, must be **judged by reference to that individual** and not just the company. In addition, **disclosure of contracts** of **significance** with **directors** is required by most **Stock Exchanges**.

(c)   Mr Satay has purchased $600,000 (12 × $50,000) worth of goods from the company and a car for $45,000, which is just over half its market value.

(d)   The transactions are not material to the company, and because Mr Satay has considerable personal wealth, they are not material to him either.

(e)   However, IAS 24 confirms that directors are related parties and transactions with directors should be disclosed. In addition, IAS 24 requires disclosure of **compensation** paid to directors. Compensation includes subsidised goods and benefits in kind. **Details of the transaction should be disclosed**, including the amount of the transactions and any outstanding balances.

Hotel property

(a)   The hotel property sold to the Managing Director's brother is a **related party transaction**, and it appears to have been undertaken at **below market price**.

(b)   IAS 24 envisages disclosure of the substance of the transaction.

(c)   IAS 24 requires disclosure of 'information about the **transaction** and **outstanding balances** necessary for an understanding of the **potential effect of the relationship upon the financial statements**'.

(d)   Not only must the transaction itself be disclosed, but the question of **impairment** needs to be **considered**. The value of the hotel has become impaired due to the **fall in property prices**, so the **carrying value needs to be adjusted** in accordance with IAS 36 *Impairment of assets*. The hotel should be shown at the lower of carrying value ($5m) and the recoverable amount. The recoverable amount is the higher of fair value less costs to sell ($4.3m – $0.2m = $4.1m) and value in use ($3.6m). Therefore the hotel should be shown at $4.1m.

The sale of the property was for $100,000 below this impaired value, and it is this amount which needs to be disclosed. This would highlight the nature of the transactions within the existing property market conditions.

Group structure

(a)   Local companies legislation and the Stock Exchange often require **disclosure of directors' interests** in a company's share capital. IAS 24 requires disclosure of the 'ultimate controlling party'. Mr Satay controls Engina as a result of his ownership of 80% of the share capital of Wheel.

(b)   IAS 24 requires disclosure of the **related party relationship** between Engina and Wheel and also of **transactions** between the two companies, despite the fact that Engina is a wholly owned subsidiary.

(c)   Engina's transactions with Car Ltd will also need to be disclosed. IAS 24 states that companies under **common control** are related parties, and the two companies are under the common control of Mr Satay.

24 Preparation question: Leases

(a)   Interest rate implicit in the lease

PV = annuity × cumulative discount factor

250,000   = 78,864 × CDF

$$\therefore CDF \quad = \frac{250,000}{78,864}$$

= 3.170

∴ Interest rate is 10%

(b)   *Property, plant and equipment*

Net book value of assets held under finance leases is $187,500.

Non-current liabilities

	$
Finance lease liabilities (W)	136,886

Current liabilities

	$
Finance lease liabilities (W) (196,136 – 136,886)	59,250

Income statement

Depreciation on assets held under finance leases	62,500
Finance charges	25,000

Working

		$
Year ended 31 December 20X1:		
1.1.20X1	Liability b/d	250,000
1.1.20X1 – 31.12.20X1	Interest at 10%	25,000
31.12.20X1	Instalment in arrears	(78,864)
31.12.20X1	Liability c/d	196,136
Year ended 31 December 20X2:		
1.1.20X2 – 31.12.20X2	Interest at 10%	19,614
31.12.20X2	Instalment in arrears	(78,864)
31.12.20X2	Liability c/d	136,886

25 Marrgrett

Text reference. These topics are covered in Chapter 12 of the BPP Study Text, apart from disposals, which is covered in Chapter 14.

Top tips. This question required a discussion of the impact of the revisions to IFRS 3 *Business combinations* on various aspects of group accounting. These topics are covered in the BPP Study Text, but unless you were very familiar with the changes from old to new, you would not have been advised to attempt this question. That said, it was not technically demanding.

Easy marks. There are no marks that are easier to gain than others – either you know the subject or you don't!

Examiner's comment. Answers were generally quite good but the main issue was that candidates found it difficult to assimilate relevant information.. Particular issues included failing to recognise that the existing 30% interest in the associate should be fair valued when control of the subsidiary is gained, also dealing with the payments to the subsidiary's directors created a problem and a minority of candidates stated that the full goodwill method was mandatory.

Marking scheme

		Marks
Consideration		6
IFRS 2 and consideration		5
Consideration		2
Intangible assets		2
NCI		5
Finalisation and reorganisation provision		2
IAS 27		3
Professional marks		2
	Available	25

Revision of IFRS 3 *Business combinations*

IFRS 3 Business combinations has been extensively revised, and the revised standard issued in January 2008. The revised IFRS 3 views **the group as an economic entity.** This means that it treats all providers of equity – including non-controlling interests – as shareholders in the group, even if they are not shareholders of the parent.

All business combinations are accounted for as **acquisitions**. The revisions to IFRS 3 affect both the consideration, and the business acquired. Specifically, **all consideration is now measured at fair value,** and there are implications for the valuation of the non-controlling interest.

Marrgrett is proposing to purchase additional shares in its associate, Josey. An increase from 30% to 70% will **give control,** as the holding passes the all-important 50% threshold. The changes to IFRS 3 have far-reaching implications for various aspects of the acquisition, which is what the standard calls a 'business combination achieved in stages'.

Equity interest already held

Consideration includes cash, assets, contingent consideration, equity instruments, options and warrants. It also includes the **fair value of any equity interest already held**, which marks a departure from the previous version of IFRS 3. This means that **the 30% holding must be re-measured to fair value** at the date of the acquisition of the further 40% holding. The revalued 30% stake, together with the consideration transferred in the form of cash and shares, is compared to the fair value of Josey's net assets at the date control was obtained, in order to arrive at a figure for goodwill.

Any **gain or loss** on the revaluation of the associate is taken to **profit or loss for the year.**

Transaction costs

The original IFRS 3 required fees (legal, accounting, valuation etc) paid in relation to a business acquisition to be included in the cost of the acquisition, which meant that they were measured as part of goodwill.

Under the revised IFRS 3 **costs relating to the acquisition must be recognised as an expense** at the time of the acquisition. They are not regarded as an asset. (Costs of issuing debt or equity are to be accounted for under the rules of IAS 39.)

Share options

As an incentive to the shareholders and employees of Josey to remain in the business, Marrgrett has offered share options in Josey. These are conditional on them remaining in employment for two years after the acquisition, that is they are contingent on future events. The question arises of whether they are **contingent consideration**, for which the treatment is specified in the revised IFRS 3, **or as compensation** for services after the acquisition, for which the treatment is given in IFRS 2 Share-based payment.

The conditions attached to the share options are employment based, rather than contingent on, say, the performance of the company. Accordingly the options must be treated as **compensation and valued under the rules of IFRS 2. The charge will be to post-acquisition earnings**, since the options are given in exchange for services after the acquisition.

Contingent consideration

The additional shares being offered to Josey's shareholders to the value of $50,000 are contingent on the achievement of a certain level of profitability. These are contingent consideration, defined in IFRS 3 as:

> Usually, an obligation of the acquirer to transfer additional assets or equity interests to the former owners of an acquiree as part of the exchange for control of the acquiree if specified future events occur or conditions are met.

The original IFRS 3 required contingent consideration to be accounted for **only if it was probable that it would become payable** and could be measured reliably. Subsequent changes in the amount of the contingent consideration were accounted for as adjustments to the cost of the business combination, and therefore generally as changes to goodwill.

However, the revised IFRS 3 recognises that, by entering into an acquisition, the acquirer becomes obliged to make additional payments. Not recognising that obligation means that the consideration recognised at the acquisition date is not fairly stated. Accordingly, the revised IFRS 3 **requires recognition of contingent consideration, measured at fair value, at the acquisition date.**

The shares worth up to $50,000 meet the IAS 32 *Financial instruments: presentation* definition of a financial liability. This contingent consideration will be **measured at fair value,** and any **changes** to the fair value on subsequent re-measurement will be taken to **profit or loss for the year.**

Intangible assets

Josey's intangible assets, which include trade names, internet domain names and non-competition agreements, will be **recognised on acquisition** by Marrgrett of a controlling stake. IFRS 3 revised gives more detailed guidance on intangible assets than did the previous version; as a result, more intangibles may be recognised than was formerly the case. The more intangibles are recognised, the lower the figure for goodwill, which is consideration transferred less fair value of assets acquired and liabilities assumed.

Non-controlling interest

As indicated above, the revised IFRS views the group as an economic entity and so non-controlling shareholders are also shareholders in the group. This means that goodwill attributable to the non-controlling interest needs to be recognised.

The non-controlling interest now forms part of the calculation of goodwill. The question now arises as to how it should be valued.

The 'economic entity' principle suggests that the non-controlling interest should be valued at fair value. In fact, IFRS 3 gives a **choice:**

> For each business combination, the acquirer shall measure any non-controlling interest in the acquiree **either at fair value or at the non-controlling interest's proportionate share of the acquiree's identifiable net assets.** *(IFRS 3)*

IFRS 3 revised suggests that the closest approximation to fair value will be the market price of the shares held by the non-controlling shareholders just before the acquisition by the parent.

Non-controlling interest at fair value will be different from non-controlling interest at proportionate share of the acquiree's net assets. The difference is goodwill attributable to non-controlling interest, which may be, but often is not, proportionate to goodwill attributable to the parent.

Effect of type of consideration

The nature of the consideration transferred – cash, shares, contingent, and so on – **does not affect the goodwill.** However, the structure of the payments may affect post-acquisition profits. For example if part of the consideration is contingent (as here), changes to the fair value will be reflected in profit or loss for the year in future years.

Partial disposal

Under the revised IFRS 3, the treatment of a partial disposal depends on whether or not control is retained. Generally, control is lost when the holding is decreased to less than 50%.

On disposal of a controlling interest, any retained interest (an associate or trade investment) is measured at fair value on the date that control is lost. This fair value is used in the calculation of the gain or loss on disposal, and also becomes the carrying amount for subsequent accounting for the retained interest.

If the **50%** boundary is **not crossed,** as when the interest in a subsidiary is reduced, the event is treated as a **transaction between owners.**

Whenever the 50% boundary is crossed, the existing interest is revalued, and a gain or loss is reported in profit or loss for the year. If the 50% boundary is not crossed, no gain or loss is reported; instead there is an **adjustment to the parent's equity.**

Margrett intends to **retain control of the first subsidiary,** so in this case there will be no gain or loss, but an adjustment to the Margrett's equity to reflect the increase in non-controlling interest. In the case of the **second subsidiary,** however, **control is lost.** A **gain will be recognised on the portion sold, and also on the portion retained,** being the difference between the fair value and the book value of the interest retained.

Re-organisation provision

IAS 27 explains that a plan to restructure a subsidiary following an acquisition is not a present obligation of the acquiree at the acquisition date, unless it meets the criteria in IAS 37 *Provisions, contingent liabilities and contingent assets.* This is very unlikely to be the case at the acquisition date. Therefore Margrett **should not recognise a liability** for the re-organisation of the group at the date of the acquisition.

This **prevents creative accounting.** An acquirer cannot set up a provision for restructuring or future losses of a subsidiary and then release this to profit or loss in subsequent periods in order to reduce losses or smooth profits.

26 Preparation question: Associate

J GROUP CONSOLIDATED STATEMENT OF FINANCIAL POSITION AS AT 31 DECEMBER 20X5

Assets		$'000
Non-current assets		
Freehold property (1,950 + 1,250 + 370 (W7))		3,570
Plant and equipment (795 + 375)		1,170
Investment in associate (W3)		480
		5,220
Current assets		
Inventories (575 + 300 – 20 (W6))		855
Trade receivables (330 + 290))		620
Cash at bank and in hand (50 + 120)		170
		1,645
		6,865

		$'000
Equity and liabilities		
Equity attributable to owners of the parent		
Issued share capital		2,000
Retained earnings		1,785
		3,785
Non-controlling interests (W5)		890
Total equity		4,675
Non-current liabilities		
12% debentures (500 + 100)		600
Current liabilities		
Bank overdraft		560
Trade payables (680 + 350)		1,030
		1,590
Total liabilities		2,190
		6,865

Workings

1   *Group structure*

	J			
600/1,000	60%		30%	225/750
	P			S

Pre acquisition profits	$200k		$150k

2   *Goodwill*

	$'000	$'000
Consideration transferred		1,000
NCI (at 'full' FV: 400 × $1.65)		660
Net assets acquired:		
Share capital	1,000	
Retained earnings at acquisition	200	
Fair value adjustment (W7)	400	
		(1,600)
		60
Impairments to date		(60)
Year-end value		–

Alternative working

	$'000	P Co $'000	NCI $'000
Consideration transferred/FV NCI (400 × $1.65)		1,000	660
Net assets acquired:			
Share capital	1,000		
Retained earnings at acquisition	200		
Fair value adjustment (W7)	400		
	1,600		
Group/NCI share (× 60%/40%)		(960)	(640)
		40	20
Impairments to date		(40)	(20)
Year-end value		–	–

3   *Investment in associate*

	$'000
Cost of associate	500.0
Share of post acquisition retained reserves ((390 – 150) × 30%)	72.0
Less impairment of investment in associate	(92.0)
	480.0

4   *Retained earnings*

	J Co $'000	P Co $'000	S Co $'000
Retained earnings per question	1,460	885	390
Unrealised profit (W6)		(20)	
Retained earnings profits at acquisition		(200)	(150)
Fair value adjustment movement (W6)		(30)	
		635	240
P Co: share of post acquisition profits 60% × 635	381		
S Co: share of post acquisition profits 30% × 240	72		
Goodwill impairments to date P Co: 60 (W2) × 60%	(36)		
S Co	(92)		
	1,785		

5   *Non-controlling interests*

	$'000
NCI at acquisition (W2)	660
NCI share of post acq'n ret'd earnings ((W4) 635 × 40%)	254
NCI share of impairment losses ((W2) 60 × 40%)	(24)
	890

Alternative working

	$'000	$'000
Net assets per question	1,885	
Unrealised profit (W5)	(20)	
Fair value adjustment (W7)	370	
	2,235 × 40% =	894
Non-controlling interest in goodwill		–
		894

6   Unrealised profit on inventories

   P Co ——————→ J Co $100k × 25/125 = $20,000

7   Fair value adjustment table

	At acquisition $'000	Movement $'000	At reporting date $'000
Land	200		200
Buildings	200	(30)	170 (200 × 34/40)
	400	(30)	370

27 Preparation question 'D'-shaped group

(a)   BAUBLE GROUP
       CONSOLIDATED STATEMENT OF FINANCIAL POSITION AS AT 31 DECEMBER 20X9

	$'000
Non-current assets	
Property, plant and equipment (720 + 60 + 70)	850
Goodwill (W2)	111
	961
Current assets (175 + 95 + 90)	360
	1,321
Equity attributable to owners of the parent	
Share capital – $1 ordinary shares	400
Retained earnings (W3)	600
	1,000
Non-controlling interest (W4)	91
	1,091
Current liabilities (120 + 65 + 45)	230
	1,321

Workings

1   *Group Structure*

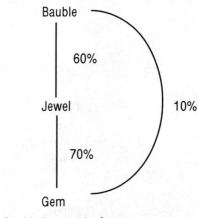

Bauble interest in Gem

	– direct	10%
	– indirect (60% × 70%)	42%
		52%
Non-controlling interest in Gem		48%

2   *Goodwill*

	Jewel		Gem	
	$'000	$'000	$'000	$'000
Consideration transferred: Bauble		142		43.0
Consideration transferred: Jewel			(100 × 60%)	60.0
NCI	(145 × 40%)	58	(90 × 48%)	43.2
Net assets at acq'n as represented by:				
Share capital	100		50	
Ret'd earnings	45		40	
		(145)		(90.0)
Goodwill		55		56.2

Total goodwill = $111,200

Alternative working

	B in J		B in G		J in G	
	$'000	$'000	$'000	$'000	$'000	$'000
Consideration transferred		142		43	60% × 100	60.0
Share of net assets acquired as represented by						
Share capital	100		50		50	
Ret'd earnings	45		40		40	
	145		90		90	
Group share	60%		10%		42%	
		87		9		37.8
Goodwill		55		34		22.2

Total goodwill = $111,200

3   *Consolidated retained earnings*

	B	J	G
	$'000	$'000	$'000
Per Q	560	90	65
Less: pre-acquisition ret'd earnings		(45)	(40)
		45	25
J – share of post acquisition ret'd earnings (45 × 60%)	27		
G – share of post acquisition ret'd earnings (25 × 52%)	13		
	600		

4   *Non-controlling interests*

	Jewel	Gem
	$'000	$'000
NCI at acquisition (W2)	58	43.2
NCI in investment in Gem (100 × 40%)	(40)	
NCI share of post acquisition retained earnings:		
Jewel ((W3) 45 × 40%)	18	
Gem ((W3) 25 × 48%)		12
	36	55.2

91.2

Alternative working

	Jewel $'000	Gem $'000
Net assets per question	190	115
Less: cost of investment in Gamma	(100)	
	90	115
Non-controlling share	× 40%	× 48%
	36	55.2
	91.2	

(b) **Goodwill**

		Jewel		Gem	
		$'000	$'000	$'000	$'000
Consideration transferred: Bauble			142		43.0
Consideration transferred: Jewel				(100 × 60%)	60.0
NCI		(160 × 40%)	64	(90 × 48%)	43.2
Net assets at acq'n as represented by:					
Share capital		100		50	
Ret'd earnings		60		40	
			(160)		(90)
Goodwill			46		56.2
			102.2		

Alternative working

		$'000	$'000
Consideration transferred			142.0
Fair value of identifiable net assets acquired:			
Jewel	Share capital	100.0	
	Retained earnings	60.0	
	Cost of investment – Gem	(100.0)	
		60.0 × 60%	(36.0)
Gem	Share capital	50.0	
	Retained earnings (1 January 20X3)	40.0	
		90.0 × 42%	(37.8)
			68.2
Bauble in Gem (per part (a))			34.0
			102.2

28 X Group

Text reference. Complex groups are covered in Chapter 18.

Top tips. This is a complicated question. However, you should be able to answer it if you work logically and methodically through the information given.

(a) X GROUP
STATEMENT OF FINANCIAL POSITION AS AT 31 MARCH 20X9

	$m
Property, plant and equipment (W7)	1,058
Goodwill (W2)	79
Investment in associate (W3)	52
Net current assets 640 + 360 + 75 − 15 (W7)	1,060
	2,249
Equity	360
Share premium	250
Retained earnings (W4)	1,114
Non-controlling interest (W5)	160
	1,884
Non current liabilities 200 + 150 + 15	365
	2,249

Workings

1 *Group structure*

		Holding	Date acquired	Retained earnings 1.4.X4	Retained earnings 1.4.X6
		$\frac{100m}{150m} = 66\frac{2}{3}\%$	1.4.X6	N/A	$120m
		$\frac{45m}{50m} = 90\%$	1.4.X4	$10m	$20m
		30%	1.4.X6	–	$7m

X
|
$66\frac{2}{3}\%$ Y
| 90%
30% Z
W

2   *Goodwill*

	Y $m	Y $m	Z $m	Z $m
Consideration transferred		320	(90 × 2/3)	60
Non-controlling interests	(375 × 1/3)	125	(85 × 40%)	34
FV of identifiable net assets at acq'n:				
Share capital	150		50	
Share premium	120		10	
Reserves	120		20	
Fair value adjustments (W6)	(15)		5	
		(375)		(85)
		70		9

79

Alternative working

	$m	$m
Consideration transferred (Y and Z)		320
Fair value of identifiable net assets acquired in Y:		
Share capital	150	
Share premium	120	
Reserves	120	
Fair value adjustments (W2)	(15)	
Investment in Z	(90)	
	285	
2/3		(190)
Fair value of identifiable net assets acquired in Z:		
Share capital	50	
Share premium	10	
Reserves	20	
Fair value adjustments (W6)	5	
60%	85	
		(51)
		79

3   *Investment in W – associate*

	$m
Cost	50
Share of post acquisition reserves (W4)	2
	52

4   *Consolidated retained earnings*

	X $m	Y $m	Z $m	W $m
Per question	1,050	210	30	17
Intragroup profit in inventories (W8)			(15)	
Fair value adjustments (W6)	–	6	2	–
Retained earnings at acquisition (W2)	–	(120)	(20)	(7)
	1,050	96	(3)	10
Post-acquisition profits of Y (2/3 × 96)	64			
Post-acquisition profits of Z (60% × (3))	(2)			
Post-acquisition profits of W (20% × 10)	2			
	1,114			

5   *Non-controlling interests*

	Y $m	Z $m
NCI at acquisition (W2)	125	34
NCI in investment in Z (90 × 1/3)	(30)	
NCI share of post acquisition retained earnings:		
Y ((W4) 96 × 1/3)	32	
Z ((W4) (3) × 40%)		(1)
	127	33

160

Alternative working

	$m	$m
Y		
Net assets at reporting date per question	480	
Fair value adjustments (W6)	(9)	
Cost of investment in Z	(90)	
Cost of investment in associate	(50)	
Investment in associate (W3)	52	
1/3	383	127
Z		
Net assets at reporting date per question	90	
Fair value adjustments (W6)	7	
Intragroup profit in inventories (44 + 16 × 25%)	(15)	
40%	82	33
		160

6   *Fair value adjustments and other adjustments to net assets*

Y	Acquisition $'m	Movement $'m	Year end $'m
Property, plant and equipment (dep'n: 30 × 10% × 3)	30	(9)	21
Intangible assets	(30)	–	(30)
Inventories (2 – 8)	(6)	6	–
Allowance for doubtful debts	(9)	9	–
	(15)	6	(9)

Z	Acquisition $'m	Movement $'m	Year end $'m
Property, plant and equipment (dep'n: 10 × 10% × 3)	10	(3)	7
Inventories	(5)	5	–
	5	(2)	7

Notes

There is no adjustment required to inventories or doubtful debts at the year end, because, practically, 3 years later, the inventories will have been sold and the doubtful debts recovered or written off.

The amount received as a result of the arbitration award was a contingent asset at the date of acquisition and is therefore not recognised as a fair value adjustment. IFRS 3 only requires recognition of contingent liabilities.

7	Property, plant and equipment	X	Y	Z
		$m	$m	$m
	Per question	900	100	30
	Fair value adjustments (W6)	–	30	10
	Amortisation (W6)	–	(9)	(3)
		900	121	37
	Y	121		
	Z	37		
		1,058		

8	Unrealised profit	
		$m
	On sales to X	44
	On sales to Y	16
		60

Unrealised profit 25% × 60 = $15m

(b) **Change of policy re goodwill**

IFRS 1 *First time adoption of International Financial Reporting Standards* is relevant as the company appears to be adopting IFRSs for the first time.

IFRS 1 requires retrospective adoption of all IFRSs in force at the reporting date for the first IFRS financial statements (31 March 20X9). Assuming that the company presents comparative figures for one year only (the minimum required by IFRS 1), it will prepare an opening IFRS statement of financial position at 1 April 20X7, which will be the date of transition to IFRSs. As all its investments were acquired before this date, it must recognise the goodwill arising as an intangible asset.

Retrospective application means that X should adjust opening retained earnings for the effect of the change. X must also test the goodwill for impairment at the date of transition.

IFRS 1 contains an exemption from applying IFRS 3 retrospectively. However, the group wishes to account for the change in policy retrospectively and therefore is not claiming the exemption.

29 Glove

Text reference. Complex groups are covered in Chapter 13.

Top tips. This question required the preparation of a consolidated statement of financial position of a group which contained a sub-subsidiary. In addition, candidates had to account for brand names, a retirement benefit plan, a convertible bond, and an exchange of plant. The question was a little easier than in previous exams, and you should not have been alarmed at getting both pensions and financial instruments, since only the straightforward aspects were being tested.

Easy marks. There are marks for standard consolidation calculations (goodwill, NCI, retained earnings) which should be familiar to you from your earlier studies, and for setting out the proforma, even if you didn't have time to do the fiddly adjustments for retirement benefits and exchange of assets. The convertible bond – don't be scared because it is a financial instrument! – is something you have covered at an earlier level.

Examiner's comment. The accounting for the sub-subsidiary was reasonably well answered but candidates found the application of the corridor approach a major problem. The convertible bond element was relatively straightforward and would have sat quite well in a lower level paper. However, candidates found this element quite difficult.

The parameters of the syllabus in the area of financial instruments have been well documented, but candidates do not seem to be able to grasp the fundamentals of the subject. The treatment of the trade name was again not well answered with the principles of recognition seldom set out correctly. Overall, the consolidation element was quite well answered but the additional technical elements were poorly treated by candidates in their answers.

	Marks
Equity	7
Reserves	6
Non-current liabilities	3
Defined benefit plan	4
Convertible bond	4
Plant	2
Trade name	3
Available	29
Maximum	25

GLOVE GROUP
CONSOLIDATED STATEMENT OF FINANCIAL POSITION AS AT 31 MAY 20X7

	$m
Non-current assets	
Property, plant and equipment	
260 + 20 + 26 + 6 (W6) + 5(W6) + 3 (W5)	320.0
Goodwill (W2)	10.1
Other intangibles: trade name (W6)	4.0
Available for sale investments	10.0
	344.1
Current assets: 65 + 29 + 20	114.0
Total assets	458.1
Equity and liabilities	
Equity attributable to owners of parent	
Ordinary shares	150.0
Other reserves (W4)	30.8
Retained earnings (W3)	150.8
Equity component of convertible debt (W8)	1.6
	333.2
Non-controlling interests (W5)	28.9
	362.1
Non-current liabilities (W10)	
45 + 2 + 3 + 0.1 (W7) − 30 + 28.9 (W8)	49.0
Current liabilities: 35 + 7 + 5	47.0
	96.0
Total equity and liabilities	458.1

Workings

1   *Group structure*

	Glove		
1 June 20X5	80%	Retained earnings	$10m
		Other reserves	$4m
	Body		
1 June 20X5	70%	Retained earnings	$6m
		Other reserves	$8m
	Fit		

		%
Effective interest: 80% × 70%		56
∴ Non-controlling interest		44
		100

Note. The acquisitions were on the same date. Our calculation of goodwill is done as if Body was acquired first, but either method would be acceptable.

2   Goodwill

	Glove in Body		*Body in Fit*	
	$m	$m	$m	$m
Consideration transferred		60	(30 × 80%)	24.00
Non-controlling interests	(65 × 20%)	13	(39 × 44%)	17.16
Fair value of net assets at acq'n:				
Per question	60		39	
Trade name (W6)	5		–	
		(65)		(39.00)
		8		2.16

10.16

Alternative working

	Glove in Body		*Body in Fit*	
	$m	$m	$m	$m
Consideration transferred		60	80% × 30	24.00
Fair value of net assets acquired				
Per question	60		39	
Trade name (W6)	5		–	
	65		39	
Group share 80%/56%		(52)		(21.84)
		8		2.16

10.16

3   Retained earnings

	Glove	Body	Fit
	$m	$m	$m
Per question	135.00	25	10
Fair value movement (W6)	–	(1)	–
Pension scheme (W7)	(0.10)		
Convertible bonds (W8) (2.3 – 1.8)	(0.50)		
Assets exchange:			
Adjustment to plant (W9)	3.00		
Less pre-acquisition		(10)	(6)
		14	4
Share of Body			
80% × 14	11.20		
Share of Fit			
56% × 4	2.24		
	150.84		

BPP
LEARNING MEDIA

4 Other reserves

	Glove $m	Body $m	Fit $m
Per question	30.0	5	8
Less pre-acquisition		(4)	(8)
		1	–
Share of body			
80% × 1	0.8		
Share of Fit			
56% × 0	0.0		
	30.8		

5 Non-controlling interests

	Body $m	Fit $m
NCI at acquisition (W2)	13	17.16
NCI in investment in Fit (30 × 20%)	(6)	
NCI share of post acquisition retained earnings:		
Body ((W3) 14 × 20%)	2.8	
Fit ((W3) 4 × 44%)		1.76
NCI share of post acquisition other reserves:		
Body ((W4) 1 × 20%)	0.2	
Fit ((W4) 0 × 44%)		0
	10	18.92

28.92

Alternative working

	Body $m	Fit $m
Net assets per question	70.0	38
Cost of investment in Fit	(30.0)	–
Fair value adjustment (W6)	10.0	5
	50	43
	× 20%	× 44%
	10.00	18.92

$28.92m

6 Fair value adjustments

	At acquisition $m	Movement (2 years) $m	At reporting date (31 May 20X7) $m
Body			
Land: 60 – (40 + 10 + 4)	6	–	6
Brand name (note)	5	(1)	4
	11	(1)	10
Fit			
Land: 39 – (20 + 8 + 6)	5	–	5

Note. The trade name is an internally generated intangible asset. While these are not normally recognised under IAS 38 *Intangible assets*, IFRS 3 *Business combinations* allows recognition if the fair value can be measured reliably. Thus this Glove should recognise an intangible asset on acquisition (at 1 June 20X5). This will reduce the value of goodwill.

The trade name is amortised over ten years, of which two have elapsed: $5m × 2/10 = $1m.

So the value is $(5 – 1)m = $4m in the consolidated statement of financial position.

BPP LEARNING MEDIA

7   *Defined benefit pension scheme*

	$m
Present value of obligation	26.0
Fair value of plan assets	(20.0)
Unrecognised actuarial losses (note) ($5m – $0.1m (note))	(4.9)
	1.1

Note. recognised actuarial losses

Corridor amounts:

10% of present value of obligation: 10% × $20m = $2m
10% of fair value of plan assets: 10% × $16m = $1.6m

∴ Use $2m

	$m
Unrecognised losses at 1 June 20X6	3
Less 10% of PV of obligation	(2)
Excess	1

Amortised over ten years ∴ $1m/10 = $0.1m

Accounting entries:

DEBIT	Retained earnings	$0.1m	
CREDIT	Unrecognised actuarial losses		$0.1m

8   *Convertible bond*

Under IAS 39, the bond must be split into a liability and an equity component:

	$'000	$'000
Proceeds: 30,000 × $1,000		30,000

Present value of principal in three years' time

$$\$30m \times \frac{1}{1.08^3}$$ 23,815

Present value of interest annuity
$30m × 6% = $1,800,000

$$\times \frac{1}{1.08}$$ 1,667

$$\times \frac{1}{(1.08)^2}$$ 1,543

$$\times \frac{1}{(1.08)^3}$$ 1,429

Liability component	(28,454)
∴ Equity component	1,546

Rounded to $1.6m

Balance of liability at 31 May 20X7

	$'000
Balance b/d at 1 June 20X6	28,454
Effective interest at 8%	2,276
Coupon interest paid at 6%	(1,800)
Balance c/d at 31 May 20X7	28,930

9   *Exchange of assets*

The cost of the plant should be measured at the fair value of the asset given up, rather than the carrying value. An adjustment must be made to the value of the plant, and to retained earnings.

	$
Fair value of land	7
Carrying value of land	(4)
∴ Adjustment required	3

DEBIT	Plant	$3m	
CREDIT	Retained earnings		$3m

10   *Non-current liabilities*

Note. This working is for additional information. To save time, you should do yours on the face of the consolidated position statement

	$m	$m
Non-current liabilities per question:		
Glove	45	
Body	2	
Fit	3	
		50.0
Unrecognised actuarial losses (W7)		0.1
Proceeds of convertible bond		(30.0)
Value of liability component		28.9
		49.0

30 Case study question: Rod

Text reference. Complex groups are covered in Chapter 13; provisions in Chapter 9; intangibles in Chapter 4; ethics in Chapter 2.

Top tips. This question required candidates to prepare a consolidated statement of financial position of a complex group. Candidates were given a basic set of data – information concerning current accounting practices – which required adjustment in the financial statements, and information about the implementation of 'new' accounting standards. This type of question will appear regularly on this paper (obviously with different group scenarios and different accounting adjustments). Candidates had to deal with adjustments relating to tangible non-current assets, inventory and defined benefit pension schemes. Part (c) is a practical question on key issues. In part (d), do not be tempted to waffle. Part (e) concerns ethics, a topic new to this syllabus.

Examiner's comment. Generally speaking, candidates performed quite well on this question but often struggled with the accounting for the defined benefit pension scheme. Many candidates treated one of the subsidiaries as an associate. In this situation, where the relationship between the companies has been incorrectly determined, marks are awarded for the methodology used in the question.

			Marks
(a)	Defined benefit pension scheme		5
(b)	Shareholding		3
	Equity – Line		6
	Non current assets – Line		4
	Equity – Reel		8
	Fair value adjustment		2
	Group properties, plant and equipment		2
	Group retained earnings		3
	Trade receivables		1
	Inventory		1
(c)	(i)	Provision: current practice	4
		acceptability	2
	(ii)	Fine: intangible asset	3
		acceptability	2
(d)	1 mark per valid point		10
(e)	For		2
	Against		2
	Conclusion		1
		Available	61
		Maximum	50

(a) **Defined benefit pension scheme**

The defined benefit pension scheme is treated in accordance with IAS 19 *Employee benefits*.

The pension scheme has a deficit of liabilities over assets:

	$m
Fair value of scheme assets	125
Less present value of obligation	(130)
	(5)

The deficit is reported as a liability in the statement of financial position.

The income statement for the year includes:

	$m
Current service cost	110
Interest cost	20
Expected return on plan assets	(10)
Actuarial gain (see note)	(15)
	105

The balance sheet includes:

	$m
Present value of pension obligation	(130)
Fair value of plan assets	125
Liability	(5)

Changes in present value of the defined benefit obligation

	$m
Opening defined benefit obligation	nil
Interest cost	20
Current service cost	110
Closing defined benefit obligation	130

Changes in fair value of plan assets

	$m
Opening fair value of plan assets	nil
Expected return on plan assets	10
Contributions	100
Actuarial gain (balancing figure)	15
Closing fair value of plan assets	125

There is an actuarial gain of $15 million on the defined benefit pension scheme assets (W). Under IAS 19 the unrecognised gains and losses at the end of the **previous** reporting period can be recognised in profit or loss for the year using the '10% corridor' approach or any other systematic approach including immediate recognition, either in retained earnings or in profit or loss for the year. Here, the directors have chosen to recognise the gain immediately in profit or loss for the year.

Adjustment to the group accounts:

	$m	$m
DEBIT Retained earnings	105	
CREDIT Trade receivables		100
CREDIT Defined benefit pension scheme		5

(b)   ROD

CONSOLIDATED STATEMENT OF FINANCIAL POSITION AT 30 NOVEMBER 20X2

	$m
Non-current assets	
Property, plant and equipment (W5)	1,930
Goodwill (W2)	132
	2,062
Current assets	
Inventories (300 + 135 + 65 – 20)	480
Receivables (240 + 105 + 49 – 100)	294
Cash at bank and in hand	220
	994
	3,056
Equity attributable to owners of the parent	
Share capital	1,500
Share premium	300
Retained earnings (W3)	586
	2,386
Non-controlling interest (W4)	265
	2,651
Non-current liabilities	
Pension scheme	5
Other	180
Current liabilities	220
	3,056

Workings

1   *Group structure*

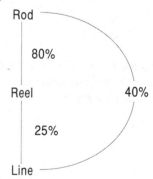

Rod's total holding in Line is 60% (40% direct + 80% × 25% indirect).

2 Goodwill

	Reel $m	Reel $m	Line $m	Line $m
Consideration transferred – Rod		640		160
Consideration transferred – Reel (100 × 80%)				80
Non-controlling interests (710 × 20%)/(300 × 40%)		142		120
FV of identifiable net assets at acq'n:				
Share capital	500		200	
Share premium	100		50	
Retained earnings	100		50	
Fair value adjustment	10		—	
		(710)		(300)
		72		60
				132

Alternative working

	Rod in Reel $m	Rod in Reel $m	Reel in Line $m	Reel in Line $m	Rod in Line $m	Rod in Line $m
Consideration transferred		640	80% × 100	80		160
Net assets acquired						
Share capital	500		200		200	
Share premium	100		50		50	
Retained earnings	100		50		50	
Fair value adjustment	10		–		–	
	710		300		300	
Group share	80%		20%		40%	
		(568)		(60)		(120)
		72		20		40

Total goodwill: $72m + $20m + $40m = $132m

3 Retained earnings

	Rod $m	Reel $m	Line $m
Per question	625.0	200	60
Fair value adjustment realised		(10)	
Development costs written off		(20)	
Trade discount on tangible assets less depreciation		(5)	
Adjustment for excess depreciation (W6)			14
At acquisition		(100)	(50)
	625.0	65	24
Group share of Reel (80% × 65)	52.0		
Group share of Line (60% × 24)	14.4		
Less defined benefit pension scheme (part (a))	(105.0)		
	586.4		

Note. The development costs do not meet the recognition criteria in IAS 38 and they cannot be treated as inventory because they have previously been written off as incurred. They were reinstated after acquisition, so they must be written off post-acquisition reserves.

4 Non-controlling interests

	Reel $m	Line $m
NCI at acquisition (W2)	142	120
NCI in investment in Line (100 × 20%)	(20)	
NCI share of post acquisition retained earnings:		
Reel ((W3) 65 × 20%)	13	
Line ((W3) 24 × 40%)		9.6
	135	129.6

264.6

Alternative working

	Reel $m	Line $m
Net assets per question	800	380
Investment in Line	(100)	–
Development costs written off	(20)	–
Trade discount on PPE less depreciation	(5)	–
Elimination of revaluation reserve (W6)	–	(70)
Adjustment for excess depreciation (W6)	–	14
	675	324
	× 20%	× 40%
	135	129.6

264.6

5 Property, plant and equipment

	$m
Rod	1,230
Reel	505
Line	256
	1,991
Less adjustment to PPE of Line (W6)	(56)
Reel: trade discount net of depreciation (6 × 5/6)	(5)
	1,930

Note. IAS 16 states that the cost of a item of PPE should be measured net of trade discounts. The trade discount must be deducted from Reel's tangible assets.

6 Adjustment to property, plant and equipment of Line

An adjustment must be made to re-state the PPE of Line from their revalued amount to depreciated historical cost, in line with group accounting policies.

The revaluation took place after acquisition, so the adjustment does not affect goodwill.

	Valuation $m	Depreciated historic cost $m
Cost at 1 December 20X1 (date of acquisition by Rod)	300	300
Depreciation (300/6)	(50)	(50)
NBV at 30 November 20X2	250	250
Revaluation	70	–
Revalued amount	320	
Depreciation (320/5)	(64)	(50)
NBV at 30 November 20X3	256	200

Adjustment required to the group accounts:	$m	$m
DEBIT Revaluation surplus	70	
CREDIT Retained earnings (64 – 50)		14
CREDIT Property, plant and equipment (256 – 200)		56

(c)   (i)   **Restructuring of the group**

IAS 37 *Provisions, contingent liabilities and contingent assets* **contains specific requirements** relating to **restructuring provisions**. The general recognition criteria apply and IAS 37 also states that **a provision should be recognised** if an entity has a **constructive obligation** to carry out a restructuring. A constructive obligation exists where **management has a detailed formal plan** for the restructuring and has also raised a **valid expectation** in those affected that it will carry out the restructuring. In this case, the company made a **public announcement** of the restructuring **after the year end**, but it had actually **drawn up the formal plan and started to implement it before the year end**, by communicating the plan to trade union representatives. Although the plan is **expected to take two years to complete**, it appears that the company **had a constructive obligation to** restructure at the year end. Therefore **a provision should be recognised**.

IAS 37 states that a restructuring provision should include **only the direct expenditure** arising from the restructuring. Costs that relate to the **future conduct of the business**, such as training and relocation costs, **should not be included**. Measuring the provision is likely to be difficult in practice, given that the restructuring will take place over two years. IAS 37 requires the provision to be the **best estimate** of the expenditure required to settle the present obligation at the reporting date, **taking all known risks and uncertainties into account**. There **may be a case for providing $50 million** (total costs of $60 million less relocation costs of $10 million) and the company **should certainly provide at least $15 million** ($20 million incurred by the time the financial statements are approved less $5 million relocation expenses). IAS 37 requires **extensive disclosures** and these **should include an indication of the uncertainties** about the amount or timing of the cash outflows.

(ii)   **Fine for illegal receipt of a state subsidy**

IAS 38 *Intangible assets* defines an **intangible asset** as a **resource controlled by the company** as a result of **past events** and **from which economic benefits are expected to flow**. The fine **does not meet this definition**. The subsidy was used to offset trading losses, not to generate future income. The fine should be **charged as an expense** in the income statement for the year ended 30 November 20X4. As it is **material** it should be **separately disclosed**.

(d)   Rod spends considerable amounts of money on research that ultimately creates economic benefits and enhances shareholder value. However, this **research does not meet the criteria for deferral** under IAS 38 *Intangible assets* because of the time lag between the expenditure and the revenue that it generates. Therefore the company's activities **appear to reduce profits, rather than increase them.** The company's expertise is **part of its inherent goodwill** and cannot be valued reliably at a monetary amount. Therefore it is **not recognised** on the statement of financial position.

There is a strong argument that traditional financial reporting is **inadequate to deal with 'knowledge led' companies** such as Rod. It is possible that the capital markets will undervalue the company because the financial statements **do not reflect the 'true' effect of the company's research activities**. The economy is becoming more 'knowledge based' and many companies find themselves in this situation.

The market value of a company is **based on the market's assessment of its future prospects**, based on available information. Analysts have developed **alternative measures of performance such as Economic Value Added (EVA).** These take factors such as expenditure on research and development expenditure into account, so that they attempt to assess estimated future cash flows. **There is a growing interest in ways of measuring shareholder value as opposed to earnings.**

Analysts and other users of the financial statements now **recognise the importance of non-financial information about a company.** Many Stock Exchanges require companies to present an Operating and Financial Review (sometimes called Management Discussion and Analysis) and some large companies do so voluntarily. This normally includes a description of the business, its objectives and its strategy. It is current best practice to analyse the **main factors and influences that may have an effect on future performance**

and to comment on how the directors have sought to **maintain and improve future performance**. In this way the directors of Rod can make the markets aware of its research activities and the way in which they give rise to future income streams and enhance shareholder value.

(e) **Internal auditor bonus**

For

The chief internal auditor is an employee of Rod, which pays a salary to him or her. As part of the internal control function, he or she is helping to **keep down costs and increase profitability**. It could therefore be argued that the chief internal auditor should have a reward for adding to the profit of the business.

Against

Conversely, the problem remains that, if the chief internal auditor receives a bonus based on results, he or she may be **tempted to allow certain actions, practices or transactions which should be stopped**, but which are increasing the profit of the business, and therefore the bonus.

Conclusion

On balance, it is **not advisable** for the chief internal auditor to receive a bonus based on the company's profit.

31 Case study question: Exotic

> **Text reference.** Complex groups are covered in Chapter 13; intangibles in Chapter 4; joint ventures in Chapter 6; environmental reporting in Chapter 3.
>
> **Top tips.** The consolidation section of this question is quite straightforward as long as you remember how to calculate the NCI of a sub-subsidiary. Points to watch in this question are the treatment of intragroup transactions and the calculation of non-controlling interest.
>
> Part (c) required candidates to advise a client about the acceptability of certain accounting practices used by that client. These related to joint ventures and intangibles. Part (d) required candidates to discuss the issues surrounding environmental reporting.
>
> **Easy marks.** With complex groups, remember to sort out the group structure first. There are enough straightforward marks available here if you remember your basic rules for consolidations. The consolidation is quite straightforward as long as you remember how to calculate the NCI of a sub-subsidiary.

(a) EXOTIC GROUP
CONSOLIDATED INCOME STATEMENT FOR THE YEAR ENDED 31 DECEMBER 20X9

	$'000
Revenue 45,600 + 24,700 + 22,800 − 740(W6) − 240(W7)	92,120
Cost of sales 15,050 + 5,463 + 5,320 + 740(W6) + 15 + 15(W6) − 240 + 32(W7)	(27,915)
Gross profit	64,205
Distribution costs (3,325 + 2,137 + 1,900)	(7,362)
Administrative expenses (3,475 + 950 + 1,900)	(6,325)
Finance costs	(325)
Profit before tax	50,193
Income tax expense (8,300 + 5,390 + 4,241)	(17,931)
Profit for the year	32,262
Profit attributable to:	
Owners of the parent	28,549
Non-controlling interest (W4)	3,713
	32,262
Dividends paid and declared for the period	9,500

(b)   EXOTIC GROUP
       CONSOLIDATED STATEMENT OF FINANCIAL POSITION AS AT 31 DECEMBER 20X9

		$'000
Non-current assets		
Property, plant and equipment (35,483 + 24,273 + 13,063 – (W7) 40 + (W7) 8)		72,787
Goodwill (W2)		4,094
		76,881
Current assets (1,568 + 9,025 + 8,883 – (W6) 15 – (W6) 15)		19,446
		96,327
Equity attributable to owners of the parent		
Share capital		8,000
Retained earnings (W3)		56,609
		64,609
Non-controlling interest (W3)		8,584
		73,193
Current liabilities (13,063 + 10,023 + 48)		23,134
		96,327

Workings

1   Group structure

     Exotic
     | 90%
     Melon
     | 80%
     Kiwi   Effective interest (90% × 80%)   72%
                 ∴ Non-controlling interest   28%
                                                 100%

2   Goodwill

	Melon		Kiwi	
	$000	$000	$000	$000
Consideration transferred		6,650	3,800 × 90%	3,420
Non-controlling interests (at 'full' fair value)		500		900
FV of identifiable net assets at acq'n:				
Share capital	3,000		2,000	
Retained earnings	1,425		950	
		(4,425)		(2,950)
		2,725		1,370
			4,095	

Alternative working

	Exotic in Melon			Melon in Kiwi		
	Group		NCI	Group		NCI
	$'000	$'000	$'000	$'000	$'000	$'000
Consideration transferred/FV NCI:		6,650	500.0	90% × 3,800	3,420	900
Share of net assets acquired:						
Share capital	3,000			2,000		
Retained earnings at acquisition	1,425			950		
	4,425			2,950		
Group/NCI share	90%		10%	72%		28%
		(3,983)	(442.5)		(2,124)	(826)
		2,667	57.5		1,296	74
			4,094.5			

3   *Retained earnings*

	Exotic $'000	Melon $'000	Kiwi $'000
Retained earnings per question	22,638	24,075	19,898
Less: PUP (W6)		(15)	(15)
Unrealised profit on transfer of equipment (W7): PUP	(32)		
Pre-acquisition retained earnings		(1,425)	(950)
		22,635	18,933
Share of Melon (22,635 × 90%)	20,372		
Share of Kiwi (18,933 × (W1) 72%)	13,631		
	56,609		

4   *Non-controlling interest (income statement)*

	$'000
Melon ((10,760 − (W6) 15) × 10%)	1,074
Kiwi ((9,439 − (W6) 15) × (W1) 28%)	2,639
	3,713

5   *Non-controlling interests (statement of financial position)*

	Melon $000	Kiwi $000
NCI at acquisition (W2)	500	900
NCI in investment in Kiwi (3,800 × 10%)	(380)	
NCI share of post acquisition retained earnings:		
Melon ((W3) 22,635 × 10%)	2,263.5	
Kiwi ((W3) 18,933 × (W1) 28%)		5,301.2
	2,383.5	6,201.2

8,584.7

Alternative working

	Melon $'000	Kiwi $'000
Net assets per question	27,075	21,898
Less: PUP (W6)	(15)	(15)
Less: Cost of investment in Kiwi	(3,800)	
	23,260	21,883
	× 10%	× 28%
Non-controlling interest share	2,326.0	6,127
Non-controlling interests in goodwill (W2)	57.5	74
	2,383.5	6,201

8,584.5

6   *Intragroup trading*

(i)   Cancel intragroup sale/purchase:

DEBIT group revenue (260 + 480) $740,000
CREDIT group cost of sales $740,000

(ii)   Unrealised profit

	$'000
Melon (60 × 33$\frac{1}{3}$/133$\frac{1}{3}$)	15
Kiwi (75 × 25/125)	15

Adjust in books of seller:

DEBIT Cost of sales/retained earnings
CREDIT Group Inventories

7   *Intragroup transfer of equipment*

(i)   Cancel intragroup sale/purchase:

DEBIT group revenue	$240,000
CREDIT group cost of sales	$240,000

(ii)   Unrealised profit on intragroup sale of equipment

Unrealised profit on transfer

240,000 – 200,000	40,000
Less proportion depreciated by year end	
40,000 × 20%	(8,000)
	32,000

Adjust in books of seller: Exotic

8   *Revenue* *

	$'000
Exotic	45,600
Melon	24,700
Kiwi	22,800
Less intragroup sales (W6)	(740)
Less intragroup transfer of equipment (W7)	(240)
	92,120

9   *Cost of sales* *

	$'000
Exotic	18,050
Melon	5,463
Kiwi	5,320
Less intragroup purchases (W6)	(740)
Less intragroup transfer of equipment (at transfer price) (W7)	(240)
Add unrealised profit on transfer of equipment (W7)	40
Less excess depreciation (240 – 200) × 20%	(8)
Add PUP (W2): Melon	15
Kiwi	15
	27,915

* **Note**. These workings are included for completeness. You should do the workings on the face of the SOCI.

(c)   **Goodwill arising on acquisition of Zest Software**

The company believes that this goodwill has an **indefinite economic life** and therefore it will be **retained in the statement of financial position** indefinitely. IFRS 3 *Business combinations* states that goodwill arising on a business combination should be **recognised as an intangible asset and is not amortised**. However, goodwill must be **reviewed for impairment annually** and impairment losses charged to the income statement where necessary. It should be noted that s**oftware products generally have short lives and the sector is not noted for stability.** This suggests that in practice the goodwill is **likely to suffer impairment** within a reasonably short time.

Interest in joint venture

Although the main standard dealing with joint ventures is IAS 31 *Interests in joint ventures,* the company uses the equity method to account for its interest. IAS 31 **allows the use of the equity method** and IAS 28 *Investments in associates* deals with its application.

IAS 28 states that **if an investor's share of the losses** of an associate **equals its interest** in the associate, it discontinues recognising its share of further losses. The investment **is reported at nil value**. In theory, IAS 28 does not prevent the company from including the loan from the joint venture as part of its investment,

Workings

1 *Timeline*

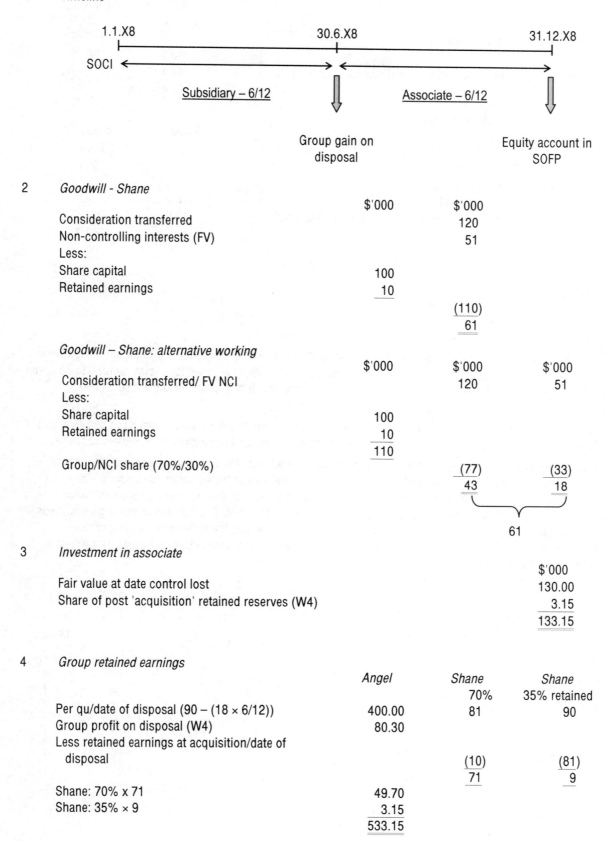

2 *Goodwill - Shane*

	$'000	$'000
Consideration transferred		120
Non-controlling interests (FV)		51
Less:		
Share capital	100	
Retained earnings	10	
		(110)
		61

Goodwill – Shane: alternative working

	$'000	$'000	$'000
Consideration transferred/ FV NCI		120	51
Less:			
Share capital	100		
Retained earnings	10		
	110		
Group/NCI share (70%/30%)		(77)	(33)
		43	18
		61	

3 *Investment in associate*

	$'000
Fair value at date control lost	130.00
Share of post 'acquisition' retained reserves (W4)	3.15
	133.15

4 *Group retained earnings*

	Angel	Shane 70%	Shane 35% retained
Per qu/date of disposal (90 – (18 × 6/12))	400.00	81	90
Group profit on disposal (W4)	80.30		
Less retained earnings at acquisition/date of disposal		(10)	(81)
		71	9
Shane: 70% x 71	49.70		
Shane: 35% × 9	3.15		
	533.15		

LEARNING MEDIA

5   *Retained earnings b/f*

	Angel	Shane
	$'000	$'000
Per Q	330.0	72
Less: Pre-acquisition retained reserves		(10)
	330.0	62
Shane – Share of post acquisition ret'd reserves (62 × 70%)	43.4	
	373.4	

6   *Group profit on disposal of Shane*

	$'000	$'000
Fair value of consideration received		120.0
Fair value of 35% investment retained		130.0
Less share of carrying value when control lost		
Net assets (190 – (18 × 6/12)) × 70%	126.7	
Goodwill belonging to owners of the parent: 61 × 70% (W2)	43.0	
		(169.7)
		80.3

33 Ejoy

Text reference. Changes in group structure are covered in Chapter 14.

Top tips. This question required the production of a consolidated income statement of a group. Candidates were expected to calculate and impairment test the investment in a subsidiary, to account for a joint venture, to deal with impairment and hedging of financial assets, and account for a pre-acquisition dividend and a discontinued operation.

Easy marks. Do not spend too long on the discontinued operation. You would not be penalised too heavily if you got this wrong and there are easy marks to be gained for adding across and other basic consolidation aspects.

Examiner's comment. Overall the question was quite well answered, with the majority of candidates achieving a pass mark. However, candidates answered the financial instruments part of the question quite poorly. The main problem seemed to be the application of knowledge; candidates could recite the principles of accounting for financial instruments but could not deal with the practical application thereof. The calculation of the goodwill was done well, as was the accounting for the pre-acquisition dividend. However, the impairment testing of the investment in the subsidiary was poorly answered. Candidates need to understand this procedure as it will be a regular feature of future papers.

Marking scheme

	Marks
Goodwill	7
Joint venture	2
Financial assets	7
Dividend	2
Income statement	7
Tbay	4
Non-controlling interest	2
Available	31
Maximum	25

EJOY: CONSOLIDATED INCOME STATEMENT FOR THE YEAR ENDED 31 MAY 20X6

	$m
Continuing operations	
Revenue (2,500 + 1,500)	4,000
Cost of sales (1,800 + 1,200 + 26 (W9))	(3,026)
Gross profit	974
Other income (70 + 10 − 3 (W12) − 24 (W4))	53
Distribution costs (130 + 120)	(250)
Administrative expenses (100 + 90)	(190)
Finance income (W7)	6
Finance costs (W8)	(134)
Profit before tax	459
Income tax expense (200 + 26)	(226)
Profit for period from continuing operations	233
Discontinued operations	
Profit for the year from discontinued operations ((30 × 6/12) − 2 (W9))	13
Profit for the year	246
Profit attributable to:	
Owners of the parent	241
Non-controlling interest (W3)	5
	246

Workings

1   *Group structure*

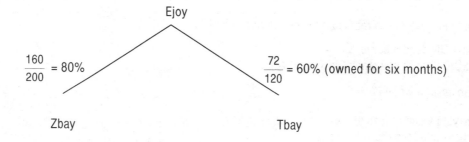

Ejoy

$\frac{160}{200}$ = 80% $\frac{72}{120}$ = 60% (owned for six months)

Zbay   Tbay

Tbay is a discontinued operation (IFRS 5).

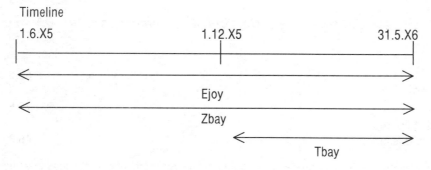

Timeline

1.6.X5   1.12.X5   31.5.X6

Ejoy

Zbay

Tbay

2   *Goodwill*

		Zbay $m		Tbay $m
Consideration transferred		520		216
Non-controlling interests	(600 × 20%)	120	(310 × 40%)	124
Less pre-acquisition dividend (W4)				(24)
Fair value of net assets at acquisition		(600)		(310)
		40		6

Alternative working

	Zbay		Tbay	
	$m	$m	$m	$m
Consideration transferred		520		216
Less pre-acquisition dividend (W4)				(24)
Fair value of net assets at				
Acquisition	600		310	
Group share (W1)	80%		60%	
		(480)		(186)
		40		6

3   *Non-controlling interest*

	Zbay	Tbay
	$m	$m
Profit for period per question	34.0	
× 6/12		15
Less impairment loss on loan asset (W5)	(42.2)	
Interest income on loan asset (W5)	1.1	
	(7.1)	15
	× 20%	× 40%
	(1.4)	6
	4.6	

4   *Pre-acquisition dividend income*

Pre-acquisition dividend income (Tbay)

	$m	$m
Dividend treated as a reduction in cost of investment (60% × 40)		24
DEBIT Dividend income	24	
CREDIT Cost of investment in Tbay (W2)		24

5   *Loan asset held by Zbay*

	$m
Carrying value of loan at 1.6.X5 (a financial asset)	60.0
Impairment loss (balancing figure)	(42.2)
Present value of expected future cash flows ($20 \times \dfrac{1}{1.06^2}$ at 1.6.X5 (note)	17.8
Interest income (6% × 17.8)	1.1
At 31.5.X6	18.9

Note. The $20 million is expected to be received on 31 May 20X7, ie. in two years' time.

6   *Hedged bond (Ejoy)*

	$m
1.6.X5	50.0
Interest income (5% × 50)	2.5
Interest received	(2.5)
Fair value loss (balancing figure)	(1.7)
Fair value at 31.5.X6 (per question)	48.3

Because the interest rate swap is 100% effective as a fair value hedge, it exactly offsets the loss in value of $1.7 million on the bond. The bond is an 'available for sale' item (per IAS 39) and therefore the loss would normally be taken to equity, but because hedge accounting is adopted both the gain on the swap and the loss on the bond are recognised in profit or loss as income and expense. The net effect on profit or loss is nil.

7   Finance income

	$m
Interest income on loan asset held by Zbay (W5)	1.1
Interest receivable on bond held by Ejoy (W6)	2.5
Interest received on interest rate swap held by Ejoy	0.5
Fair value gain on interest rate swap	1.7
	5.8

8   Finance costs

	$m
Per draft income statements (50 + 40)	90.0
Impairment loss (loan asset held by Zbay) (W5)	42.2
Fair value loss on hedged bond (W6)	1.7
	133.9

9   Impairment losses

	Zbay $m	Tbay $m
Notional goodwill (40 × 100%/80%) (6 × 100%/60%) (W2)	50.0	10.0
Carrying amount of net assets (W10)/(W11)	612.9	285.0
	662.9	295.0
Recoverable amount 630/(300 − (5 × 100/60))	(630.0)	(291.7)
Impairment loss: gross	32.9	3.3
Impairment loss recognised: all allocated to goodwill (80% × 32.9)/(60% × 3.3)	26.3	2.0

10   Carrying amount of net assets at 31 May 20X6 (Zbay)

	$m
Fair value of identifiable assets and liabilities acquired (1 June 20X4)	600.0
Profit for year to 31 May 20X5	20.0
Profit for year to 31 May 20X6 per draft income statement	34.0
Less impairment loss (loan asset) (W5)	(42.2)
Interest income (loan asset) (W5)	1.1
	612.9

11   Carrying amount of net assets (Tbay)

	$m
Carrying value of investment in Tbay at 31 May 20X6:	
Fair value of net assets at acquisition (1 December 20X5)	310
Post acquisition profit (30 × 6/12)	15
Less dividend	(40)
	285

12   Joint venture

	$m	$m
Elimination of other venturer's share of gain on disposal (50% × 6)		3
DEBIT Other income	3	
CREDIT Investment in joint venture		3

34 Case study question: Bravado

Text reference. Business combinations achieved in stages are covered in Chapter 14. Ethics are covered in Chapter 2.

Top tips. This question required the preparation of a consolidated statement of financial position where the non-controlling interest on acquisition was at fair value. This is often called the full goodwill method. There was also a calculation and explanation of the impact on the calculation of goodwill if the non-controlling interest was calculated on a proportionate basis and a discussion of the ethics of showing a loan to a director as cash and cash equivalents. The main body of the question required candidates to deal with the calculation of goodwill in a simple situation, the calculation of goodwill where there was a prior holding in the subsidiary, an investment in an associate, a foreign currency transaction, deferred tax and impairment of inventory. Don't be put off by the fact that the goodwill on Message is negative (gain on a bargain purchase). This is unusual, and can sometimes mean your calculation is wrong, but you don't lose many marks for arithmetical mistakes

Easy marks. Part (b) is very generously marked, since the calculation is similar to that in part (a) – you just need the NCI share of the subsidiary's net assets. If you're pushed for time you should ignore the foreign currency AFSFA, as it's fiddly and only carries 3 marks.

Examiner's comment. In general the basic calculation of goodwill under the full goodwill method was well done by candidates. However, they dealt less well with the business combination achieved in stages, the contingent consideration and the deferred tax. Many candidates did not complete the retained earnings calculation and often there was doubt over where the gain on bargain purchase should be recorded. (Group retained profits) The calculation of the impairment of inventories was dealt with quite well by candidates, as was the increase in the value of PPE and land. Often the increase in the depreciation charge as a result of the revaluation of PPE was not calculated correctly, nor was the deferred taxation effect. Many candidates got muddled with Part (b) and omitted Part (c) altogether, but those who attempted Part (c) did well on it.

Marking scheme

		Marks
(a)	Message	5
	Mixted	6
	Clarity	4
	AFS instrument	3
	Retained earnings	3
	Post acquisition reserves	2
	Other components of equity	2
	Current liabilities	1
	NCI	2
	Inventories	2
	PPE	2
	AFS	1
	Deferred tax	1
	Trade receivables	1
		35
(b)	Message	3
	Mixted	3
	Explanation	2
		8
(c)	Subjective	7
	Available	50

(a)   BRAVADO GROUP
      CONSOLIDATED STATEMENT OF FINANCIAL POSITION AS AT 31 MAY 20X9

	$m
Non-current assets	
Property, plant and equipment: 265 + 230 + 161 + 40 (W7) + 12 (W7)	708.0
Goodwill (W2)	25.0
Investment in associate (W3)	22.5
Available-for-sale financial assets: 51 + 6 + 5 – 17.4 (W9)	44.6
	800.1
Current assets	
Inventories: 135 + 55 + 73 – 18 (W10)	245.0
Trade receivables: 91 + 45 + 32	168.0
Director's loan (W11)	1.0
Cash and cash equivalents: 102 + 100 + 8 – 1 (W11)	209.0
	623.0
	1,423.1
Equity attributable to owners of the parent	
Share capital	520.0
Retained earnings (W4)	256.2
Other components of equity (W5)	9.5
	785.7
Non-controlling interests (W6)	148.8
	934.5
Non-current liabilities	
Long-term borrowings: 120 + 15 + 5	140.0
Deferred tax: 25 + 9 + 3 + 2.6 (W7)	39.6
	179.6
Current liabilities	
Trade and other payables: 115 + 30 + 60 + 12 (W2)	217.0
Current tax payable: 60 + 8 + 24	92.0
	309.0
	1,423.1

Workings

1   *Group structure*

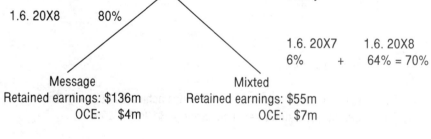

2　　Goodwill

	Message $m	Message $m	Mixted $m	Mixted $m
Consideration transferred				
Cash		300		118
Contingent (at FV)		–		12
		300		130
Non-controlling interest (at fair value)		86		53
Fair value of previously held equity interest				15
Less fair value of net assets at acquisition				
Per question/170 + 6	400		176	
Deferred tax liability (W7)	–		(3)	
		(400)		(173)
(Gain on bargain purchase)/Goodwill		(14)*		25

***Note**. This is a gain on a bargain purchase and should be recorded in profit or loss for the year (W4).

Alternative working

Message:

	$m	$m	$m
Consideration transferred/fair value NCI		300	86
Less fair value of net assets at acquisition per question	400		
Group/NCI share 80%/20%		(320)	(80)
		(20)	(6)
Gain on bargain purchase*		(14)	

***Note**. This is to be recorded in profit or loss for the year.

Mixted:

	$m	$m	$m
Consideration transferred/FV NCI			
Cash		118	53
Contingent		12	
Fair value of previously held equity interest		15	
Less fair value of net assets at acqn.			
Per question: 170 + 6	176		
Deferred tax liability (W7)	(3)		
	173		
Group/NCI share: 70%/30		(121)	(52)
		24	1
		25	

3　　Investment in associate

	$m
Cost = fair value at date significant influence achieved: $9m + $11m	20.0
Share of post 'acquisition' retained earnings $10m* × 25%	2.5
	22.5

***Note**. The profit for the year to 31 May 20X9 is the relevant figure, as the investment only became an associate at the beginning of that year.

Realisation of profit on achievement of significant influence.

	$m
Value at date significant influence achieved	9
Value at date of acquisition	8
Increase (originally to other components of equity)	1

Realisation of profit:

DEBIT	Other components of equity	$1m
CREDIT	Profit or loss for the year, and retained earnings	$1m

4 *Retained earnings*

	Bravado $m	Message $m	Mixted $m	Clarity $m
Per question	240.0	150	80.0	10
Clarity (realisation of profit (W3))	1.0			
Fair value movement			(1.6)	
Derecognition of AFSFA (W8)	5.0			
Foreign AFSFA (W9)	(15.9)			
Loss on inventory (W10)	(18.0)			
Gain on bargain purchase (W2)	14			
Pre-acquisition		(136)	(55.0)	(0)
		14	23.4	10

Group share

Message: 80% × 14	11.2
Mixted: 70% × 23.4	16.4
Clarity: 25% × 10	2.5
	256.2

5 *Other components of equity*

	Bravado $m	Message $m	Mixted $m
Per question	12.0	4	7
Realisation of profit on associate (W3)	(1.0)		
Derecognition of AFSFA (W8)	0.0		
Foreign AFSFA (W9)	(1.5)		
Pre-acquisition		(4)	(7)
Group share post acqn: Message	0.0	0	0
Mixted	0.0		
	9.5		

6 *Non-controlling interests*

	Message $m	Mixted $m
At date of control (FV/W2)	86.0	53
Post acquisition share of reserves		
Message: 14 (W4) × 20%	2.8	
Mixted: 23.4 (W4) × 30%		7
	88.8	60
	148.8	

Alternative working

	Message $m	Mixted $m
Net assets per question	374	187.0
Fair value adjustments (W7)	40	9.4
	414	196.4
NCI share: 20%/30%	82.8	58.92
Add: goodwill attributable to NCI (W2)	6.0	1.00
	88.8	59.92
	148.8	

7   *Fair value adjustments*

Message:

	At acqn $m	Movement $m	At year end $m
Land: 400 − (220 + 136 + 4)	40	–	40

Mixted:

	At acqn	Movement	At year end
Property, plant and equipment:		$\left(\dfrac{1}{7}\right)$	
170 + 6 − (100 + 55 + 7)	14	(2.0)	12.0
Deferred tax liability (176 − 160) × 30%	(3)	0.4	(2.6)
	11	(1.6)	9.4

8   *Derecognition of available-for-sale financial asset (Mixted)*

		$m	$m
DEBIT	Previously held equity interest – (goodwill)	15	
CREDIT	Other components of equity		0*
CREDIT	Available-for-sale financial asset		10
CREDIT	Profit or loss for the year		5

*****Note**. The AFSFA is restated at cost on Mixted becoming a subsidiary so all the gain on derecognition goes to profit or loss for the year.

9   *Foreign currency available-for-sale instrument*

	$m
Value on initial recognition: 11m dinars × 4.5 =	49.50
Value at 31 May 20X8: 10m dinars × 5.1 =	51.00
Gain	1.50

At 31 May 20X8, this gain would be recorded in equity.

		$1.5m	
DEBIT	Instrument	$1.5m	
CREDIT	Other components of equity		$1.5m

	$m
Value at 31 May 20X8	51.00
Value at 31 May 20X9: 7 × 4.8	33.60
Impairment	17.40

This is recorded as follows		$m	$m
DEBIT	Other components of equity	1.5	
DEBIT	Profit or loss for the year	15.9	
CREDIT	Instrument		17.4

10   *Inventories*

	$m	$m
Cost in financial statements		
1st stage (100,000 × 1,000)	100	
2nd stage (200,000 × 1,500)		300
Net realisable value		
1st stage (100,000 × (950 − 10))	(94)	
2nd stage (200,000 × (1,450 − 10))		(288)
	6	12
	18	

11   *Director's loan*

DEBIT	Loan receivable	$1m	
CREDIT	Cash		$1m

(b) **Goodwill if non-controlling interest is calculated on a proportionate basis**

	Message		Mixted	
	$m	$m	$m	$m
Consolidated transferred				
Cash		300		118.0
Contingent (at FV)		–		12.0
		300		130.0
Non-controlling interest (20% × 400)/(30% × 173)		80		51.9
Fair value of previously held equity interest				15.0
Less fair value at net assets at acquisition				
Per question	400		176	
Deferred tax liability (W7)	–		(3)	
		400		(173.0)
(Gain on bargain purchase)/goodwill		(20)		23.9

In the case of **Message**, if non-controlling interest is valued on a **proportionate basis**, the **gain on the bargain purchase is greater**. This is logical if the fair value of the non-controlling interest is seen as part of the cost of the acquisition, and the fair value of this NCI is greater than the NCI's proportionate share of the subsidiary's net assets.

In the case of **Mixted**, the **goodwill is less** because, as for Message, Bravado has 'paid' less. The non-controlling interest is, as for Message, seen as part of the cost of the acquisition.

Alternative working

	Message		Mixted	
	$m	$m	$m	$m
Consolidated transferred				
Cash		300		118.0
Contingent (at FV)				12.0
		300		130.0
Fair value of previously held equity interest				15.0
Less fair value at net assets at acquisition				
Per question	400		176	
Deferred tax liability (W7)	–		(3)	
	400		173	
Group share 80%/70%		(320)		(121.1)
		(20)		23.9

(c) **Treatment of loan to director**

Although there is no specific prohibition against this treatment in IFRS, there is a requirement not to be misleading. The treatment is in **breach of certain concepts** prescribed in the IASB's *Framework for the Preparation and Presentation of Financial Statements,* namely:

(i) **Understandability.** If the loan is shown in cash, it hides the true nature of the practices of the company, making the financial statements less understandable to users.

(ii) **Relevance.** The information should be disclosed separately as it is relevant to users.

(iii) **Reliability.** The reliability concept states that information must be free from bias and faithfully represent transactions. Clearly this is not the case if a loan to a director is shown in cash.

(iv) **Comparability.** For financial statements to be comparable year-on-year and with other companies., transactions must be correctly classified, which is not the case here. If the cash balance one year includes a loan to a director and the next year it does not, then you are not comparing like with like.

In some countries, loans to directors are **illegal**, with directors being personally liable. Even if this is not the case, there is a potential **conflict of interest** between that of the director and that of the company, which is why separate disclosure is required as a minimum. Directors are responsible for the financial statements required by statute, and thus it is their responsibility to put right any errors that mean that the financial statements do not comply with IFRS. There is generally a legal requirement to maintain proper accounting records, and recording a loan as cash conflicts with this requirement.

There is, in addition, an **ethical aspect**. In obscuring the nature of the transaction, it is possible that the directors are **motivated by personal interest**, and are thus failing in their duty to act honestly and ethically. If one transaction is misleading, it casts doubt on the credibility of the financial statements as a whole.

In conclusion, the treatment is problematic and **should be rectified**.

35 Case study question: Base Group

Text reference. Changes in group structure are covered in Chapter 14. Revenue recognition is in Chapter 1. Social and environmental reporting is in Chapter 3.

Top tips. This question required a consolidated income statement. This included the calculation of the profit/loss on a disposal of shares, adjustments for intragroup profit, retirement benefits, convertible debt instruments and share options as well as dealing with accounting for associates, non-controlling interests and goodwill. Part (b) deals with revenue recognition. In part (c) there are easy marks to be had for backing up your arguments.

Easy marks. There are a lot of easy marks here for basic consolidation technique, which, even if you missed complications you could still gain.

Examiner's comment. In general this question was well answered. However, some candidates used proportional consolidation for the subsidiary, and few treated the share options correctly.

Marking scheme

			Marks
(a)	Revenue		1
	Cost of sales		3
	Distribution/administration		1
	Interest expense		2
	Investment income		1
	Taxation		1
	Goodwill		3
	Inter-company profit		2
	Retirement benefit – explanation		2
	Debt – explanation		2
	Share options – explanation		2
	Associate		4
	Non-controlling interest		2
	Gain on disposal/adjustment to parent equity		4
(b)	Revenue recognition		5
(c)	(i)	Strategic issue	1
		Sustainable performance	1
		Transparency	1
		Best practice	1
		Responsible ownership	1
		Reduction of risks	1
		Reputation	1
		Governments	1
		Cultural/social pressures	1
	(ii)	1 mark per point up to a maximum	6
		Maximum	50

(a) BASE GROUP
CONSOLIDATED INCOME STATEMENT FOR THE YEAR ENDED 31 MAY 20X3

	$m
Revenue (3,000 + 2,300 + (600 × 9/12))	5,750
Cost of sales (W4) (2,000 + 1,600 + 225 – 5 + (3 – 1))	(3,822)
Gross profit	1,928
Distribution costs (240 + 230 + (120 × 9/12))	(560)
Administrative expenses (200 + 220 + (80 × 9/12))	(480)
Profit on disposal of shares in subsidiary (W8)	35
Finance costs (W5) (20 + 10 + 9 + 1.1 + 3)	(43)
Investment income receivable (100 – (200/350 × 70))	60
Share of loss of associate (W7)	(6)
Profit before tax	934
Income tax expense (130 + 80 + 27)	(237)
Profit for the year	697
Profit attributable to	
Owners of the parent	624
Non-controlling interests (W2)	73
	697

Because Base retained control of Zero, the gain on the sale of the 50 million shares in Zero is treated as an adjustment to the parent's equity in the consolidated statement of financial position. It is calculated as $12m (W9). In the SOFP, goodwill on the acquisition of Zero will remain at $8m. Non-controlling interests will increase.

Workings

1 *Group structure*

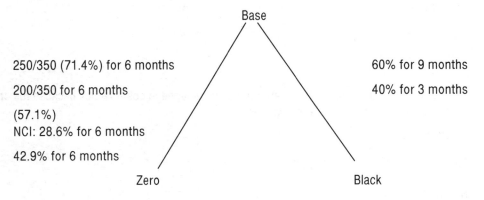

Zero was a subsidiary throughout the year.

Black became an associate on 1 March 20X3.

2 *Non-controlling interests*

	$m
Zero to 1 December 20X2 (160 × 6/12 × 28.6%/350)	23
Zero to 31 May 20X3 (160 × 6/12 × 42.9%/350)	34
Black to 1 March 20X3 (52 × 9/12× 40%)	16
	73

3 Goodwill

	Zero $m	Black $m
Consideration transferred	600	270
Non-controlling interests $(770 \times 28.6\%)/180$	220	180
Less: fair value of net assets acquired:	(770)	(400)
	50	50
Impairment losses to 1 June 20X2	(10)	(10)
Goodwill not yet written off at date of disposal	40	40

Alternative working

	Zero $m	Black $m	NCI in Black $m
Consideration transferred/FV NCI	600	270	180
Less: fair value of net assets acquired:			
$(250/350 \times 770)$	(550)		
$(60\%/40\% \times 400)$		(240)	(160)
	50	30	20
Impairment losses to 1 June 20X2	(10)	(6)	(4)
Goodwill not yet written off at date of disposal	40	24	16

40

Note It is assumed that the impairment losses are in proportion as between group and NCI.

4 Cost of sales

	$m
Base	2,000
Zero	1,600
Black $(300 \times 9/12)$	225
	3,825
Retirement benefit (W6)	(5)
Share options $(3-1)$	2
	3,822

Note. The loss in the value of the share options is included in cost of sales because the options were received in exchange for trade receivables.

5 Finance costs

	$m
Base	20
Zero	10
Black $(12 \times 9/12)$	9
	39
Redeemable debt $(20 \times 5.4\%)$	1.1
Retirement benefit plan	3
	43.1

6 Retirement benefits

	$m
Amount originally included in cost of sales	10
Amount that should be included (current service cost only)	(5)
Adjustment (reduction)	5

10% 'corridor' (based on amounts at 31 May 20X2)

10% of present value of defined benefit obligation ($54m)	$5.4m
10% of fair value of plan assets ($48 m)	$4.8 m

The unrecognised actuarial loss is only $3 million and therefore no loss is recognised during the year.

7 Share of loss of associate

	$m
Profit for the year ($52 \times 3/12 \times 40\%$)	5.2
Provision for unrealised profit (90 (W10))	(10.8)
	(5.6)

8 Profit on disposal of shares in Black

	$m	$m
Fair value of consideration received ($40m \times \$2.65$)		106.0
Fair value of 40% investment retained		240.0
Base's share of consolidated carrying value when control lost		
Share capital	200	
Retained earnings at start of year	190	
Profit for current year ($52 \times 9/12$)	39	
Fair value adjustment (($400 - (200 + 150)$))	50	
	$479 \times 60\%$	(287.4)
Goodwill not yet written off attributable to owners of parent:		
$60\% \times 40$ (W2)		(24.0)
		34.6

9 Adjustment to parent's equity on disposal of Zero

	$m	$m
Fair value of consideration received		155
Less change in non-controlling interest		
NCI at acquisition	220.00	
NCI share of post acquisition reserves $\left(400 + \left(160 \times \dfrac{6}{12}\right) - 250\right) \times 28.6\%$	65.78	
	285.78	
$\times$ charge in NCI $\dfrac{42.9\% - 28.6\%}{28.6\%}$		(143)
		12

Alternative working

Adjustment to parent's equity on disposal of Zero

	$m	$m
Fair value of consideration received		155
Increase in NCI in net assets at disposal		
Share capital	350	
Retained earnings at start of year	400	
Profit for current year ($160 \times 6/12$)	80	
Fair value adjustment ($770 - 350 - 250$)	170	
	1,000	
Increase in NCI 50/350		(143)
		12

Note: No adjustment is made to the non-controlling interests in goodwill as they are not recognised as a group policy is to hold non-controlling interests at their proportionate share of the fair because value of the identifiable net assets not at fair value.

10 Provision for unrealised profit

$90 \times 30\%$	= $25m
Group share: 40%	= $10.8m

(b) Revenue from the sale of software under licences

At present the company must comply with **IAS 18 *Revenue***, although this standard **only sets out general principles**. There have recently been several high profile cases in which companies have been criticised for adopting questionable revenue recognition policies. As a result, **many companies have turned to US GAAP where this provides further guidance** on reporting specific types of transaction. In itself, **this does not contravene IAS 18.**

However, IAS 18 does require that where a transaction consists of **more than one distinct element**, each element should be **accounted for separately**. An Appendix to IAS 18 states that where the selling price of the product includes an identifiable amount for subsequent servicing, that amount, including a profit element, should be **deferred and recognised as revenue over the period during which the service is performed**. Alternatively, it could be argued that the provision of the software and the services are **linked** and should be **treated as one transaction**. The correct accounting treatment **depends on the economic substance** of the transactions.

The Appendix to IAS 18 also states that fees from the development of customised software should be recognised **by reference to the stage of completion of the development**. At present the company only recognises revenue at the completion of the contract and therefore **this accounting policy should be changed.**

(c) (i) There are a number of factors which encourage companies to disclose social and environmental information in their financial statements.

Public interest in corporate social responsibility is steadily increasing. Although financial statements are primarily intended for investors and their advisers, there is growing recognition that companies actually have **a number of different stakeholders**. These include **customers, employees and the general public,** all of whom are **potentially interested** in the way in which a company's operations affect the natural environment and the wider community. These stakeholders can have a **considerable effect on a company's performance**. As a result many companies now deliberately attempt to build a **reputation for social and environmental responsibility**. Therefore the disclosure of environmental and social information is essential. There is also growing recognition that **corporate social responsibility is actually an important part of an entity's overall performance.** Responsible practice in areas such as reduction of damage to the environment and recruitment **increases shareholder value**. Companies that act responsibly and make social and environmental disclosures are **perceived as better investments** than those that do not.

Another factor is **growing interest by governments and professional bodies**. Although there are **no IFRSs** that specifically require environmental and social reporting, it may be required by **company legislation**. There are now a number of **awards for environmental and social reports** and high quality disclosure in financial statements. These provide further encouragement to disclose information.

At present companies are normally able to disclose **as much or as little information as they wish in whatever manner that they wish**. This causes a number of **problems**. Companies tend to disclose information **selectively** and it is difficult for users of the financial statements to **compare the performance of different companies**. However, there are **good arguments** for continuing to allow companies a certain amount of freedom to determine the information that they disclose. If detailed rules are imposed, **companies are likely to adopt a 'checklist' approach** and will **present information in a very general and standardised way**, so that it is of very little use to stakeholders.

(ii) The Base Group could improve its disclosure of 'Corporate Environmental Governance' by including the following information in its financial statements:

(1) a general description of its **policies** relating to the environment

(2) descriptions of the **ways in which the company seeks to manage and minimise environmental risks**

(3) **details** of any **serious pollution incidents** that have occurred during the year and details of any **fines** imposed for environmental offences

(4) a report on the company's **environmental performance** including **details of acid gas and other emissions** and details of how the company's activities affect the natural environment in other ways. The report should include **narrative information** (descriptions of how the risks are reduced) and **numerical information** if this is verifiable

(5) details of the company's **targets (key performance indicators)** for reducing emissions and other forms of pollution and whether these have been met; **historical data** should be included here if this is practicable

There exist a number of **guidelines** that set out the information that should be disclosed in an environmental report (for example, the Global Reporting Initiative (GRI) framework of performance indicators). The guidance is **non-mandatory, but represents best practice**. Ideally, the environmental information should be **audited**.

36 Case study question: Beth

Text reference. Piecemeal acquisitions are covered in Chapter 14; ethics in Chapter 2; the environment in Chapter 3.

Top tips. There is a lot of information in this question, but do not let this put you off. As so many marks are available for consolidation aspects, the key is to establish the group structure and work out the goodwill. This needs to be calculated only once: when Lose gains control. Note that the group aspects can be dealt with separately from the adjustments.

Easy marks. Marks are available for standard consolidation calculations, for example five marks for goodwill in Lose, which is easy once you have established the group structure. Parts (b) and (c) are fairly open ended.

Examiner's comment. In Part (a),the piecemeal acquisition was well answered, but not the effect of the above on the group reserve. Many candidates did not correctly deal with the elimination of inter group profit between the associate and the holding company generally taking out the whole of the profit rather than 30% of it. Several candidates did not consider the impairment of the associate. Many did not realise that if a payment to the supplier is a deposit and is refundable, then the amount is deemed to be a monetary amount which should be retranslated at the year end. Similarly, many candidates did not realise that the factored trade receivables should not have been derecognised and therefore should remain on the SOFP. The calculation of the share options was generally well done but the calculation of the non-controlling interest was surprisingly poorly done considering that there was relatively little adjustment required to the subsidiary's closing reserves. Candidates often had differing views as to the nature of the environmental provision and markers were instructed to give credit for a well argued case. Parts (b) and (c) of the question were quite well answered although many candidates did not spend long enough on them. The main problem with the answers to this part was failure to consider the ethical issues involved. Two professional marks were awarded for the quality of the appraisal and analysis of the position of the company in respect of its environmental and social policy. This would mean not simply regurgitating the facts of the case but having the ability to conceptualise the facts and produce key conclusions from those facts.

Marking scheme

		Marks
(a)	Goodwill – Lose	5
	Non-controlling interest	1
	Group reserves	2
	Associate and impairment	5
	Intra-group profit	2
	Foreign currency	4
	Debt factoring	4
	Share options	4
	Provision	3
	Operating lease	3
	Other statement of financial position items	2
	Maximum	35
(b)	Benefits of environmental report – Maximum	8
(c)	Discussion of ethical and social responsibility – subjective	5
	Professional marks	2
	Maximum	7
	Maximum	50

(a) BETH GROUP
CONSOLIDATED STATEMENT OF FINANCIAL POSITION
AS AT 30 NOVEMBER 20X7

	$m
Non-current assets	
Property, plant and equipment: 1,700 + 200 + (W6) 10 + 2 – 2	1,910
Goodwill (W2)	17
Other intangible assets	300
Investment in associate (W3)	183
	2,410
Current assets	
Inventories: 800 + 100	900
Trade receivables: 600 + 60 – 1 (W8) + 50 (W9)	709
Cash: 500 + 40	540
	2,149
Total assets	4,559

	$m
Equity and liabilities	
Equity attributable to owners of the parent	
Share capital	1,500
Retained earnings (W4)	447
Other reserves: 300 + 9 (W10)	309
	2,256
Non-controlling interests (W5)	65
	2,321
Non-current liabilities: 700 + 2 (W7) + 11 (W11)	713
Current liabilities: 1,380 + 100 + 45 (W9)	1,525
Total equity and liabilities	4,559

Workings

1   Group structure

	1 Dec X5		1 Dec X6	Beth			1 Dec X6
	20%	+	60% = 80%				30%
Pre-acquisition retained earnings	$80m		$150m			Pre-acquisition retained earnings	$260m

Lose   Gain

2   Goodwill: Lose (at date control obtained)

	$m	$m
Consideration transferred		160.00
Non-controlling interests		53.33
Fair value of previously held equity interest		53.33
Fair value of identifiable assets acquired and liabilities assumed		
Share capital	100	
Retained earnings	150	
		(250.00)
		16.66

Alternative working

	$m	$m	$m
Consideration transferred/FV NCI		160.00	53.33
Fair value of previously held equity interest		53.33	
Fair value of identifiable assets acquired and liabilities assumed			
Share capital	100		
Retained earnings	150		
	250		
× 80%/20%		(200.00)	(50.00)
		13.33	3.33
		16.66	

3   *Investment in associate*

	$m
Cost	180
Share of post acquisition retained earnings (W4)	12
Unrealised profit in inventories (W6)	(3)
Impairment loss (to profit or loss/retained earnings) (bal fig)	(6)
Recoverable amount: $610 × 30%	183

4   *Retained earnings*

	Beth	Lose 80%	Gain
	$m	$m	$m
Per question	400.00	200	300
Profit on derecognition of investment*	13.33		
Unrealised profit (W6)	(3.00)		
Operating lease (W7): 10 - 2		8	
Foreign currency (W8)	(1.00)		
Debt factoring reversal (W9)	5.00		
Share-based payment (W10)	(9.00)		
Provision (W11)	(11.00)		
Pre-acquisition		(150)	(260)
		58	40
Group share			
Lose: 58 × 80%	46.40		
Gain: 40 × 30%	12.00		
Impairment (W3)	(6.00)		
	446.73	rounded up to 447	

*Profit on derecognition of investment:

	$m
Fair value at date control obtained	53.33
Cost	(40.00)
	13.33

5   *Non-controlling interests: Lose*

	$m
NCI at acquisition	53.33
NCI share of post acquisition retained earnings ((W4) 58 × 20%)	11.60
	64.93

Non-controlling interest: $64.93m rounded up to $65m.

Alternative working

	$
Net assets per question	300
Operating lease corrections (W7): 10 – 2	8
	308

	$m
Non-controlling interest: $308m × 20% =	61.60
Add goodwill attributable to NCI	3.33
	64.93 rounded up to $65m

6   *Unrealised profit on intra-group trading with associate (Gain)*

	$m
Inventories: selling price	28
Cost	(18)
Profit	10

IAS 28 requires that Beth's share of this profit should be eliminated. Beth's share is 30% × $10m = $3m.

DEBIT	Cost of sales/retained earnings (Beth)	$3m	
CREDIT	Investment in associate		$3m

Note. The unrealised profit is eliminated from retained earnings in the books of the seller (Beth) and from inventories in the books of the holder (Gain), ie the investment in associate.

7   *Lease*

IAS 16 *Property, plant and equipment* requires that Lose should capitalise the leasehold improvements of $10m and depreciate them over the term of the lease. The requirement in the lease to return the building in its original condition is an obligation arising from past events, so a provision of $2m should be made for the estimated costs.

Capitalise leasehold improvements

DEBIT	Property, plant and equipment	$10m	
CREDIT	Cost of sales /retained earnings		$10m

Provide for conversion costs

DEBIT	Property, plant and equipment	$2m	
CREDIT	Non-current liability		$2m

Adjust for depreciation

DEBIT	Cost of sales/retained earnings	$2m	
	(10 + 2) ÷6		
CREDIT	Property, plant and equipment		$2m

Note. The PPE adjustment will affect non-controlling interest in Lose.

8   *Foreign currency contract*

The payment to the supplier is a refundable deposit. It is deemed to be a monetary amount and is re-translated at the year end.

At 1 September 20X7	$m
€12m × 50% ÷ 0.75	= 8.00

At y/e (30 November 20X7)	
€12m × 50% ÷ 0.85	= 7.06
Loss	= 0.94 (rounded to $1m)

DEBIT	Retained earnings	$1m	
CREDIT	Receivables		$1m

9   *Debt factoring*

Under IAS 39 *Financial instruments: recognition and measurement*, a financial asset must be de-recognised:

(i)   If the contractual rights to the cash flows have expired
(ii)   If the financial asset has been transferred, together with the risks and rewards

Condition (ii) has not been met. Beth still bears the risks and rewards of ownership . Accordingly, the receivable must be reinstated.

DEBIT	Receivables	$50m	
CREDIT	Retained earnings		$5m
CREDIT	Loan (current liabilities)		$45m

10   *Share options*

Following IFRS 2, a charge must be made to profit or loss and a corresponding credit to equity, as follows.

200 options × (10,000 − (600+500)) × ½ × $10
= $8.9m, rounded to $9m

DEBIT	Retained earnings	$9m	
CREDIT	Equity (Share-based payment reserve/other reserves)		$9m

11   *Provision for contamination clear up*

Following IAS 37, a provision must be recognised if and only if:

(i)   A present obligation (legal or constructive) has arisen as a result of a past event
(ii)   Payment is probable
(iii)   The amount can be measured reliably

In this case, a provision must be made for the costs of contamination only where there is a legal obligation to clean it up. A moral obligation does not justify a provision. $4m relates to costs where there is an existing law. $7m relates to a law that will come in December 20X7, but it is assumed that the law will apply retrospectively. The total provision that must be made is $(7+4)m = $11m.

DEBIT	Profit and loss/retained earnings	$11m	
CREDIT	Non-current liability		$11m

(b)   **Advantages of a separate environmental report**

Most countries do not have any legal requirements to produce an environmental report, and until fairly recently, environmental reporting was not seen as important. However, there would be a number of advantages for Beth in producing an environmental report.

(i)   Producing a separate report will force Beth to **improve its practices** on environmental matters, an area the group has neglected.

(ii)   Customers will see the efforts the group is making, and this will **increase customer confidence** in the group and its products.

(iii)   The oil industry has a negative image when it comes to environmental matters. If Beth can be shown to be making an effort, and giving a detailed report on the changes made, this will **give the group an edge over its competitors.**

(iv)   Beth has a **poor reputation as a good corporate citizen**. This needs to be put right and **be seen to be put right.**

(v)   The group is facing potential litigation. If it takes steps to improving environmental performance and reporting on this, it can **improve relationships with regulators,** and therefore reduce the potential threat.

(vi)   Beth operates in a number of different countries, and so needs to **improve its international reputation.** The international trend is towards improving environmental performance and increased provision of environmental information. Sustained efforts in this area will enhance the group's standing in the international arena.

(vii)   Environmental performance covers areas such as waste management, resources and costs. Improvements in these areas will bring **economies and efficiencies** which will improve the group's profitability.

(viii) **Management information systems will be enhanced** in order to provide environmental information.

(ix)   A good quality environmental report will make Beth **attractive to investors** and financial analysts, who are keen to see evidence of sustainability.

(x)   Companies Beth supplies and contracts with may have to demonstrate to their own investors that they are dealing with reputable suppliers and contractors. Good environmental practices and reporting will **make Beth a more attractive supplier and contractor** to deal with.

A separate environmental report on its own is clearly not enough to give these benefits – the report must be underpinned by **sustained action**.

(c)   **Ethical and social responsibilities**

Ethics and corporate social responsibility are important in themselves, but also because they can improve business performance. At present the company is stagnating, because it has focused on maintaining market share and on its own shareholders at the expense of other stakeholders. Corporate social responsibility is concerned with a company's **accountability to a wide range of stakeholders**, not just shareholders. For Beth, the most significant of these include:

(i)   Regulators
(ii)   Customers
(iii)   Creditors
(iv)   Employees

Regulators

The relationship with regulators is not good, mainly because of a poor reputation on environmental matters. Beth just does the bare minimum, for example cleaning up contamination only when legally obliged to do so. Adopting **environmentally friendly policies** and reporting in detail on these in an environmental report will go some way towards mending the relationship. **Litigation costs**, which have a direct impact on profit, can be **avoided.**

Customers

Currently Beth provides poor customer support, and makes no effort to understand the customs and cultures of the countries in which it operates. Moreover, it makes no positive contributions and does not promote socially responsible policies. This attitude could easily **alienate its present customers and deter new ones**. A **competitor** who does make positive contributions to the community, for example in sponsoring education or environmental programmes, will be **seen as having the edge** and could take customers away from Beth. Corporate social responsibility involves **thinking long-term** about the community rather than about short-term profits, but in the long term, profits could suffer if socially responsible attitudes are not adopted.

Creditors

Suppliers are key stakeholders, who must be handled responsibly if a reputation in the wider business community is not to suffer. **Beth's policy of not paying small and medium-sized companies is very short-sighted**. While such companies may not be in a position to sue for payment, the effect on goodwill and reputation will be very damaging in the long term. Suppliers may be put off doing business with Beth. Perhaps a key component can only be sourced from a small supplier, who will not sell to Beth if word gets around that it does not pay. This **unethical and damaging policy must be discontinued** and relationships with all suppliers fostered.

Employees

Employees are very important stakeholders. Beth's authoritarian approach to management and its refusal to value employees or listen to their ideas, is **potentially damaging to business performance**. High staff turnover is costly as new staff must be recruited and trained. Employees who do not feel valued will not work as hard as those who do. In addition, **employees may have some good ideas** to contribute that would benefit performance; at the moment Beth is missing out on these ideas.

Acting responsibly and ethically is not just right; it is also profitable.

37 Preparation question: Foreign operation

CONSOLIDATED STATEMENT OF FINANCIAL POSITION

	Standard $'000	Odense Kr'000	Rate	Odense $'000	Consol $'000
Property, plant and equipment	1,285	4,400	8.1	543	1,828
Inv in Odense	520	–		–	–
Goodwill (W2)	–	–		–	277
	1,805	4,400		543	2,105
Current assets	410	2,000	8.1	247	657
	2,215	6,400		790	2,762
Share capital	500	1,000	9.4	106	500
Retained earnings (W3)	1,115				1,395
Pre-acq'n		2,100	9.4	224	
Post acq'n	–	2,200	Bal fig	324	
	1,615	5,300		654	1,895
Non-controlling interest (654 × 20%)					131
					2,026
Loans	200	300	8.1	37	237
Current liabilities	400	800	8.1	99	499
	600	1,100		136	736
	2,215	6,400		790	2,762

CONSOLIDATED STATEMENT OF COMPREHENSIVE INCOME

	Standard $'000	Odense Kr'000	Rate	Odense $'000	Consol $'000
Revenue	1,125	5,200	8.4	619	1,744
Cost of sales	(410)	(2,300)	8.4	(274)	(684)
Gross profit	715	2,900		345	1,060
Other expenses	(180)	(910)	8.4	(108)	(288)
Impairment loss (W2)					(21)
Dividend from Odense	40				–
Profit before tax	575	1,990		237	751
Income tax expense	(180)	(640)	8.4	(76)	(256)
Profit for the year	395	1,350		161	495

OTHER COMPREHENSIVE INCOME

	Standard $'000	Odense Kr'000	Rate	Odense $'000	Consol $'000
Exchange difference on translating foreign operations (W4)	–	–		–	72
TOTAL COMPREHENSIVE INCOME FOR THE YEAR	395	1,350		161	567

Profit attributable to:
Owners of the parent	463
Non-controlling interest (161× 20%)	32
	495

Total comprehensive income for the year attributable to:
Owners of the parent	525
Non-controlling interest (161 + 48) × 20%	42
	567

CONSOLIDATED STATEMENT OF CHANGES IN EQUITY (EXTRACT)

	Retained earnings $'000
Balance at 20X5	1,065
Dividends paid	(195)
Total comprehensive income for the year (per SOCI)	525
Balance at 31/12/X6 (W3)/(W5)	1,395

Workings

1   *Group structure*

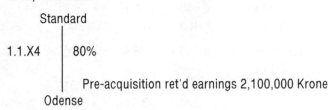

Standard

1.1.X4   80%

Pre-acquisition ret'd earnings 2,100,000 Krone

Odense

2   *Goodwill*

	Kr'000	Kr'000	Rate	$'000
Consideration transferred (520 × 9.4)		4,888		520
Non-controlling interests (3,100 × 20%)		620		66
Share capital	1,000		9.4	
Reserves	2,100			
		(3,100)		(330)
		2,408		256
Exchange differences 20X4-20X5		–	β	18
At 31.12.X5		2,408	8.8	274
Impairment losses 20X6		(168)	8.1	(21)
Exchange differences 20X6		–	β	24
At 31.12.X6		2,240	8.1	277

Alternative working

	Kr'000	Kr'000	Rate	$'000
Consideration transferred		4,888		
Share capital	1,000			
Retained earnings	2,100			
	3,100			
Group share (80%)		(2,480)		
		2,408	9.4	256
Exchange differences 20X4-20X5		–	β	18
At 31.12.X5		2,408	8.8	274
Impairment losses 20X6		(168)	8.1	(21)
Exchange differences 20X6		–	β	24
At 31.12.X6		2,240	8.1	277

3   *Consolidated retained earnings carried forward*

	Standard $'000
Standard	1,115
Group share of post acquisition reserves at Odense (324 × 80%)	259
	1,374
Less goodwill impairment losses (W2)	(21)
Exchange on differences on goodwill (18 + 24)	42
	1,395

4   *Consolidated retained earnings b/f proof*

		$'000
Standard		915
Add post-acquisition retained earnings of Odense		
(4,355 @ 8.8 – 3,100 @ 9.4) × 80%		132
Less goodwill impairment losses (W2)		0
Exchange differences on goodwill (W2)		18
		1,065

5   *Exchange differences*

	$'000	$'000
On translation of net assets:		
Closing NA @ CR	654	
Opening NA @ OR (5,300 – 1,350 + 405 = 4,355 @ 8.8)	(495)	
Less retained profit as translated (161 (SOCI) – 405 @ 8.1)	(111)	
Exchange gain		48
On goodwill (W2)		24
		72

6   *Non-controlling interests (statement of financial position)*

	$'000
NCI at acquisition (W2)	66
NCI share of post acquisition reserves of Odense (324 × 20%)	65
	131

38 Memo

Text reference. Foreign currency is covered in Chapter 16.

Top tips. In this question, you had to produce a consolidated income statement and statement of financial position for a parent company and its foreign subsidiary. Adjustments had to be made for intragroup items such as loans and inventory, and candidates had to deal with the treatment of goodwill as a foreign currency asset. Exchange gains and losses had to be recognised in the financial statements.

Easy marks. Just setting out the proforma and doing the mechanics of translation will earn you easy marks, even if you struggle with more difficult aspects.

Examiner's comment. This question was well answered. Candidates generally made good attempts at the translation of the foreign subsidiary, the calculation of goodwill, intragroup profit in inventory, and the gain on translation. At the same time, there were problems with the treatment of goodwill as a foreign currency asset, and the exchange gain on the intra group loan.

Marking scheme

	Marks
Consolidated statement of financial position	7
Translation of subsidiary's statement of financial position	5
Goodwill	1
Non-controlling interest	2
Post acquisition reserves	5
Consolidated income statement	5
Unrealised profit	4
Loan	3
Available	32
Maximum	32

(Movement on reserves and exchange gain analysis not asked for)

MEMO
CONSOLIDATED STATEMENT OF FINANCIAL POSITION AT 30 APRIL 20X4

	$m
Assets	
Property, plant and equipment: 297 + 70(W5)	367
Goodwill (W2)	8
Current assets (355 + 48.6 – 0.6) (W7)	403
	778
Equity and liabilities	
Equity attributable to owners of the parent:	
Share capital	60
Share premium	50
Retained earnings (W3)	372
	482
Non-controlling interest (W4)	18
	500
Non-current liabilities (30 + 18.6 – 5)	44
Current liabilities: 6205 + 29 (W5)	234
	778

MEMO
CONSOLIDATED STATEMENT OF COMPREHENSIVE INCOME FOR THE YEAR ENDED 30 APRIL 20X4

	$m
Revenue (200 + 71 – 6)	265
Cost of sales (120 + 48 – 6 + 0.6 (W8)	(163)
Gross profit	102
Distribution costs and administrative expenses: 30 + 10 (W6)	(40)
Impairment of goodwill (W2)	(2)
Finance costs (W6)	(1)
Interest receivable	4
Exchange gains (W8)	1
Profit before tax	64
Income tax expense: 20 + 4.5 (W6)	(24)
Profit for the year	40
Other comprehensive income	
Exchange differences on foreign operations (W9) (9.7 + 1.6)	11
Total comprehensive income for the year	51
Profit attributable to	
Owners of the parent	38
Non-controlling interest (25% × 7.9) (W4)	2
	40
Total comprehensive income for the year attributable to	
Owners of the parent	47
Non-controlling interest (7.9 + 9.7) × 25%	4
	51

Workings

1   *Group structure*

Memo

1 May 20X3 | 75%

Random

Cost = 120m crowns
PAR = 80m crowns

2 Goodwill

	CRm	CRm	Rate	$m
Consideration transferred		120.0		48
Non-controlling interests (132 × 25%)		33.0		13.2
Less fair value of net assets at acq'n:				
Share capital	32		2.5	
Share premium	20			
Retained earnings	80			
		(132.0)		(52.8)
		21.0		8.4
Impairment losses		(4.2)	2.1	(2.0)
FX gain		–	β	1.6
At 30.4.X4		16.8	2.1	8.0

Alternative working

	CRm	CRm	Rate	$m
Consideration transferred		120.0		
Less fair value of net assets acquired				
Share capital	32			
Share premium	20			
Retained earnings	80			
	132			
Group share (75%)		(99.0)		
		21.0	2.5	8.4
Impairment losses		(4.2)	2.1	(2.0)
FX gain		–	β	1.6
At 30.4.X4		16.8	2.1	8.0

3 Retained earnings

	$m
Memo	360.0
Random (75% × 17.6 (W6))	13.2
Provision for unrealised profit (W7)	(0.6)
Impairment of goodwill (W2)	(2.0)
Exchange differences on goodwill (W2)	1.6
	372.2

4 Non-controlling interests

	$m
NCI at acquisition (W1)	13.2
NCI share of post acquisition reserves of Random ((W3) 17.6 × 25%)	4.4
	17.6

Alternative working

	$m
Non-controlling interest share of net assets (25% × 70.4 (W2))	17.6

5 Translation of statement of financial position

	CRm	Rate	$m
Property, plant and equipment	146.0	2.1	69.5
Current assets	102.0	2.1	48.6
	248.0		118.1
Share capital	32.0	2.5	12.8
Share premium	20.0	2.5	8.0
Retained earnings:			
Pre-acquisition	80.0	2.5	32.0
	132.0		52.8

	CRm	Rate	$m
Post-acquisition: 15 + (2 − 1.2) (W8)	15.8	β	17.6
	147.8		70.4
Non-current liabilities (41 − 2 (W8))	39.0	2.1	18.6
Current liabilities (60 + 1.2 (W8))	61.2	2.1	29.1
	248.0		118.1

6   *Translation of income statement*

	CRm	Rate	$m
Revenue	142	2	71
Cost of sales	(96)	2	(48)
Gross profit	46		23
Distribution and administrative expenses	(20)	2	(10)
Interest payable	(2)	2	(1)
Exchange gain (2 − 1.2) (W8)	0.8	2	0.4
Profit before tax	24.8		12.4
Income tax expense	(9)	2	(4.5)
Profit for the year	15.8		7.9

7   *Provision for unrealised profit*

	$m
Sale by parent to subsidiary (6 million × 20% × ½)	0.6

8   *Exchange gains and losses in the accounts of Random*

Loan to Random (non-current liabilities)

	CRm
At 1 May 20X3 ($5 million × 2.5)	12.5
At 30 April 20X4 ($5 million × 2.1)	(10.5)
Gain	2.0

Intro-group purchases (current liabilities)

	CRm
Purchase of goods from Memo ($6 million × 2)	12
Payment made ($6 million × 2.2)	(13.2)
Loss	(1.2)

Exchange differences in income statement (retranslated to dollars)

	$m
Gain on loan (2 ÷ 2)	1.0
Loss on current liability/purchases (1.2 ÷ 2)	(0.6)
	0.4

(*Note.* This has been rounded up to $1 million.)

9   *Exchange differences arising during the year*

	$m	$m
Closing net assets at closing rate (W5)	70.4	
Less opening net assets at opening rate (W5)	(52.8)	
		17.6
Less retained profit as translated (W6)		(7.9)
		9.7
Exchange gain on retranslation of goodwill (W2)		1.6
		11.3

	$m
B/Fwd	282.1
Non-current liabilities	
90 + 5 + 4 (W2) − 4 (W8) − 10 (W10) + 4 (W12) − 1 (W12) + 0.5 (W12)	88.5
Current liabilities	
110 + 7 + 6 (W2) + 10 (W10) + 1 (W10) + 3 (W11) + 6 (W13)	143.0
	513.6

*Note: Hall's 'other components of equity' are all pre-acquisition.

Workings

1   Group structure

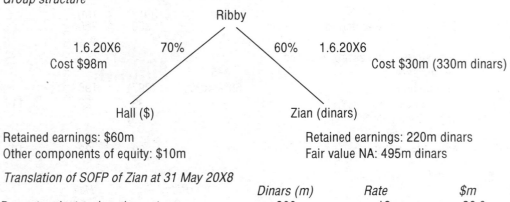

Ribby

1.6.20X6   70%   60%   1.6.20X6
Cost $98m   Cost $30m (330m dinars)

Hall ($)   Zian (dinars)

Retained earnings: $60m   Retained earnings: 220m dinars
Other components of equity: $10m   Fair value NA: 495m dinars

2   *Translation of SOFP of Zian at 31 May 20X8*

	Dinars (m)	Rate	$m
Property, plant and equipment	360	12	30.0
Financial assets	148	12	12.3
Current assets	120	12	10.0
	628		52.3
Share capital	209	11	19.0
Retained earnings			
Pre-acqn	220	11	20.0
	429		39.0
Post-acqn. (307 − 220 − 8 (W8)	79	ß	3.3
	508		42.3
Non-current liabilities 40 + 8 (W8)	48	12	4.0
Current liabilities	72	12	6.0
	628		52.3

3   *Goodwill: Hall*

	$m	$m
Consideration transferred		98
Fair value of non-controlling interests		42
Fair value of identifiable net assets at acq'n (per question)		(120)
		20

Alternative working

		Group	NCI
	$m	$m	$m
Consideration transferred/FV NCI		98	42
Fair value of identifiable			
net assets acquired (per question)	120		
Group NCI share: 70%/30%		(84)	(36)
		14	6

20

4 Goodwill: Zian

	Dinars (m)	Rate	$m
Consideration transferred (30 × 11)	330		30.0
Non-controlling interests	220		20.0
		11	
Less: fair value of net assets at acq'n per question	(495)		(45.0)
At 1 June 20X6	55		5.0
Impairment loss	(0)		(0.0)
Exchange loss	-		(0.4)
At 31 May 20X8	55	12	4.6

Alternative working

	Dinars (m)	Dinars (m)	Dinars (m)	Rate	$m	$m
Consideration transferred (30 × 11)/ FU NCI		330	220			
Less share of net assets acquired						
Per question	495					
Group share:	60%/40%	(297)	198			
At 1 June 20X6		33	22	11	3.0	2.0
Impairment loss		(0)			(0.0)	(0.0)
Exchange loss		-			(0.2)	(0.1)
At 31 May 20X8		33	22	12	2.8	1.9

5 Retained earnings

	Ribby $m	Hall $m	Zian $m
Per question/as translated (W2)	120.0	80.0	23.3
Adjustments			
Fair value movement (W7)			(0.5)
Impairment (W9)	(0.8)		
Loan penalty (W10)	(1.0)		
Bonus/share options (W11)	(4.8)		
Past service cost (W12): 3 + 0.5	(3.5)		
Unrealised profit in inventory (W13)		(4)	
Pre-acquisition: per question		(60)	
as translated (W2)			(20.0)
		16	2.8
Group share: Hall: 16 × 70%	11.2		
Zian: 2.8 × 60%	1.7		
Exchange loss on goodwill (W4)	(0.4)		
	122.4		

6 Non-controlling interests

	Hall $m	Zian $m
NCI at acquisition (W6)/(W4)	42.0	20.0
NCI share of post acquisition retained earnings:		
Hall ((W5) 16 × 30%)	4.8	
Zian ((W5) 2.8 × 40%)		1.1
	46.8	21.1
		67.9

Non-controlling interests: alternative working

	Hall $m	Zian $m
Net assets per qu/per (W2)	130	42.3
Fair value adjustments (W7)	10	5.5
Unrealised profit (W13)	(4)	
	136	47.8
	30%	40%
	40.8	19.2
Add goodwill on NCI	6.0	1.9
	46.8	21.1

67.9

7   *Fair value adjustments*

Hall:

	Acquisition 1 June 20X6 $m	Movement 2 years $m	Year end 31 May 20X8 $m
Land: 120 – 40 (SC) – 60 (RE) – 10 (other)	10	–	10

Zian:

	Acquisition 1 June 20X6	Movement (exchange diff)	Year-end 31 May 20X8 $m
Land (in dinars (m))			
495 – 209 (SC) – 220 (RE) = 66			
In dollars: 66/11 (66/12)	6	(0.5)	5.5

Note: The land is non-depreciable so the movement for Zian is the change in exchange rate.

8   *Intragroup loan*

	Dinar
Initial value 1 June 20X7 ($4m × 10)	40
Year-end value 31 May 20X8 ($4m × 12)	48
Foreign exchange loss	8

Adjust in Zian's books (W6)

DEBIT Profit and loss (retained earnings)	8 dinars	
CREDIT Non-current liabilities		8 dinars

The intra-group loan will be eliminated from the consolidated SOFP.

DEBIT Non-current liabilities	$4m	
CREDIT Financial assets		$4m

9   *Impairment loss on building*

	$
Cost at 1 June 20X7: 40m dinar/10	4.0
Depreciation: 4m/20	(0.2)
	3.8
Impairment loss (bal. fig.)	(0.8)
Impaired value at 31 May 20X8: 36m dinar/12	3.0

10   *Early repayment of loan*

The decision to repay the loan early has two implications:

(i)   The loan must be transferred from non-current liabilities to current liabilities.

(ii)   A penalty for early re-payment. The double entries are:

DEBIT	Non-current liabilities	$10m	
CREDIT	Current liabilities		$10m

Being transfer to current liabilities

DEBIT	Profit or loss for the year	$1m
CREDIT	Current liabilities	$1m

Being accrual of early repayment penalty

11   *Bonus and share options*

Half the bonus is to be paid in cash, so a liability of $(6m × ½) = $3m must be accrued.

The remainder of the bonus is to be paid in share options. The grant date will be 30 November 20X8, as this is when the terms of the share options become fixed. However, the services must be recognised as received, and so 12 months of the 18 month service period up to the grant date must be recognised.

The double entry is as follows:

DEBIT   Profit or loss (retained earnings) $4.8m

CREDIT   Current liabilities (cash bonus (6m × ½)) $3m

CREDIT   Other components of entity 90% × $6m × ½ × $\dfrac{12\,\text{months}}{18\,\text{months}}$ $1.8m

12   *Past service cost*

A past service cost of $3m must be recognised immediately, as this benefit has already been vested. The remaining $1m relates to an entitlement that has not yet fully vested, as it is given in return for services over the remaining two-year period. It should therefore be recognised on a straight line basis over two years.

The double entry is as follows:

On 1 June 20X7:

DEBIT	Profit or loss (retained earnings)	$3m
DEBIT	Unrecognised past service cost	$1m
CREDIT	Present value of obligation (non-current liabilities)	$4m

On 31 May 20X8:

DEBIT	Profit or loss (retaining earnings) $1m/2	$0.5m
CREDIT	Unrecognised past service cost (non-current liability)	$0.5m

13   *Sale of inventory*

This transaction is known as 'window dressing'. It should not be shown as a sale; the sale must be cancelled and the inventory re-instated at $2m (cost) rather than $6m sales price.

The entries for the cancellation of the sale are:

DEBIT	Sales	$6m
CREDIT	Cash (current liabilities)	$6m

For the cancellation of the purchase:

DEBIT	Cash (current assets)	$6m
CREDIT	Purchases	$6m

The above entries have no effect on retained earnings, but the elimination of unrealised profit, reducing inventory from $6m to $2m, will affect it.

DEBIT	Closing inventory/cost of sales (Hall's books): 6 – 2 $4m	
CREDIT	Inventory (current asset)	$4m

(c) **Ethical implications of sale of inventory**

Members of the accounting profession enjoy a number of privileges. These include:

(i)   Special status and respect within the community.

(ii)   Self-regulation, that is regulation by the accountants' professional body

(iii)   An exclusive right to certain functions. For example, auditors must be members of certain professional bodies.

Like other professions, the accounting profession has **features that distinguish it** from non-professional jobs. The most important of these is specialist knowledge, but also recognition as being committed to the good of society, rather than just commercial gain.

To **earn this status and these privileges**, accountants should, as a minimum:

(a)   Be committed to the presentation of true, fair and accurate financial statements.

(b)   Show independence and objectivity in applying financial reporting standards.

(c)   Be committed to an ethical approach to business, and apply this in the preparation of financial statements.

Ethical behaviour in the preparation of financial statements, and in other areas, is of **paramount importance**. This applies equally to preparers of accounts, to auditors and to accountants giving advice to directors. Company accountants act unethically if they use 'creative' accounting in accounts preparation to make the figures look better.

In treating the inventory as sold, Ribby is indulging in '**window dressing**'. This is not a genuine sale; its purpose is purely **to show Ribby's subsidiary Hall in a better financial position** than is truly the case, in order to increase the likelihood of the sale of Hall. The 'sale' of inventory would increase cash and retained earnings by $4m, boosting the appearance of both profitability and liquidity. This would **mislead a potential buyer**. Nor would this manipulation be a 'one-off'; if the subsidiary is not sold, the transaction would be carried out again in the interim accounts. Neither the final accounts for 31 May 20X8, nor the interim accounts would give a fair presentation of the true picture.

The treatment of the inventory is therefore **unethical**, and should be reversed when preparing the consolidated financial statements.

40 Preparation question: Consolidated statement of cash flows

STATEMENT OF CASH FLOWS FOR THE YEAR ENDED 31 DECEMBER 20X5

	$'000	$'000
Cash flows from operating activities		
Profit before tax	16,500	
Adjustments for:		
Depreciation	5,800	
Impairment losses (W2)	240	
	22,540	
Increase in trade receivables (9,800 – 7,500 – 600)	(1,700)	
Increase in inventories (16,000 – 10,000 – 1,600)	(4,400)	
Increase in trade payables (7,600 – 6,100 – 300)	1,200	
Cash generated from operations	17,640	
Income taxes paid (W1)	(4,200)	
Net cash from operating activities		13,440
Cash flows from investing activities		
Acquisition of subsidiary net of cash acquired	(600)	
Purchase of property, plant and equipment (W2)	(13,100)	
Net cash used in investing activities		(13,700)
Cash flows from financing activities		
Proceeds from issue of share capital		
(12,300 + 5,800 – 10,000 – 2,000 – (5,000 – 1,000))	2,100	
Dividends paid	(900)	
Dividends paid to non-controlling interest (W3)	(40)	
Net cash from financing activities		1,160
Net increase in cash and cash equivalents		900
Cash and cash equivalents at the beginning of the period		1,500
Cash and cash equivalents at the end of the period		2,400

Workings

1   *Additions to property, plant and equipment*

PROPERTY, PLANT AND EQUIPMENT

	$'000			$'000
b/d	25,000			
Revaluation surplus	500			
On acquisition	2,700	Depreciation		5,800
∴ Additions	13,100	c/d		35,500
	41,300			41,300

2   *Goodwill impairment losses*

GOODWILL

	$'000			$'000
b/d	0	∴ Impairment loss		240
On acquisition (5,000 +				
(4,800 × 30%) – 4,800)	1,640	c/d		1,400
	1,640			1,640

Alternative working

GOODWILL

	$'000		$'000
b/d	0	∴ Impairment loss	240
On acquisition			
(5,000 – (4,800 × 70%))	1,640	c/d	1,400
	1,640		1,640

3   *Dividends paid to non-controlling interest*

NON-CONTROLLING INTEREST

	$'000		$'000
		b/d	0
∴ Dividends paid	40	Acquisition (4,800 × 30%)	1,440
c/d	1,750	TCI	350
	1,790		1,790

4   *Income taxes paid*

INCOME TAX PAYABLE

	$'000		$'000
		b/d	4,000
∴ Income taxes paid	4,200	Acquisition	200
c/d	5,200	I/S	5,200
	9,400		9,400

41 Portal

Text reference. Group statements of cash flow are covered in Chapter 17.

Top tips. The examiner for this paper has stated that the emphasis is on advising management and on realistic scenarios. Part (b) could come under the heading of advice and Part (a), which involves using your knowledge to correct the accountant's work, could come under both headings.

Marking scheme

			Marks
(a)	Net cash inflow		8
	Taxation		3
	Sale of property, plant and equipment		4
	Non-controlling interest		2
	Joint venture		2
	Disposal of subsidiary and cash disposed of		2
		Available	21
		Maximum	18
(b)	Subjective		7
		Available	28
		Maximum	25

(a)   PORTAL GROUP
       STATEMENT OF CASH FLOWS FOR THE YEAR ENDED 31 DECEMBER 20X0

	Working	$m	$m
Cash generated from operations	1		712
Interest paid		(9)	
Income taxes paid	2	(115)	
			(124)
Net cash from operating activities			588
Cash flows from investing activities			
Disposal of subsidiary		75	
Subsidiary's cash disposed of		(130)	
Purchase of property, plant and equipment		(380)	
Sale of property, plant and equipment	3	195	
Purchase of interest in joint venture		(25)	
Interest received		26	
Dividend received from joint venture		10	
Net cash used in investing activities			(229)
Cash flows from financing activities			
Increase in short term deposits		(143)	
Dividend paid to non-controlling interest	4	(31)	
Net cash used in financing activities			(174)
Net increase in cash and cash equivalents			185
Cash and cash equivalents at 1 January 20X0			600
Cash and cash equivalents at 31 December 20X0			785

Workings

1   *Cash generated from operations*

	$m
Per question	875
Add back loss on disposal	25
Adjustments for current assets/liabilities of subsidiary *	
Inventory	(60)
Trade receivables	(50)
Current liabilities (130 – 25)	105
Deduct post-tax profit on joint venture	(55)
Interest receivable	(27)
Interest payable	19
Deduct profit on sale of non current assets	(120)
	712

Note. The movements in current assets used by the accountant to calculate net cash inflow from operating activities incorrectly include amounts relating to the subsidiary disposed of.

2   *Income taxes paid*

	$m
Per question (position statement movement)	31
Tax on subsidiary disposed of	25
Tax on profit	(171)
Cash outflow	(115)

3   *Sale of property, plant and equipment*

	$m
Per question (carrying value)	1,585
Transferred to joint venture	(200)
Subsidiary disposed of	(310)
Sale and leaseback	(1,000)
Profit on sale	120
Cash inflow	195

(a) ANDASH
STATEMENT OF CASH FLOWS FOR YEAR ENDED 31 OCTOBER 20X6

	$m	$m
Cash flows from operating activities		
Profit before taxation (400 + 1 (W3) – 78 (W7)	323	
Adjustments for:		
Depreciation	260	
Impairment of goodwill (W7)	78	
Share of profit of associate (W3)	(1)	
Gain on disposal of subsidiary	(8)	
Interest expense	148	
	800	
Increase in trade receivables (2,400 – 1,500 + 4)	(904)	
Increase in inventories (2,650 – 2,300 + 8)	(358)	
Increase in trade payables (4,700 – 2,800 + 6)	1,906	
Cash generated from operations	1,444	
Interest paid (W6)	(118)	
Income taxes paid (W5)	(523)	
Net cash from operating activities		803
Cash flows from investing activities		
Acquisition of associate	(10)	
Purchase of property, plant and equipment (W1)	(1,320)	
Proceeds from sale of subsidiary, net of cash disposed (32 – 5)	27	
Net cash used in investing activities		(1,303)
	$m	$m
Cash flows from financing activities		
Proceeds from issue of share capital (400 + 120 – 270 – 80 – 10 – 50)	10	
Proceeds from long-term borrowings (3,100 – 2,700)	400	
Dividends paid	(50)	
Dividends paid to non-controlling interest shareholders (W4)	(20)	
Net cash from financing activities		340
Net decrease in cash and cash equivalents		(160)

Workings

1 *Purchase of property, plant and equipment*

PROPERTY, PLANT AND EQUIPMENT

	$m		$m
Balance b/d	4,110	Disposal of subsidiary	10
Share options (10 – 1) (W8)	9	Depreciation	260
Additions	1,320	Balance c/d (5,170 – 1)	5,169
	5,439		5,439

2 *Goodwill*

GOODWILL

	$m		$m
Balance b/d	130	Disposal of subsidiary	10
		Impairment loss	78
		Balance c/d (120 – 78)	42
	130		130

3   *Share of profit of associate and dividend from associate*

INVESTMENT IN ASSOCIATE

	$m		$m
Balance b/d	–	Dividends received	–
Acquisition (50 + 10)	60	Balance c/d	61
Post-acquisition profit	1		
	61		61

	$m
Share of post-acquisition reserves:	
25% × ($32m – $20m)	3
Intragroup profit:	
25% × ($16m – $8m)	2
Profit from associate	1

As there is no information about the profit earned by the associate, the only possible assumption is that it paid no dividends.

4   *Dividend paid to non-controlling interest*

NON-CONTROLLING INTEREST

	$m		$m
∴ Cash paid	20	Balance b/d	180
Balance c/d	200	Income statement	40
	220		220

5   *Tax paid*

TAX PAYABLE

	$m		$m
Disposal	7	Balance b/d (deferred)	300
∴ Taxes paid	523	Balance b/d (current	770
Balance c/d (deferred)	400	Income statement	160
Balance c/d (current)	300		
	1,230		1,230

6   *Interest paid*

INTEREST PAYABLE

	$m		$m
∴ Interest paid	118	Balance b/d	40
Balance c/d (current)	300	Income statement	148
	1,230		1,230

7   *Impairment loss*

	$m
Net assets at 31 October 20X6	240
Goodwill (90 × 100/60)	150
	390
Recoverable amount	(260)
	130
Recognised (130 × 60%)	78

8   *Share options*

The basic rule in IFRS 2 *Share-based payment* is that when equity instruments are issued to acquire goods or services, they should be measured at the fair value of those goods and services. An adjustment is required to reduce the options and the plant by £1m to £9m.

(b)   (i)   The IASB's *Framework for the Preparation and Presentation of Financial Statements* sets out the **principles that underpin the preparation of general purpose financial statements**. The purpose of the *Framework* is to **assist the IASB in the preparation of future standards** and to **assist preparers of financial statements in applying standards** and in **dealing with topics that are not yet covered** by international accounting standards. This means that in theory, IFRSs are based on the *Framework*, which covers:

- The objective of financial statements
- Underlying assumptions
- The qualities that make the information in financial statements useful
- The elements of financial statements
- When elements should be recognised in financial statements
- Measurement in financial statements
- Concepts of capital and capital maintenance

IAS 8 *Accounting policies, changes in accounting estimates and errors* recognises the *Framework* as one of the **authoritative sources of guidance** in situations where a transaction is not covered by a specific IAS or IFRS.

The *Framework* adopts an **approach based** on the **statement of financial position**. It **defines assets and liabilities** and explains the conditions that must be met before they are recognised. **Income and expenses are defined in relation to assets and liabilities**; a gain is recognised when assets increase or liabilities decrease; a loss is recognised where liabilities increase or assets decrease. There are advantages of this approach, not least that it **helps to prevent 'creative accounting'** where the economic substance of a transaction is different from its legal form. However, it is **very different from the way in which most preparers of accounts view the basis of accounting**: the allocation of transactions to accounting periods.

There are other problems. The *Framework* is a **theoretical document** and financial statements are used for **practical purposes** including determining dividend payments, tax payments and directors' remuneration. Standards based on the *Framework* are sometimes **difficult to apply**, particularly for smaller entities.

A further issue is that the IASB's work is now largely being driven by the **need to converge with US GAAP** and is in fact **moving away from the *Framework* in some respects**. For example, IFRSs make increasing use of **fair value accounting**, but arguably the *Framework* does not deal with this. The IASB is now **developing a new conceptual *Framework*** jointly with the US Financial Accounting Standards Board (FASB).

(ii)   **Situation 1**

IAS 37 *Provisions, contingent liabilities and contingent assets* states that a provision should be recognised if:

- There is a **present obligation** as a result of a **past transaction or event** and
- It is **probable** that a **transfer of economic benefits** will be required to settle the obligation and
- A **reliable estimate** can be made of the **amount** of the obligation.

In this case, the obligating event is the **installation of the facility** and it occurred before the year end. The operating licence has created a **legal obligation** to incur the cost of decommissioning the facility, the expenditure is **probable** and the **amount can be measured reliably.**

Because the entity cannot operate the facility without incurring an obligation to pay for decommissioning, **the expenditure also enables it to acquire economic benefits** (income from operating the facility). Therefore Andash **recognises an asset** as well as a provision and **depreciates the asset over its useful life of 20 years**.

Andash **recognises a provision for the cost of removing the facility**, but **does not include the cost of rectifying the damage** caused by the extraction of natural gas until it is incurred. This means that a provision for rectifying the damage caused by extraction is **recognised over the life of the facility**. The provision is **discounted** to its net present value as the time value of money is material.

The accounting treatment is as follows:

STATEMENT OF FINANCIAL POSITION AT 31 OCTOBER 20X7 (EXTRACTS)

	$m
Tangible non-current assets	
Extraction facility	200
Decommissioning costs (W)	40
	240
Depreciation (240 ÷ 20)	(12)
	228
Provisions	
Provision for decommissioning at 1 November 20X6	40.00
Plus unwinding of discount (40 × 5%)	2.00
	42.00
Provision for damage caused by extraction (W)	1.33
	43.33

INCOME STATEMENT FOR THE YEAR ENDED 31 OCTOBER 20X7 (EXTRACTS)

	$m
Depreciation	12
Provision for damage caused by extraction	1.33
Unwinding of discount	2

Working

	$m
Provision for decommissioning costs at 1 November 20X6 (80% × 50)	40
Provision for damage caused by extraction at 31 October 20X7	
$20\% \times 50 \times \dfrac{1.05^{20}}{20}$	1.33

Note: the extraction costs (20% × $50m) are payable in 20 years' time but they must be built up over the period of twenty years.

Situation 2

The company should **recognise a provision for deferred tax relating to the building** and there is a **deferred tax asset relating to the warranty**. Per IAS 12 *Income taxes* the calculation is as follows.

	$m	$m
Building		
Tax written down value (75% × 8)	6	
Net book value (9 − 1.8)	(7.2)	
		1.2
Other temporary differences		40.0
Total temporary differences (liabilities)		41.2
Warranty provision		4.0
Tax losses		70.0
Total temporary differences (assets)		74.0

Therefore the company **recognises a deferred tax liability of $12.4 million** (41.2 × 30%) and **can also recognise a deferred tax asset for the same amoun**t. It will only be able to recognise the full amount of the deferred tax asset if it can prove that **suitable taxable profits are available to offset the losses** in future.

(iii) **Treatment of the items and the *Framework***

It can be argued that some of the assets and liabilities involved are **not 'true' assets and liabilities** and therefore that they **should not be recognised**.

Under the *Framework*, the company would have to **recognise the full discounted liability** for the decommissioning costs and a corresponding asset. An **asset** is defined as a **resource controlled by**

the company as a result of past events and from which **future economic benefits** are expected to flow.

The *Framework* defines a **liability** as a **present obligation arising from a past event**, the settlement of which is expected to result in an **outflow of economic benefits**. Strictly speaking, the deferred tax provision **does not meet this definition**; only an **actual liability** to the tax authorities can be an obligation at the reporting date. A deferred tax liability **can be avoided,** for example, with tax planning, or if a company makes future losses. Still less does the deferred tax asset meet the definition of an asset, because it **depends on the availability of future profits.**

In addition, the **grant** towards the building has been treated as a **deferred credit** and is therefore a liability. It **does not meet the definition of a liability** unless it has to be repaid.

43 Case study question: Squire

Text reference. Group statements of cash flow are covered in Chapter 17. Ethics is covered in Chapter 2.

Top tips. Part (a) of his question required candidates to prepare a group statement of cash flows. There were adjustments to be made for impairment, interest on a deferred consideration, retirement benefits and the purchase of a subsidiary in the year.

You need to use a bit of imagination in (b). Try to use your own experience to think of what you can find out about resource usage, also what you would like to know and how you can obtain evidence of what you would like to know.

In (c) observation is likely to be the most useful audit technique, although if staff are being observed, they may behave differently. You may have come up with other means for informing staff.

Part (d) focuses on the impact of stakeholder views and voluntary principles-based disclosure versus compulsory rules-based disclosure.

Examiner's comment (Part (a) only. The question was quite straightforward and candidates performed very well. There are several quite easy marks to be earned in a cash flow question and many candidates gained these marks. The only major criticism of candidates' answers was that the workings were sometimes difficult to follow or were not presented at all. This latter point is critical. Many candidates simply showed a line of numbers without any narrative. This is acceptable but if these numbers are wrong or not easily recognisable then marks are difficult to award.

(a) SQUIRE
GROUP STATEMENT OF CASH FLOWS FOR THE YEAR ENDED 31 MAY 20X2

	$m	$m
Cash flows from operating activities:		
Profit before tax	420	
Adjustments for:		
Share of profit in associate	(45)	
Exchange differences on property, plant and equipment	9	
Interest	75	
Depreciation	129	
Retirement benefit expense	20	
	608	
Decrease in inventories (1,300 − 1,160 − 180)	40	
Increase in trade receivables (1,220 − 1,060)	(160)	
Increase in trade payables (2,355 − 2,105)	250	
Cash generated from operations	738	
Interest paid (W5)	(51)	
Income taxes paid (W6)	(140)	
Contributions paid to retirement benefit scheme	(26)	
Net cash from operating activities		521
Cash flows from investing activities:		
Purchase of property, plant and equipment (W5)	(451)	
Purchase of subsidiary (200 + 30)	(230)	
Dividends received from associate (W3)	50	
Net cash used in investing activities		(631)
Cash flows from financing activities:		
Issue of shares (200 + 60 − 170 −30)	60	
Repayment of loans (1,320 − 1,270)	(50)	
Equity dividends paid (90 − 5)(W5)	(85)	
Dividends paid to non-controlling interests (W4)	(5)	
Net cash used in financing activities		(80)
Decrease in cash and cash equivalents for the period		(190)
Cash and cash equivalents at 1 April 20X1		280
Cash and cash equivalents at 31 March 20X2		90

Workings

1   PROPERTY, PLANT AND EQUIPMENT

	$m		$m
Balance b/d	2,010	Depreciation	129
Payables balance c/d	351	Impairment losses	194
Acquisition	150	Balance c/d	2,630
Additions (balancing figure)	**442**		2,953
	2,953		

	$m
Cash flow:	
Non-current asset additions	442
Exchange difference (income statement)	9
	451

2   GOODWILL (PROOF)

	$m		$m
Balance b/d	65	Balance c/d	105
Acquisition (note)	40		
	105		105

Note

	$m
Goodwill on acquisition:	
Consideration transferred:	
Cash	200
Deferred consideration	50
	250
Non-controlling interests (300 × 30%)	90
Less: fair value of identifiable net assets at acquisition	(300)
	40

ALTERNATIVE WORKING: GOODWILL (PROOF)

	$m		$m
Balance b/d	65	Balance c/d	105
Acquisition (note)	40		
	105		105

Note

	$m
Purchase consideration:	
Cash	200
Deferred consideration	50
	250
Less group share of identifiable net assets acquired (70% × 300)	(210)
	40

3   DIVIDENDS RECEIVED FROM ASSOCIATE

	$m		$m
Balance b/d	550	Foreign exchange loss	10
Share of profit	45	**Dividends received (balancing figure)**	**50**
	595	Balance c/d	535
			595

4   NON-CONTROLLING INTERESTS

	$m		$m
Dividend paid (balancing figure)	**5**	Balance b/d	345
Balance c/d	522	Acquisition (30% × 300)	90
		TCI for year	92
	527		527

5   INTEREST PAYABLE

	$m		$m
		Balance b/d	45
Cash paid (balancing figure)	**51**	Income statement (75 − (154 − 50))	71
Balance c/d	65		
	116		116

6   INCOME TAXES

	$m		$m
Cash paid (balancing figure)	**140**	Balance b/d:	
Balance c/d:		Current	160
Current	200	Deferred	175
Deferred	200	Income statement	205
	540		540

(b)   **The planning process**

The planning process for any investigative activity revolves around a consideration of **what information is needed,** where it **may be found** and **how to obtain it.**

Available information

In the case of an environmental audit, much information is probably already available in the form of accounting records; **heating and lighting costs**, for instance can be related to factors such as numbers employed, floor space and building volumes.

There are some fairly **standard aspects of good practice** in terms of energy conservation such as provision of wall and roof insulation; and thermostatic and time clock control of space and water heating systems. The existence and maintenance of such factors can be established from the appropriate records. In the UK, the energy utilities offer free advice on energy conservation and this should be considered. **Use of renewable resources** should be a matter of policy and the purchasing department should be able to comment on the extent to which it is achieved.

Expert advice

Other aspects of energy consumption require expert advice. For instance, the **compressed air circuits** used in many factories to power hand and machine tools can be extremely wasteful of energy if they are leaky, since this causes the compressor to be run for excessive periods to maintain pressure. However, it is a specialised engineering task to measure the actual efficiency of a pneumatic system.

If the organisation is a manufacturer, it would be appropriate to consider the extent to which the **products themselves** were **energy efficient** in use and made use of renewable resources both in use and in their construction. These are largely matters of design and it would be necessary to take technical advice.

(c) **Testing for employee awareness**

Employee awareness could be measured by **observation, questionnaire and interview.** In a large organisation a sampling approach could be taken. Observation could be largely unobtrusive and might provide a useful control on the results of interview, since some staff might make exaggerated claims about their environmental awareness.

Involvement of employees

The techniques of **internal marketing** could be used to involve employees. Internal marketing is the use of marketing techniques that are normally associated with communications flowing out from the organisation, for internal purposes. It is a concept associated with change management and therefore may be appropriate here.

A concerted campaign could be created. This could include messages in salary advices, posters, presentations, the **formation of discussion groups**, and the creation of a **suggestion scheme** specifically aimed at environmental issues. If there are any existing empowerment schemes such as quality circles, it may be possible to introduce an environmental dimension into them.

(d) **Stakeholder interest**

Public interest in corporate social responsibility is steadily increasing. Although financial statements are primarily intended for investors and their advisers, there is growing recognition that companies actually have **a number of different stakeholders**. These include **customers, employees and the general public,** all of whom are **potentially interested** in the way in which a company's operations affect the natural environment and the wider community. These stakeholders can have a **considerable effect on a company's performance**. As a result many companies now deliberately attempt to build a **reputation for social and environmental responsibility**. Therefore the disclosure of environmental and social information is essential.

Regulatory and professional interest

Another factor is **growing interest by governments and professional bodies**. Although there are **no IFRSs** that specifically require environmental and social reporting, it may be required by **company legislation**. There are now a number of **awards for environmental and social reports** and high quality disclosure in financial statements. These provide further encouragement to disclose information.

Performance impact

There is also growing recognition that **corporate social responsibility is actually an important part of an entity's overall performance.** Responsible practice in areas such as reduction of damage to the environment and recruitment **increases shareholder value**. Companies that act responsibly and make social and environmental disclosures are **perceived as better investments** than those that do not.

Compulsory or voluntary disclosure

At present companies are normally able to disclose **as much or as little information as they wish in whatever manner that they wish**. This causes a number of **problems**. Companies tend to disclose information **selectively** and it is difficult for users of the financial statements to **compare the performance of different companies**. However, there are **good arguments** for continuing to allow companies a certain amount of freedom to determine the information that they disclose. If detailed rules are imposed, **companies are likely to adopt a 'checklist' approach** and will **present information in a very general and standardised way**, so that it is of very little use to stakeholders.

44 Case study question: Zambeze

Text reference. Group statements of cash flow are covered in Chapter 17. Ethics are covered in Chapter 2.

Top tips. Some students don't like group statements of cash flows, but they really are a gift. You can simply ignore any complications – at least to start off with – and concentrate on getting the easy marks (see below). Set out your proforma, and, if you can, try to set out your workings in the order shown in our answer. This order has been designed so that the easy workings come first. Part (b) requires straightforward bookwork knowledge of the criteria for consolidation, but also application of this knowledge to the matter of River. Part (c) requires a general discussion of ethical behaviour, but also, more specifically, how these general principles may be applied in the case of River.

Easy marks. Look at the marking scheme for Part (a). There are six marks for operating activities – most of which you know from your non-group cash flow studies at earlier levels. The property plant and equipment working has a few complications, but the same complications come up regularly, so if you learn our working you can't go too far wrong. Tax, interest and dividends are all straightforward. Turning to parts (b) and (c), as indicated above, there are easy marks for a more general discussion, as well as trickier marks for specific application. And write clearly, so you earn those extra two marks for communication.

Marking scheme

		Marks
(a)	Operating activities	6
	Retirement benefit	3
	Associate	3
	Subsidiary treatment	4
	Property, plant and equipment	3
	Goodwill	2
	Non-controlling interest	3
	Taxation	3
	Dividend paid	3
	Interest	2
	River	2
	Issue of shares	1
		35
(b)	Issues	9
(c)	Ethical discussion	3
	River	3
	Two marks for professional communication	2
		50

(a) ZAMBEZE

GROUP STATEMENT OF CASH FLOWS FOR THE YEAR ENDED 30 JUNE 20X6

	$m	$m
Cash flow from operating activities		
Profit before tax	680	
Adjustments for		
Share of profit in associate	(20)	
Depreciation	60	
Impairment of goodwill (W2)	8	
Interest	40	
Retirement benefit expense	13	
	781	
Decrease in inventories (650 – 580 – 90)	20	
Increase in trade receivables (610 – 530)	(80)	
Increase in trade payables (1,341 – 1,200)	141	
Cash generated from operations	862	
Interest paid (W5)	(31)	
Income taxes paid (W6)	(190)	
Contributions paid to retirement benefit scheme	(7)	
Net cash from operating activities		634
Cash flows from investing activities		
Purchase of property, plant and equipment (W1)	(251)	
Purchase of subsidiary	(100)	
Dividends received from associate (W3)	35	
Investment in River	(400)	
Net cash used in investing activities		(716)
Cash flows from financing activities		
Issue of shares	30	
Increase in loans (621 – 555)	66	
Dividends paid (W6)	(46)	
Dividend to non-controlling interest (W4)	(58)	
Net cash used in financing activities		(8)
Decrease in cash and cash equivalents		(90)
Cash and cash equivalents at 1 July 20X5		140
Cash and cash equivalents at 30 June 20X6		50

Workings

1   *Purchase of property, plant and equipment*

PROPERTY, PLANT AND EQUIPMENT

	$m		$m
Balance b/fwd	1,005	Depreciation	60
Payable c/d	144	Impairment losses	95
Acquisition: Damp	70	Balance c/fwd	1,315
Additions (balancing figure)	251		
	1,470		1,470

2   *Impairment of goodwill*

GOODWILL

	$m		$m
Balance b/fwd	25	Impairment (balancing figure)	8
Acquisition (note)	13	Balance c/fwd	30
	38		38

Note: Goodwill on acquisition

	$m
Consideration transferred:	
Cash	100
Deferred	25
	125
Non-controlling interests: 160 × 30%	48
Less: fair value of identifiable net assets at acquisition	(160)
Goodwill	13

3   *Dividend received from associate*

INVESTMENT IN ASSOCIATE

	$m		$m
Balance b/fwd	290	Foreign exchange loss	5
Share of profit after tax	20	Dividend received (balancing figure)	35
		Balance c/fwd	270
	310		310

4   *Dividend paid to non-controlling interest*

NON-CONTROLLING INTEREST

	$m		$m
Dividend paid (balancing figure)	58	Balance b/fwd	45
		Acquisition: 30% × 160	48
Balance c/fwd	60	TCI for the year	25
	118		118

5   *Interest paid*

INTEREST PAYABLE

	$m		$m
Unwinding of discount on purchase (29 – 25)	4	Balance b/fwd	45
		Income statement	40
Cash paid (balancing figure)	31		
Balance c/fwd	50		
	85		85

6   *Income taxes paid*

TAX PAYABLE

	$m		$m
Cash paid (balancing figure)	190	Balance b/fwd	
Balance c/fwd		Current	185
Current	190	Deferred	25
Deferred	30	Income statement	200
	410		410

7   *Dividend paid*

	$
Per SOCIE	504
Less dividend to NCI (W4)	58
Less investment in River	400
Dividend paid	46

Note: Goodwill on acquisition

	$
Purchase consideration	
Cash	100
Deferred	25
	125
Less group share of identifiable net assets acquired: 70% × 160	(112)
Goodwill	13

(b)   The requirement to consolidate an investment is determined by **control**, not merely by ownership. Both IFRS 3 *Business combinations* and IAS 27 *Consolidated and separate financial statements* state that control can usually be assumed to exist when the parent **owns more than half (ie over 50%) of the voting power** of an entity *unless* it can be clearly shown that **such ownership does not constitute control** (these situations will be very rare).

However, IFRS 3 and IAS 27 also list the certain situations where control exists, even when the parent owns only 50% or less of the voting shares of an entity. Control exists if any one of the following apply:

(i)   The parent has power over more than 50% of the voting rights by virtue of **agreement with other investors**

(ii)   The parent has power to **govern the financial and operating policies** of the entity by statute or under an agreement

(iii)   The parent has the power to **appoint or remove a majority of members of the board of directors** (or equivalent governing body)

(iv)   The parent has power to cast a **majority of votes at meetings of the board of directors**

Control exists by virtue of having certain powers, regardless whether those powers are actually exercised. Control of decision making is not enough, however: the reporting entity must control the decision making with a view to **obtaining benefits** from the entity over which it has control.

Applying the above criteria to Zambese's relationship with River:

Zambese has power to govern the financial and operating policies of River, through its **operating guidelines.**

The control is exercised with a view to **obtaining financial benefits** from River. Zambese receives 95% of the profits and 100% of the losses of River.

Zambese therefore **controls** River, and **River should be consolidated.**

(c)   **Ethical behaviour** in the preparation of financial statements, and in other areas, is of **paramount importance**. This applies equally to preparers of accounts, to auditors and to accountants giving advice to directors. Accountants act unethically if they use 'creative' accounting in accounts preparation to make the figures look better, and they act unethically if, in the role of adviser, they fail to point this out.

The creation of River is **a device to keep activities off Zambese's balance sheet**. In hiding the true nature of Zambese's transactions with River, **the directors are acting unethically.** Showing the payment of $400 to river as a dividend is **deliberately misleading,** and may, depending on the laws that apply, be illegal.

The creation of River, and the failure to disclose and account for the transactions properly, puts Zambese's directors **in breach of three important principles** which must apply to the preparation of financial statements:

Compliance with generally accepted accounting principles (GAAP). IAS 27 is not complied with.

Fair presentation, sometimes called the principle of **substance** over form. River is an example of off balance sheet finance, where the form does not reflect the economic substance of the transaction.

Transparency of disclosure. Disclosure must be sufficient for the reader of financial statements to understand fully the nature of the transaction.

The directors must correct this unethical behaviour by consolidating River, and by disclosing the true nature of the payment to River.

45 Case study question: Warrburt

Marking scheme

		Marks
(a)	Net loss before tax	1
	AFS financial instruments	4
	Retirement benefit	3
	Property, plant and equipment	6
	Insurance proceeds	2
	Associate	4
	Goodwill and intangibles	1
	Finance costs	2
	Taxation	4
	Working capital	4
	Proceeds of share issue	1
	Repayment of borrowings	1
	Dividends	1
	Non-controlling interest	1
		35
(b)	Operating cash flow and discussion	10
(c)	Discussion including professional marks	5
	Available	50

(a) WARRBURT GROUP
STATEMENT OF CASH FLOWS
FOR THE YEAR ENDED 30 NOVEMBER 20X8

	$m	$m
Operating activities		
Net loss before tax	(23)	
Adjustments for		
Profit on sale of available-for-sale financial assets:		
45 – 38 + 24 (per question)	(31)	
Retirement benefit expense	10	
Depreciation	36	
Profit on sale of property plant and equipment: $63m – $56m	(7)	
Profit on insurance claim: $3m – $1m	(2)	
Foreign exchange loss (W9) $1.1m + $0.83m	2	
Share of profit of associate	(6)	
Impairment losses: $20m + $12m	32	
Interest expense	9	
	20	
Decrease in trade receivables: $92m – $163m	71	
Decrease in inventories: $135m – $198m	63	
Decrease in trade payables: $115m – $180m – $20.83m (W9)	(86)	
Cash generated from operations	68	
Retirement benefit contributions*	(10)	
Interest paid (W8)	(8)	
Income taxes paid (W7)	(39)	
Net cash from operating activities		11
Investing activities		
Purchase of property, plant and equipment: $56m (W1) + $1.1m (W9)	(57)	
Proceeds from sale of property, plant and equipment:	63	
Proceeds from sale of available-for-sale financial assets	45	
Acquisition of associate (W4)	(96)	
Dividend received from associate: 25% × $8m	2	
Net cash used in investing activities		(43)
Financing activities		
Proceeds from issue of share capital: $650m – $595m	55	
Repayment of long-term borrowings: $20m – $64m	(44)	
Dividends paid	(9)	
Dividends paid to non-controlling shareholders (W6)	(5)	
Net cash used in financing activities		(3)
Net decrease in cash and cash equivalents		(35)
Cash and cash equivalents at beginning of year		323
Cash and cash equivalents at end of year		288

*Note. Only the contributors paid are reported in the cash flow, because this is the only movement of cash. The amounts paid by the trustees are not included, because they are not paid by the company.

Workings

1   *Property plant and equipment*

PROPERTY, PLANT AND EQUIPMENT

	$m		$m
Balance b/fwd	360	Disposals	56
Gain on property revaluation		Depreciation	36
Per SOCI 2		Asset destroyed	1
Deferred tax 2	4	Balance c/fwd	350
Replacement asset from insurance			
company (at F V)	3		
Additions (on credit)*	20		
Additions (cash)*	56		

*Note. The additions are translated at the historic rate. Adjustment for exchange rate differences are dealt with in (W9).

		$m
Additions (cash) $\dfrac{280}{5}$ =		56
Additions (credit) $\dfrac{100}{5}$		20
Total (excluding destroyed assets replaced): 78 – (3 – 1)		$\overline{76}$

2   *Impairment of goodwill*

GOODWILL

	$m		$m
Balance b/fwd	100	Impairment (Bal. fig.)	20
		Balance c/fwd	80
	$\overline{100}$		$\overline{100}$

3   *Impairment of other intangible assets*

OTHER INTANGIBLE ASSETS

	$m		$m
Balance b/fwd	240	Impairment (bal.fig.)	12
		Balance c/fwd	228
	$\overline{240}$		$\overline{240}$

4   *Purchase of associate*

INVESTMENT IN ASSOCIATE

	$m		$m
Balance b/fwd	Nil		
Statement of comprehensive income		Dividend received: $8m × 25%	2
(profit or loss)	6	Balance c/fwd	100
Purchase of associate (bal.fig.)	96		
	$\overline{102}$		$\overline{102}$

5   *Available for sale financial assets*

AVAILABLE FOR SALE FINANCIAL ASSETS

	$m		$m
Balance b/fwd	150	Disposals	38
Other comprehensive income*		Balance c/fwd	142
(gain on revaluation)*	30		
	$\overline{180}$		$\overline{180}$

* **Note**: This is the gain on revaluation, which is shown in the statement of comprehensive income net of deferred tax of $3m (W7), that is at $27m. The gross gain is therefore $30m and is the amount reflected in this working.

6   *Dividends paid to non-controlling interests*

NON-CONTROLLING INTERESTS

	$m		$m
Dividends paid (bal.fig.)	5	Balance b/fwd	53
Balance c/fwd	70	Total comprehensive income	22
	$\overline{75}$		$\overline{75}$

7   Income taxes paid

INCOME TAX PAYABLE

	$m		$m
Income taxes paid (bal. fig.)	39	Balance b/fwd (deferred)	26
Balance c/fwd (deferred)	28	Balance b/fwd (current)	42
Balance c/fwd (current)	35	Profit/loss for year	29
		Other comprehensive income for year (AFS FA) (W5)	3
		Other comprehensive income for year (PPE) (W1)	2
	102		102

8   Interest paid

INTEREST PAYABLE

	$m		$m
Interest paid (bal. fig.)	8	Balance b/fwd (short-term provisions)	4
Balance c/fwd (short-term provisions)	5	SOCI (profit or loss for year)	9
	13		13

9   Exchange loss

At 30 June 20X8:

DEBIT	Property, plant and equipment (W1) $\dfrac{380}{5}$	$76m	
CREDIT	Payables $\dfrac{380}{5}$		$76m

To record purchase of property, plant and equipment

At 31 October 20X8;

DEBIT	Payables $\dfrac{280}{5}$	$56m	
DEBIT	Profit/loss (loss)	$1.1m	
CREDIT	Cash $\dfrac{280}{4.9}$		$57.1

Being payment of 280 million dinars

At 30 November 20X8;

DEBIT	P/L (loss)	$0.83	
CREDIT	Payables $\left(\dfrac{100}{4.8} = 20.83\right) - \left(\dfrac{100}{5} = 20\right)$		$0.83m

Being loss on re-translation of payable at the year end.

Notes

1   The $20.83m was wrongly included in trade payables, so must be removed from the decrease in trade payables in the SOCF.

2   The unrealised loss on retranslation of the payable ($0.83m) must always be adjusted. The realised loss on the cash payment of $1.1 would not normally be adjusted, but it relates to a non-operating item, so is transferred to 'purchase of PPE'.

(b)   Key issues arising from the statement of cash flows

The statements of financial position and comprehensive income, and the ratios associated with these statements, can provide useful information to users, but it is the **statement of cash flows** which gives the **key insight** into a company's liquidity. Cash is the life-blood of business, and less able to be manipulated than profit. It is particularly important to look at where the cash has come from. If the cash is from trading activity, it is a healthy sign.

Although Warrburt has made a loss before tax of $23m, net cash from operating activities is a modest but healthy $11m. Before working capital changes, the cash generated is $20m. The question arises, however, as to **whether this cash generation can continue if profitability does not improve.**

Of some concern is the fact that **a large amount of cash has been generated by the sale of available-for-sale financial assets.** This source of cash generation is not sustainable in the long term.

Operating cash flow **does not compare favourably with liabilities** ($115m). In the long term, operating cash flow should finance the repayment of long-term debt, but in the case of Warrburt, working capital is being used to **for investing activities,** specifically the purchase of an associate and of property, plant and equipment. It remains to be seen whether these investments generate future profits that will sustain and increase the operating cash flow.

The company's **current ratio** (515/155 = 3.3) and **acid test ratio** (380/155 = 2.45) are **sound;** it appears that cash is tied up in long-term, rather than short-term investment. An encouraging sign, however, is that the cash used to repay long-term loans has been nearly replaced by cash raised from the issue of share capital. This means that **gearing will reduce**, which is particularly important in the light of possible problems sustaining profitability and cash flows from trading activities.

(c) **Ethical responsibility of accountant**

Directors may, particularly in times of falling profit and cash flow, wish to **present a company's results in a favourable light.** This may involve manipulation by creative accounting techniques such as window dressing, or, as is proposed here, an **inaccurate classification.**

If the proceeds of the sale of available-for-sale financial assets and property, plant and equipment are presented in the cash flow statement as part of 'cash generated from operations', the picture is **misleading**. Operating cash flow is crucial, in the long term, for the survival of the company, because it derives from trading activities, which is what the company is there to do. **Sales of assets generate short term cash flow,** and cannot be repeated year-on-year, unless there are to be no assets left to generate trading profits with.

As **a professional, the accountant has a duty,** not only to the company he works for, but to his professional body, stakeholders in the company, and to **the principles of independence and fair presentation of financial statements.**

It is essential that the accountant **tries to persuade the directors not to proceed with the adjustments**, which he or she must know violates IFRS 1, and may well go against the requirements of local legislation. If, despite his protests, the directors insist on the misleading presentation, then the accountant has a duty to **bring this to the attention of the auditors.**

46 Mineral

Text reference. Ethics is covered in Chapter 2 and environmental matters in Chapter 3. Reporting performance is covered in Chapters 6, 10 and 18.

Top tips. This question required candidates to discuss the nature of information, which could be disclosed in annual reports in order to better assess the performance of a company.

The question was case study based although many candidates ignored the information in the question. This type of question will arise regularly.

Where you are required to write a report, develop a plan or structure. Identify headings and sub-headings before you begin writing that will help you stick to the question requirements.

Examiner's comment. Too often candidates simply wrote about environmental reporting, or produced a ratio analysis type answer, or assessed the current performance of the company. The question was about the information content of published financial statements and how this might be improved. This was clearly set out in the question.

Answers were often wide-ranging and irrelevant and candidates sometimes spent a disproportionate amount of time on this question. However, generally speaking the layout and style of the reports were quite good and marks were awarded accordingly.

		Marks
Reporting business performance:	Strategy and targets	3
	Operating performance	2
	Risks	2
	Investment	2
Analysis of financial position:	Long term capital structure	2
	Liquidity	2
	Treasury management	2
Corporate citizenship:	Corporate governance	2
	Ethics	1
	Employee reports	1
	Environment	1
Use of information in question		4
Style and layout		4
	Available	**28**
	Maximum	**25**

REPORT

To: The Directors, Mineral
From: Accountant
Date: 12 November 20X1

Information to improve assessment of corporate performance

In addition to the main financial statements, annual reports need to contain information about **key elements of corporate activity**. This report focuses on three main areas.

- Reporting business performance
- Analysis of the financial position
- Nature of corporate citizenship

(a) **Reporting business performance**

A report on business performance may include a ratio analysis, with a year on year comparison. The ratios commonly selected are those concerned with **profitability and liquidity**:

Profitability

	20X1	*20X0*
Return on capital employed	$\frac{10}{59+13} = 13.9\%$	$\frac{9}{46+9} = 16.4\%$
$\dfrac{\text{Gross profit}}{\text{Sales}}$	$\frac{45}{250} = 18\%$	$\frac{35}{201} = 17.4\%$
$\dfrac{\text{PBIT}}{\text{Sales}}$	$\frac{10}{250} \times 100\% = 4\%$	$\frac{9}{201} \times 100\% = 4.5\%$

Long- and short-term liquidity

	20X1	*20X0*
$\dfrac{\text{Current assets}}{\text{Current liabilities}}$	$\frac{55}{25} = 2.2$	$\frac{43}{24} = 1.8$
$\dfrac{\text{Long-term liabilities}}{\text{Equity}}$	$\frac{13}{59} \times 100\% = 22\%$	$\frac{9}{46} \times 100\% = 19.6\%$

These ratios raise a number of questions.

Use of ratios

(i) **Gross profit margin** has **risen**, while **operating profit margin** and **return on capital employed** have **fallen**. Possible problems with **control of overheads?**

(ii) **Short-term liquidity** has **improved**, but **gearing** has **deteriorated**. Is the company using long-term loans to finance expansion? The company has **expanded**, both in revenue and non-current assets.

(iii) **Standard ratios** are a useful tool, but must be discussed in relation to the **specific circumstances of the company.**

- The **impact of the increase in production** through the **acquisition** of the **competitor company** and the **regeneration** of **old plants** needs to be taken into account when considering revenue and non-current asset ratios and other comments in the report.

- When considering profit ratios, the **effectiveness of the cost control programme** might be assessed.

(iv) As well as **year on year comparison**, a report on business performance might usefully **compare actual performance against targets**. To enhance the usefulness of the information, the targets should be industry specific, measurable and realistic.

- The targets set for growth in retained earnings are 20% for 20X2 and between 20% to 25% thereafter. Reporting on actual performance would be informative.

- An objective is to generate the growth by the introduction of new products and improved efficiency. The actual performance in these areas might also be worthy of comment.

(v) The discussion of **business performance** also takes into consideration the **risks** that the business faces. In the context of Mineral, such a discussion would cover:

- The proposed $40m **expenditure on research and development and investment in non-current assets.** Are the directors justified in assuming the **predicted growth** in **retained earnings** that this **large expenditure** is meant to bring about?

- The **joint project** to develop a new aluminium car body will be very lucrative if successful, but is the risk v return decision appropriate?

- The company's pricing strategy and projected increase in demand should be discussed.

(vi) **Knowledge management** is also an important issue where new processes and products are being developed.

(vii) As modern investors become more sophisticated, they are also likely to want to learn about the company's **strategic objectives** including the maintenance and development of **income and profit streams**, future projects and capital expenditure projects.

(b) Analysis of the financial position

(i) Annual reports should contain a review of the company's **financing arrangements** and **financial position** as well as a review of its **operating activities**.

(ii) In the case of Mineral plc, such a review is likely to note that:

- **Gearing has increased, but it is still low**, so the expenditure on research and development could be financed by borrowing, if not by retained earnings.

- Of the long-term loans of $13m, debentures of $4m could be converted into shares or redeemed.

- Should the debentures be **converted**, the **existing shareholders' interest will be diluted**, and they should be made aware of this.

- Current assets are comfortably in excess of current liabilities (by $30m), so the company should have little problem in redeeming the debentures.

(iii) The report will need to disclose information about the **treasury management policies** of the company. This would cover such issues as the potential adverse movement in **foreign exchange risk** and details of the use of **financial instruments** for **hedging**.

(iv)   **Currency risk and interest rate risk** need to be **managed and minimised**, and the report needs to disclose the **company's approach** for dealing with this.

(v)   **Credit risk** is also an **important issue**, particularly as the company operates in the **global market place**.

(vi)   A **statement of cash flows** will be provided as part of the financial statements, but the annual report should also indicate the **maturity profile of borrowings**.

(vii)   Finally, the financial analysis might benefit from the use of techniques such as **SWOT analysis,** covering **potential liquidity problems** and **market growth**. Reference would be made to the **cartel** of car manufacturers aiming to prevent the increased use of aluminium in the car industry.

(c)   **Nature of corporate citizenship**

(i)   Increasingly businesses are expected to be **socially responsible as well as profitable**.

(ii)   **Strategic decisions** by businesses, particularly global businesses nearly always have wider **social consequences**. It could be argued, as Henry Mintzburg does, that a company produces two outputs:

- goods and services
- the social consequences of its activities, such as pollution.

(iii)   One **major development** in the area of corporate citizenship is the **environmental report.**

- This is not a legal requirement, but a large number of UK FTSE 100 companies produce them.
- Worldwide there are around 20 award schemes for environmental reporting, notably the ACCA's.

(iv)   Mineral shows that it is responsible with regard to the environment by disclosing the following information.

- The use of the **eco-productivity index** in the financial performance of sites and divisions. This **links environmental and financial performance**
- The **regeneration of old plants**
- The development of **eco-friendly cars**. Particularly impressive, if successful, is the project to develop a new aluminium alloy car body. Aluminium is rust-free, and it is also lighter, which would reduce fuel consumption.

(v)   Another environmental issue which the company could consider is **emission levels** from factories. Many companies now **include details** of this in their **environmental report**.

(vi)   The other main aspect of corporate citizenship where Mineral plc scores highly is in its **treatment of its workforce.** The company sees the workforce as the **key factor** in the **growth** of its business. The car industry had a reputation in the past for **restrictive practices,** and the annual report could usefully discuss the extent to which these have been eliminated.

(vii)   **Employees** of a businesses are **stakeholders** in that business, along with shareholders and customers. A company wishing to demonstrate good corporate citizenship will therefore be concerned with **employee welfare**. Accordingly, the annual report might usefully contain information on details of **working hours**, **industrial accidents** and **sickness of employees**.

(viii) In conclusion, it can be seen that the annual report can, and should go **far beyond the financial statements** and traditional ratio analysis.

47 Value relevance

Text reference. Performance measures are covered in Chapter 21.

Top tips. This question required candidates to discuss the importance of published financial statements as a source of information, how financial reporting is changing to meet various needs, the problem of reliance on the earnings figure and the use of fair values. Part (c) of the question required a discussion about 'fair value' accounting.

Marking scheme

		Marks
(a)	Subjective	11
(b)	Subjective	8
(c)	Subjective	6
		25

(a)   **The importance of published financial statements**

The objective of published financial statements is to satisfy the information needs of users. Some types of user will always need financial statements as their main source of information about a company. **Companies are normally required to file financial statements with the regulatory authorities** so that a certain amount of information is available to the general public. The government uses financial statements in order to assess taxation and to regulate the activities of businesses.

Financial reporting has evolved to meet the needs of investors in large public companies and their advisers. Yet **published financial statements have serious limitations**: they are based on historic information and they only reflect the financial effects of transactions and events. **Investors need to predict a company's future performance**, including changes in shareholder value. These are affected by the development of new products, the quality of management, the use of new technology and the economic and political environment.

Traditional financial statements are **only one of many sources of information used by investors**. Other sources include **market data, product information, quarterly earnings announcements, press conferences and other briefings given by the directors to institutional investors, analysts and financial journalists**.

Traditional ratio analysis is becoming outdated. The Association for Investment Management and Research (AIMR) has developed global investment performance standards. These are based on 'total return', which includes realised and unrealised gains and income and rates of return that are adjusted for daily-weighted cash flows. **Earnings per share and the price earnings ratio continue to be important, but analysts now calculate a range of other measures. These include cash flow per share, market value per share and 'consensus earnings per share', which predicts future performance.**

Free cash flow is a key performance measure used by analysts to value a company. Free cash flow is cash revenues less cash expenses, taxation paid, cash needed for working capital and cash required for routine capital expenditure. **This can be compared with the cost of capital employed to assess whether shareholder value has increased or decreased**. It can also be projected and discounted to provide an approximate market value.

(b)   **How financial reporting is changing**

Financial reporting practice develops over time in response to changes in the business environment. For example, because businesses are entering into more sophisticated transactions, financial reporting **standards are now based on principles rather than rules**. Businesses increasingly operate across national boundaries and so there is an **emphasis on international convergence of accounting standards**. These developments improve the transparency and comparability of the information available to investors and other users of the financial statements.

Businesses increasingly recognise the **limitations of traditional financial statements** and **non-financial information is now routinely included in the annual report**. Companies disclose information about **risks and opportunities, long term goals, products, human resources, intangible assets and research and development activities**. They may also report the effects of their operations on the **natural environment** and on the **wider social community**. These disclosures reflect a growing awareness that **an entity's performance goes far beyond its earnings for the year**.

Despite this, **many users and preparers of financial statements still focus narrowly on the earnings figure**. As a result, earnings before interest, tax, depreciation and amortisation **(EBITDA) has been developed as a key performance measure**. 'Aggressive earnings management' (inappropriate methods of revenue recognition) and other forms of 'creative accounting' may be used in an attempt to enhance EBITDA**. Emphasis on profits means that quite small changes in earnings can bring about major fluctuations in a company's share price.

(c)   **The use of fair values**

Financial statements should provide information that helps users to predict the future performance of a company. Fair values are more relevant than historic costs for this purpose. In theory fair values reflect the present value of future cash flows and the fair value of an asset shows its potential contribution to future cash flows.

However, **there will always be a difference between the overall value of a company and the aggregate fair values of its assets and liabilities**. (This difference is often described as goodwill.) There may not be a direct relationship between future cash flows and the assets and liabilities on the statement of financial position. In addition, **investors and others may use financial statements for purposes other than predicting future performance and cash flows**.

It can be difficult to arrive at a fair value for an asset or liability because there may not always be a reliable market price. If this is the case, (in theory) fair values are based on the company's own predictions of future cash flow and can only be subjective.

Historic cost accounting has the advantages of being **objective and reliable**. It is **based on actual transactions which can be verified**. Therefore **traditional historic cost financial statements may better meet the needs of users than financial statements based on fair values**.

48 Rockby and Bye

Text reference. Discontinued operations are covered in Chapter 15.

Top tips. This question required candidates to have knowledge of IFRS 5 and discontinued operations. The question has been amended to reflect the publication of a full IFRS, rather than the original exposure draft. In part (b), you had to discuss whether certain assets would be considered to be 'held for sale'.

Easy marks. The obvious easy marks are for Part (a), which is straight out of your Study Text. But as the examiner said, 'Often in questions of this nature, candidates assume certain facts about the scenario. If the assumptions are reasonable, due regard is taken and credit given.'

Examiner's comment. This question was well answered, though candidates did not use the facts of the question in formulating their answer as much as they should have done.

			Marks
(a)	Discussion – IAS		3
	Impairment – IAS		5
(b)	(i)	Operating lease	4
		Plant	3
	(ii)	Property	6
		Available	21
		Maximum	19

(a)   **Sale of the subsidiary**

IFRS 5 *Non-current assets held for sale and discontinued operations* requires an asset or disposal group to be classified as held for sale where it is **available for immediate sale** in its **present condition** subject only to **terms that are usual** and customary and the sale is **highly probable**. For a sale to be highly probable:

- Management must be **committed** to the sale.
- An **active programme to locate a buyer** must have been initiated.
- The **market price** must be **reasonable** in relation to the asset's current fair value.
- The sale must be **expected to be completed within one year** from the date of classification.

The proposed sale of Bye **appears to meet these conditions**. Although the sale had not taken place by the time that the 20X4 financial statements were approved, **negotiations were in progress** and the sale is expected to take place on 1 July 20X4, well **within a year** after the decision to sell. Rockby had **committed** itself to the sale **before its year-end of 31 March 20X4.**

Where a subsidiary is held for sale it **continues to be included** in the consolidated financial statements, but it is **presented separately** from other assets and liabilities in the statement of financial position and its assets and liabilities should not be offset. If Bye represents a **separate major line of business or geographical area** of operations it will also qualify as a **discontinued operation**, which means that on the **face of the income statement** the group must disclose a single amount comprising the **total of its post-tax loss for the year** and **any post-tax gain or loss recognised on its remeasurement. Further analysis is required in the notes** and the notes must also disclose a description of the facts and circumstances leading to the expected disposal and the expected manner and timing of the disposal.

Bye must be **reviewed for** impairment immediately before its classification as 'held for sale'. The calculation is as follows:

	$'000
Net assets at 31 March 20X4	5,000
Goodwill	1,000
	6,000
Value in use at 15 May 20X4	3,900
Add losses incurred from 1 April 20X4 to 15 May 20X4	500
Value in use at 31 March 20X4	4,400
Fair value less costs to sell	4,500

Recoverable amount is the **higher of fair value less costs to sell** and **value in use**. In this case, recoverable amount **is fair value less costs to sell** and so there is an **impairment loss of $1.5 million.** IFRS 5 requires items held for sale to be measured at the **lower of carrying amount and fair value less costs to sell** and therefore Bye will be carried **at $4.5 million** in the statement of financial position and the loss of $1.5 million will be recognised in profit or loss.

(b)   **Items of plant**

If the items of plant are to be classified as 'held for sale', management must be **committed** to the sale and the sale must be **highly probable** and **expected to take place within one year**. The operating leases **do not appear to qualify** as the company is **undecided** as to whether to sell or lease the plant under finance leases. Therefore the company should **continue to treat them as non-current assets** and to depreciate them. The value in use of the items is greater than their carrying value and so they are **not impaired**.

The other items of plant will also **not be classified as 'held for sale'**. Although they were no longer in use at 31 March 20X4 and were sold subsequently, a **firm decision** to sell them **had not been made by the year-end**. IFRS 5 **prohibits retrospective use** of the 'held for sale' classification if, as in this case, assets are sold after the year end but before the financial statements are authorised for issue, although the sale should be **disclosed as an event after the reporting period**. IFRS 5 also requires **disclosure** of the **facts and circumstances** of the sale and a **description** of the items, together with the segment in which they are presented under IFRS 8 *Operating segments* (if applicable).

Head office land and buildings

In order to qualify as 'held for sale' an asset must be **available for immediate sale** in its **present condition**, subject to the usual terms. Although the company had taken the decision to sell the property at 31 March 20X3, the **subsidence** would have meant that a buyer was **unlikely to be found** for the property until the renovations had taken place. Therefore the property **did not qualify as 'held for sale' at 31 March 20X3**.

At 31 March 20X4 the property **had been on the market for nine months** at the price of $10 million. **No buyer** had yet been found. Despite the fact that the **market had deteriorated significantly** the company had **not reduced the price**. The property was eventually sold for $7.5 million on 1 June 20X4. To qualify as being held for sale at the year-end the **market price must be reasonable** in relation to the asset's current fair value. It appears that the market price of $10 million is **not reasonable when compared with the eventual selling price** of $7.5 million, the **offer** of $8.3 million received on 20 April or the **carrying value** of $7 million. Therefore the property **should not be classified as 'held for sale' at 31 March 20X4**.

49 Ashlee

Text reference. Financial instruments are in Chapter 7; provisions in Chapter 9; revenue recognition in Chapter 1; impairment in Chapter 4.

Top tips. This question was a case study which described mistakes or problems occurring in the financial statements of a company. Candidates had to discuss the implications for the financial statements. The case study dealt with going concern, reorganisation provisions, discontinuance, revenue recognition, impairment, financial instruments, and breach of loan covenants. The answer required a discussion of the implications of the events, together with relevant computations. In the answer, it is important to set out the basic principles relating to the event, then quantify (if possible) the impact on the financial statements and, finally, to discuss the implications/solutions to the problem.

Easy marks. There are no obviously easy marks in this question, which does not specify a mark allocation for each item. It is best to assume that marks are allocated equally.

Examiner's comment. The question was quite well-answered but candidates do not seem to be able to apply their knowledge to the case study. Instead, rote knowledge was set out in answers and not application of that knowledge. This is a continuing problem. In addition, the areas covered by this question appear frequently in this paper and yet the standard of answers is not really improving.

	Marks
Introduction	3
Pilot	9
Gibson	8
Ashlee	6
Available	26
Maximum	25

General

The **mistakes** which have been found in the financial statements **must be adjusted** before the financial statements are approved by the directors and published.

Loan covenants have been breached. This means that **the directors should determine whether the company continues to be a going concer**n. If this is not the case, the financial statements for the year ended 31 March 20X5 should not be prepared on a going concern basis. The company appears to have come to an arrangement with the loan creditors and this suggests that **in practice it will be able to carry on trading** at least in the short term. Any **material uncertainties** that **cast doubts on the company's ability to continue as a going concern** should be **disclosed** in the notes to the financial statements, as required by IAS 1 *Presentation of financial statements*.

The fact that the loan covenants have been breached suggests that **the assets of the group may have become impaired**. An **impairment review should be carried out** in accordance with IAS 36 *Impairment of assets* and **any impairment loss should be recognised** in the financial statements for the year ended 31 March 20X5.

Pilot

IAS 37 *Provisions, contingent liabilities and contingent assets* states that **a provision for reorganisation costs cannot be recognised** unless the entity had a **constructive obligation** to carry out the reorganisation at the year end. The **decision** to reorganise Pilot **was not taken until after the year end.** Therefore the reorganisation costs of $4 million **cannot be recognised** in the financial statements for the year ended 31 March 20X5. The financial statements should **disclose** details of the planned reorganisation in the notes as it is a **non-adjusting event** as defined by IAS 10 *Events after the reporting period*.

A major reorganisation indicates that **the assets of Pilot may be impaired** and so an **impairment review is required**. Because the **reorganisation costs** cannot be recognised, these **should not be included in any calculation of recoverable amount**. The **recoverable amount** (value in use) of Pilot is **$82 million** without the reorganisation, this is **less than the carrying value of $85 million** and therefore the company should **recognise an impairment loss of $3 million**. This reduces the carrying value of Pilot's **goodwill**. IAS 36 **prohibits** any **subsequent reversal** of impairment losses **relating to goodwill.**

Gibson

The **decision** to sell Gibson was **made before the year end**. Therefore **IFRS 5 *Non-current assets held for sale and discontinued operations* may apply.** The contract for sale **was being negotiated** at the time of preparation of the financial statements and the sale **appears to be certain**. Therefore Gibson **meets the definition of a 'disposal group'**: a group of assets to be disposed of in a single transaction.

A disposal group is **measured at the lower of its carrying amount and fair value less costs to sell**. The **carrying amount is $450 million** and **fair value less costs to sell is $410 million** ($415 million less selling costs of $5 million) and therefore **an impairment loss of $40 million is recognised**. The loss is **allocated as set out in IAS 36**: first to goodwill, then to the other non-current assets on a pro-rata basis.

Impairment calculation:

	Before impairment $m	Impairment loss $m	After impairment $m
Goodwill	30	(30)	–
Property, plant and equipment at cost	120	(4)	116
Property, plant and equipment at valuation	180	(6)	174
Inventory	100	–	100
Net current assets	20	–	20
	450	(40)	410

(An impairment review would have been required even if there had been no plans to sell Gibson, because of the reorganisation.)

A disposal group is **separately disclosed on the face of the statement of financial position** and **details** of the disposal **are disclosed in the notes** to the financial statements.

Revenue recognition

IAS 18 *Revenue* states that **where properties are sold**, sales **revenue should be recognised when title passes**. Ashlee has followed this policy in previous years and **the change seems questionable**. Therefore the **profit of $10 million on sale should not be recognised** in profit or loss and the properties should **continue to be recognised at their carrying value in the statement of financial position**.

Financial instruments

IAS 39 *Financial instruments: Recognition and measurement* allows some financial assets to be designated as 'at fair value through profit or loss'. The shares are **neither derivatives**, **nor held for trading** and there is **no evidence** that they are **part of a portfolio** of financial assets evaluated on a fair value basis and so they **cannot be classified as 'at fair value through profit or loss'**. Investments in equity instruments that **do not have a quoted market price** in an active market and **whose fair value cannot be reliably measured cannot be designated in this way**.

The shares should be classified as **'available for sale'** and **valued on a fair value basis. Transaction costs are included in the initial measurement**. Therefore the shares are **initially valued at $3.1 million**. At the year end they are **remeasured to $3.75 million as before**. The **gain of $650,000 is recognised in other comprehensive income**, rather than as part of the profit for the year. When the shares are eventually **sold**, the cumulative **gains and losses on remeasurement are reclassified** from other comprehensive income to profit or loss as a reclassification adjustment.

50 Enterprise

Text reference. Segment reporting is in Chapter 18. Related parties are in Chapter 10.

Top tips. This was a case study question, testing accounting standards on segment reporting, related party disclosures, accounting for employee benefits namely pension schemes and impairment of assets.

Easy marks. The segment reporting aspect is easier than the other parts of this question.

Examiner's comment. Answers to the segment reporting part of the question were disappointing, though the examiner considers it an important area. The related parties question was answered better but some candidates adopted an approach whereby all parties in the question were deemed to be related. The discussion of the effect of the sale of a subsidiary on the pension scheme was required but this question produced relatively weak answers.

			Marks
(a)	(i)	Segment reporting	6
	(ii)	Related parties	5
(b)		Pension fund	7
(c)		Impairment	7
		Available/Maximum	25

(a) (i) **Segment reporting**

IFRS 8 *Operating segments* states that an operating segment is a reported **separately** if:

1 It **meets the definition of an operating segment**, ie:

- It engages in business activities from which it may **earn revenues** and **incur expenses**,
- Its operating results are **regularly reviewed by the entity's chief operating decision maker** to make decisions about resources to be allocated to the segment and assess its performance, and
- **Discrete financial information** is available for the segment,

and

2 It exceeds **at least one** of the following quantitative thresholds:

- Reported revenue is **10% or more the combined revenue** of all operating segments (external and intersegment), or
- The absolute amount of its reported profit or loss is **10% or more of the greater of,** in absolute amount, **all operating segments not reporting a loss, and all operating segments reporting a loss**, or
- Its assets are **10% or more of the total assets** of all operating segments.

At 30 April 20X4 **all four** operating segments are **reportable segments,** assuming the segment information is regularly reviewed by the entity's chief operating decision maker. IFRS 8 states that total external revenue reported by operating segments **should be at least 75% of total external revenue** and this **condition will only be met** if at least the **property letting, vehicle sales and one other segment** are reported separately.

After the sale of Carp, the vehicle leasing segment represents only 3% of total revenue, 5% of total segment losses (1/17) and 4% of total assets. Although it falls below the 10% thresholds it **can still be reported as a separate operating segment** provided it meets the operating segment definition and management believes that **information about the segment would be useful** to users of the financial statements. Alternatively the group could consider **amalgamating it with vehicle sales** as long as the segments have **similar economic characteristics**, and the segments are **similar in each of the following respects**:

- The nature of the products and services;
- The nature of the production process;
- The type or class of customer;
- The methods used to distribution the products or provide the services; and
- If applicable, the nature of the regulatory environment.

The radio station may be reported as a separate segment, rather than combining it with the insurance segment, as it passes the 10% threshold test for segment assets (30/239), but only if its separate operating results will be **regularly reviewed by the entity's chief operating decision maker**.

(ii)   **Related parties**

IAS 24 *Related party disclosures* defines a **related party** as a party that **controls**, or **is controlled** by the entity or has **significant influence** or **joint control** over the entity. **Directors** are **key management personnel** and therefore are **related parties**. The director of Carp has leased a number of vehicles from Carp for his family's use and therefore **the transaction must be disclosed** in the financial statements of Carp. However, he is not a director of Enterprise and the directors of Carp and Enterprise are **not related parties simply by virtue of their investment in Carp**. Whether director is a related party of Enterprise (and therefore whether the leasing transaction is disclosed in the financial statements of Enterprise) will depend on **whether the director is key management of the Enterprise group**. In reaching a conclusion the directors of Enterprise will need to consider a number of factors, including whether the director had a significant amount of authority in relation to Enterprise. On balance, the transaction probably need not be disclosed.

Carp was a related party of Enterprise (a subsidiary) for the year ended 30 April 20X4 and therefore **any transactions between the two companies must be disclosed** in the financial statements of **both**.

Under the revised IAS 24 (revised December 2003) a pension scheme is automatically considered a related party. The fact that the directors are Board members is no longer relevant to this.

(b)   **Effect of the sale of Carp on the pension scheme**

There has been a **curtailment** of the scheme. The effect of the sale is to **reduce the net present value of the obligation by $10 million** and a **proportionate amount** of the **unrecognised actuarial gains and unrecognised actuarial losses** is also **eliminated**.

	Before sale $m	Reduction $m	After sale $m
Net present value of obligation	40.0	(10.0)	30.0
Fair value of plan assets	(25.0)	–	(25.0)
	15.0	(10.0)	5.0
Unrecognised actuarial gains	12.0	(3.0)*	9.0
	27.0	(13.0)	14.0

$$* \ 12 \times \frac{10}{40}$$

There is a **gain on sale of $13 million** and the net **pension fund liability is reduced to $14 million**.

(c)   **Nature of impairment reviews**

An impairment review took place **at 30 April 20X2**. Goodwill arising on the acquisition of Fish and Near **cannot be allocated** between the two subsidiaries, so the impairment review takes place in two stages:

	Fish $m	Near $m
Carrying value of net assets	20	5
Recoverable amount	16	8
Impairment	4	Nil

The **impairment loss on Fish is recognised** and then the **two subsidiaries are combined** in order to carry out the impairment review on the goodwill:

	$m
Fish	16
Near	5
	21
Goodwill (30 – 22)	8
	29
Total recoverable amount (16 + 8)	24
Additional impairment loss (goodwill)	5

There are two reasons why a further impairment review needs to be carried out at 30 April 20X4: both Fish and Near are **making losses**; and it now appears that the **original impairment review was inaccurate**.

	Fish $m	Near $m	Goodwill $m	Total $m
Carrying value of net assets (per segment information)	23	8	3	34
Recoverable amount	29	10		39

Neither company is impaired at 30 April 20X4, nor is the goodwill impaired. Because the actual cash flows were better than forecast, it is possible that the original impairment loss may have **reversed**. The carrying value of the assets is compared with depreciated historic cost:

	Fish $m	Near $m
Carrying value of net assets (per segment information)	23	8
Depreciated historic cost	26	8
Reversal	3	–

Under IAS 36 *Impairment of assets*, an impairment loss **can be reversed** where there has been a **favourable change in estimates**. The carrying value of the net assets can be increased up to the **lower of recoverable amount ($29 million) and depreciated historical cost ($26 million)**. Therefore a **gain of $3 million is recognised** in profit or loss. The impairment loss on goodwill is **not reversed** as IAS 36 now **prohibits** this.

51 Carpart

Text reference. Leasing is covered in Chapter 11, revenue recognition in Chapter 1 and property, plant and equipment in Chapter 4.

Top tips. In this question you had to discuss certain transactions of a vehicle part manufacturer, which sells vehicles purchased from manufacturers. Also you had to discuss certain arrangements for the supply of car seats to two local companies. To answer this question you needed knowledge of IAS 17 *Leases*, IFRIC 4 *Determining whether an arrangement contains a lease*, IAS 16 Property, plant and equipment and IAS 18 *Revenue*. You could have answered it without detailed knowledge of IFRIC 4 by applying the *Framework*.

Easy marks. There are no obviously easy marks for any one part, but an advantage of this kind of multi-standard question is that you can gain the first few marks on each issue fairly easily by outlining the basic principles.

Examiner's comment. Candidates found this question difficult. The nature of the risks and rewards of ownership and the principles it embodies is essential to any P2 examination, but candidates often could not apply this principle to the question.

Marking scheme

		Marks
Vehiclex	IAS 18	2
	IAS 11	1
	IAS 16	1
Autoseat	IFRIC 4	3
	Discussion	3
	Finance lease	3
Sale of vehicles	IAS 18	3
	Repurchase four years	2
	Repurchase two years	3
	Demonstration	2
Professional marks		2
	Available	25

(a)   **Vehiclex**

Generally, IAS 18 *Revenue* looks at each transaction **as a whole**. Sometimes, however, transactions are more complicated, and it is necessary to break a transaction down into its **component parts**. For example, a sale may include the transfer of goods and the provision of future servicing, the revenue for which should be deferred over the period the service is performed. The revenue for **each component part needs to be assessed separately** in applying the recognition criteria, and the transaction should be viewed from the customer's perspective, not that of the seller.

In this case, the construction of machinery needs to be considered separately from the sale of the car seats.

Machinery

No revenue should be recognised in respect of the machinery because:

(i)   There is no contract to sell the machinery to Vehiclex.
(ii)   The machinery is for the use of Carpart only, and will not be sold elsewhere.
(iii)   The contract with Vehiclex is not a construction contract under IAS 11 *Construction contracts*.

Accordingly, the machinery **must be accounted for under IAS 16** *Property, plant and equipment.* Assuming that the future economic benefits of the asset will flow to Carpart, and that the cost can be measured reliably, it should be recorded at cost and depreciated. The machinery should be **reviewed for impairment** so that it is not carried above its recoverable amount. For the purposes of an impairment review, the machinery would probably need to be treated as part of a cash generating unit. One indicator of impairment would be if seat orders are not at the minimum required to cover costs.

Sale of car seats

The contract to manufacture and sell seats is a **contract for the sale of goods**, not a service contract or a construction contract. Therefore, following IAS 18, revenue should be **recognised on sale**.

(b)   **Autoseat**

The form and the substance of this transaction are not the same. There is no lease in legal form, but there may be one in substance if the contract conveys the right to use the asset in return for payment.

Guidance on whether this arrangement contains a lease can be found in IFRIC 4 *Determining whether an arrangement contains a lease*. IFRIC 4 looks at the substance of the arrangement, and if the arrangement is, in substance, a lease, then it is accounted for under IAS 17 *Leases*. The following criteria must be met.

(i)   Fulfilment of the arrangement depends upon **a specific asset.**

(ii)   The arrangement conveys a **right to control the use of the underlying asset**. This is the case if any of the following conditions is met:

    (1)   The purchaser in the arrangement has the **ability or right to operate the asset** or direct others to operate the asset (while obtaining more than an insignificant amount of the output of the asset).

    (2)   The purchaser has the **ability or right to control physical access to the asset** (while obtaining more than an insignificant amount of the output of the asset).

    (3)   There is **only a remote possibility that parties other than the purchaser will take more than an insignificant amount of the output of the asset** and the price that the purchaser will pay is neither fixed per unit of output nor equal to the current market price at the time of delivery.

Applying these criteria to the contract with Autoseat, the contract **contains a lease** for the following reasons.

(i)   Fulfilment of the arrangement depends on the construction and use of **a specific asset**, namely the specialised machinery, which can be used only for the production of seats, and only for Autoseat, which sets the level of production and controls quality through the right to reject defective seats.

(ii)   Autoseat has the ability to **control the use of the asset**, and no other party will take more than an insignificant amount of the asset's output. In fact Autoseat is the sole customer.

The fleet of vehicles will therefore be included as property, plant and equipment and **depreciated** over their useful lives in accordance with IAS 16 *Property, plant and equipment*. Because the discount is normal for this type of transaction, the fair value of the vehicles will be measured at their actual purchase price, not the discounted price. **Income from the lease** should be **recognised over the lease term** on a straight line basis.

The **buyback option** may meet the definition of a **financial liability** under IAS 39 *Financial instruments: Recognition and measurement*. If this is the case, the liability should be **measured initially at its fair value** and subsequently at **amortised cost**.

(b)   **Former administrative centre**

The land and the building must be considered separately. The decision to demolish the building was taken **during the year** and this indicates that it was **impaired** at 31 May 20X6. The **recoverable amount** of the building is **zero** and therefore it should be written down to that amount, and the **impairment loss recognised in profit or loss** for the year ended 31 May 20X6.

The **demolition costs** must be **charged** to the income statement **in the period in which they occur** (the year ended 31 May 20X7). **No provision** for remedial environmental work **should be recognised at 31 May 20X6**, because the company **did not have an obligation** to incur costs at that date (the building had not yet been demolished).

Although the company has decided to sell the land, it **does not meet the definition** of an asset **'held for sale'** under IFRS 5 *Non-current assets held for sale and discontinued operations*. In order to be treated as 'held for sale' the land would have to be **actively marketed** and **available for immediate sale in its present condition**. Remedial work must be carried out and the directors have decided to delay the sale to take advantage of rising prices. Therefore **the criteria have clearly not been met**.

The land is measured at **cost** as Tyre uses the cost model of IAS 16. It was acquired many years ago and prices are rising, so it **cannot be impaired**. When the remedial work has been completed, it may be possible to treat the land as an **investment property** using the **fair value model** in IAS 40 *Investment Property*. **Subsequent gains or losses** in value could then be **recognised in profit and loss** each period.

(c)   **Lease premiums**

Because one lease is a **finance lease** and the other is an **operating lease** the two lease premiums must be **treated differently**.

IAS 17 *Leases* states that costs that are **directly attributable to a finance lease** should be **added to the amount recognised as an asset**. Therefore the **amount capitalised** at the start of the finance lease should **include the premium**, which will then be **depreciated** over the lease term or the property's useful life (whichever is the shorter). The premium is also **included in the liability** for future payments under the lease.

The premium paid to enter into the **operating lease** is treated as **part of the lease rentals**. In effect, this is a prepayment of rent. Therefore the premium is **recognised as an expense** over the lease term on a **straight line basis** (unless some other systematic basis is more appropriate).

(d)   **Car accessories**

The main issue here is whether the company has **incurred an obligation** to supply the free car accessories at 31 May 20X6 and therefore whether a **provision** should be recognised in the financial statements.

IAS 37 *Provisions, contingent liabilities and contingent assets* states that a provision should only be recognised if:

- there is a **present obligation** as the result of a **past event**
- an **outflow of resources embodying economic benefits is probable**; and
- a **reliable estimate** of the amount can be made.

The accessories can only be obtained by presenting a coupon when a vehicle is purchased. The **purchase of the car is the obligating event** and an **outflow of resources embodying economic benefits occurs at the**

same time. The company does not have an obligation to provide free goods relating to sales that have not yet happened. **No provision should be recognised.**

The cost of the accessories is included in the **cost of sales**. The **revenue recognised should be the actual amount received** from the customer; the sales price of the car only, not grossed up to include the value of the accessories.

53 Ghorse

Text reference. Group re-organisations are covered in Chapter 14; deferred tax in Chapter 6; impairment in Chapter 4 and leases in Chapter 10.

Top tips. This is a 'mixed bag' question, dealing with a group re-organisation, deferred tax and revaluation, impairment and re-classification of a lease. These are all linked in with a calculation of the effect on return on capital employed. In Part (a) there is no need to spend time giving the IFRS 5 criteria for classification as held for sale, since we are told in the question that these criteria have been met.

Easy marks. None of this question is easy except for the calculation of ROCE; however, because it split equally across four topics, it is a good question to do. Do the parts you feel sure about, but have a go at all parts as the first few marks are the easiest to pick up.

Examiner's comments. Part (a) of the question was not well answered as many candidates did not realise that there was a disposal group as the two manufacturing units were being sold in a single transaction. Part (b) was quite well answered although many did not realise that the resultant balance was a deferred tax asset with the recognition issues that this represents. In Part (c), many candidates calculated the 'value in use' of the equipment but failed to apply the principles which often had correctly been described earlier in the answer. The answers to Part (d) were quite good with candidates realising that the operating lease was now a finance lease but several candidates then could not outline the accounting treatment of an operating lease. The adjustments to ROCE were poorly done; in fact many candidates did not even attempt this part of the question. The issues required a degree of thought and understanding of the impact on the financial statements of the adjustments and ROCE. For example there were instances (deferred tax) where profit before tax was not affected but the capital employed was affected. The professional marks were awarded for analysing the impact of the information, drawing conclusions and considering the implications for ROCE.

(a)   The criteria in IFRS 5 *Non-current assets held for sale and discontinued operations* have been met for Cee and Gee. As the assets are to be disposed of in a single transaction, Cee and Gee together are deemed to be a **disposal group** under IFRS 5.

The disposal group as a whole is **measured on the basis required for non-current assets held for sale**. Any impairment loss reduces the carrying amount of the non-current assets in the disposal group, the loss being allocated in the order required by IAS 36 *Impairment of assets*. Before the manufacturing units are classified as held for sale, impairment is tested for on an individual cash generating unit basis. Once classified as held for sale, the impairment testing is done on a **disposal group basis**.

Impact on performance ratios

Three key performance ratios have been calculated as follows:

	Local GAAP	IFRS
Return on capital employed	$\dfrac{130}{520} \times 100\% = 25\%$	$\dfrac{151.7}{607.45} \times 100\% = 24.9\%$
Gearing ratio	$\dfrac{40}{480} \times 100\% = 8.3\%$	$\dfrac{120.9}{486.55} \times 100\% = 24.9\%$
Price earnings ratio	$\dfrac{\$6}{\$0.5} = 12$	$\dfrac{\$6}{\$0.558} = 10.8$

There is very **little effect on return on capital employed**. **Profit has increased** by $21.7 million, mainly because the operating lease rentals have been excluded and the gain on revaluation has been included. However, **capital employed has also increased**, due to the recognition of the finance lease liability.

Gearing has increased significantly, mainly because of the recognition of the finance lease liability.

As a consequence of the increase in profits, **earnings per share has risen** and therefore the **price earnings ratio has fallen.**

Appendix: impact of the change to IFRS on profit, taxation and the statement of financial position

1   *Effect on profit*

	$m	$m
Profit before interest and tax under local GAAP		130.00
Add back operating lease rentals		10.00
Less: depreciation on building (86 ÷ 20)		(4.30)
Effect of increase in residual value: add back excess depreciation (W2)		1.00
Investment property: revaluation gain (5 + 10)		15.00
Profit before interest and tax under IFRS		151.70
Interest:		
Under local GAAP	5.0	
Add interest on finance leases (W1)	5.2	
		(10.20)
Taxation:		
Under local GAAP	25.00	
Add increase in charge under IFRS (Appendix 2)	4.95	
		(29.95)
Profit after interest and tax under IFRS		111.55

Earnings per share under IFRS: $\dfrac{111.58}{200} = 55.8c$

2   *Effect on taxation*

	Current tax $m	Deferred tax $m	Total $m
Operating lease rentals (increase in profit)	10		
Interest expense on finance lease (decrease in profit)	(5.2)		
Tax deductable depreciation on plant (deincrease in profit)	(4.3)	1	
Gain on investment property (increase in profit)		15	
	0.5	16	16.5
Increase in tax charge at 30%	0.15	4.8	4.95

3 *Effect on statement of financial position amounts*

	Equity $m	Non-current liabilities $m	Net assets $m
At 31 May 20X5 under local GAAP	480.00	40.0	520.0
Lease (W1):			
Liability		86.0	86.0
Operating lease rentals	10.00	(10.0)	
Depreciation	(4.30)		(4.3)
Interest	(5.20)	5.2	
Current liability		(5.1)	(5.1)
Plant: depreciation (W2)	1.00		1.0
Investment property: gain	10.00		10.0
Tax (Appendix 2)	(4.95)	4.8	(0.15)
At 31 May 20X5 under IFRS	486.55	120.9	607.45

Workings

1 *Finance lease*

	$m
Net present value of future lease commitments	86.0
Interest at 6%	5.2
Repayment	(10.0)
Total liability at 31 May 20X5	81.2
Interest at 6%	4.9
Repayment	(10.0)
Total liability at 31 May 20X6	76.1

Therefore $5.1 million (10 – 4.9) is included in current liabilities.

2 *Excess depreciation*

	$m
Cost	20
Depreciation for year ended 31 May 20X4 (20 – 4 ÷ 8)	(2)
Carrying value at 1 June 20X4	18
Residual value at 1 June 20X4	(11)
Depreciable amount	7
Annual depreciation charge (7 ÷ 7)	1

55 Fair values

Text reference. Current issues are covered in Chapter 19.

Top tips. This question required candidates to discuss the problems relating to fair value measurement and related disclosures, and the relevance of fair values as opposed to historical cost. The Discussion Paper was not specifically mentioned in the question, so you would not have needed to know it in detail, but it was a very good starting point for your answer, and we have included it in ours.

Easy marks. Part (b) is fairly open ended, and credit will be given for valid points if you back up your arguments.

Examiner's comment. The uses of judgment, independent verification of fair values, and problems with markets were explained by candidates quite well. However, many candidates gave disappointing answers when contrasting the relevance of fair value as opposed to historical cost. Candidates would perform better in questions such as this if more reference was made to The Framework. Relevance and reliability are concepts that can be discussed regularly in this context.

			Marks
(a)	Reliability and measurement		10
	Disclosures		3
		Available/Maximum	13
(b)	Market values		3
	Value received		2
	Entity specific		4
	Matching		2
	Pre-acquisition costs		2
	Reliable/relevant		3
		Available	16
		Maximum	12
		Available	29
		Maximum	25

(a) **Reliability and measurement**

There are a number of **definitions** of fair value. For example, it could be defined as an **'exit price'**, that is a selling price, or more specifically the price that would be received to sell an asset or paid to transfer a liability. The use of an exit price assumes that a transaction to sell the asset or transfer the liability occurs in the **principal market** for such an asset or, failing that, the most **advantageous market**. **Different approaches may give different exit prices**, for example, IAS 39 *Financial instruments: recognition and measurement* requires an entity to use the most advantageous active market to fair value assets and liabilities, whereas IAS 41 *Agriculture* requires the most relevant market, which will vary depending on the nature of the biological asset. As well as these differences, current replacement cost and various valuation techniques may be used to determine exit value.

Current IFRS, for example IFRS 3 *Business combinations,* **does not confine its definition to an exit price**. IFRS 3 defines fair value as 'the amount for which an asset could be exchanged, or a liability settled, between knowledgeable, willing parties in an arm's length transaction.' This is neutral between buyer and seller, so fair value is neither an exit price nor an entry (buying) price.

Current IFRS is **not entirely consistent** in treatment of fair value. For example, inventories that are impaired are measured at net realisable value using selling price as a measure of fair value, while inventories acquired in a business combination are measured at expected selling price less costs to completion and a reasonable profit margin. Similarly, intangible assets can only be revalued to fair value under IAS 38 where there is an active market price, whereas IFRS 3 allows their fair value in a business combination to be measured on an arm's length basis where there is no active market (in order to separate them from goodwill). Such inconsistencies, the IASB believes, are unsatisfactory and that there should be a **single source of guidance** for all fair value measurements required by IFRS. For this reason it issued a **Discussion Paper** *Fair value measurement* in November 2006. This uses the recent US standard SFAS 157 as a starting point for ironing out some of the inconsistencies.

SFAS 157 establishes a three-level hierarchy for the inputs that valuation techniques use to measure fair value:

Level 1   Quoted prices (unadjusted) in active markets for identical assets or liabilities that the reporting entity has the ability to access at the measurement date

Level 2   Inputs other than quoted prices included within Level 1 that are observable for the asset or liability, either directly or indirectly, eg quoted prices for similar assets in active markets or for identical or similar assets in non active markets or use of quoted interest rates for valuation purposes

Level 3 Unobservable inputs for the asset or liability, ie using the entity's own assumptions about market exit value.

In order to establish this single set of guidance there will be a **need for changes to other IFRSs** which will change how fair value is measured in some standards and how the requirements are interpreted and applied. This will take some time. In the meantime entities are faced with a variety of options for fair value measurement, and this means that **reliability may be an issue**. Specifically:

(i)   Markets are not all liquid and transparent.

(ii)   Many assets and liabilities do not have an active market, and methods for estimating their value are more subjective.

(iii)   Management must exercise judgement in the valuation process, and may not be entirely objective in doing so.

(iv)   Because fair value, in the absence of an active market, represents an estimate, additional disclosures are needed to explain and justify the estimates. These disclosures may themselves be subjective.

(v)   Independent verification of fair value estimates is difficult for all the above reasons.

(b)   **Fair value measurement or historical cost**

The debate between historical cost accounting and fair value measurement centres on **reliability versus relevance**. Very broadly speaking, fair values are perceived as relevant but not reliable. Historical cost accounting is perceived as reliable but not relevant.

Fair value can be said to be more relevant than historical cost because it is based on current market values rather than a value that is in some cases many years out of date. Fair values for an entity's assets, it is argued, will be give a closer approximation to the value of the entity as a whole, and are more useful to a decision maker or an investor.

If there is **more standardisation in fair valuing** – the Discussion Paper mentioned above is a step towards this – then in the future, if not immediately, fair value measurement will have the advantage of being both relevant and reliable.

Historical cost accounting traditionally matches cost and revenue. The objective has been to match the cost of the asset with the revenue it earns over its useful life. It has a number of **disadvantages.**

(i)   If the historical cost differs from its fair value on initial recognition, the **matching process in future periods becomes arbitrary**.

(ii)   Non-current asset **values are unrealistic**, particularly those of property.

(iii)   **Holding gains on inventory are included in profit.** During a period of high inflation the **monetary value of inventories held may increase significantly** while they are being processed. The conventions of historical cost accounting lead to the **realised part of this holding gain** (known as *inventory appreciation*) being **included** in **profit** for the year.

(iv)   **Comparisons over time are unrealistic**, because they do not take account of inflation.

(v)   **Costs incurred before an asset is recognised are not capitalised**. This is particularly true of development expenditure, and means that the historical cost does not represent the fair value of the consideration given to create the asset.

However, historical cost has a number of **advantages** over fair values, mainly as regards reliability.

(i)   It is **easy to understand**.
(ii)   It is grounded in **real transaction amounts**, and is therefore **objective** and objectively verifiable.
(iii)   There is **less scope for manipulation**.

Until there is **more uniformity and objectivity in fair valuing**, it is likely that historical cost accounting will continue to be used.

(iv)   IFRSs allow **choice** in many cases, which leads to subjectivity.

(v)   Selection of **valuation method** requires judgement, and many IFRS leave the choice of method open. This affects areas such as pensions, impairment, intangible assets acquired in business combinations, onerous contracts and share-based payment.

Financial reporting infrastructure

As well as sound management judgement, implementation of IFRS requires a sound financial reporting infrastructure. Key aspects of this include the following.

(i)   A **robust regulatory framework**. For IFRS to be successful, they must be rigorously enforced.

(ii)   **Trained and qualified staff**. Many preparers of financial statements will have been trained in local GAAP and not be familiar with the principles underlying IFRS, let alone the detail. Some professional bodies provide conversion qualifications – for example, the ACCA's Diploma in International Financial Reporting – but the availability of such qualifications and courses may vary from country to country.

(iii)   **Availability and transparency of market information**. This is particularly important in the determination of fair values, which are such a key component of many IFRSs.

(iv)   **High standards of corporate governance and audit**. This is all the more important in the transition period, especially where there is resistance to change.

Overall, there are significant advantages to the widespread adoption of IFRS, but if the transition is to go well, there must be a realistic assessment of potential challenges.

57 IFRS and SMEs

Text reference. Current issues are covered in Chapter 19; specialised entities in Chapter 20.

Top tips. This question required candidates to discuss the need to develop a set of IFRSs especially for small to medium-sized enterprises (SMEs). Do not be tempted to waffle or repeat yourself. Since this question was set, the IASB has published an IFRS for SMEs.

Easy marks. This is a knowledge-based question, so all marks are easy if you know it.

Examiner's comment. This question was generally well answered and the topic will feature in future exams.

Marking scheme

			Marks
(a)	Subjective		7
(b)	Purpose		3
	Definition of entity		4
	How to modify		6
	Items not dealt with		3
	Full IFRS		3
		Available	26
		Maximum	25

(a)   Originally, International Accounting Standards (IASs) issued by the International Accounting Standards Committee (IASC) were **designed to be suitable for all types of entity**, including small and medium entities (SMEs) and entities in developing countries. Large listed entities based their financial statements on national GAAP which normally **automatically complied** with those IASs due to choices permitted in the past. In recent years, IASs and IFRSs have become **increasingly complex and prescriptive**. They are now designed primarily to meet the information needs of **institutional investors in large listed entities** and their advisers. In many countries, IFRSs are **used mainly by listed companies**.

There is a case for continued use of full IFRSs by SMEs. It can be argued that the **main objectives** of general purpose financial statements **are the same for all types of company**, of whatever size. Compliance with full IFRSs ensures that the financial statements of SMEs **present their financial performance fairly** and gives them greater **credibility**. It also ensures their **comparability** with those of other entities.

There were also many arguments for developing a separate set of standards for SMEs, and these have been taken into account (see below) Full IFRSs have become very **detailed and onerous** to follow. The **cost** of complying may **exceed the benefits** to the entity and the users of its financial statements. At present, an entity cannot describe their financial statements as IFRS financial statements unless they have complied with every single requirement.

SME financial statements are normally **used by a relatively small number of people**. Often, the **investors** are also **involved in day to day management**. The **main external users** of SME financial statements tend to be **lenders and the tax authorities**, rather than institutional investors and their advisers. These users have **different information needs** from those of investors. For these users, the accounting treatments and the detailed disclosures required may sometimes **obscure the picture** given by the financial statements. In some cases, **different, or more detailed information may be needed.** For example, related party transactions are often very significant in the context of SME activities and expanded disclosure may be appropriate.

The *IFRS for Small and Medium-Sized Entities* (IFRS for SMEs) was published in July 2009, and therefore falls to be examinable in 2010. It is only 230 pages, and has **simplifications** that reflect the needs of users of SMEs' financial statements and cost-benefit considerations. It is designed to facilitate financial reporting by small and medium-sized entities in a number of ways:

(a)   It provides significantly **less guidance** than full IFRS.

(b)   Many of the **principles** for recognising and measuring assets, liabilities, income and expenses in full IFRSs are **simplified**.

(c)   Where full IFRSs allow accounting policy choices, the IFRS for SMEs **allows only the easier** option.

(d)   **Topics not relevant** to SMEs are **omitted**.

(e)   Significantly **fewer disclosures** are required.

(f)   The standard has been written in **clear language** that can easily be translated.

(b)   **Issues in developing IFRSs for SMEs**

(i)   **The purpose of the standards and type of entity to which they should apply**

The main objective of accounting standards for SMEs is that they should provide the users of SME financial statements with **relevant, reliable and understandable information**. The standards should be **suitable for SMEs globally** and should **reduce the financial reporting burden** on SMEs. It is generally accepted that SME standards should be built on the **same conceptual framework** as full IFRSs.

It could also be argued that SME standards should **allow for easy transition** to full IFRS as some SMEs will become listed entities or need to change for other reasons. This would mean that SME standards **could not be separately developed from first principles** (as many would prefer) but instead would be a **modified version of full IFRS**. Some argue that ease of transition is not important as relatively few SMEs will need to change to IFRS in practice.

The **definition** of an SME could be based on **size** or on **public accountability** or on a combination of the two. There are several disadvantages of basing the definition on size limits alone. Size limits are **arbitrary** and **different limits are likely to be appropriate in different countries.** Most people believe that SMEs are **not simply smaller versions of listed entities**, but differ from them in more fundamental ways.

The most important way in which SMEs differ from other entities is that they are **not usually publicly accountable**. Using this as the basis of a definition raises other issues: which types of company are publicly accountable? Obviously the **definition would include** companies which have **issued shares** or other instruments **to the public**. It has been suggested that this category should also include companies **holding assets in a fiduciary capacity** (such as banks or providers of pensions), companies that provide **essential public services** (utility companies) and any entity with **economic significance in its country** (which in turn would have to be defined). This would mean that SME standards could potentially be used by a very large number of entities covering a very large range in terms of size.

There is a case for allowing **national standard setters** to **impose size limits** or otherwise **restrict** the types of entities that could use SME standards. There is also a case for allowing national standard setters to **define 'publicly accountable'** in a way that is appropriate for their particular jurisdiction.

The IFRS for SMEs published in July 2009 does not use size or quantitative thresholds, but qualification is determined by public accountability. It is up to legislative and regulatory authorities and standard-setters in individual jurisdictions to decide who may or must use the IFRS for SMEs.

(ii)   **How existing standards could be modified to meet the needs of SMEs**

The starting point for modifying existing standards should be the most likely **users** of SME financial statements and their **information needs**. SME financial statements are mainly used by **lenders** and **potential lenders, the tax authorities** and **suppliers**. In addition, the **owners and management** (who are often the same people) may be dependent on the information in the financial statements. SME financial statements must **meet the needs** of their users, but the **costs** of providing the information **should not outweigh the benefits.**

There is considerable scope for **simplifying disclosure and presentation requirements**. Many of the existing requirements, for example those related to financial instruments, discontinued operations and earnings per share, are **not really relevant** to the users of SME financial statements. In any case, lenders and potential lenders are normally able to ask for additional information (including forecasts) if they need it.

The SME standards are likely to be a **simplified version of existing standards**, using only those principles that are likely to be relevant to SMEs. The IASB has proposed that the **recognition and measurement principles** in full IFRSs should **remain unchanged** unless there is a good argument for modifying them. Clearly the SME standards will have to be sufficiently rigorous to produce information that is relevant and reliable. However, many believe that there is a **case for simplifying** at least some of the more **complicated measurement requirements** and that it will be difficult to reduce the financial reporting burden placed on SMEs otherwise.

(iii)   **How items not dealt with by SME standards should be treated**

Because SME standards are **unlikely to cover all possible transactions** and events, there will be occasions where an SME has to **account for an item that the standards do not deal with**. There are several alternatives.

(a)   The entity is **required to apply the relevant full IFRS**, while still following SME standards otherwise.

(b)   Management can **use its judgement** to develop an accounting policy based on the relevant full IFRS, or the *Framework*, or other IFRSs for SMEs and the other sources of potential guidance cited in IAS 8.

(c)   The entity could continue to follow its **existing practice**.

In theory, the **first alternative is the most appropriate** as this is the most likely to result in relevant, reliable and comparable information. The argument against it is that SMEs may then effectively have to comply with **two sets of standards**.

Another issue is whether an SME should be able to **opt to comply** with a specific full IFRS or IFRSs while still following SME standards otherwise. There is an argument that SMEs should be able to, for example, make the additional disclosures required by a full IFRS if there is a good reason to do so. The argument against optional reversion to full IFRSs is that it would lead to **lack of comparability**. There would also need to be safeguards against entities attempting to 'pick and mix' accounting standards.

58 Seejoy

(a) **Sale and leaseback of football stadium**

The proposal is for a sale and leaseback which be treated as a **finance lease**. The accounting treatment for such a transaction is dealt with by IAS 17 *Leases*. As the **substance of the transaction is a financing transaction** this would not be dealt with as a sale so the **stadium would remain on the statement of financial position as an item of property, plant and equipment** and be depreciated but it will now be valued at the sales value of $15 million. The **excess of the sales value over the carrying value** will be recognised as **deferred income** and credited to the income statement over the period of the finance lease.

When the sale takes place on 1 January 20X7 the double entry will be:

		$m	$m
DEBIT	Cash	15	
CREDIT	Properties, plant and equipment		12
CREDIT	Deferred income		3

On this same date the finance lease will also be recognised:

DEBIT	Properties, plant and equipment	15	
CREDIT	Finance lease payables		15

In the financial statements for the year ending 31 December 20X7 the effects will be as follows:

INCOME STATEMENT

	$'000
Depreciation of stadium ($15m/20 years)	(750)
Finance charge (($15m − $1.2m) × 5.6%)	(773)
Deferred income ($3m/20 years)	150

STATEMENT OF FINANCIAL POSITION

	$'000
Properties, plant and equipment	
Stadium ($15m − $0.75m)	14,250
Current liabilities	
Rental payment	1,200
Non-current liabilities	
Finance lease payables ($15m − ($1.2m × 2) + $0.773m)	13,373
Deferred income ($3m − $0.15m)	2,850

There is little doubt that this form of sale and leaseback will improve the cash flow of the club as $15 million will be received on 1 January 20X7. However, the required accounting treatment by IAS 17 will mean that the sale and leaseback has **significant and detrimental affects** on the financial statements. The **profit** shown in the income statement is likely to **decrease** as the finance charge on the lease significantly outweighs the deferred income credit to the income statement. If the $15 million receipt is not used to pay off existing long term loans then the overall **gearing** of the club will **increase** as the finance lease payables are included on the statement of financial position.

It might be worth investigating the possibility of a **sale and leaseback** agreement which **results in an operating lease rather** than a finance lease. In such a leaseback, as the sale is at fair value, the **profit can be recognised immediately** in profit or loss and the stadium will be deemed to have been sold and removed from the statement of financial position. There will also be no finance leases payables as liabilities on the statement of financial position. The downside however is that any increase in the residual value of the stadium would be lost.

(b) **Player registrations**

The player registrations are **capitalised** by the club as intangible non-current assets under IAS 38 *Intangible assets*. This is an **acceptable** accounting treatment; the transfer fees classify as assets as it is probable that expected future benefits will flow to the club as a result of the contracts and the cost can be measured reliably at the amount of the transfer fees actually paid.

According to IAS 38, intangible non-current assets which are capitalised should be **amortised over their useful life**. Therefore on the face of it claiming a useful life of 10 years might be acceptable. However IAS 38 recommends that amortisation reflects the useful life of the assets and the pattern of economic benefits. Therefore the proposal to amortise the transfer fees over a period of **10 years is not acceptable as the contracts are only for 5 years and 3 years**.

In terms of **cash flow** this proposal regarding the amortisation would have **no effect** at all. It would simply be a bookkeeping entry which would reduce the amortisation charge to the income statement.

The potential payment to the two players' former clubs of $5 million would **not** appear to be **probable** due to the current form of the club. Therefore under IAS 37 *Provisions, contingent liabilities and contingent assets* no provision would be recognised for this amount. However, the possible payment does fall within the IAS 37 definition of a contingent liability which is a possible obligation arising out of past events whose existence will be confirmed only by the occurrence or non-occurrence of one or more uncertain future events not wholly within the control of the entity. Therefore as a contingent liability the amount and details would be **disclosed** in the notes to the financial statements.

(c) **Issue of bond**

What the club is proposing here is known as **securitisation**. This particular type of securitisation is often called 'future flow' securitisation. In some forms of securitisation a special purpose vehicle is set up to administer the income stream or assets involved in which case there is potentially an off balance sheet effect. However, in this case there is **no special purpose vehicle** and therefore the only accounting issue is how the bond is to be treated under IAS 39 *Financial instruments: recognition and measurement*.

The bond will be recorded as a **financial liability** and will either be classified as a financial liability at fair value through profit or loss or as a financial liability measured at amortised cost. To be a financial liability at fair value through profit or loss the bond must either be held for trading or be part of a group of financial assets, financial liabilities, or both, that are managed on a fair value basis. It is unlikely that this is the case, therefore the bond will be **classified as measured at amortised cost**.

The bond will be **initially recognised at its fair value** which is the amount for which the liability can be settled between knowledgeable and willing parties in an arm's length transaction. Fair value at inception will normally be the amount of the consideration received for the instrument. Subsequent to initial recognition the instrument will be measured using amortised cost or fair value. In this case the club does not wish to use the valuation model therefore the bond will be measured at amortised cost.

When the bond is issued on 1 January 20X7 it will be measured at the value of the consideration received of $47.5 million ($50m × 95%).

At 31 December 20X7 the valuation will be:

	$m
Initial value	47.5
Interest at 7.7%	3.7
Cash paid	(6.0)
Value in statement of financial position	45.2

In terms of cash flow the issue of the bond will **bring $47.5 million into the club**. The bond is effectively secured on the income stream of the future corporate hospitality sales and season tickets receipts and due to this security the coupon rate of interest is lower than the market rates. The money is to be used to improve the grounds which is an appropriate use of long-term funds. However, the proposal to pay the **short term costs of the players' wages** out of these long term funds is a **misuse of long-term capital** which is likely to lead to future liquidity problems.

(d) **Player trading**

In accounting terms there is no issue to deal with at 31 December 20X6 as the potential sale of the players will not fall to be classified as 'held for sale' non-current assets under IFRS 5 *Non-current assets held for sale and discontinued operations*. In order for these players to classify as held for sale they would need to be available for immediate sale which they are not.

However, the club must consider carrying out an **impairment review** of these assets at 31 December 20X6. If the players are sold for the anticipated figure of $16 million then the following loss will be incurred:

	$m
Carrying value at 1 May 20X7	
A Steel ($20m − ($4m + 4/12 × $4m)	14.7
R Aldo ($15m − ($10 + 4/12 × $5)	3.3
	18.0
Potential sales value	16.0
Potential loss	2.0

This potential loss of $2 million on the sale of these players may be evidence of impairment and a review should be carried out at 31 December 20X6 and the **players' value written down to recoverable amount** if necessary.

In terms of cash flow, the sale of the players would **provide much needed cash**. However, as the club is performing poorly currently the sale of the two best players **may lead to even worse performance** which is likely to have a detrimental affect on ticket sales and the liquidity of the club in future.

59 Norman

		Marks
(a)	Identification of segments	2
	Definition	2
	Reporting information	2
	Normal applicability	5
		11
(b)	Sale of businesses	4
	Vouchers	4
	Grant income	4
	Quality of discussion	2
		14
	Maximum	25

(a) **Determining operating segments**

IFRS 8 *Operating segments* states that an operating segment is a reported **separately** if:

(i) It **meets the definition of an operating segment**, ie:

(1) It engages in business activities from which it may **earn revenues** and **incur expenses**,

(2) Its operating results are **regularly reviewed by the entity's chief operating decision maker** to make decisions about resources to be allocated to the segment and assess its performance, and

(3) **Discrete financial information** is available for the segment,

and

(ii) It exceeds **at least one** of the following quantitative thresholds:

(1) Reported revenue is **10% or more the combined revenue** of all operating segments (external and intersegment), or

(2) The absolute amount of its reported profit or loss is **10% or more of the greater of**, in absolute amount, **all operating segments not reporting a loss, and all operating segments reporting a loss**, or

(3) Its assets are **10% or more of the total assets** of all operating segments.

At least **75% of total external revenue** must be reported by operating segments. Where this is not the case, additional segments must be identified (even if they do not meet the 10% thresholds).

Two or more operating segments **below** the thresholds may be aggregated to produce a reportable segment if the segments have similar economic characteristics, and the segments are similar in a **majority** of the following aggregation criteria:

(1) The nature of the products and services
(2) The nature of the production process
(3) The type or class of customer for their products or services
(4) The methods used to distribute their products or provide their services
(5) If applicable, the nature of the regulatory environment

Operating segments that do not meet **any of the quantitative thresholds** may be reported separately if management believes that information about the segment would be useful to users of the financial statements.

For Norman, **the thresholds are as follows.**

(i)   Combined revenue is $1,010 million, so 10% is $101 million.
(ii) Combined reported profit is $165 million, so 10% is $16.5 million.
(iii) Combined reported loss is $10 million, so 10% is $1 million.
(iv) Total assets are $3,100 million, so 10% is $310 million.

The **South East Asia segment** meets the criteria, passing all three tests. Its combined revenue is $302 million; its reported profit is $60 million, and its assets are $800 million.

The **European segment** also meets the criteria, but only marginally. Its reported revenue, at $203 million is greater than 10% of combined revenue, and only one of the tests must be satisfied. However, its loss of $10 million is less than the greater of 10% of combined profit and 10% of combined loss, so it fails this test. It also fails the assets test, as its assets, at $300 million are less than 10% of combined assets ($310 million).

IFRS 8 requires further that at least 75% of total external revenue must be reported by operating segments. Currently, only 50% is so reported. Additional operating segments (the 'other regions') must be identified until this 75% threshold is reached.

IFRS 8 may result in a **change** to the way Norman's operating segments are reported, depending on how segments were previously identified.

(b)   **Sale of hotel complex**

The issue here is one of **revenue recognition**, and the accounting treatment is governed by IAS 18 *Revenue*. It can be argued in some cases where property is sold that the seller, by continuing to be involved, has **not transferred the risks and rewards of ownership**. In such cases, the sale is not genuine, but is often in substance a **financing arrangement**. IAS 18 requires that the substance of a transaction is determined by looking at the transaction as a whole. If two or more transactions are linked, they should be treated as one transaction to better reflect the commercial substance.

Norman continues to operate and manage the hotel complex, receiving the bulk (75%) of the profits, and the residual interest reverts back to Norman; effectively, Norman retains the risks and rewards of ownership. Conquest does not bear any risk: its minimum annual income is guaranteed at $15m. The sale should not be recognised. In substance it is a financing transaction. The **proceeds** should be treated as a **loan**, and the payment of **profits** as **interest**.

Discount vouchers

The treatment of the vouchers is governed by IAS 18 *Revenue* and by IFRIC 13 *Customer loyalty programmes*. The principles of the standard and the IFRIC require that

(i)   The voucher should be accounted for as a **separate component** of the sale
(ii) The amount of the proceeds allocated to such vouchers should be measured at **fair value**.

The vouchers are issued as part of the sale of the room and redeemable against future bookings. The substance of the transaction is that **the customer is purchasing both a room and a voucher**. This means that revenue should be reported as the amount of consideration received less the fair value of the voucher. In determining the fair value, the following considerations apply:

(i)   The value to the holder, not the seller
(ii) The discount the customer obtains
(iii) The percentage of vouchers that will be redeemed
(iv) The time value of money

Vouchers worth $20 million are eligible for discount as at 31 May 20X8. However, based on past experience, it is likely that only one in five vouchers will be redeemed, that is vouchers worth $4 million. Room sales are $300 million, **so effectively, the company has made sales worth $(300m + 4m) = $304 million in exchange for $300 million**. The proceeds need to be split proportionally, that is the discount of $4 million needs to be allocated between the room sales and the vouchers, as follows:

Room sales: $\dfrac{300}{304} \times \$300m = \$296.1m$

Vouchers (balance) = $3.9m

The $3.9 million attributable to the vouchers is only recognised when the obligations are fulfilled, that is when the vouchers are redeemed.

Government grant

The applicable standard relating to this transaction is IAS 20 *Accounting for government grants and disclosure of government assistance.* The principle behind the standard is that of accruals or matching: the **grant received must be matched with the related costs**.

Government grants are assistance by government in the form of transfers of resources to an entity in return for past or future compliance with certain conditions relating to the operating activities of the entity. There are two main types of grants:

(i)   **Grants related to assets**: grants whose primary condition is that an entity qualifying for them should purchase, construct or otherwise acquire long-term assets. Subsidiary conditions may also be attached restricting the type or location of the assets or the periods during which they are to be acquired or held. In this case the condition relates to the cost of building the hotels, which must be $500m or more.

(ii)   **Grants related to income**: These are government grants other than grants related to assets.

It is not always easy to match costs and revenues if the terms of the grant are not explicit about the expense to which the grant is meant to contribute. In the case of Norman, the intention of the grant is to create employment in the area, and the building of hotels is for that purpose. However, on balance, the grant can be seen as **capital based,** because the amount is not tied into payroll expenditure or numbers of jobs created, and the repayment clause is related to the cost of the asset (building of hotels). Accordingly, IAS 20 allows two possible approaches:

(i)   Match the grant against the depreciation of the hotels using a deferred income approach.
(i)   Deduct the grant from the carrying value of the asset.

Mock exams

ACCA

Paper P2

Corporate Reporting (International)

Mock Examination 1

Question Paper	
Time allowed	
Reading and planning	**15 minutes**
Writing	**3 hours**
This paper is divided into two sections	
Section A This **ONE** question is compulsory and **MUST** be attempted	
Section B **TWO** questions **ONLY** to be answered	

DO NOT OPEN THIS PAPER UNTIL YOU ARE READY TO START UNDER EXAMINATION CONDITIONS

SECTION A – This ONE question is compulsory and MUST be attempted

Question 1

(a) Jay, a public limited company, has acquired the following shareholdings in Gee and Hem, both public limited companies.

Date of Acquisition	Holding acquired	Fair value of net assets	Purchase Consideration
		$m	$m
Gee			
1 June 20X3	30%	40	15
1 June 20X4	50%	50	30
Hem			
1 June 20X4	25%	32	12

The following statements of financial position relate to Jay, Gee and Hem at 31 May 20X5.

	Jay	Gee	Hem
	$m	$m	$m
Property, plant and equipment	300	40	30
Investment in Gee	52		
Investment in Hem	22		
Current assets	100	20	15
Total assets	474	60	45
Share capital of $1	100	10	6
Share premium account	50	20	14
Revaluation surplus	15		
Retained earnings	139	16	10
Total equity	304	46	30
Non-current liabilities	60	4	3
Current liabilities	110	10	12
Total equity and liabilities	474	60	45

The following information is relevant to the preparation of the group financial statements of the Jay Group.

(i) Gee and Hem have not issued any new share capital since the acquisition of the shareholdings by Jay. The excess of the fair value of the net assets of Gee and Hem over their carrying amounts at the dates of acquisition is due to an increase in the value of Gee's non-depreciable land of $10 million at 1 June 20X3 and a further increase of $4 million at 1 June 20X4, and Hem's non-depreciable land of $6 million at 1 June 20X4. There has been no change in the value of non-depreciable land since 1 June 20X4. Before obtaining control of Gee, Jay did not have significant influence over Gee but has significant influence over Hem. Jay has accounted for the investment in Gee at market value with changes in value being recorded in profit or loss. The market price of the shares of Gee at 31 May 20X5 had risen to $6.50 per share as there was speculation regarding a takeover bid.

(ii) On 1 June 20X4, Jay sold goods costing $13 million to Gee for $19 million. Gee has used the goods in constructing a machine which began service on 1 December 20X4. Additionally, on 31 May 20X5, Jay purchased a portfolio of investments from Hem at a cost of $10 million on which Hem had made a profit of $2 million. These investments have been incorrectly included in Jay's statement of financial position under the heading 'Investment in Hem'.

(iii) Jay sold some machinery with a carrying value of $5 million on 28 February 20X5 for $8 million. The terms of the contract, which was legally binding from 28 February 20X5, was that the purchaser would pay a non-refundable initial deposit of $2 million followed by two instalments of $3·5 million (including total interest of $1 million) payable on 31 May 20X5 and 20X6. The purchaser was in financial difficulties at the year end and subsequently went into liquidation on 10 June 20X5. No payment is expected from the liquidator. The deposit had been received on 28 February 20X5 but the first instalment was not received. The terms of the agreement were such that Jay maintained title to the machinery until the first instalment was paid. The machinery was still physically held by Jay and the machinery had been treated as sold in the financial statements. The amount outstanding of $6 million is included in current assets and no interest has been accrued in the financial statements.

(iv) Group policy on depreciation of plant and equipment is that depreciation of 10% is charged on a reducing balance basis.

(v) There are no intra-group amounts outstanding at 31 May 20X5.

(vi) It is the group's policy to value the non-controlling interest on acquisition at fair value. The fair value at the non-controlling interest in Gee on 1 July 20X4 was $12m.

Required

Prepare the consolidated statement of financial position of the Jay Group as at 31 May 20X5 in accordance with International Financial Reporting Standards.

(Candidates should calculate figures to one decimal place of $ million.) **(29 marks)**

(b) In the year ended 31 May 20X6 Jay purchased goods from a foreign supplier for 8 million euros on 28 February 20X6. At 31 May 20X6, the trade payable was still outstanding and the goods were still held by Jay. Similarly Jay has sold goods to a foreign customer for 4 million euros on 28 February 20X6 and it received payment for the goods in euros on 31 May 20X6. additionally Jay had purchased an investment property on 1 June 20X5 for 28 million euros. At 31 May 20X6, the investment property had a fair value of 24 million euros. The company uses the fair value model in accounting for investment properties.

Jay would like advice on how to treat this transaction in the financial statements for the year ended 31 May 20X6. Its functional and presentation currency is the dollar.

Exchange rates	*Euro: $*	*Average rate (Euro: $) for year to*
1 June 20X5	1.4	
28 February 20X6	1.6	
31 May 20X6	1.3	1.5

(10 marks)

(c) Jay has a reputation for responsible corporate behaviour and sees the workforce as the key factor in the profitable growth of the business. The company is also keen to provide detailed disclosures relating to environmental matters and sustainability.

Discuss what matters should be disclosed in Jay's annual report in relation to the nature of corporate citizenship, in order that there might be a better assessment of the performance of the company. **(11 marks)**

(Total = 50 marks)

Answers

DO NOT TURN THIS PAGE UNTIL YOU HAVE
COMPLETED THE MOCK EXAM

A PLAN OF ATTACK

If this were the real Corporate Reporting exam and you had been told to turn over and begin, what would be going through your mind?

The answer may be 'I can't do this to save my life'! You've spent most of your study time on groups and current issues (because that's what your tutor/BPP Study Text told you to do), plus a selection of other topics, and you're really not sure that you know enough. The good news is that this may get you through. The first question, in Section A, is very likely to be on groups. In Section B you have to choose three out of four questions, and at least one of those is likely to be on current issues – a new IFRS, ED or discussion paper. So there's no need to panic. First spend **five minutes or so looking at the paper**, and develop a **plan of attack**.

Looking through the paper

The compulsory question in Section A is, as a case study on groups, in this case a complex group. You also have a fairly easy bit on corporate citizenship. In **Section B** you have **four questions on a variety of topics:**

- Question 2 requires you to adjust and redraft financial statements.
- Question 3 requires a discussion about issues concerning a change in a accounting policy.
- Question 4 is about the implications of a move to IFRS.

You **only have to answer three out of these four questions.** You don't have to pick your optional questions right now, but this brief overview should have convinced you that you have enough **choice** and variety to have a respectable go at Section B. So let's go back to the compulsory question in Section A.

Compulsory question

Question 1 requires you to **prepare a consolidated statement of financial position for a complex group**. This question looks daunting, partly because of the piecemeal acquisition aspects. However, there are easy marks to be gained for basic consolidation techniques such as intragroup trading. Part (c) is a good source of easy marks too.

Optional questions

Deciding between the optional questions is obviously a personal matter – it depends how you have spent your study time. However, here are a few pointers.

Question 2 is about a specialised entity. However, it uses knowledge from standards you have covered, so you should be able to find a way in.

Question 3 has easy marks for knowledge of IAS 8, and looks worse than it is.

Question 4 is fairly straight forward if you know the topic. In our opinion, everyone should do this question.

Allocating your time

BPP's advice is always allocate your time **according to the marks for the question** in total and for the parts of the question. But **use common sense.** If you're doing Question 1 but have no idea about fair value, jot down something (anything!) and move onto Part (b), where most of the easy marks are to be gained.

Forget about it!

And don't worry if you found the paper difficult. More than likely other candidates will too. The paper is marked fairly leniently and always has a good pass rate. If this were the real thing, you would need to **forget** the exam the minute you left the exam hall and **think about the next one**. Or, if it's the last one, **celebrate**!

Question 1

Marking scheme

		Marks
(a)	Property, plant and equipment	4
	Goodwill	5
	Associate	4
	Investment	1
	Current assets	1
	Share capital	1
	Revaluation surplus	1
	Retained earnings	7
	Non-controlling interest	
	Non-current liabilities	4
	Current liabilities	
(b)	Inventory, goods sold	10
(c)	Corporate citizenship:	
	Corporate governance	3
	Ethics	3
	Employee reports	3
	Environment	3
	Maximum	50

(a)   JAY GROUP
       CONSOLIDATED STATEMENT OF FINANCIAL POSITION AT 31 MAY 20X5

	$m
Assets	
Property, plant and equipment (W9) 300 + 40 + 14 + (5 – 0.1) – 5.7 (W9)	353.2
Goodwill (W2)	10.0
Investment in associate (W3)	13.0
Investment (10 – 0.5) (W6)	9.5
Current assets (120 – 6) (W7)	114.0
	499.7
Equity and liabilities	
Share capital	100.0
Share premium	50.0
Revaluation surplus (W8)	15.0
Retained earnings (W4)	136.7
	301.7
Non-controlling interest (W5)	14.0
	315.7
Non-current liabilities	64.0
Current liabilities	120.0
	499.7

Workings

1   *Group structure*

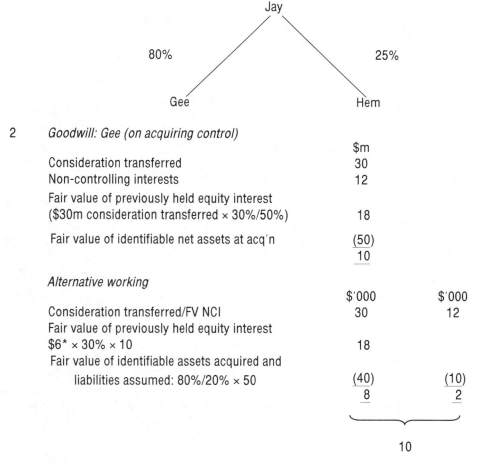

2   *Goodwill: Gee (on acquiring control)*

	$m
Consideration transferred	30
Non-controlling interests	12
Fair value of previously held equity interest ($30m consideration transferred × 30%/50%)	18
Fair value of identifiable net assets at acq'n	(50)
	10

Alternative working

	$'000	$'000
Consideration transferred/FV NCI	30	12
Fair value of previously held equity interest $6* × 30% × 10	18	
Fair value of identifiable assets acquired and liabilities assumed: 80%/20% × 50	(40)	(10)
	8	2

10

*At 1 June 20X4, the share price of Gee was $\dfrac{\$30m}{50\% \times \$10m}$ = $6

3   Investment in associate

	$m
Cost of investment	12
Share of profit for year ended 31 May 20X5 (W5)	1
	13

4   Retained earnings

	Jay $m	Gee $m	Hem $m
Per question	139.00	16	10
Profit on derecognition of investment *	3.00		
PUP on machinery (W6)	(5.70)		
PUP on investment (associate)	(0.5)		
Impairment loss on receivable	(1.10)		
Pre-acquisition (NA excl FV adjustments, SC and SP):			
50 – 14 – 10 – 20		(6)	
32 – 6 – 6 – 14			(6)
		10	4
Group share			
Gee: 80% × 10	8.0		
Hem: 25% × 4	1		
Less fair value gain recognised in Jay's separate			
FS: 52 – 30 – 15	(7.0)		
	136.7		

		$m
* Profit on derecognition of 30% investment:		
Fair value at date control obtained (W2)		18
Cost		(15)
		3

5   Non-controlling interests

	$m
NCI at acquisition (date of control)	12
NCI share of post acquisition retained earnings ((W4) 10 × 20%)	2
	14

Alternative working

	$m
Net assets at reporting date	46
Plus fair value adjustment (W9)	14
	60
NCI share (20%)	12
Add goodwill attributable to NCI	2
	14

6   Provision for unrealised profit

Sales from Jay to Gee

	$m
Profit (19 – 13)	6.0
Less depreciation on machine constructed with goods: (6 × 10% × 6/12)	(0.3)
	5.7

Sale of investments from Hem to Jay

	$m
Group share of profit (25% × 2)	0.5

7   *Impairment of receivable*

	$m
Cost of machinery	8.0
Less deposit received	(2.0)
Bad debt written off	6.0
Less net book value of machine (included in tangible assets) (W9)	(4.9)
Impairment loss deducted from retained earnings	1.1

8   *Revaluation surplus*

	$m
Jay	15.00
Gee: at date control acquired (80% × 14 – 14)	0.00
	15.00

9   *Property, plant and equipment*

	$m	$m
Jay		300.0
Gee		40.0
Fair value adjustment (land)		14.0
Machine		
Cost	5.0	
Less depreciation (3/12 × 10% × 5)	(0.1)	
		4.9
Provision for unrealised profit (W6)		(5.7)
		353.2

Note that Jay has retained title to the machinery because the first instalment has not been paid.

(b)   The initial transaction of the purchase of goods from the foreign supplier would be **recorded in the ledger accounts at $5 million (€8/1.6)**. Therefore both the purchase and the payables balance would be recorded at this amount. At the **year end** the payables balance is **restated to the closing rate** but the **inventories remain at $5 million**. Therefore the payable is restated to $6.2 million (€8m/1.3) and an **exchange loss** is taken to the income statement of $1.2 million ($6.2 – 5m).

On the **sale**, the original transaction is recorded at $2.5 million (€4m/1.6) as both a sale and a receivable. When payment is made the amount actually received is $3.1 million (€4m/1.3) and an **exchange gain** is recognised in profit or loss of $0.6 million ($3.1 – 2.5m).

When the investment property was first purchased it should have been recognised in the statement of financial position at $20 million (€28m/1.4). At the year end the investment property has fallen in value to €24 million and the exchange rate has changed to 1.3. Therefore at 31 May 20X6 the property would be valued at $18.5 million (€24m/1.3).

The **fall in value** of $1.5 million ($20 – 18.5m) is recognised in **profit or loss**. The loss is a mixture of a fall in value of the property and a gain due to the exchange rate movement. However, as the investment property is a **non-monetary asset the foreign currency element is not recognised separately**.

(c)   **Nature of corporate citizenship**

Increasingly businesses are expected to be **socially responsible as well as profitable**. Strategic decisions by businesses, particularly global businesses nearly always have wider social consequences. It could be argued, as Henry Mintzburg does, that a company produces two outputs: goods and services, and the social consequences of its activities, such as pollution.

One major development in the area of corporate citizenship is the **environmental report.** While this is not a legal requirement, a large number of major companies produce them. Worldwide there are around 20 award schemes for environmental reporting, notably the ACCA's.

Jay might be advised to adopt the guidelines on sustainability given in the **Global Reporting Initiative**. These guidelines cover a number of areas (economic, environmental and social). The GRI specifies key performance indicators for each area. For environmental reporting, the indicators are:

(i)   Energy
(ii)   Water
(iii)   Biodiversity
(iv)   Emissions
(v)   Energy and waste
(vi)   Products and services
(vii)   Compliance
(viii) Transport

Another environmental issue which the company could consider is **emission levels** from factories. Many companies now include details of this in their environmental report.

The other main aspect of corporate citizenship where Jay scores highly is in its **treatment of its workforce**. The company sees the workforce as the key factor in the growth of its business. The car industry had a reputation in the past for **restrictive practices,** and the annual report could usefully discuss the extent to which these have been eliminated.

Employees of a businesses are **stakeholders** in that business, along with shareholders and customers. A company wishing to demonstrate good corporate citizenship will therefore be concerned with **employee welfare**. Accordingly, the annual report might usefully contain information on details of working hours, industrial accidents and sickness of employees.

In conclusion, it can be seen that the annual report can, and should go **far beyond the financial statements** and traditional ratio analysis.

Question 2

Text reference. Specialised entities are covered in Chapter 20.

Top tips. This question dealt with issues pertinent to a specialised industry, namely the entertainment industry. The examiner has said that specialised industry questions will not require specific accounting knowledge of a specialised industry, but will instead test the application of standard knowledge to unusual scenarios. Here the question tested revenue recognition, property, plant, and equipment (PPE), leasing, and investments in other entities. Part (a) dealt with revenue recognition issues such as reliability of measurement, probability of flow of economic benefits, etc. Part (b) dealt with PPE and the lease of land and buildings. Parts (c) and (d) dealt with investments in other entities, the calculation of a gain/loss on the disposal of an investment, and the accounting under IAS 27, 28 and 39.

Easy marks. Part (c) is very straightforward, with a simple gain on disposal calculation and status of investment comments able to earn easy marks.

Examiner's comment. This question, in particular Parts (a) (c) and (d), was quite well answered. In Part (b), candidates did not realise that derecognition of a lease liability must be assessed under IAS 39. Leases are financial instruments which normally are accounted for under IAS 17, but reference to IAS 39 is made when determining whether the lease is to be taken off the balance sheet.

			Marks
(a)	Revenue recognition		5
(b)	Studios and offices		10
(c)	Film distribution company		7
(d)	Playtime		4
		Available	26
		Maximum	25

(a) **Recognition of income from the film**

IAS 18 *Revenue* states that **revenue** on a service contract may **only be recognised** when the outcome of the transaction can be **measured reliably**. If **certain criteria** are met, the stage of completion method may be used, that is revenue should be recognised by reference to the stage of completion of the transaction at the reporting date. The criteria are as follows.

(i)   The amount of revenue can be measured reliably.
(ii)   It is probable that economic benefits will flow to the seller.
(iii)   The stage of completion at the reporting date can be measured reliably.
(iv)   The costs incurred, or costs to be incurred, can be measured reliably.

If these criteria are not met, revenue arising from the rendering of services should be recognised **only to the extent that that expenses recognised are recoverable**.

In the case of Router, the **fee for making the film of $5m can** be measured reliably, has been paid and **can therefore be recognised** and matched against the costs incurred of $4m. However, the **anticipated future income of $400,000 should not be recognised**. The $100,000 will only be received when the film is shown, which is expected to be four times. However, the revenue should not be recognised before then because there is a **'performance' condition**, namely the substantial editing that is required before the film can be shown.

The **costs of editing need to be assessed** and matched against any revenue in future years. However, costs incurred to date **cannot be carried forward** and matched against future income unless they meet the IAS 38 definition of an intangible asset, and this does not appear to be the case.

(b) **Land and buildings**

IAS 16 *Property, plant and equipment* allows assets to be revalued, provided all assets within one class are treated in the same way. While the Router's buildings (office buildings and film studios) have different characteristics and could be **classified differently under IAS 16**, to change from the revaluation model to the cost model for the film studios involves a change in accounting policy, and may conflict with IAS 8 *Accounting policies, changes in accounting estimates and errors*.

The **general rule** under IAS 8 is that an entity should apply accounting policies **consistently** from year to year. Accounting policies may be changed only in two specific cases:

(i)   There has been a **new accounting standard** or interpretation or changes to an accounting standard.
(ii)   The change results in the financial statements providing **more reliable and more relevant information** about the effects of transactions, other events or conditions on the entity's financial position, financial performance or cash flows.

The first criterion does not apply here, and Routers will have to ascertain whether the second is appropriate. If the 'cost model' is adopted, the following **adjustments** will need to be made:

(i)   Calculate depreciated historical cost at the beginning of the period.
(ii)   Adjust the opening balance on the revaluation surplus and any other component of equity affected.
(iii)   Present comparative amounts, as if the accounting policy had always been applied.

Currently the theme park land and buildings are classified as a **finance lease**. This is unusual. Land is normally classified as an **operating lease** because it is considered to have an **indefinite life**, the exception being when ownership passes to the lessee during the lease term. The policy is not appropriate and **adjustments** need to be made:

(i)   Separate the land out from the lease.
(ii)   Remove the asset and liability relating to the land from the statement of financial position.
(iii)   Treat the lease payments as rentals in the income statement
(iv)   Make a prior period adjustment to reflect this change.

The **buildings may continue to be treated as property, plant and equipment**, and no adjustment needs to be made to the carrying value. However, in future years the carrying value will be **depreciated over a shorter**

period, reflecting the decrease in the remaining useful life of the building, following the **change in the lease terms** on 31 May 20X7.

The change in the lease term will also require the lease liability to be **assessed for derecognition** under IAS 39 *Financial instruments: recognition and measurement.* This would be appropriate if the new lease terms are **substantially different** from the current terms, but that **does not appear to the case here**. The change appears to be a **modification, not an extinguishment**. After separating out the land, the lease liability will then be amended further by **deducting the one off payment of $10m** from the carrying amount, together with any transaction costs. The **liability will be remeasured** (taking any difference on remeasurement to profit or loss) to the present value of revised future cash flows discounted using the original effective interest rate.

(c)   **Sale of 15% holding in Wirerles**

Wireless is **currently an associate** and is accounted for under the equity method in accordance with IAS 28 *Investments in associates.* The reduction from a 25% holding to a 10% holding and the loss of significant influence means that, **after the sale**, it must be accounted for in **accordance with IAS 39**. Router must recognise in profit or loss a gain on disposal, calculated as follows:

	$m
Fair value of consideration received	40
Fair value of interest retained	23
Equity valuation at disposal:	
Net assets (200 × 25%)	(50)
Goodwill	(5)
	8

The gain to be recognised is therefore $8m.

At 1 January 20X7, after the disposal, the 10% financial asset remaining is held at its fair value of $23m.

Under IAS 39, the remaining investment will be classified as **an available for sale financial asset or a financial asset at fair value through profit and loss**. In either case the asset will be **recorded at fair value**. If it is classified as an available for sale financial asset, changes in fair value will be reported in other comprehensive income. If it is classified at fair value through profit and loss, changes will be reported in profit or loss. (It can only be so classified if the IAS 39 criteria are met.)

At 31 May 20X7, the asset will be remeasured and a **gain** of $26m – $23m = $3m **reported in other comprehensive income or in profit or loss.**

(d)   **Investment in Playtime**

Although Router owns 60% of the shares of Playtime, which would normally give it control, the warrants held by the competitor company, currently exercisable, mean that this **control is in doubt.** IAS 27 *Consolidated and separate financial statements* states that warrants with the potential to give the holder voting power or reduce another party's voting power should be taken into account when assessing control. The **competitor would gain control** over Playtime if it exercised the warrants, and should therefore **consolidate Playtime**. Playtime cannot be controlled by both Router and the competitor, so it is probably more appropriate for **Router** to account for its investment in Playtime **under IAS 28, or even IAS 39** if significant influence is reduced. All circumstances that affect voting rights, and not just share ownership, will need to be considered in reaching a decision.

Question 3

Marking scheme

				Marks
(a)	IASB explanation		4	
	Cost centres		6	
		Available	10	
		Maximum		9
(b)	Hardware		3	
	Revenue recognition		3	
		Available/maximum		6
(c)	Provisions	Available	8	
		Maximum		7
(d)	Going concern	Available/maximum		3
	Report		2	
		Available	29	
		Maximum		25

REPORT

To: Directors of Gear Software
From:
Subject: Implications of various transactions for the financial statements for the year ended 31 May 20X3
Date: June 20X3

As requested, I explain below the implications of several transactions for the financial statements.

(a) **Cost centres**

The relevant standard here is IAS 8 *Accounting policies, changes in accounting estimates and errors.*

It is necessary to distinguish between changes in accounting policy and changes in accounting estimates. A change to an accounting policy involves a change in the way in which an item is recognised, measured or presented.

The indirect overhead costs are directly attributable to the two cost centres and are included in the inventory valuation in the statement of financial position. The only change has been a change to the way in which the costs are allocated. There have been **no changes to the way in which they are recognised, measured or presented**. This change is **not a change in accounting policy**, but a **change in an accounting estimate**.

Direct labour and overhead costs were previously carried forward as work in progress and included in the statement of financial position as part of inventories. They are now written off to the income statement as they are incurred. There has been a change in the way in which these costs are recognised and presented and therefore there is a **change in accounting policy**.

Overhead costs relating to the sale of computer games were previously included in cost of sales and are now included in distribution costs. There has been a **change in the way in which these costs are presented** and again, there has been a **change in accounting policy**.

IAS 8 states that a change in accounting policy is **only allowed if** the change is **required by a standard** or an interpretation or if it results in the financial statements providing **more reliable and more relevant information** about the effects of transactions, other events or conditions on the entity's financial position, performance or cash flows. Both accounting policy changes are voluntary, so there **must be a clear case** for them on the grounds that they do result in more useful information.

The effect of the change in accounting estimate is **included in the income statement for the current period (ie, recognised prospectively).**

IAS 8 requires the effect of changes in accounting policy to be recognised **retrospectively**, by making a **prior period adjustment**. The opening balance of retained earnings is adjusted and comparative figures are restated. IAS 8 also requires the company to **disclose the effect** of the changes, including the reason why the change provides improved information and the effect of the adjustment on the financial statements for the current period (in detail) and for each prior period presented. Therefore the company is required to disclose the effect of the write off of the development costs on the current year's income statement. It is unlikely that it is impracticable to do so.

(b)   **Computer hardware and revenue on contracts**

IAS 23 *Borrowing costs* **now requires the capitalisation of interest** relating to qualifying non-current assets. The computer hardware is **likely to meet the definition of a qualifying asset** as it requires a substantial amount of time to bring it to a saleable condition. There is a change to the way in which the interest is recognised and presented and therefore there is a **further change in accounting policy** following the transitional provisions of IAS 23 (revised 2007).

The change in the method of depreciation is a **change in an accounting estimate**, rather than a change in accounting policy. However, there has also been a **change in the way in which depreciation is presented** in the financial statements and this *is* a **change in accounting policy**, following the translational provisions of IAS 23 (revised 2007).

The requirements of IAS 8 will again apply. The accounting policy changes must be **applied retrospectively** and the effect of the changes **must be disclosed**.

It is proposed to change the way in which contract revenue is recognised. The company's current policy of recognising revenue as the contract progresses is acceptable under IAS 11 *Construction Contracts* and IAS 18 *Revenue*. However, **IASs 11 and 18 may not specifically apply to this situation.** IAS 8 states that where there is **no specifically applicable standard**, management should **select a policy** that results in information that is **relevant to the needs of users and reliable**. Management should **refer to standards dealing with similar issues** and to the **IASB *Framework***, but it may also consider **accepted industry practice** (revenue is recognised when the product is shipped to customers). The advantage of adopting this policy is that revenue would increase and this is particularly important given that significant provisions may have to be recognised (see below). Provided that there is no conflict between the industry practice and IASs 11 and 18, the company **should change to the new policy**. Again, the **accounting and disclosure requirements of IAS 8 apply**.

(c)   **Provisions**

IAS 37 *Provisions, contingent liabilities and contingent assets* states that a provision should only be recognised if:

(i)   There is a **present obligation** as a result of a **past event**, and

(ii)   It is **probable** (more likely than not) that an **outflow of resources** embodying economic benefits will be required to settle the obligation, and

(iii) A **reliable estimate** can be made of the **amount** of the obligation.

In the case of the disputed invoice, the company's solicitors apparently do not believe that any further sums will be payable. On this basis, **no provision should be recognised**, but the company has a **contingent liability**. Information about the contingent liability should be **disclosed** in the financial statements, including the estimated financial effects and any uncertainties relating to the amount or timing of any outflow.

ACCA

Paper P2

Corporate Reporting (International)

Mock Examination 2

Question Paper	
Time allowed	
Reading and planning	**15 minutes**
Writing	**3 hours**
This paper is divided into two sections	
Section A	This ONE question is compulsory and MUST be attempted
Section B	TWO questions ONLY to be answered

DO NOT OPEN THIS PAPER UNTIL YOU ARE READY TO START UNDER EXAMINATION CONDITIONS

SECTION A – This ONE question is compulsory and MUST be attempted

Question 1

Lateral, a public limited company, acquired two subsidiary companies, Think and Plank, both public limited companies. The details of the acquisitions are as follows:

Subsidiary	Date of acquisition	Retained earnings at acquisition $m	Share capital acquired $1 shares m	Fair value of net assets at acquisition $m
Think	1 November 20X3	150	200	400
Plank	1 November 20X3	210	300	800

The draft statements of financial position as at 31 October 20X5 are:

	Lateral $m	Think $m	Plank $m
Assets			
Non-current assets			
Property, plant and equipment	700	390	780
Investment in subsidiaries:			
Think	380		
Plank	340		
Held to maturity investments	30	–	–
	1,450	390	780
Current assets			
Inventories	200	185	90
Trade receivables	170	80	100
Cash and cash equivalents	40	30	50
	410	295	240
Non-current assets classified as held for sale		15	
		310	
Total assets	1,860	700	1,020
Equity and Liabilities:			
Share capital – shares of $1	400	250	500
Retained earnings	850	280	290
Total equity	1,250	530	790
Non-current liabilities	250	60	80
Current liabilities	360	110	150
Total liabilities	610	170	230
Total equity and liabilities	1,860	700	1,020

The following information is relevant to the preparation of the group financial statements.

(i)   There have been no new issues of shares in the group since 1 November 20X3 and the fair value adjustments have not been included in the subsidiaries' financial records.

(ii)   Any increase in the fair values of the net assets over their carrying values at acquisition is attributable to plant and equipment. Plant and equipment is depreciated at 20% per annum on the reducing balance basis.

(iii) Think sold plant and equipment to Lateral on 12 November 20X5. The transaction was completed at an agreed price of $15 million after selling costs. The transaction complies with the conditions in IFRS 5 *Non-current assets held for sale and discontinued operations* for disclosure as assets 'held for sale'. The plant and equipment had been valued at 'fair value less costs to sell' in the individual accounts of Think. At 1

November 20X4, this plant and equipment had a carrying value of $10 million and no depreciation on these assets has been charged for the year ended 31 October 20X5.

(iv) Lateral had purchased a debt instrument with five years remaining to maturity on 1 November 20X3. The purchase price and fair value was $30 million on that date. The instrument will be repaid in five years time at an amount of $37·5 million. The instrument carries fixed interest of 4·7% per annum on the principal of $37·5 million and has an effective interest rate of 10% per annum. The fixed interest has been received and accounted for but no accounting entry has been made other than the recognition of the original purchase price of the instrument.

(v) Goodwill arising on the acquisition of the subsidiaries was impairment tested on 31 October 20X4 and 31 October 20X5 in accordance with IAS 36 *Impairment of assets*. There was no impairment of goodwill on the acquisition of Think or Plank.

(vi) On 31 October 20X5 Lateral sold 100 million shares in Plank for $180 million. Lateral still maintains significant influence over Plank after the disposal of the shares. The fair value of the remaining investment was $400m at that date. The receipt of the sale proceeds has been recorded in the cash book and as a reduction in the carrying value of the cost of the investment in the subsidiary.

(vii) It is the group's policy to value the non-controlling interest at its proportionate share of the fair value of the subsidiary's identifiable net assets.

Required

(a) Calculate the gain or loss that would be recorded in the group financial statement on the sale of the shares in Plank. **(4 marks)**

(b) Prepare a consolidated statement of financial position as at 31 October 20X5 for the Lateral Group in accordance with International Financial Reporting Standards. **(24 marks)**

(c) In the year ended 31 October 20X6, Lateral entered into a contract to purchase plant and equipment from a foreign supplier on 30 June 20X7. The purchase price is 4 million euros. A non-refundable deposit of 1 million euros was paid on signing the contract on 31 July 20X6 with the balance of 3 million euros payable on 30 June 20X7. Lateral was uncertain as to whether to purchase a 3 million euro bond on 31 July 20X6 which will not mature until 30 June 20Y0, or to enter into a forward contract on the same date to purchase 3 million euros for a fixed price of $2 million on 30 June 20X7 and to designate the forward contract as a cash flow hedge of the purchase commitment. The bond carries interest at 4% per annum, payable on 30 June 20X7. Current market rates are 4% per annum. The company chose to purchase the bond with a view to selling it on 30 June 20X7 in order to purchase the plant and equipment. The bond is not to be classified as a cash flow hedge but at fair value through profit and loss.

Lateral would like advice as to whether it made the correct decision and as to the accounting treatment of the items for 20X6 and 20X7. The company's functional and presentational currency is the dollar.

(12 marks)

Exchange rates	Euro: $	Average rate (Euro: $) for year to
31 July 20X6	1.6	
31 October 20X6	1.3	1.5

(d) Lateral discloses the following information relating to employees in its financial statements.

Its full commitment to equal opportunities
Its investment in the training of staff
The number of employees injured at work each year.

The company wishes to enhance disclosure in these areas, but is unsure as to what the benefits would be. The directors are particularly concerned that the disclosures on management of the workforce (human capital management) has no current value to the stakeholders of the company.

Discuss the general nature of the current information disclosed by companies concerning 'human capital management' and how the link between the company performance and its employees could be made more visible. **(10 marks)**

(Total = 50 marks)

SECTION B – TWO questions ONLY to be attempted

Question 2

Barking, an unlisted company, operates in the house building and commercial property investment development sector. The sector has seen an upturn in activity during recent years and the directors have been considering future plans with a view to determining their impact on the financial statements for the financial year to 30 November 20X4.

(a) Barking wishes to obtain a stock exchange listing in the year to 30 November 20X4. It is to be acquired by Ash, a significantly smaller listed company in a share for share exchange whereby Barking will receive sufficient voting shares of Ash to control the new group. Due to the relative values of the companies, Barking will become the majority shareholder with 80% of the enlarged capital of Ash. The executive management of the new group will be that of Barking.

As part of the purchase consideration, Ash will issue zero dividend preference shares of $1 to the shareholders of Barking on 30 June 20X4. These will be redeemed on 1 January 20X5 at $1·10 per share. Additionally Ash will issue convertible interest free loan notes. The loan notes are unlikely to be repaid on 30 November 20X5 (the redemption date) as the conversion terms are very favourable. The management of Ash have excluded the redemption of the loan notes from their cash flow projections. The loan notes are to be included in long term liabilities in Ash's statement of financial position. As part of the business combination Ash will change its name to Barking inc. **(9 marks)**

(b) The acquisition will also have other planned effects on the company. Barking operates a defined benefit pension scheme. On acquisition the scheme will be frozen and replaced by a group defined contribution scheme, and as a result no additional benefits in the old scheme will accrue to the employees. Ash's employees are also in a defined benefit scheme which has been classified as a multi-employer plan but it is currently impossible to identify its share of the underlying assets and liabilities in the scheme. After acquisition, Ash's employees will be transferred to the group's defined contribution scheme, with the previous scheme being frozen. **(5 marks)**

(c) As a result of the acquisition the company will change the way in which it recognises sales of residential properties. It used to treat such properties as sold when the building work was substantially complete, defined as being when the roof and internal walls had been completed. The new policy will be to recognise a sale when a refundable deposit for the sale of the property has been received and the building work is physically complete. Legal costs incurred on the sale of the property are currently capitalised and shown as current assets until the sale of the property has occurred. Further, it has been decided by the directors that as at 30 November 20X4, the financial year end, some properties held as trading properties of both companies would be moved from the trading portfolio to the investment portfolio of the holding company, and carried at fair value. **(7 marks)**

(d) The directors intend to carry out an impairment review as at 30 November 20X4 in order to ascertain whether the carrying amount of goodwill and other non-current assets can be supported by their value in use. The plan is to produce cash flow projections up to 20Y4 with an average discount rate of 15% being used in the calculations. The ten year period is to be used as it reflects fairly the long term nature of the assets being assessed. Any subsequent impairment loss is to be charged against the income statement. **(4 marks)**

Required

Draft a report to the directors of Barking, setting out the financial reporting implications of the above plans for the financial statements for the year to 30 November 20X4. **(Total = 25 marks)**

Question 3

The Gow Group, a public limited company, and Glass, a public limited company, have agreed to create a new entity, York, a limited liability company on 31 October 20X6. the companies' line of business is the generation, distribution, and supply of energy. Gow supplies electricity and Glass supplies gas to customers. Each company has agreed to subscribe net assets for a 50% share in the equity capital of York. York is to issue 30 million ordinary shares of $1. There was no written agreement signed by Gow and Glass but the minutes of the meeting where the creation of the new company was discussed have been formally approved by both companies. Each company provides equal numbers of directors to the Board of Directors. The net assets of York were initially shown at amounts agreed between Gow and Glass, but their values are to be adjusted so that the carrying amounts at 31 October 20X6 are based on International Financial Reporting Standards.

Gow had contributed the following assets to the new company in exchange for its share of the equity:

	$m
Cash	1
Trade receivables – Race	7
Intangible assets – contract with Race	3
Property, plant and equipment	9
	20

The above assets form a cash generated unit (an electricity power station) in its own right. The unit provided power to a single customer, Race. On 31 October 20X6 Race went into administration and the contract to provide power to Race was cancelled. On 1 December 20X6, the administrators of the customer provisionally agreed to pay a final settlement figure of $5 million on 31 October 20X7, including any compensation for the loss of the contract. Gow expects York will receive 80% of the provisional amount. On hearing of the cancelled contract, an offer was received for the power station of $16 million. York would be required to pay the disposal costs estimated at $1 million.

The power station has an estimated remaining useful life of four years at 31 October 20X6. it has been agreed with the government that it will be dismantled on 31 October 20Y0. The cost at 31 October 20Y0 of dismantling the power station is estimated to be $5 million.

The directors of Gow and York are currently in the final stages of negotiating a contract to supply electricity to another customer. As a result the future net cash inflows (undiscounted) expected to arise from the cash generating unit (power station) are as follows:

	$m
31 October 20X7	6
31 October 20X8	7
31 October 20X9	8
31 October 20Y0	8
	29

The dismantling cost has not been provided for, and future cash flows are discounted at 6 per cent by the companies.

Glass had agreed to contribute the following net assets to the new company in exchange for its share of the equity:

	$m
Cash	10
Intangible asset	2
Inventory at cost	6
Property at carrying value	4
Lease receivable	1
Lease payable	(3)
	20

The property contributed by Glass is held on a 10 year finance lease which was entered into on 31 October 20X0. The property is being depreciated over the life of the lease on the straight line basis. As from 31 October 20X6, the terms of the lease have been changed and the lease will be terminated early on 31 October 20X8 in exchange for a payment of $1 million on 31 October 20X6 and a further two annual payments of $600,000. The first annual

A PLAN OF ATTACK

Managing your nerves

As you turn the pages to start this exam a number of thoughts are likely to cross your mind. At best, examinations cause anxiety so it is important to stay focused on your task for the next three hours! Developing an awareness of what is going on emotionally within you may help you manage your nerves. Remember, you are unlikely to banish the flow of adrenaline, but the key is to harness it to help you work steadily and quickly through your answers.

Working through this mock exam will help you develop the exam stamina you will need to keep going for three hours.

Managing your time

Planning and time management are two of the key skills which complement the technical knowledge you need to succeed. To keep yourself on time, do not be afraid to jot down your target completion times for each question, perhaps next to the title of the question on the paper.

Focusing on scoring marks

When completing written answers, remember to communicate the critical points, which represent marks, and avoid padding and waffle. Sometimes it is possible to analyse a long sentence into more than one point. Always try to maximise the mark potential of what you write.

As you read through the questions, jot down on the question paper, any points you think you might forget. There is nothing more upsetting than coming out of an exam having forgotten to write a point you knew!

Also remember you can only score marks for what is on paper; you must write down enough to help the examiner to give you marks!

Structure and signpost your answers

To help you answer the examiner's requirements, highlight as you read through the paper the key words and phrases in the examiner's requirements.

Also, where possible try to use headings and subheadings, to give a logical and easy-to-follow structure to your response. A well structured and signposted answer is more likely to convince the examiner that you know your subject.

Your approach

This paper has two sections. The first section contains one question which is compulsory. The second has three questions and you must answer two of them.

You have a choice.

- Read through and answer the Section A question before moving on to Section B
- Go through Section B and select the two questions you will attempt. Then go back and answer the question in Section A first
- Select the two questions in Section B, answer them and then go back to Section A

You will have fifteen minutes before the start of the exam to go through the questions you are going to do.

Time spent at the start of each question confirming the requirements and producing a plan for the answers is time well spent.

Question selection

When selecting the two questions from Section B make sure that you read through all of the requirements. It is painful to answer part (a) of a question and then realise that parts (b) and (c) are beyond you, by then it is too late to change your mind and do another question.

When reviewing the requirements look at how many marks have been allocated to each part. This will give you an idea of how detailed your answer must be.

Generally, you need to be aware of your strengths and weaknesses and select accordingly.

Doing the exam

Actually doing the exam is a personal experience. There is not a single *right way*. As long as you submit complete answers to question 1 and any two from questions 2 to 4 after the three hours are up, then your approach obviously works.

Looking through the paper

The compulsory case study question is, as will always be the case, on groups, in this case, disposal of a subsidiary. You also have some foreign currency transactions and a ten marker on human capital management. In Section B you have three questions on a variety of topics:

- Question 2 a wide ranging question covering the accounting implications of various policies.
- Question 3 is a multi-standard question, covering leasing, financial instruments, impairment and revenue recognition.
- Question 4 is on the management commentary.

You only have to answer three out of these four questions. You don't have to pick your optional questions right now, but this brief overview should have convinced you that you have enough choice and variety to have a respectable go at Section B. So let's go back to the compulsory question in Section A.

Compulsory question

Question 1 requires you to prepare a consolidated statement of financial position for a group in which there has been a disposal. Additional complications are presentation of non-current assets held for sale, a debt instrument and an impairment loss. The key with this question, which you cannot avoid doing, is not to panic. There is a lot of number crunching, and you might not be able to complete the question. The thing to do is to set out your proformas and then patiently, but briskly, work through the workings, doing as much as you can. By using a strategy of picking the low hanging 'fruit' you could get 80% of the group aspects right which enables you to put 22 marks in the bank!

Optional questions

Deciding between the optional questions is obviously a personal matter – it depends how you have spent your study time.

One thing is clear – the optional questions all contain a discursive element and are all based around a scenario. The Examiner has said that the emphasis in this paper is on giving advice in a practical situation.

The secret is to plan your answer; break it down into bite sized subsections, clearly labelled to help your examiner to quickly conclude you understand the problem and have a logical answer.

Allocating your time

The golden rule is always allocate your time according to the marks for the question in total and for the parts of the question. But be sensible. If (for example) you have committed yourself to answering Question 5, but can think of nothing to say about fair value, you may be better off trying to pick up some extra marks on the questions you can do.

Afterwards

Don't be tempted to do a post mortem on the paper with your colleagues. It will only worry you and them and it's unlikely you'll be able to remember exactly what you wrote anyway. If you really can't resist going over the topics covered in the paper, allow yourself a maximum of half an hour's 'worry time', then put it out of your head! Relax as it's all out of your hands now!

Question 1

Marking scheme

		Marks
(a)	Gain/loss on sale of shares	4
(b)	Plant and equipment	4
	Associate	3
	Investment	4
	Goodwill	7
	Sundry assets and liabilities	2
	Retained earnings	6
	Non-controlling interests	2
(c)	Plant and machinery	
	Deposit	3
	Cash flow hedge	3
	Bond	3
	Forward contract	3
(d)	Nature of current information	5
	Visibility	5
	Available	54
	Maximum	50

minimum amount of information required. Other companies may be more proactive. In practice, publishing information about human capital management **can enhance the reputation of a company** and **help it to recruit and retain high quality staff**.

The company wishes to help stakeholders to **understand the link** between its **performance** and **the way that it manages its employees**. As well as **information on equal opportunities** and **health and safety** at work it could disclose the following:

(i)   A **description** of the company's **policies** relating to the **recruitment, retention and motivation of employees**

(ii)   Employee **numbers** and other appropriate information about the **composition of the workforce**

(iii) Details of **staff remuneration**

(iv)   Details of **amounts invested** in **training** and **developing employees** and also **descriptions** of the company's **policies and practices** in this area

(v)   A description of the way in which the company ensures **management succession**.

Information should be provided **consistently** from period to period and should be **comparable with previous periods**. This means that the company will need to develop **key performance indicators**.

The most obvious vehicle for these disclosures is the **Operating and Financial Review (Management Discussion and Analysis)** as this is management's analysis of the key factors and risks affecting the company's performance. Many companies also publish **separate social or employee reports,** which can be targeted at particular stakeholder groups, such as investors or current and potential employees and the general public.

Question 2

Text reference. Reverse acquisitions are covered in Chapter 14; retirement benefits in Chapter 5; revenue in Chapter 1; investment properties in Chapter 4; impairment in Chapter 4.

Top tips. This was a wide ranging question, requiring you to set out the financial reporting implications of certain future plans that a company was considering. The question required quite detailed knowledge of certain accounting standards although a good mark could be attained by outlining the main areas of concern. Retirement benefits, revenue recognition, investment properties, impairment and reverse acquisitions were examined.

Easy marks. The advantage of this kind of question is that if you are on shaky ground on one area you can gain marks on another. To that extent it is easier than a question on a single topic. Easy marks were available for setting out the principles underlying the problem, for using the report format and for clarity of the report.

Examiner's comment. This question was well answered, because candidates obtained the easy marks available.

Marking scheme

	Marks
Reverse acquisition	4
Preference capital	2
Loan notes	3
Retirement benefits	5
Revenue recognition	5
Investment properties	3
Impairment review	4
Report	3
Available	29
Maximum	25

To: Directors of Barking

From:

Subject: Financial reporting implications of plans for the financial statements for the year ended 30 November
           20X4

Date: December 20X3

I set out below my comments on the financial reporting implications of your future plans.

(a)   **Acquisition of Ash**

This type of acquisition is known as a **'reverse acquisition'**. Technically it is Ash which acquires Barking and the **legal form of the transaction is that Ash is the parent**. However, Ash will issue a large number of shares to the shareholders of Barking and the **directors of Barking will control the acquired entity**. The **substance** of the transaction is that **Barking is the acquirer.**

IFRS 3 *Business combinations* applies to the acquisition and states that **Barking will be treated as the acquirer** for the purpose of the consolidated financial statements. This means that the **assets and liabilities of Ash**, rather than the assets and liabilities of Barking are **remeasured to fair value**; the **retained earnings and equity balances of Barking are not revalued**. The **equity shares issued by Ash** must be **included in the cost of the combination** at their **fair value** at the date of exchange.

Part of the purchase consideration will be in the form of **zero rated preference shares** and **interest free loan notes**. **Both** of these **must be included in the cost of the combination at their fair value**. The preference shares are redeemable and therefore must be treated as **liabilities, not equity**. IAS 39 *Financial instruments: recognition and measurement* requires them to be carried at **amortised cost**. Although there is no interest charge as such **there is a finance cost**, because the shares will be **redeemed at a premium** and a **finance cost must be recognised in profit or loss for the year ended 30 November 20X4**. This is **based on the effective interest rate**. The discounted redemption proceeds could be taken as the fair value of the shares if there is no market price that can be used.

The **loan rates are** convertible debt. Although it is likely that they will be converted, rather than redeemed, this does not mean they should all be included in equity. Following IAS 32 *Financial instruments: presentation*, the equity and liability components must be classified separately. This is done by deducting the value for the liability component from the value for the instrument as a whole, leaving a residual value for the equity component.

(b)   **Pension schemes**

The defined benefit pension scheme of Barking is to be frozen. Under IAS 19 *Employee benefits*, an **estimate of the present value of the scheme** is made and **recognised in the statement of financial position** of the company. Because there will be **no new entrants** to the scheme, the **current service cost will probably increase** as the present members grow older and get nearer to retirement age.

The **defined contribution scheme** will present few accounting problems. The **cost** of providing pensions is the **amount of the contributions payable in the current period**. The employer has no further obligations.

Ash's defined benefit pension scheme will also be frozen. There is an added complication here because the existing scheme is a **multi-employer plan**. IAS 19 states that where (as in this case) it is **not possible to identify the company's share of the underlying assets and liabilities** in the scheme, **a defined benefit scheme can be accounted for as if it were a defined contribution scheme**. The fact that this has been done must be **disclosed** in the notes to the financial statements; the company will also have to disclose any available information about the **existence of a surplus or deficit** in the scheme that may affect future contributions; and the **basis used** to determine that surplus or deficit and the **implications, if any, for the company**. Ash will need to **determine the net assets** of the scheme in order to establish the net asset or liability that will be recognised when the employees are transferred to the new scheme.

(c) **Revenue recognition and investment properties**

IAS 18 *Revenue* states that revenue for the sale of goods **cannot be recognised before** the entity has **transferred the significant risks and rewards** of ownership to the buyer. Where property is sold, this is **normally when legal title passes** to the buyer. Although the new policy will mean that revenue is recognised at a **later stage than previously** it allows revenue from the sale of a property to be **recognised before there is a legal contract**. The deposit is **refundable** and this **suggests that there is not yet a legal contract**. It is necessary to look at the various acts which have to be performed under a sales contract. It may be possible to **recognise revenue when cash is received**, but **only if there are no substantial acts still to be performed**. It is also necessary to **look at industry practice** as users of the financial statements will need to be able to **compare Barking's performance with that of other companies in the same sector**.

It is **not appropriate** to **recognise legal costs as an asset**. They **do not qualify** either as **development expenditure** or as **any other intangible asset**. They represent **expenses** of the company and should be treated as such.

IAS 40 *Investment property* states that **transfers** to or from investment property **can only be made when there is a change of use**, for example, where the company starts to lease a property under an operating lease. Assuming that this is the case, any **difference between the fair value of the property at the date of transfer and its previous carrying amount should be recognised in profit or loss.**

(d) **Impairment review**

An impairment review **compares the carrying value of assets with their recoverable amount. Recoverable amount** is the **higher of fair value less costs to sell and value in use.** Because there has been an upturn in the property market, **fair value less costs to sell is likely to be higher than recoverable amount** and there will be **no impairment** and no need to calculate value in use.

However, there will be potential **problems if it is necessary to calculate value in use**. IAS 36 *Impairment of assets* states that cash flow projections should cover a **maximum of five years** unless a longer period can be justified; it is planned to use a period of ten years. The proposed discount rate of 15% appears **high**, particularly in view of the long time period to be used and it is **likely to produce inaccurate figures**. It is possible that a **shorter period and a lower discount rate will have to be used.**

Impairment losses are normally **recognised in profit or loss**, but where properties have been **revalued upwards** any loss should **first be set against the revaluation surplus** in equity (the revaluation reserve) with **only the excess being taken to the income statement**.

Question 3

Text reference. Impairment is covered in Chapter 4; IAS 39 in Chapter 7; leasing in Chapter 10; revenue in Chapter 1.

Top tips. As this is a multi-issue question, it is important to allocate your time sensibly between the different aspects. Do not spend too long on Gow's net assets at the expense of Glass's.

Easy marks. Part (a) is straightforward. Marks can be gained for backing up your arguments even if you come to the wrong conclusion.

		Marks
(a)	Nature of relationship and accounting treatment	5
(b)	Impairment and calculation	7
	IAS 39	3
	Lease	5
	Revenue	4
	Issues with values contributed	2
	Available	26
	Maximum	25

(a) IAS 31 *Interests in joint ventures* defines a joint venture as a contractual arrangement between two or more parties that undertake an economic activity that is subject to joint control on a long-term basis. Control is defined as the power to direct the financial and operating policies of the entity with a view to gaining economic benefits from its activities. Joint control in turn is where none of the entities alone can control the joint venture but together they can do so and decisions on financial and operating policy, economic performance and financial position require each venturer's consent.

On the face of it, it would appear that York is a joint venture jointly controlled by Gow and Glass. Both venturers appear to have joint control and have contributed assets and other resources to the joint venture. The only issue however is that there is **no written contract** and the definition of a joint venture is that it is a contractual arrangement. However, the **substance of the arrangement** should be considered and with the **minutes** of the discussions about the setting up of the venture being formally approved by both companies this would certainly **imply a contractual arrangement**.

In terms of the accounting for such a joint venture it should be **either the proportionate consolidation method or the equity method** which should be used in the group accounts of both Gow and Glass.

(b) **Gow's net assets**

The loss of the only customer of the power station (a cash generating unit) would be an **indicator** of a possible impairment of that cash generating unit. Therefore according to IAS 36 *Impairment of assets* an **impairment test** must be carried out on the power station. The power station has a current carrying value of $20 million. This must be **compared to the recoverable amount** of the power station which is the higher of the power station's fair value less costs to sell and its value in use.

The fair value less costs to sell is the potential sale proceeds (offer of $16m) less the disposal costs ($1m). The value in use is the discounted value of the expected future cash flows from the power station. The future dismantling costs of $5 million must also be included in this calculation as it has been agreed with the government that this will take place therefore it is a liability.

Carrying value = $20 million
Fair value less costs to sell = $16 million – $1 million = $15 million
Value in use (W1) = $21 million

Therefore the recoverable amount is the higher of $21 million and $15 million. As this recoverable amount of $21 million is actually higher than the carrying value of the power station ($20 million) then there is **no impairment**. The discounted present value must be shown as a long term provision and as part of the cost of land and buildings.

There is however a further issue with Gow's assets and that is the debt from Race. IAS 39 *Financial instruments: recognition and measurement* states that **financial assets must be assessed at each reporting date for impairment**. It is highly likely that the **debt from Race is impaired** as Race has gone into receivership. The value of the amount to be received is the anticipated cash from the final settlement. As the cash is not likely to be received for a year then it should be discounted.

Value of receivable (W2) = $3.8 million

A further factor here is that the **value of the contract with Race** shown as an intangible asset will now be **zero**.

Glass's net assets

The building **remains an asset** of the joint venture and there is no reason to alter its carrying value. However, its **remaining useful life will change** and the future depreciation charges will be $2 million each year for the next two years. As this is a change in estimate it is accounted for **prospectively not retrospectively**. Therefore this **does not affect the current statement of financial position**.

The lease liability must be assessed under IAS 39 to determine whether it is to be derecognised. In this case there is a change to the lease term but it **will not be derecognised**. The lease liability, however, will change and will be measured at the **present value of the future cash payments**.

Value of lease liability (W3) = $£1.1 million

The **lease receivable is also extinguished** as this is the payment of $1 million on 31 October 20X6.

IAS 38 states that if intangible non-current assets are to be recognised in the statement of financial position they must give a right to future economic benefits, be capable of being disposed of separately from the business and have a readily ascertainable market value. The **payment to the agency of $0.5 million** does not meet any of these criteria and **cannot be recognised as an intangible asset** and must be removed from the statement of financial position.

The terms of the contract with the overseas retailer can in fact be split into **two separate contracts** in accordance with IAS 18 *Revenue*. There is one contract to provide gas to the overseas retailer and the income from this will be accounted for in the normal way when gas is supplied. The other element of the contract is not to supply gas to any other company in that country over the four year period. Therefore the **$1.5 million deposit** received should not be taken to the income statement immediately but spread over the four year period. The deposit should not have been deducted from intangible assets but instead should be shown as **deferred income**.

Intangible assets (W4) = $3m
Deferred income (W5) = $1.5m

STATEMENT OF FINANCIAL POSITION OF YORK AS AT 31 OCTOBER 20X6

	$m	$m
Land and buildings (9 + 4 + 4) (W1)		17.0
Intangible assets (W4)		3.0
		20.0
Current assets		
Inventory		
Receivables (W2)	6.0	
Cash (1 + 10)	3.8	
	11.0	
Total assets		20.8
		40.8
Share capital		
Reserves (bal fig)		30.0
		4.2
Lease liability (W3)		1.1
Long-term provision (W1)		4.0
Deferred income (W5)		1.5
		40.8

Workings

1   *Value in use – power station*

$m

Cash flow

31 Oct 20X7 $\left(6 \times \dfrac{1}{1.06}\right)$ 5.7

31 Oct 20X8 $\left(7 \times \dfrac{1}{1.06^2}\right)$ 6.2

31 Oct 20X9 $\left(8 \times \dfrac{1}{1.06^3}\right)$ 6.7

31 Oct 20Y0 $\left((8-5) \times \dfrac{1}{1.06^4}\right)$ 2.4

                                                                21.0

The dismantling costs must also be discounted and added into the value of property, plant and equipment $5 million $\times \dfrac{1}{1.06^4}$ 0.792 = $4 million

2   *Value of receivable – Race*

Discounted present value = $5 million × 80% × 1/1.06
                          = $3.8 million

3   *Value of lease payable*

$0.6 million × 1/1.07   = $0.56 million
$0.6 million × 1/(1.07 × 1.07) = $0.52 million
                                  $1.08 rounded to $1.1 million

4   *Intangible assets in Glass*

	$m
Per statement of financial position	2.0
Less agency fee	(0.5)
Add value of overseas deposit	1.5
	3.0

5   *Deferred income*

Deposit from overseas retailer = $1.5 million

Question 4

> **Text reference.** This topic is covered in Chapter 1 of the text.
> **Top tips.** In part (b), make full use of the information in the question, but do not simply regurgitate it.
> **Easy marks.** Part (a) is very straightforward book work. Part (b) also has easy marks for style and layout.

Marking scheme

			Marks
(a)	Principle		6
	Mandatory discussion		7
		Available/ maximum	13
(b)	Principal risks		9
	Treasury policies		3
		Available/ maximum	12
	Style and presentation		2
		Available	27
		Maximum	25

(a)   In 2005, the IASB issue a discussion paper *Management Commentary*, which is the international equivalent of the UK's Operating and Financial Review. The purpose of these statements is to explain the main factors underlying a company's **financial position and performance**. The principles and objectives of a Management Commentary (MC) are as follows:

(i)   It is specifically prepared **for the shareholders of the company** not for investors in general, although it may be of interest to other parties.

(ii)   The MC **reflects the directors' view** of the business.

(iii)   It should be a **clear and balanced analysis** of the strategic position and direction of the business which should help members to assess those strategies and their potential for success.

(iv)   The MC should **be forward looking** and should identify those trends and factors that will help members to assess the current and future performance of the business.

(v)   Members should be **warned** that some information is not verifiable and of **any uncertainties** underpinning the information.

(vi)   The MC should **complement** the financial statements by providing useful financial and non-financial information which is not to be found in the financial statements.

(vii)   The MC should provide **all information** that might reasonably be expected **to influence** the shareholders.

(viii) The MC should be **balanced and neutral** and deal equally with favourable and unfavourable information.

(ix)   The MC and key performance indicators should be comparable over time.

The arguments for a mandatory MC are largely to do with content and comparability. It is argued that a mandatory MC will make it easier for companies themselves to judge what is required in such a report and the required standard of reporting, thereby making such reports more **robust, transparent and comparable**. If an MC is not mandatory then there may be **uncertainty** as to content and the possibility of **misinformation**. There is also the risk that without a mandatory MC directors may take a **minimalist approach** to disclosure which will make the MC less useful and the information to be disclosed will be in hands of senior executives and directors.

However, the **arguments against** a mandatory MC are that it could **stifle the development of the MC as a tool** for communication and may lead to a **checklist approach** to producing it. It is argued that a mandatory MC is not required as market forces and the needs of investors should lead to companies feeling the pressure to provide a useful and reliable report.

(b)

Jones and Cousin
Annual Report 20X6
Management Commentary

Introduction

Jones and Cousin is a public quoted company and the group develops, manufactures and markets products in the medical sector. This report is designed to assist members of the group in understanding and assessing the strategies of the group and the potential success of these strategies.

Risks

The group faces a number of risks which will be considered under the headings of:

*   Market risk
*   Product risk
*   Currency risk

Market risk

The market in which the group operates is quite fiercely competitive and contains a number of different competitors including specialised and large international corporations. There is the risk that any technical advances or product innovations by these competitors could adversely affect the group's profits. Also this element of competition also means that there is a risk of loss of market share or lower than expected sales growth which could affect the share price.

The sector in which the group operates is heavily monitored by local governments and the group's share of revenue in a market sector is often determined by government policy. The group is therefore heavily dependent upon governments providing the funds for health care. Any reduction in funds by governments would almost certainly lead to a fall in revenue for the group.

Product risk

The products of the group are essentially a low health risk. However, there is always the possibility of a problem with products which may lead to legal action which would be costly and damage the group's reputation and goodwill. The industry is highly regulated in terms of both medical and environmental laws. Any such claims would have an adverse effect on sales, profit and share price.

There will always be innovations in this market sector and the group is careful to protect its products with patents and will enter into legal proceedings where necessary to protect those patents. There is also the problem of infringing the patents of others. If claims were brought for infringement of patents of other companies this would be costly and damaging and alternative products would have to be found.

There are constantly new products being developed by the group which is costly in terms of research and development expenditure. Product innovation may not always be successful and this highly regulated market may not always gain the regulatory approval required.

Currency risk

The group operates in twenty-seven different countries and earns revenue and incurs costs in several different currencies. Although the dollar is the group's functional currency only 5% of its business is in the country of incorporation. Therefore exchange fluctuations in the main currencies in which it trades may have a material effect on the group's profits and cash flows.

Relationships

The group has a positive ethical programme. It sources its products from a wide range of suppliers largely in the form of long term contracts for the supply of goods. The group has a policy of ensuring that such suppliers are suitable from both qualitative and ethical perspectives.

The group has a set of corporate and social responsibility principles for which the Board of Directors is responsible. The risks that the group bears from these responsibilities are managed by the Managing Director. The group operates in many geographical areas and encourages its subsidiaries to help local communities to reinvest in local educational projects. Great care is taken by the group to ensure that obsolete products are disposed of responsibly and safely. Wherever possible reusable materials are used.

Group policy is to attract and retain employees and to maintain an equal opportunities policy for all employees. To this end employees regularly receive in-house training and are kept informed of management policies.

Treasury policies

The group uses derivative products to protect against both currency risk and interest rate risk. This is done by the used of fixed rate currency swaps and using floating to fixed rate interest rate swaps. All financial instruments are accounted for as cash flow hedges which means that gains and losses are recognised initially in reserves and are only released to profit or loss when the hedged item also affects profit or loss.

ACCA

Paper P2

Corporate Reporting (International)

Mock Examination 3:

December 2009

Question Paper	
Time allowed	
Reading and planning	**15 minutes**
Writing	**3 hours**
This paper is divided into two sections	
Section A	This ONE question is compulsory and MUST be attempted
Section B	TWO questions ONLY to be answered

DO NOT OPEN THIS PAPER UNTIL YOU ARE READY TO START UNDER EXAMINATION CONDITIONS

SECTION A – This ONE question is compulsory and MUST be attempted

Question 1

Grange, a public limited company, operates in the manufacturing sector. The draft statements of financial position of the group companies are as follows at 30 November 20X9.

	Grange $m	Park $m	Fence $m
Assets			
Non-current assets			
Property, plant and equipment	257	311	238
Investment in subsidiaries:			
Park	340		
Fence	134		
Investment in Sitin	16		
	747	311	238
Current assets	475	304	141
Total assets	1,222	615	379
Equity and liabilities			
Share capital	430	230	150
Retained earnings	410	170	65
Other components of equity	22	14	17
Total equity	862	414	232
Non-current liabilities	172	124	38
Current liabilities			
Trade and other payables	178	71	105
Provisions for liabilities	10	6	4
Total current liabilities	188	77	109
Total liabilities	360	201	147
Total equity and liabilities	1,222	615	379

The following information is relevant to the preparation of the group financial statements.

(i) On 1 June 20X8, Grange acquired 60% of the equity interests of Park, a public limited company. The purchase consideration comprised cash of $250 million. Excluding the franchise referred to below, the fair value of the identifiable net assets was $360 million. The excess of the fair value of the net assets is due to an increase in the value of non-depreciable land.

Park held a franchise right, which at 1 June 20X8 had a fair value of $10 million. This had not been recognised in the financial statements of Park. The franchise agreement had a remaining term of five years to run at that date and is not renewable. Park still holds this franchise at the year-end.

Grange wishes to use the 'full goodwill' method for all acquisitions. The fair value of the non-controlling interest in Park was $150 million on 1 June 20X8. The retained earnings of Park were $115 million and other components of equity were $10 million at the date of acquisition.

Grange acquired a further 20% interest from the non-controlling interests in Park on 30 November 20X9 for a cash consideration of $90 million.

(ii) On 31 July 20X8, Grange acquired 100% of the equity interests of Fence for a cash consideration of $214 million. The identifiable net assets of Fence had a provisional fair value of $202 million, including any contingent liabilities. At the time of the business combination, Fence had a contingent liability with a fair value of $30 million. At 30 November 20X9, the contingent liability met the recognition criteria of IAS 37

Provisions, contingent liabilities and contingent assets and the revised estimate of this liability was $25 million. The accountant of Fence is yet to account for this revised liability.

However, Grange had not completed the valuation of an element of property, plant and equipment of Fence at 31 July 20X8 and the valuation was not completed by 30 November 20X8. The valuation was received on 30 June 20X9 and the excess of the fair value over book value at the date of acquisition was estimated at $4 million. The asset had a useful economic life of 10 years at 31 July 20X8.

The retained earnings of Fence were $73 million and other components of equity were $9 million at 31 July 20X8 before any adjustment for the contingent liability.

On 30 November 20X9, Grange disposed of 25% of its equity interest in Fence to the non-controlling interest for a consideration of $80 million. The disposal proceeds had been credited to the cost of the investment in the statement of financial position.

(iii) On 30 June 20X8, Grange had acquired a 100% interest in Sitin, a public limited company, for a cash consideration of $39 million. Sitin's identifiable net assets were fair valued at $32 million.

On 30 November 20X9, Grange disposed of 60% of the equity of Sitin when its identifiable net assets were $36 million. Of the increase in net assets, $3 million had been reported in profit or loss and $1 million had been reported in other comprehensive income as profit on an available-for-sale asset. The sale proceeds were $23 million and the remaining equity interest was fair valued at $13 million. Grange could still exert significant influence after the disposal of the interest. The only accounting entry made in Grange's financial statements was to increase cash and reduce the cost of the investment in Sitin.

(iv) Grange acquired a plot of land on 1 December 20X8 in an area where the land is expected to rise significantly in value if plans for regeneration go ahead in the area. The land is currently held at cost of $6 million in property, plant and equipment until Grange decides what should be done with the land. The market value of the land at 30 November 20X9 was $8 million but as at 15 December 20X9, this had reduced to $7 million as there was some uncertainty surrounding the viability of the regeneration plan.

(v) Grange anticipates that it will be fined $1 million by the local regulator for environmental pollution. It also anticipates that it will have to pay compensation to local residents of $6 million, although this is only the best estimate of that liability. In addition, the regulator has requested that certain changes be made to the manufacturing process in order to make the process more environmentally friendly. This is anticipated to cost the company $4 million.

(vi) Grange has a property located in a foreign country, which was acquired at a cost of 8 million dinars on 30 November 20X8 when the exchange rate was $1 = 2 dinars. At 30 November 20X9, the property was revalued to 12 million dinars. The exchange rate at 30 November 20X9 was $1 = 1.5 dinars. The property was being carried at its value as at 30 November 20X8. The company policy is to revalue property, plant and equipment whenever material differences exist between book and fair value. Depreciation on the property can be assumed to be immaterial.

(vii) Grange has prepared a plan for reorganising the parent company's own operations. The board of directors has discussed the plan but further work has to be carried out before they can approve it. However, Grange has made a public announcement as regards the reorganisation and wishes to make a reorganisation provision at 30 November 20X9 of $30 million. The plan will generate cost savings. The directors have calculated the value in use of the net assets (total equity) of the parent company as being $870 million if the reorganisation takes place and $830 million if the reorganisation does not take place. Grange is concerned that the parent company's property, plant and equipment have lost value during the period because of a decline in property prices in the region and feel that any impairment charge would relate to these assets. There is no reserve within other equity relating to prior revaluation of these non-current assets.

(viii) Grange uses accounting policies, which maximise its return on capital employed. The directors of Grange feel that they are acting ethically in using this approach as they feel that as long as they follow 'professional rules', then there is no problem. They have adopted a similar philosophy in the way they conduct their business affairs. The finance director had recently received information that one of their key customers, Brook, a public limited company, was having serious liquidity problems. This information was received from a close friend who was employed by Brook. However, he also learned that Brook had approached a rival company Field, a public limited company, for credit and knew that if Field granted Brook credit then there was a high probability that the outstanding balance owed by Brook to Grange would be paid. Field had approached the director for an informal credit reference for Brook who until recently had always paid promptly. The director was intending to give Brook a good reference because of its recent prompt payment history, as the director felt that there was no obligation or rule which required him to mention the company's liquidity problems. (There is no change required to the financial statements as a result of the above information.)

Required

(a) Calculate the consolidated gain or loss arising on the disposal of the equity interest in Sitin. **(6 marks)**

(b) Prepare a consolidated statement of financial position of the Grange Group at 30 November 20X9 in accordance with International Financial Reporting Standards. **(35 marks)**

(c) Discuss the view that ethical behaviour is simply a matter of compliance with professional rules and whether the finance director should simply consider 'rules' when determining whether to give Brook a good credit reference. **(7 marks)**

Professional marks will be awarded in part (c) for clarity and expression. **(2 marks)**

(Total = 50 marks)

Section B – TWO questions ONLY to be attempted

Question 2

(a)   Key, a public limited company, is concerned about the reduction in the general availability of credit and the sudden tightening of the conditions required to obtain a loan from banks. There has been a reduction in credit availability and a rise in interest rates. It seems as though there has ceased to be a clear relationship between interest rates and credit availability, and lenders and investors are seeking less risky investments. The directors are trying to determine the practical implications for the financial statements particularly because of large write downs of assets in the banking sector, tightening of credit conditions, and falling sales and asset prices. They are particularly concerned about the impairment of assets and the market inputs to be used in impairment testing. They are afraid that they may experience significant impairment charges in the coming financial year. They are unsure as to how they should test for impairment and any considerations which should be taken into account.

Required

Discuss the main considerations that the company should take into account when impairment testing non-current assets in the above economic climate.   **(8 marks)**

Professional marks will be awarded in part (a) for clarity and expression.   **(2 marks)**

(b)   There are specific assets on which the company wishes to seek advice. The company holds certain non-current assets, which are in a development area and carried at cost less depreciation. These assets cost $3 million on 1 June 20X3 and are depreciated on the straight-line basis over their useful life of five years. An impairment review was carried out on 31 May 20X4 and the projected cash flows relating to these assets were as follows:

Year to	31 May 20X5	31 May 20X6	31 May 20X7	31 May 20X8
Cash flows ($'000)	280	450	500	550

The company used a discount rate of 5%. At 30 November 20X4, the directors used the same cash flow projections and noticed that the resultant value in use was above the carrying amount of the assets and wished to reverse any impairment loss calculated at 31 May 20X4. The government has indicated that it may compensate the company for any loss in value of the assets up to 20% of the impairment loss.

Key holds a non-current asset, which was purchased for $10 million on 1 December 20X1 with an expected useful life of 10 years. On 1 December 20X3, it was revalued to $8.8 million. At 30 November 20X4, the asset was reviewed for impairment and written down to its recoverable amount of $5.5 million.

Key committed itself at the beginning of the financial year to selling a property that is being under-utilised following the economic downturn. As a result of the economic downturn, the property was not sold by the end of the year. The asset was actively marketed but there were no reasonable offers to purchase the asset. Key is hoping that the economic downturn will change in the future and therefore has not reduced the price of the asset.

Required

Discuss with suitable computations, how to account for any potential impairment of the above non-current assets in the financial statements for the year ended 30 November 20X4.   **(15 marks)**

Note: The following discount factors may be relevant

Year 1	0.9524
Year 2	0.9070
Year 3	0.8638
Year 4	0.8227

(Total = 25 marks)

Answers

DO NOT TURN THIS PAGE UNTIL YOU HAVE
COMPLETED THE MOCK EXAM

6   **Non-controlling interest**

	Park $m	Fence $m	Sitin/* $m
NCI at acquisition	150.0	–	–
NCI share of post-acquisition:			
Retained earnings: 52(W4) × 40%	20.8		
Other components: 4(W5) × 40%	1.6		
NCI at 30.11.X9 before changes	172.4		
Change in NCI on 30.11.X9			
Park (W12)	(86.2)		
Fence (W13)		54.62	
	86.2	54.62	–

140.82

*Note. There is no NCI in Sitin because it goes from being a 100% subsidiary to being an associate.

Alternative working

	Park $m	Fence $m
Net assets per question	414	232.00
Fair value adjustments (W7)	12	(21.53)
Goodwill (W2)		8.00
	426	218.47
× 20%/× 25%	85.2	54.62

139.82

7   **Fair value adjustments**

Park

	At acqn (1.6.X8) $m	Movement $m	Year-end (30.11.X9) $m
Land*			
360 – (230 + 115 + 10)	5	–	5
Franchise: at 1.6.X8	10		
Depn. $10 \times 1\frac{1}{2}/5$		(3)	7
	15	(3)	12

*Note. For the purposes of the goodwill calculation, the fair value uplift is already included in the $360m given in the question for the fair value of the net assets of Park on acquisition.

Fence

	At acqn $m	Movement $m	Year-end (30.11.X9) $m
Contingent liability*			
at 31.7.X8	(30)	5	(25)
Property, plant and equipment			
excess at acquisition per qu.	4		
Depreciation 16 months ÷	–	–	–
120 months	–	(0.53)	3.47
	(26)	4.47	(21.53)

Note. For the purposes of the goodwill calculation, the contingent liability of $30 million is already included in the fair value of the net assets.

8   *Investment land (Grange)*

The land should be re-classified as investment property. IAS 40 states that land held for indeterminate use (Grange has not decided what to do with it) is investment property. The entries to re-classify are:

DEBIT	Investment property	$6m	
CREDIT	Property, plant and equipment		$6m

As Grange's policy is to maximise return on capital employed, it will use the fair value model, and the gain for the year end of $8m – $6m = $2m will be taken to profit or loss for the year shown in retained earnings.

DEBIT	Investment property	$2m	
CREDIT	Profit or loss (retained earnings)		$2m

The fall in value after the year end to $7m will be disclosed as a non-adjusting event after the reporting period.

9   *Provision for environmental claim*

The environmental obligations of $1m and $6m are a present obligation arising from past events and should be provided for:

DEBIT	Profit or loss (retained earnings)	$7m	
CREDIT	Provision		$7m

However, no provision should be made for the costs of changing the manufacturing process because the events to date do not provide sufficient detail to recognise a constructive obligation. Grange still has the option of making other changes such as buying a new machine, shutting down production or changing the product.

10   *Foreign property*

	$m
Value at 30 November 20X8 ($8m/2$)	4
Value at 30 November 20X9 ($12m/1.5$)	8
Gain	4

DEBIT	Property, plant and equipment	$4m	
CREDIT	Other comprehensive income (OCE)		$4m

11   *Restructuring*

No provision should be recognised for the restructuring because there is no constructive obligation. A constructive obligation arises when an entity:

(i)   Has a formal plan, and
(ii)   Makes an announcement of the plan to those affected.

There is insufficient detail to recognise a constructive obligation. However, there is evidence that Grange's property, plant and equipment (and Grange itself) is impaired. An impairment test should be performed on Grange.

	$m
Net assets per question	862
Revaluation of investment property (W8)	2
Provision (W9)	(7)
Revaluation of property (W10)	4
Impairment of Sitin (W3)	(3)
	858
Fair value at y/e if restructured	(830)
Impairment loss	28

All the loss of $28m is taken to profit or loss for the year (in retained earnings) as none of it relates to previously revalued assets.

programme to locate a buyer. However, **Key has not reduced the price of the asset, which is in excess of its market value** – one of the IFRS 5 criteria is that the market price must be reasonable in relation to the asset's current fair value. In addition, the asset has remained unsold for a year, so it **cannot be assumed that the sale will be completed within one year** of classification.

The property does not meet the IFRS 5 criteria, so it **cannot be classified as held for sale**. However, an **impairment** has taken place and, in the circumstances, the **recoverable amount** would be **fair value** less **costs to sell**.

Question 3

Text reference. Revenue recognition is covered in Chapter 21 of your text. Joint ventures are covered in Chapter 12 and intangibles in Chapter 4.

Top tips. This is a specialised entity question, based in the energy industry. Although the question relates to one company, it is a multi-topic question, dealing with revenue recognition, joint ventures, decommissioning costs and intangibles. Revenue recognition is a favourite topic for this examiner, so make sure you fully understand our answer to this and the other questions in the kit on this topic. Intangibles, likewise, comes up regularly (in December 2008, for example), so you need to be familiar with criteria for recognition and derecognition of assets. Joint ventures/jointly controlled entities are examined only in P2.

Easy marks. Listing the criteria for revenue recognition (Part (a)) and joint control (Part (b)) will get you some easy marks.

Marking scheme

		Marks
(a)	Joint venture*	1
	Revenue recognition	3
	Inventory	3
	Events after reporting period	2
(b)	Jointly controlled	3
	Accounting for entity	2
	Decommissioning	5
	Asset definition/IAS 38/IAS 36	4
	Professional marks	2
		25

Note. BPP has given a mark for recognising the joint venture. This was not in the original marking scheme.

(a)   Revenue from the sale of goods should only be recognised when **all the following conditions** are satisfied.

   (i)   The entity has transferred the **significant risks and rewards** of ownership of the goods to the buyer

   (ii)   The entity has **no continuing managerial involvement** to the degree usually associated with ownership, and no longer has effective control over the goods sold

   (iii) The amount of revenue can be **measured reliably**

   (iv)   It is probable that the **economic benefits** associated with the transaction will flow to the enterprise

   (v)   The **costs incurred** in respect of the transaction can be measured reliably

The transfer of risks and rewards can only be decided by examining each transaction. In the case of the oil sold to third parties, all the revenue should be recognised as all the criteria have been met.

Revenue up to 1 October 20X9

The arrangement between Burley and Slite is a **joint venture,** since both entities jointly control an asset – the oilfield. This means that **each company accounts for its share of revenue** in respect of oil produced up to 1 October 20X9, calculated, using the selling price to third parties of $100 per barrel, as:

Burley: 60%
Slite: 40%

Excess oil extracted

Burley has over-extracted and Slite under-extracted by 10,000 barrels of oil. The **substance** of the transaction is that **Burley has purchased the oil from Slite** at the point of production at the market value ruling at that point, namely $100 per barrel. Burley should therefore **recognise a purchase** from Slite in the amount of 10,000 × $100 = $1m.

The accounting entries would be:

DEBIT	Purchases	$1m	
CREDIT	Slite – financial liability		$1m

The **amount payable to Slite at the year end** will **change with the movement in the price of oil** and therefore the financial liability recorded at the year end should reflect the best estimate of the cash payable. By the year end the price of oil has risen to $105 per barrel, so the financial liability will be 10,000 × $105 = $1,050,000, an **increase of $50,000**. The accounting entries to reflect this increase in liability and expense to profit or loss at the year end will be:

DEBIT	Expense (P/L)	$50,000	
CREDIT	Slite – financial liability		$50,000

After the year end the price of oil changes again, and the transaction is settled at $95 per barrel. The cash paid by Burley to Slite on 12 December 20X9 is 10,000 × $95 = $950,000. This means that a **gain arises after the year end** of $1,050,000 - $950,000 = $100,000. This gain will be **taken to profit or loss** in the **following accounting period**:

DEBIT	Slite – financial liability	$100,000	
CREDIT	Profit or loss		$100,000

The gain arising is an **event after the reporting period.** These are defined by IAS 10 *Events after the reporting period* as events, both favourable and unfavourable, that occur between the end of the reporting period and the date that the financial statements are authorised for issue.

The question arises of whether this is an **adjusting or non-adjusting** event. An adjusting event is an event after the reporting period that provides further evidence of conditions that existed at the end of the reporting period. A non-adjusting event is an event after the reporting period that is indicative of a **condition that arose after the end of the reporting period**. The price of oil changes frequently in response to a number of factors, reflecting events that arose after the year end. It would therefore not be appropriate to adjust the financial statements in response to the decline in the price of oil. The gain is therefore a **non-adjusting** event after the reporting period.

Inventory

IAS 2 *Inventories* requires that inventories should be stated at the **lower of cost and net realisable value.** Net realisable value (NRV) is the estimated selling price in the ordinary course of business less the estimated cost of completion and the estimated costs of making the sale.

In estimating NRV, entities must use reliable evidence of the **market price** available at the time. Such evidence includes any movements in price that reflect conditions at the year end, including prices recorded after the year end to the extent that they confirm these conditions. In the case of Burley, the appropriate market price to use is that recorded at the year end, namely **$105 per barrel**, since the decline to $95 results from conditions arising after the year end. Selling costs are $2 per barrel, so the amount to be used for NRV in valuing the inventory is $105 - $2 = $103 per barrel.

Net realisable value, in this instance, is higher than cost, which was $98 per barrel. The inventory should be stated at the lower of the two, that is at $98 per barrel, giving a total inventory value of $98 × 5,000 = $490,000. No loss is recorded as no write-down to NRV has been made.

(b)   **Arrangement with Jorge and Heavy**

Burley wishes to account for its arrangement with Jorge and Heavy using proportionate consolidation. It can only do so if the arrangement meets the criteria for a **jointly controlled entity.**

A jointly controlled entity is a form of joint venture, that is a contractual arrangement (a corporation, partnership or other entity) where two or more parties undertake an economic activity which is subject to joint control. In jointly controlled entities, the venturers have a **contractual arrangement establishing their joint control** over the economic activity of the entity.

A jointly controlled entity effectively operates as a **separate entity**: it controls the joint venture's assets, incurs liabilities and expenses and earns income. It can, as a separate entity, enter into contracts in its own name and raise finance to fund the activities of the joint venture. The venturers share the results of the jointly controlled entity, and in some cases they may also share the output of the joint venture.

Joint control is the contractually agreed sharing of control over an economic activity.

Jointly controlled entities may be accounted for in different ways:

*   **Proportionate consolidation:** combine items on a line by line basis
*   **Equity method:** as for associates

For **joint control** to exist, financial and operating decisions relating to the activity require the **unanimous consent** of the parties sharing control (the venturers). The arrangement entered into by Burley does not require unanimous consent for all decisions – the operating and financial decisions of Wells may be approved by two thirds of the venturers. This means that **Wells is not jointly controlled**, and therefore that **proportionate consolidation may not be used.**

The three investors have **significant influence but not control**. Accordingly, each must account for its interest in the entity **as an associate, using equity accounting.**

Decommissioning costs

Decommissioning costs are not payable until some future date, therefore the **amount of costs** that will be incurred is generally **uncertain**. IAS 16 *Property, plant and equipment* requires that management should record **its best estimate** of the entity's obligations. Since the cash flows are delayed, **discounting is used.** The estimate of the amount payable is discounted to the date of initial recognition and the discounted amount is capitalised. A corresponding credit is recorded in provisions. Changes in the liability and resulting from changes in the discount rate adjust the cost of the related asset in the current period (IFRIC 1 *Changes in existing decommissioning, restoration and similar liabilities*).

The decommissioning costs of Wells are accounted for as follows:

	$m
Cost ten years ago	240.0
Depreciation: 240 ×10/40	(60.0)
Decrease in decommissioning costs: 32.6 – 18.5	(14.1)
Carrying value at 1 December 20X8	165.9
Less depreciation: 165.9 ÷ 30 years	(5.5)
Carrying amount at 30 November 20X9	160.4

The provision as restated at 1 December 20X8 would be increased at 30 November 20X9 by the unwinding of the discount of the new rate of 7%.

Decommissioning liability: 32.6 – 14.1	18.5
Finance costs: 18.5 × 7%	1.3
Decommissioning liability at 30 November 20X9	19.8

Jointly controlled assets

Since Burley has joint control over the pipeline, even though its interest is only 10%, it would not be appropriate to show the pipeline as an investment. The pipeline is a **jointly controlled asset** and the arrangement is a **joint venture.**

In this type of joint venture, the venturers have **joint control**, and often **joint ownership** of some or all of the assets in the joint venture. These assets may have been contributed to the joint venture or purchased for the purpose of the joint venture, but in any case they are **dedicated to the activities of the joint venture**. These assets are used to produce benefits for the venturers; each venturer takes a share of the output and bears a share of the incurred expenses.

As with jointly controlled operations, this type of joint venture does **not** involve setting up a corporation, partnership or any other kind of entity. The venturers **control their share of future economic benefits** through their share in the jointly controlled asset.

IAS 31 requires each venturer to recognise (ie include in their financial statements) the following in respect of its interest in jointly controlled assets.

(i)   Its **share of the jointly controlled assets**, classified by their nature, eg a share of a jointly controlled oil pipeline should be classified as property, plant and equipment

(ii)   Any **liabilities** it has incurred, eg in financing its share of the assets

(iii)   Its share of any **liabilities incurred jointly** with the other venturers which relate to the joint venture

(iv)   Any **income** from the sale or use of its share of the joint venture's output, together with its share of any **expenses** incurred by the joint venture

(v)   Any **expenses** which it has incurred in respect of its interest in the joint venture, eg those relating to financing the venturer's interest in the assets and selling its share of the output

Burley must show the asset not as an investment, but as **property, plant and equipment,** and record any income from it or liabilities incurred.

(c)   **Intangible asset**

The relevant standard here is IAS 38 *Intangible assets.* An intangible asset may be recognised if it meets the **identifiability criteria** in IAS 38, if it is probable that **future economic benefits** attributable to the asset will flow to the entity and if its **fair value can be measured reliably.** For an intangible asset to be identifiable, the asset must be separable, or it must arise from contractual or other legal rights.

It appears that these **criteria have been met.** The licence has been acquired separately, and its value can be measured reliably at the purchase price.

Burley does not yet know if the extraction of oil is commercially viable, and does not know for sure whether oil will be discovered in the region. If, on further exploration, some or all activities must be discontinued, then the licence must be **tested for impairment** following IAS 36 *Impairment of assets.* (IAS 36 has a number of impairment indicators, both internal and external.)

It is possible that the licence may **increase in value** if commercial viability is proven. However, IAS 38 does not allow revaluation unless there is an **active market** for the asset.

Question 4

Text reference. Financial instruments are covered in Chapter 7 of the BPP Study Text.

Top tips. A regular topic – financial instruments – is examined in a current issues context. Recently the examiner has started to insert a calculation element into his current issues question. On past form, the calculations have not been difficult, but have served to illustrate the impact of a change or proposed change. The Discussion Paper on Reducing Complexity, from which many of the ideas in this question are drawn, is covered in your Study Text and flagged as a current issue.

Easy marks. The calculation is a good source of easy marks as it is straightforward. And there are marks for bookwork – listing the problems of complexity and advantages of fair value.

			Marks
(a)	(i)	1 mark per point up to maximum	9
	(ii)	1 mark per point up to maximum	9
		Professional marks	2
(b)		Identical payment	2
		Carrying amount	1
		Fair value	2
			25

(a)   (i)   Many users and preparers of accounts have found financial instruments to be **complex**. There are a number of reasons for this complexity and resulting confusion, many of which are covered in a Discussion Paper, *Reducing Complexity in Reporting Financial Instruments*, issued by the IASB in 2008.

As the Discussion Paper acknowledges, the main reason for complexity in accounting for financial instruments is the **many different ways in which they can be measured**. A table lists twenty-four! The measurement method depends on:

(1)   The **applicable financial reporting standard.** A variety of IFRS and IAS apply to the measurement of financial instruments. For example, financial assets may be measured using consolidation for subsidiaries (IAS 27), the equity method for associates (IAS 28), proportionate consolidation for joint ventures or IAS 39 for most other financial assets.

(2)   The **categorisation of the financial instrument** under IAS 39 *Financial instruments: Recognition and measurement.* Where IAS 39 applies, there are still four categories: fair value through profit or loss, available for sale financial assets, loans and receivables and held to maturity.

(3)   Whether **hedge accounting** has been applied. Hedge accounting is **complex**, for example when cash flow hedge accounting is used, gains and losses may be split between profit or loss for the year and other comprehensive income. In addition, there may be mismatches when hedge accounting applies reflecting the underlying mismatches under the non-hedging rules.

Some measurement methods use an estimate of **current value, and others use historical cost.** Some include impairment losses, others do not.

Management intentions play a role in deciding the measurement method: if management decides that an asset is to be held to maturity, it will have a different value from an identical asset that is treated at fair value through profit or loss.

The different measurement methods for financial instruments creates a number of **problems for preparers and users** of accounts:

(1)   The treatment of a particular instrument **may not be the best**, but may be determined by other factors. For example management may not have documented the investment or risk strategy so that an instrument must be classified as available-for-sale rather than as fair value through profit or loss.

(2)   Gains or losses resulting from different measurement methods may be combined in the same line item in the statement of comprehensive income. **Comparability** is therefore compromised.

(3)   Comparability is also affected when it is **not clear** what measurement method has been used.

(4)   It is **difficult to apply the criteria** for deciding which instrument is to be measured in which way. As new types of instruments are created, the criteria may be applied in ways that are not consistent.

(ii)   There is pressure to reduce complexity in accounting for financial instruments. One idea, put forward in the Discussion Paper, is that **fair value is the only measure that is appropriate for all types of financial instruments**, and that a full fair value model would be much simpler to apply than the current mixed model. A single measurement method would, it is argued:

(1)   Significantly **reduce complexity in classification**. There would be no need to classify financial instruments into the four categories of fair value through profit or loss, available for sale financial assets, loans and receivables and held to maturity.

(2)   **Reduce complexity in accounting**. There would be no need to account for transfers between the above categories, or to report how impairment losses have been quantified.

(3)   **Eliminated measurement mismatches** between financial instruments and reduce the need for fair value hedge accounting.

(4)   Eliminate the need to identify and separate **embedded derivatives.**

(5)   **Better reflect the cash flows** that would be paid if liabilities were transferred at the re-measurement date.

(6)   Make reported information **easier to understand**

(7)   **Improve the comparability** of reported information between entities and between periods

However, while fair value has some obvious advantages, it has problems too. **Uncertainty** may be an issue for the following reasons

(1)   Markets are not all liquid and transparent.

(2)   Many assets and liabilities do not have an active market, and methods for estimating their value are more subjective.

(3)   Management must exercise judgement in the valuation process, and may not be entirely objective in doing so.

(4)   Because fair value, in the absence of an active market, represents an estimate, additional disclosures are needed to explain and justify the estimates. These disclosures may themselves be subjective.

(5)   Independent verification of fair value estimates is difficult for all the above reasons.

(b)   Different valuation methods bring comparability problems, as indicated in Part (a), and this can be seen with the examples in this part of the question.

Amortised cost

Using amortised cost, both the initial loan and the new loan result in **single payments that are almost identical** on 30 November 20X9:

Initial loan: $47m × 1.05 for 5 years = $59.98m

New loan: $45m ×1.074 for 4 years = $59.89m

However, the **carrying amounts at 30 November 20X5 will be different:**

Initial loan: $47m + ($47m × 5%) = $49.35m

New loan: $45m

Fair value

If the two loans were carried at fair value, both **the initial loan and the new loan would have the same value,** and be carried at $45m. There would be a net profit of $2m, made up of the interest expense of $47m × 5% = $2.35m and the unrealised gain of $49.35m - $47m = $4.35m.

Arguably, since the obligation on 30 November 20X9 will be the same for both loans, fair value is a more appropriate measure than amortised cost.

ACCA examiner's answers:
June and December 2009 papers

1   (a)

Bravado plc
Consolidated Statement of Financial Position at 31 May 2009

	$m
Assets:	
Non-current assets:	
Property, plant and equipment W9	708
Goodwill W2	25
Investment in associate W3	22·5
Available for sale financial assets W10	44·6
	800·1
Current assets:	
Inventories W10	245
Trade receivables W11	168
Loans to directors	1
Cash and cash equivalents	209
	623
Total assets	1,423·1
Equity and liabilities	
Equity attributable to owners of parent	
Share capital	520
Retained earnings W5	256·32
Other components of equity W5	9·5
	785·82
Non-controlling interest W7	148·88
	934·7
Non-current liabilities	
Long-term borrowings	140
Deferred tax W10	39·4
Total non-current liabilities	179·4
Current liabilities	
Trade and other payables W6	217
Current tax payable	92
Total current liabilities	309
Total liabilities	488·4
Total equity and liabilities	1,423·1

Working 1

Message

	$m
Fair value of consideration for 80% interest	300
Fair value of non-controlling interest	86
	386
Amount of identifiable net assets acquired	(400)
Gain on bargain purchase	(14)

Essentially the entries would be:

		$m	$m
DR	Net identifiable assets	400	
CR	Cash		300
CR	Gain on bargain purchase		14
CR	Equity – non-controlling interest		86
		400	400

Working 2

Mixted

	$m
1 June 2008 (128 – 10)	118
Contingent consideration	12
Total consideration transferred	130
Fair value of equity interest held before business combination	15
Fair value of consideration	145
Fair value of non-controlling interest	53
	198
Identifiable net assets	(170)
Increase in value	(6)
Deferred tax (176 – 166) x 30%	3
Goodwill	25

Working 3

Clarity

The gain of 1 recorded within other equity should now be deemed realised once the shareholding has been increased to 25%. An adjustment is required to reclassify this gain.

DR Other components of equity (9 – 8)	1
CR Profit or Loss (Retained Earnings)	1

The amount included in the consolidated statement of financial position would be:

	$m
Cost ($9 million + $11 million)	20
Share of post acquisition profits ($10 million x 25%)	2·5
	22·5

(There is an alternative way of dealing with Clarity which is reduce the value of the original investment to cost as it has been classified as available for sale.

DR Other components of equity (9 – 8)	1
CR Investment in associate	1

The amount included in the consolidated statement of financial position would be:

	$m
Cost ($8 million + $11 million)	19
Share of post acquisition profits ($6 million x 10% + $10 million x 25%)	3·1
	22·1

This would affect the statement of financial position.)

Working 4

Available for sale instrument

Date	Exchange rate	Value Dinars m	$m	Change in fair value $m
1 June 2007	4·5	11	49·5	
31 May 2008	5·1	10	51	1·5
31 May 2009	4·8	7	33·6	(17·4)

The asset's fair value in the overseas currency has declined for successive periods. However, no impairment loss is recognised in the year ended 31 May 2008 as there is no loss in the reporting currency ($). The gain of $1·5 million would be recorded in equity. However, in the year to 31 May 2009 an impairment loss of $17·4 million will be recorded as follows:

	$m
DR Other components of equity	1·5
DR Profit or loss	15·9
CR AFS investments	17·4

Working 5

Retained earnings

	$m
Bravado:	
Balance at 31 May 2009	240
Associate profits W3	2·5
AFS impairment W4	(15·9)
Increase in fair value of Clarity now realised	1
Write down of inventory W8	(18)
Increase in fair value of equity interest – Mixted (15 – 10)	5
Gain on bargain purchase	14
Post acquisition reserves: Message	11·2
Mixted	16·52
	256·32

	$m
Message:	
Post acquisition reserves (150 – 136) i.e. $14m	
Group reserves – 80%	11·2
NCI – 20%	2·8
	14

	$m
Mixted:	
Post acquisition reserves:	
at 31 May 2009 (80 – 55)	25
Less increase in depreciation	(2)
Add deferred tax movement	0·6
	23·6
Group reserves – 70%	16·52
NCI – 30%	7·08
	23·6

	$m
Bravado: other components of equity	
Balance at 31 May 2009	12
Investment in associate W3	(1)
Impairment loss – AFS W4	(1·5)
	9·5

Working 6

	$m
Current liabilities – trade payables	
Balance at 31 May 2009	
Bravado	115
Message	30
Mixted	60
	205
Contingent consideration	12
	217

Working 7

	$m
Non-controlling interest	
Message	86
Post acquisition reserves	2·8
	88·8
Mixted	53
Post acquisition reserves	7·08
	60·08
Total	148·88

Working 8

Inventories

IAS2 'Inventories' states that estimates of net realisable value should take into account fluctuations in price occurring after the end of the period to the extent that it confirms conditions at the year end. The new model would have been developed over a period of time and, therefore, would have existed at the year end. The loss in value should be adjusted for. Additionally, although the selling price per stage can be determined, net realisable value (NRV) is based on the selling price of the finished product, and this should be used to calculate NRV.

	$
Selling price of units	1,450
Less selling costs	(10)
NRV	1,440
Less conversion costs	(500)
NRV at 1st stage	940

	$m
Write down	
200,000 units x (1,500 − 1,440)	12
100,000 units x (1,000 − 940)	6
	18

There will have to be an investigation of the difference between the total value of the above inventory and the amount in the financial statements.

Working 9

Property, plant and equipment

	$m	$m
Bravado	265	
Message	230	
Mixted	161	
		656
Increase in value of land – Message (400 − 220 − 136 − 4)		40
Increase in value of PPE – Mixted (176 − 100 − 55 − 7)		14
Less: increased depreciation (14 ÷ 7)		(2)
		708

Working 10

	$m	$m
Available for sale financial assets		
Bravado	51	
Message	6	
Mixted	5	
		62
Less: impairment loss		(17·4)
		44·6

	$m	$m
Inventories		
Bravado	135	
Message	55	
Mixted	73	
		263
Less: write down to NRV		(18)
		245

	$m	$m
Deferred tax		
Bravado	25	
Message	9	
Mixted	3	
		37
Arising on acquisition		3
Movement to year end		(0·6)
		39·4

Working 11

Trade receivables

	$m	$m
Bravado	91	
Message	45	
Mixted	32	
		168

(b) Message:

Gain on bargain purchase if proportionate interest method is used.

	$m
Consideration	300
Identifiable net assets	(400)
Non-controlling interest (20% x 400)	80
Gain on bargain purchase	(20)

	$m
Mixted:	
Purchase consideration	145
Identifiable net assets less deferred tax	
(170 initial fair value + 6 additional fair value – 3 deferred tax)	(173)
Non-controlling interest (30% x 173)	51·9
Goodwill	23·9

Thus in the case of Mixted, the proportionate interest method results in lower net assets in the statement of financial position where goodwill is created with the result that impairment of goodwill may be less. Additionally in the case of Message, it results in a higher gain on the bargain purchase which increases the reported income.

(c) Showing a loan as cash and cash equivalents is misleading. The Framework says that financial statements should have certain characteristics:

(a) understandability
(b) relevance
(c) reliability
(d) comparability

These concepts would preclude the showing of directors' loans in cash. Such information needs separate disclosure as it is relevant to users as it shows the nature of the practices carried out by the company. Reliability requires information to be free from bias and faithfully represent transactions. Comparability is not possible if transactions are not correctly classified. Directors are responsible for the statutory financial statements and if they believe that they are not complying with IFRS, they should take all steps to ensure that the error or irregularity is rectified. Every director will be deemed to have knowledge of the content of the financial statements. In some countries loans to directors are illegal and directors can be personally liable. Directors have a responsibility to act honestly and ethically and not be motivated by personal interest and gain. If the ethical conduct of the directors is questionable then other areas of the financial statements may need scrutiny. A loan of this nature could create a conflict of interest as the directors' personal interests may interfere or conflict with those of the company's. The accurate and full recording of business activities is essential to fulfil the financial and legal obligations of a director as is the efficient use of corporate assets. The loan to a director conflicts with the latter principle.

2 (a) Discussion of fair value and its relevance

The fair value of an asset is the amount at which that asset could be bought or sold in a current transaction between willing parties, other than in a liquidation. The fair value of a liability is the amount at which that liability could be incurred or settled in a current transaction between willing parties, other than in a liquidation. If available, a quoted market price in an active market is the best evidence of fair value and should be used as the basis for the measurement. If a quoted market price is not available, preparers should make an estimate of fair value using the best information available in the circumstances. This may include discounting future cash flows or using pricing models such as Black-Scholes. However these methods all use an element of estimation which in itself can create discrepancies in the values that result. In an efficient market these differences should be immaterial.

The IASB has concluded that fair value is the most relevant measure for most financial instruments. Fair value measurements provide more transparency than historical cost based measurements. Reliability is as important as relevance because relevant information that is not reliable is of no use to an investor. Fair value measurements should be reliable and computed in a manner that is faithful to the underlying economics of the transaction. Measuring financial instruments at fair value should not necessarily mean abandoning historical cost information.

However, market conditions will affect fair value measurements. In many circumstances, quoted market prices are unavailable. As a result, difficulties occur when making estimates of fair value. It is difficult to apply fair value measures in illiquid markets and to decide how and when models should be used for fair valuation. Fair value information can provide a value at the point in time that it is measured but its relevance will depend on the volatility of the market inputs and whether the instruments are actively traded or are held for the long term. Fair value provides an important indicator of risk profile and exposure but to fully understand this and to put it into context, the entity must disclose sufficient information.

(b) (i) Convertible bond

Some compound instruments have both a liability and an equity component from the issuer's perspective. In this case, IAS32 'Financial Instruments: Presentation' requires that the component parts be accounted for and presented separately according to their substance based on the definitions of liabilities and equity. The split is made at issuance and not revised for subsequent changes in market interest rates, share prices, or other events that changes the likelihood that the conversion option will be exercised. (IAS32.28)

A convertible bond contains two components. One is a financial liability, namely the issuer's contractual obligation to pay cash in the form of interest or capital, and the other is an equity instrument, which is the holder's option to convert into shares. When the initial carrying amount of a compound financial instrument is required to be allocated to its equity and liability components, the equity component is assigned the residual amount after deducting from the fair value of the instrument as a whole the amount separately determined for the liability component. (IAS32.31)

In the case of the bond, the liability element will be determined by discounting the future stream of cash flows which will be the interest to be paid and the final capital balance assuming no conversion. The discount rate used will be 9% which is the market rate for similar bonds without the conversion right. The difference between cash received and the liability component is the value of the option.

	$000
Present value of interest at end of:	
Year 1 (31 May 2007) ($100m x 6%) ÷ 1·09	5,505
Year 2 (31 May 2008) ($100m x 6%) ÷ 1·09^2	5,050
Year 3 (31 May 2009) ($100m + ($100m x 6%)) ÷ 1·09^3	81,852
Total liability component	92,407
Total equity element	7,593
Proceeds of issue	100,000

The issue cost will have to be allocated between the liability and equity components in proportion to the above proceeds.

	$000 Liability	$000 Equity	$000 Total
Proceeds	92,407	7,593	100,000
Issue cost	(924)	(76)	(1,000)
	91,483	7,517	99,000

The credit to equity of $7,517 would not be re-measured. The liability component of $91,483 would be measured at amortised cost using the effective interest rate of 9·38%, as this spreads the issue costs over the term of the bond. The interest payments will reduce the liability in getting to the year end. The initial entries would have been:

	$000		$000
Dr Cash	100,000	Cr Cash	1,000
Cr Liability	92,407	Dr Liability	924
Cr Equity	7,593	Dr Equity	76

The liability component balance on 31 May 2009 becomes $100,000 as a result of the effective interest rate of 9·38% being applied and cashflows at 6% based on nominal value.

B/f	Effective Interest 9·38%	Cashflow 6%	C/f
91,483	8,581	6,000	94,064
94,064	8,823	6,000	96,887
96,887	9,088	6,000	~100,000

On conversion of the bond on 31 May 2009, Aron would issue 25 million ordinary shares of $1 and the original equity component together with the balance on the liability will become the consideration.

	$000
Share capital – 25 million at $1	25,000
Share premium	82,517
Equity and liability components (100,000 + 7,593 – 76)	107,517

(ii) Shares in Smart

In this situation Aron has to determine if the transfer of shares in Smart qualifies for derecognition. The criteria are firstly to determine that the asset has been transferred, and then to determine whether or not the entity has transferred

Marks

1 **(a)** Message — 5
Mixted — 6
Clarity — 4
AFS instrument — 3
Retained earnings — 3
Post acquisition reserves — 2
Other components of equity — 2
Current liabilities — 1
NCI — 2
Inventories — 2
PPE — 2
AFS — 1
Deferred tax — 1
Trade receivables — 1
—
35

(b) Message — 3
Mixted — 3
Explanation — 2
—
8

(c) Subjective — 7

AVAILABLE — 50

2 **(a)** Fair value – subjective — 4

(b) Convertible bond: explanation — 2
calculation — 4
Shares in Smart: explanation — 2
calculation — 2
Foreign subsidiary: explanation of principles — 2
accounting treatment — 3
Interest free loan: explanation of principles — 2
accounting treatment — 2
Quality of explanations — 2
—
21

AVAILABLE — 25

3 Vehiclex — IAS18 — 2
IAS11 — 1
IAS16 — 1
Autoseat — IFRIC4 — 3
Discussion — 3
Finance lease — 3
Sale of vehicles — IAS18 — 3
Repurchase four years — 2
Repurchase two years — 3
Demonstration — 2
Professional marks — 2

AVAILABLE — 25

			Marks
4	**(a)**	Subjective	17
		Professional marks	2
			19
	(b)	Calculation	3
		Discussion	3
			6
		AVAILABLE	25

1   (a)   Disposal of equity interest in Sitin
          The gain recognised in profit or loss would be as follows:

	$m
Fair value of consideration	23
Fair value of residual interest	13
Gain reported in comprehensive income	1
	37
less net assets and goodwill derecognised	
net assets	(36)
goodwill ($39 – $32 million)	(7)
Loss on disposal	(6)

    (b)   Grange plc
          Consolidated Statement of Financial Position at 30 November 2009

	$m
Assets:	
Non-current assets	
Property, plant and equipment (W6)	784·47
Investment property (W7)	8
Goodwill (30 + 8)	38
Intangible assets (10 – 3)	7
Investment in Associate (Part a)	13
	850·47
Current assets	920
Total assets	1,770·47
Equity and liabilities:	
Share capital	430
Retained earnings (W3)	401·67
Other components of equity (W3)	57·98
	889·65
Non-controlling interest (W5)	140·82
Total equity	1,030·47
Non-current liabilities	334
Current liabilities	
Trade and other payables	354
Provisions for liabilities (W4)	52
Total current liabilities	406
Total liabilities	740
Total equity and liabilities	1,770·47

          Working 1 Park goodwill and subsequent acquisition

	$m	$m
Fair value of consideration for 60% interest	250	
Fair value of non-controlling interest	150	400
Fair value of identifiable net assets acquired		(360)
Franchise right		(10)
Goodwill		30

          Amortisation of Franchise right
          1 June 2008 to 30 November 2009 – $10m divided by five years multiplied by 1·5 years is $3 million

Dr Profit or loss	$3 million
Cr Franchise right	$3 million

Acquisition of further interest

The net assets of Park have increased from $370 million to $(414 + 5 + 10 – 3) i.e. $426 million at 30 November 2009. They have increased by $56 million and therefore the NCI has increased by 40% of $56 million i.e. $22·4 million.

	$m
Park – NCI 1 June 2008	150
Increase in net assets – NCI to 30 November 2009	22·4
NCI – 30 November 2009	172·4
Transfer to equity 20/40	(86·2)
Balance at 30 November 2009	86·2
Fair value of consideration	90
Transfer from NCI	(86·2)
Negative movement in equity	3·8

Alternatively the acquisition could have been calculated as consideration of $90m less 20% of net assets at second acquisition (20% x (net assets per question 414 + land fair value 5 + franchise fair value 10 less franchise amortisation 3)), resulting in a negative movement in equity of $4·8m. The NCI would therefore be $87·2 million.

Working 2 Fence goodwill and disposal

	$m
Fair value of consideration	214
Fair value of net assets held	(202)
Increase in value of PPE	(4)
Goodwill	8

	$m
Sale of equity interest in Fence	
Fair value of consideration received	80
Amount recognised as non-controlling interest (Net Assets per question at year end 232 – provision created 25 + Fair value of PPE at acquisition 4 – depreciation of fair value adjustment 0·53 (4 x 16/12 x 1/10) + goodwill 8) x 25%	(54·62)
Positive movement in parent equity	25·38

Because a provisional fair value had been recognised for the non-current asset and the valuation was received within 12 months of the date of the acquisition, the fair value of the net assets at acquisition is adjusted thus affecting goodwill.

Contingent liability – Fence

IFRS 3 (2004) required the contingent liabilities of the acquiree to be recognised and measured in a business combination at acquisition-date fair value. IFRS 3 (2008) effectively reapplies the requirement of IFRS 3 (2004) to measure at acquisition-date fair value regardless of probability, but retains a filter based on whether fair value can be measured reliably. This may result in the recognition of contingent liabilities that would not qualify for recognition under IAS 37 *Provisions, Contingent Liabilities and Contingent Assets*. The following consolidation adjustment would have been made:

Dr Retained earnings	$30 million
Cr Contingent liability	$30 million

IFRS 3(2008) requires the acquirer to measure contingent liabilities subsequent to the date of acquisition at the higher of the amount that would be recognised in accordance with IAS 37, and the amount initially recognised, less any appropriate cumulative amortisation. These requirements should be applied only for the period in which the item is considered to be a contingent liability, and usually will result in the contingent liability being carried at the value attributed to it in the initial business combination.

In this case, the contingent liability has subsequently met the requirements to be classified as a provision and has been measured in accordance with IAS 37. As a result the provisions for liabilities of Fence will be reduced by $5 million as the contingent liability consolidation adjustment is no longer required and the provision is created as an entry in the financial statements of Fence. No adjustment will be made to goodwill arising on acquisition.

Dr Contingent Liability/Provisions	$5 million
Cr Profit or loss	$5 million

Working 3 Retained earnings and other components of equity

Retained earnings

	$m
Grange:	
Balance at 30 November 2009	410
Associate profits Sitin (post acquisition profit 3 x 100%)	3
Loss on disposal of Sitin	(6)
Impairment	(28)
Investment property – gain	2
Provision for legal claims	(7)
Post acquisition reserves: Park (60% x (year end retained earnings 170 – acquisition profit 115 – franchise amortisation 3)	31·2
Fence (100% x (year end retained earnings 65 – acquisition retained earnings 73 + conversion of contingent liability to provision and reduction 5 – FV PPE depreciation 0·53))	(3·53)
	401·67

Other components of equity	$m
Balance at 30 November 2009	22
Post acqn reserves – Park (60% x (14 – 10))	2·4
– Fence (17 – 9)	8
– Sitin (post acquisition 1 – recycled on disposal 1)	(nil)
Revaluation surplus – foreign property	4
Park – negative movement in equity	(3·8)
Fence – positive movement in equity	25·38
	57·98

Working 4 Provisions

	$m
Balance at 30 November 2009	
Grange	10
Park	6
Fence	4
	20
Contingency	30
Cancellation of contingency and introduction of provision	(5)
Provision for environmental claims	7
	52

Working 5 Non-controlling interest

	$m
Park (W1)	86·2
Fence (W2)	54·62
Total	140·82

Working 6 Property, plant and equipment

	$m	$m
Grange	257	
Park	311	
Fence	238	
		806
Increase in value of land – Park (360 – 230 – 115 – 10)		5
Investment property – reclassified		(6)
Impairment – Grange (W9)		(28)
Increase in value of PPE – Fence		4
Less: increased depreciation (4 x 16/12 ÷ 10)		(0·53)
Revaluation surplus foreign property		4
		784·47

Working 7

The land should be classified as an investment property. Although Grange has not decided what to do with the land, it is being held for capital appreciation. IAS 40 'Investment Property' states that land held for indeterminate future use is an investment property where the entity has not decided that it will use the land as owner occupied or for short-term sale. The land will be measured at fair value as Grange has a policy of maximising its return on capital employed. The fall in value of the investment property after the year-end will not affect its year-end valuation as the uncertainty relating to the regeneration occurred after the year-end.

Dr Investment property	$6 million
Cr PPE	$6 million
Dr Investment property	$2 million
Cr Profit or loss	$2 million

No depreciation will be charged

Working 8 Provision for environmental claims

The environmental obligations of $1 million and $6 million (total $7 million) arise from past events but the costs of $4 million relating to the improvement of the manufacturing process relate to the company's future operations and should not be provided for.

Dr Profit or loss	$7 million
Cr Provision	$7 million

Working 9 Restructuring

A provision for restructuring should not be recognised, as a constructive obligation does not exist. A constructive obligation arises when an entity both has a detailed formal plan and makes an announcement of the plan to those affected. The events to date do not provide sufficient detail that would permit recognition of a constructive obligation. Therefore no provision for reorganisation should be made and the costs and benefits of the plan should not be taken into account when determining the impairment loss. Any impairment loss can be allocated to non-current assets, as this is the area in which the directors feel that loss has occurred.

	$m
Carrying value of Grange's net assets	862
Revaluation surplus	4
Provision for legal claims	(7)
Investment property	2
Impairment of investment in Sitin (16 – 13)	(3)
	858
Value-in-use (pre-restructuring)	830
Impairment to PPE	(28)

Working 10 Foreign property

	$m
Value at 30 November 2009 (12m dinars/1·5)	8
Value at acquisition 30 November 2008	4
Revaluation surplus to equity	4
Change in fair value (4m dinars at 1·5)	2·67
Exchange rate change	1·33
(8m dinars at 2 minus 12 million dinars at 1·5)	4

(c) Rules are a very important element of ethics. Usually this means focusing upon the rules contained in the accounting profession's code of professional conduct and references to legislation and corporate codes of conduct. They are an efficient means by which the accounting profession can communicate its expectations as to what behaviour is expected.

A view that equates ethical behaviour with compliance to professional rules could create a narrow perception of what ethical behaviour constitutes. Compliance with rules is not necessarily the same as ethical behaviour. Ethics and rules can be different. Ethical principles and values are used to judge the appropriateness of any rule.

Accountants should have the ability to conclude that a particular rule is inappropriate, unfair, or possibly unethical in any given circumstance. Rules are the starting point for any ethical question and rules are objective measures of ethical standards. In fact, rules are the value judgments as to what is right for accountants and reflect the profession's view about what constitutes good behaviour. Accountants who view ethical issues within this rigid framework are likely to suffer a moral crisis when encountering problems for which there is no readily apparent rule.

An overemphasis on ethical codes of behaviour tends to reinforce a perception of ethics as being punitive and does not promote the positive aspects of ethics that are designed to promote the reputation of an accounting firm and its clients, as well as standards within the profession. The resolution of ethical problems depends on the application of commonly shared ethical principles with appropriate skill and judgment. Ethical behaviour is based on universal principles and reasoned public debate and is difficult to capture in 'rules'.

Accountants have to make accounting policy choices on a regular basis. Stakeholders rely on the information reported by accountants to make informed decisions about the entity at hand. All decisions require judgment, and judgment depends on personal values with the decision needing to be made on some basis such as following rules, obeying authority, caring for others, justice, or whether the choice is right. These values and several others compete as the criterion for making a choice. Such personal values incorporate ethical values that dictate whether any accounting value chosen is a good or poor surrogate for economic value. To maintain the faith of the public, accountants must be highly ethical in their work. The focus on independence (conflict of interest) and associated compliance requirements may absorb considerable resources and conceptual space in relation to ethics in practice. This response is driven by a strong commitment within the firms to meet their statutory and regulatory obligations. The primary focus on independence may have narrowed some firms' appreciation of what constitutes broader ethical performance. As a result it may be that the increasing codification and compliance focus on one or two key aspects of ethical behaviour may be in fact eroding or preventing a more holistic approach to enabling ethics in practice.

If the director tells Field about the liquidity problems of Brook, then a confidence has been betrayed but there is a question of honesty if the true situation is not divulged. Another issue is whether the financial director has a duty to several stakeholders including the shareholders and employees of Grange, as if the information is disclosed about the poor liquidity position of Brook, then the amounts owing to Grange may not be paid. However, there is or may be a duty to disclose all the information to Field but if the information is deemed to be insider information then it should not be disclosed.

The finance director's reputation and career may suffer if Brook goes into liquidation especially as he will be responsible for the amounts owing by Brook. Another issue is whether the friend of the director has the right to expect him to keep the information private and if the shareholders of Grange stand to lose as a result of not divulging the information there may be an expectation that such information should be disclosed. Finally, should Field expect any credit information to be accurate or simply be a note of Brook's credit history? Thus it can be seen that the ethical and moral dilemma's facing the director of Grange are not simply a matter of following rules but are a complex mix of issues concerning trust, duty of care, insider information, confidentiality and morality.

2   (a)   IAS 36 'Impairment of Assets' states that an asset is impaired when its carrying amount will not be recovered from its continuing use or from its sale. An entity must determine at each reporting date whether there is any indication that an asset is impaired. If an indicator of impairment exists then the asset's recoverable amount must be determined and compared with its carrying amount to assess the amount of any impairment. Accounting for the impairment of non-financial assets can be difficult as IAS 36 'Impairment of Assets' is a complex accounting standard. The turbulence in the markets and signs of economic downturn will cause many companies to revisit their business plans and revise financial forecasts. As a result of these changes, there may be significant impairment charges. Indicators of impairment may arise from either the external environment in which the entity operates or from within the entity's own operating environment. Thus the current economic downturn is an obvious indicator of impairment, which may cause the entity to experience significant impairment charges.

Assets should be tested for impairment at as low a level as possible, at individual asset level where possible. However, many assets do not generate cash inflows independently from other assets and such assets will usually be tested within the cash-generating unit (CGU) to which the asset belongs. Cash flow projections should be based on reasonable assumptions that represent management's best estimate of the range of economic conditions that will exist over the remaining useful life of the asset. The discount rate used is the rate, which reflects the specific risks of the asset or CGU.

The basic principle is that an asset may not be carried in the statement of financial position at more than its recoverable amount. An asset's recoverable amount is the higher of:

(a)   the amount for which the asset could be sold in an arm's length transaction between knowledgeable and willing parties, net of costs of disposal (fair value less costs to sell); and

(b)   the present value of the future cash flows that are expected to be derived from the asset (value in use). The expected future cash flows include those from the asset's continued use in the business and those from its ultimate disposal. Value in use (VIU) is explicitly based on present value calculations.

This measurement basis reflects the economic decisions that a company's management team makes when assets become impaired from the viewpoint of whether the business is better off disposing of the asset or continuing to use it.

The assumptions used in arriving at the recoverable amount need to be 'reasonable and supportable' regardless of whether impairment calculations are based on fair value less costs to sell or value in use. The acceptable range for such assumptions will change over time and forecasts for revenue growth and profit margins are likely to have fallen in the economic climate. The assumptions made by management should be in line with the assumptions made by industry commentators or analysts. Variances from market will need to be justified and highlighted in financial statement disclosures.

Whatever method is used to calculate the recoverable amount; the value needs to be considered in the light of available market evidence. If other entities in the same sector are taking impairment charges, the absence of an impairment charge have to be justified because the market will be asking the same question.

It is important to inform the market about how it is dealing with the conditions, and be thinking about how different parts of the business are affected, and the market inputs they use in impairment testing. Impairment testing should be commenced as soon as possible as an impairment test process takes a significant amount of time. It includes identifying impairment indicators, assessing or reassessing the cash flows, determining the discount rates, testing the reasonableness of the assumptions and benchmarking the assumptions with the market. Goodwill does not have to be tested for impairment at the year-end; it can be tested earlier and if any impairment indicator arises at the balance sheet date, the impairment assessment can be updated. Also, it is important to comply with all disclosure requirements, such as the discount rate and long-term growth rate assumptions in a discounted cash flow model, and describe what the key assumptions are and what they are based on.

It is important that the cash flows being tested are consistent with the assets being tested. The forecast cash flows should make allowance for investment in working capital if the business is expected to grow. When the detailed calculations have been completed, the company should check that their conclusions make sense by comparison to any market data, such as share prices and analysts reports. Market capitalisation below net asset value is an impairment indicator, and calculations of recoverable amount are required. If the market capitalisation is lower than a value-in-use calculation, then the VIU assumptions may require reassessment. For example, the cash flow projections might not be as expected by the market, and the reasons for this must be scrutinised. Discount rates should be scrutinised in order to see if they are logical. Discount rates may have risen too as risk premiums rise. Many factors affect discount rates in impairment calculations. These include corporate lending rates, cost of capital and risks associated with cash flows, which are all increasing in the current volatile environment and can potentially result in an increase of the discount rate.

(b) An asset's carrying amount may not be recovered from future business activity. Wherever indicators of impairment exist, a review for impairment should be carried out. Where impairment is identified, a write-down of the carrying value to the recoverable amount should be charged as an immediate expense in the income statement. Using a discount rate of 5%, the value in use of the non-current assets is:

Year to	31 May 2010	31 May 2011	31 May 2012	31 May 2013	Total
Discounted cash flows ($000)	267	408	431	452	1,558

The carrying value of the non-current assets at 31 May 2009 is $3 million – depreciation of $600,000. i.e. $2·4 million. Therefore the assets are impaired by $842,000 ($2·4m – $1·558m).

IAS 36 requires an assessment at each balance sheet date whether there is an indication that an impairment loss may have decreased. This does not apply to goodwill or to the unwinding of the discount. In this case, the increase in value is due to the unwinding of the discount as the same cash flows have been used in the calculation. Compensation received in the form of reimbursements from governmental indemnities is recorded in the statement of comprehensive income when the compensation becomes receivable according to IAS 37 *Provisions, Contingent Liabilities and Contingent Assets*. It is treated as separate economic events and accounted for as such. At this time the government has only stated that it may reimburse the company and therefore credit should not taken of any potential government receipt.

For a revalued asset, the impairment loss is treated as a revaluation decrease. The loss is first set against any revaluation surplus and the balance of the loss is then treated as an expense in profit or loss. The revaluation gain and the impairment loss would be treated as follows:

	Depreciated historical cost ($m)	Revalued carrying value ($m)
1 December 2006	10	10
Depreciation (2 years)	(2)	(2)
Revaluation		0·8
1 December 2008	8	8·8
Depreciation	(1)	(1·1)
Impairment loss	(1·5)	(2·2)
30 November 2009 after impairment loss	5·5	5·5

The impairment loss of $2·2 million is charged to equity until the carrying amount reaches depreciated historical cost and thereafter it goes to profit or loss. It is assumed that the company will transfer an amount from revaluation surplus to retained earnings to cover the excess depreciation of $0·1 million as allowed by IAS 16. Therefore the impairment loss charged to equity would be $(0·8 – 0·1) million i.e. $0·7 million and the remainder of $1·5 million would be charged to profit or loss.

A plan by management to dispose of an asset or group of assets due to under utilisation is an indicator of impairment. This will usually be well before the held for sale criteria under IFRS 5 *'Non Current Assets Held-for-sale and Discontinued Activities'* are met. Assets or CGUs are tested for impairment when the decision to sell is made. The impairment test is updated immediately before classification under IFRS 5. IFRS 5 requires an asset held for sale to be measured at the lower of its carrying amount and its fair value less costs to sell. Non-current assets held for sale and disposal groups are re-measured at the lower of carrying amount or fair value less costs to sell at every balance sheet date from classification until disposal. The measurement process is similar to that which occurs on classification as held for sale. Any excess of carrying value over fair value less costs to sell is a further impairment loss and is recognised as a loss in the statement of comprehensive income in the current period. Fair value less costs to sell in excess of carrying value is ignored and no gain is recorded on classification. The non-current assets or disposal group cannot be written up past its previous (pre-impairment) carrying amount, adjusted for depreciation, that would have been applied without the impairment. The fact that the asset is being marketed at a price in excess of its fair value may mean that the asset is not available for immediate sale and therefore may not meet the criteria for 'held for sale'.

3 **(i)** Revenue arising from the sale of goods should be recognised when all of the following criteria have been satisfied: [IAS 18 Para 14]

(a) The seller has transferred to the buyer the significant risks and rewards of ownership;
(b) The seller retains neither continuing managerial involvement to the degree usually associated with ownership nor effective control over the goods sold;
(c) The amount of revenue can be measured reliably;
(d) It is probable that the economic benefits associated with the transaction will flow to the seller; and
(e) The costs incurred or to be incurred in respect of the transaction can be measured reliably.

Burley should recognise a purchase from Slite for the amount of the excess amount extracted (10,000 barrels x $100). The substance of the transaction is that Slite has sold the oil to Burley at the point of production at market value at that time. Burley should recognise all of the oil it has sold to the third parties as revenue including that purchased from Slite as the criteria in IAS 18 are met. The amount payable to Slite will change with movements in the oil price. The balance at the year-end is a financial liability, which should reflect the best estimate of the amount of cash payable, which at the year-end would be $1,050,000. The best estimate will be based on the price of oil on 30 November 2009. At the year-end there will be an expense of $50,000 as the liability will have increased from $1 million. The amount payable will be revised after the year-end to reflect changes in the price of oil and would have amounted to $950,000. Thus giving a gain of $100,000 to profit or loss in the following accounting period.

Events after the reporting period are events, which could be favourable or unfavourable, and occur between the end of the reporting period and the date that the financial statements are authorised for issue. [IAS 10 Para 3]

An adjusting event is an event after the reporting period that provides further evidence of conditions that existed at the end of the reporting period, including an event that indicates that the going concern assumption in relation to the whole part or part of the enterprise is not appropriate. A non-adjusting event is an event after the reporting period that is indicative of a condition that arose after the end of the reporting period. [IAS 10 Para 3]

Inventories are required to be stated at the lower of cost and net realisable value (NRV). [IAS 2 Para 9] NRV is the estimated selling price in the ordinary course of business, less the estimated cost of completion and the estimated costs necessary to make the sale. Any write-down to NRV should be recognised as an expense in the period in which the write-down occurs. Estimates of NRV are based on the most reliable evidence available at the time the estimates are made. These estimates consider fluctuations in price directly relating to events occurring after the end of the financial period to the extent that they confirm conditions at the end of the accounting period.

Burley should calculate NRV by reference to the market price of oil at the balance sheet date. The price of oil changes frequently in response to many factors and therefore changes in the market price since the balance sheet date reflect events since that date. These represent non-adjusting events. Therefore the decline in the price of oil since the date of the financial statements will not be adjusted in those statements. The inventory will be valued at cost of $98 per barrel as this is lower than NRV of $(105 – 2) i.e. $103 at the year-end.

Workings 1

	DR($)	CR($)
Purchases/Inventory (10,000 x 100)	1m	
Slite – financial liability		1m
At year end		
Expense	50,000	
Slite – financial liability (10,000 x $(105 – 100))		50,000
After year end		
Slite – financial liability (10,000 x $(105 – 95)	100,000	
Profit or loss		100,000

Cash paid to Slite is $950,000 on 12 December 2009

(ii) A jointly controlled entity is a corporation, partnership, or other entity in which two or more venturers have an interest, under a contractual arrangement that establishes joint control over the entity. [IAS 31.24]

IAS 31 allows two treatments of accounting for an investment in jointly controlled entities:

(a) Proportionate consolidation.
(b) Equity method of accounting.

Joint control is the contractually agreed sharing of control over an economic activity and only exists when strategic, financial and operating decisions relating to the activity require the unanimous consent of the parties sharing control i.e. the venturers. [IAS 31 Para 3] Thus Burley cannot use proportionate consolidation, as Wells is not jointly controlled. A decision can be made by gaining the approval of two thirds of the venturers and not by unanimous agreement. Two out of the three venturers can make the decision. Thus each investor must account for their interest in the entity as an associate since they have significant influence but not control. Equity accounting will be used.

One of the key differences between decommissioning costs and other costs of acquisition is the timing of costs. Decommissioning costs will not become payable until some future date. Consequently, there is likely to be uncertainty over the amount of costs that will be incurred. Management should record its best estimate of the entity's obligations. [IAS 16.16]

Discounting is used to address the impact of the delayed cash flows. The amount capitalised, as part of the assets will be the amount estimated to be paid, discounted to the date of initial recognition. The related credit is recognised in provisions. An entity that uses the cost model records changes in the existing liability and changes in discount rate are added to, or deducted from, the cost of the related asset in the current period. [IFRIC 1.5]

Thus in the case of Wells, the accounting for the decommissioning is as follows.

The carrying amount of the asset will be

	$m
Carrying amount at 1 December 2008	
(240 – depreciation 60 – 14·1 decrease	
In decommissioning costs)	165·9
Less depreciation 165·9 ÷ 30 years	(5·5)
Carrying amount at 30 November 2009	160·4
Finance cost ($32·6 million – $14·1 million) at 7%	1·3
Decommissioning liability will be ($32·6m – $14·1m)	18·5
Decommissioning liability at 30 November 2009	19·8

Jointly controlled assets involve the joint control, and often the joint ownership, of assets dedicated to the joint venture. Each venturer may take a share of the output from the assets and each bears a share of the expenses incurred. [IAS 31 Para 18]

IAS 31 requires that the venturer should recognise in its financial statements its share of the joint assets, any liabilities that it has incurred directly and its share of any liabilities incurred jointly with other venturers, income from the sale or use of its share of the output of the joint venture, its share of expenses incurred by the joint venture and expenses incurred directly in the respect of its interest in the joint venture. [IAS 31 Para 21] The pipeline is a jointly controlled asset. Therefore, Burley should not show the asset as an investment but as property, plant and equipment. Any liabilities or expenses incurred should be shown also.

(iii) An asset is a resource controlled by the enterprise as a result of past events and from which future economic benefits are expected to flow to the enterprise. [Framework. Para 49(a)] An asset is recognised in the statement of financial position when it is probable that the future economic benefits will flow to the enterprise and the asset has a cost or value that can be measured reliably. [Framework. Para 89]

IAS 38 *'Intangible Assets'* also requires an enterprise to recognise an intangible asset, whether purchased or self-created (at cost) if, and only if: [IAS 38]

(a)   it is probable that the future economic benefits that are attributable to the asset will flow to the enterprise; and

(b)   the cost of the asset can be measured reliably.

This requirement applies whether an intangible asset is acquired externally or generated internally.

The probability of future economic benefits must be based on reasonable and supportable assumptions about conditions that will exist over the life of the asset. [IAS 38] The probability recognition criterion is always considered to be satisfied for intangible assets that are acquired separately or in a business combination. [IAS 38] IAS 36 *'Impairment of Assets'* also says that at each balance sheet date, an entity should review all assets to look for any indication that an asset may be impaired (its carrying amount may be in excess of the greater of its net selling price and its value in use). IAS 36 has a list of external and internal indicators of impairment. If there is an indication that an asset may be impaired, then the asset's recoverable amount should be calculated. [IAS 36] Thus the licence can be capitalised and if the exploration of the area does not lead to the discovery of oil, and activities are discontinued in the area, then an impairment test will be performed.

4   (a)   (i)   Financial instruments can be measured under IFRS in a variety of ways. For example financial assets utilise the equity method for associates, proportionate consolidation for joint ventures, fair value with gains and losses in earnings, fair value with gains and losses in other comprehensive income until realised. Financial liabilities can also utilise different measurement methods including fair value with gains and losses in earnings and amortised cost. The measurement methods used under IFRS sometimes portray an estimate of current value and others portray original cost. Some of the measurements include the effect of impairment losses, which are recognised differently under IFRS. For example financial assets at fair value through profit/loss (FVTPL) recognise changes in value in earnings, whilst those classified as 'available for sale' are measured at fair value with changes in other comprehensive income except for those impairments that are required to be reported in earnings.

The above can result in two identical instruments being measured differently by the same entity because management's intentions for realising the value of the instrument may determine the way it is measured (FVTPL compared to held to maturity investments). Management also has the option of valuing a financial instrument at fair value or at amortised cost ('available for sale' compared to 'loans and receivables'). Also the percentage of the ownership interest acquired will determine how the holding is accounted for (associate – equity method, subsidiary – acquisition method).

The different ways in which financial instruments can be measured creates problems for preparers and users of financial statements because of the following:

(a) the criteria for deciding which instrument can be measured in a certain way are complex and difficult to apply. It is sometimes difficult to determine whether an instrument is equity or a liability and the criteria can be applied in different ways as new types of instruments are created.

(b) Management can choose how to account for an instrument or can be forced into a treatment that they would have preferred to avoid. For example if there is no proper documentation of the risk management or investment strategy then the FVTPL category may not be available for use and the default category of 'available for sale' may have to be utilised.

(c) Different gains or losses resulting from different measurement methods may be combined in the same line item in the statement of comprehensive income.

(d) It is not always apparent which measurement principle has been applied to which instrument and what the implications are of the difference. Comparability is affected and the interpretation of financial statements is difficult and time consuming.

(ii) There are several approaches that can be taken to solve the measurement and related problems. There is pressure to develop standards, which are principle-based and less complex. It has been suggested by IASB members that the long-term solution is to measure all financial instruments using a single measurement principle thus making reported information easier to understand and allowing comparisons between entities and periods. If fair value was used for all types of financial instrument then

(a) There would be no need to 'classify' financial instruments
(b) There would be no requirement to report how impairment losses have been quantified
(c) There would be no need for rules as regards transfers between measurement categories
(d) There would be no measurement mismatches between financial instruments and the need for fair value hedge accounting would be reduced
(e) Identification and separation of embedded derivatives would not be required (this may be required for non-financial instruments)
(f) A single measurement method would eliminate the confusion about which method was being used for different types of financial instruments
(g) Entities with comparable credit ratings and obligations will report liabilities at comparable amounts even if borrowings occurred at different times at different interest rates. The reverse is true also. Different credit ratings and obligations will result in the reporting of different liabilities
(h) Fair value would better reflect the cash flows that would be paid if liabilities were transferred at the re-measurement date

Fair value would result in an entity reporting the same measure for security payment obligations with identical cash flow amounts and timing. At present different amounts are likely to be reported if the two obligations were incurred at different times if market interest rates change.

There is uncertainty inherent in all estimates and fair value measurements, and there is the risk that financial statements will be seen as more arbitrary with fair value because management has even more ability to affect the financial statements. Accountants need to be trained to recognise biases with respect to accounting estimates and fair value measurements so they can advise entities. It is important to demonstrate consistency in how an entity has applied the fair value principles and developed valuations to ensure credibility with investors, lenders and auditors. Although entities may select which assets and liabilities they wish to value under IAS 39, outside parties will be looking for consistency in how the standard was applied. Circumstances and market conditions change. Markets may become illiquid and the predicative models may not provide an ongoing advantage for the entity.

(b) Using amortised cost, both financial liabilities will result in single payments, which are almost identical at the same point in time in the future ($59·9 million). ($47m x 1·05 for 5 years and $45m x 1·074 for 4 years) However, the carrying amounts at 30 November 2009 would be different. The initial loan would be carried at $47 million plus interest of $2·35 million, i.e. $49·35 million, whilst the new loan would be carried at $45 million even though the obligation at 30 November 2013 would be approximately the same.

If the two loans were carried at fair value, then the initial loan would be carried at $45 million thus showing a net profit of $2 million (interest expense of $2·35 million and unrealised gain of $4·35 million).

Marks

1 **(a)** Fair value of consideration — 1
Fair value of residual interest — 1
Gain reported in comprehensive income — 1
Net assets — 1
Goodwill — 2
—
6
—

(b) Property, plant and equipment — 6
Investment property — 2
Goodwill — 3
Retained earnings — 7
Other components of equity — 5
Non-controlling interest — 2
Non-current liabilities/Trade and other payables — 1
Provisions for liabilities — 3
Intangible assets — 2
Current assets/Available for sale financial assets — 1
Investment in Associate — 2
Share capital — 1
—
35
—

(c) Subjective up to — 7
Professional marks — 2
—
Total — **50**
—

2 **(a)** Impairment process — • 4
General considerations — 4
Professional marks — 2

(b) Non-current asset at cost — 6
Non-current assets at valuation — 6
Non-currents asset held for sale — 3
—
25
—

3 Revenue recognition — 4
Inventory — 3
Events after reporting period — 2
Jointly controlled — 3
Accounting for entity — 2
Decommissioning — 5
Asset definition /IAS38 /IAS 36 — 4
Professional marks — 2
—
25
—

4 **(a)** **(i)** 1 mark per point up to maximum — 9

(ii) 1 mark per point up to maximum — 9

Professional marks — 2

(b) Identical payment — 2
Carrying amount — 1
Fair value — 2
—
AVAILABLE — **25**
—

Mathematical tables

Present value table

Present value of 1 = $(1+r)^{-n}$ where r = discount rate, n = number of periods until payment.

This table shows the present value of £1 per annum, receivable or payable at the end of *n* years.

Periods					Discount rates (r)					
(n)	1%	2%	3%	4%	5%	6%	7%	8%	9%	10%
1	0.990	0.980	0.971	0.962	0.952	0.943	0.935	0.926	0.917	0.909
2	0.980	0.961	0.943	0.925	0.907	0.890	0.873	0.857	0.842	0.826
3	0.971	0.942	0.915	0.889	0.864	0.840	0.816	0.794	0.772	0.751
4	0.961	0.924	0.888	0.855	0.823	0.792	0.763	0.735	0.708	0.683
5	0.951	0.906	0.863	0.822	0.784	0.747	0.713	0.681	0.650	0.621
6	0.942	0.888	0.837	0.790	0.746	0.705	0.666	0.630	0.596	0.564
7	0.933	0.871	0.813	0.760	0.711	0.665	0.623	0.583	0.547	0.513
8	0.923	0.853	0.789	0.731	0.677	0.627	0.582	0.540	0.502	0.467
9	0.914	0.837	0.766	0.703	0.645	0.592	0.544	0.500	0.460	0.424
10	0.905	0.820	0.744	0.676	0.614	0.558	0.508	0.463	0.422	0.386
11	0.896	0.804	0.722	0.650	0.585	0.527	0.475	0.429	0.388	0.350
12	0.887	0.788	0.701	0.625	0.557	0.497	0.444	0.397	0.356	0.319
13	0.879	0.773	0.681	0.601	0.530	0.469	0.415	0.368	0.326	0.290
14	0.870	0.758	0.661	0.577	0.505	0.442	0.388	0.340	0.299	0.263
15	0.861	0.743	0.642	0.555	0.481	0.417	0.362	0.315	0.275	0.239
16	0.853	0.728	0.623	0.534	0.458	0.394	0.339	0.292	0.252	0.218
17	0.844	0.714	0.605	0.513	0.436	0.371	0.317	0.270	0.231	0.198
18	0.836	0.700	0.587	0.494	0.416	0.350	0.296	0.250	0.212	0.180
19	0.828	0.686	0.570	0.475	0.396	0.331	0.277	0.232	0.194	0.164
20	0.820	0.673	0.554	0.456	0.377	0.312	0.258	0.215	0.178	0.149

Periods					Discount rates (r)					
(n)	11%	12%	13%	14%	15%	16%	17%	18%	19%	20%
1	0.901	0.893	0.885	0.877	0.870	0.862	0.855	0.847	0.840	0.833
2	0.812	0.797	0.783	0.769	0.756	0.743	0.731	0.718	0.706	0.694
3	0.731	0.712	0.693	0.675	0.658	0.641	0.624	0.609	0.593	0.579
4	0.659	0.636	0.613	0.592	0.572	0.552	0.534	0.516	0.499	0.482
5	0.593	0.567	0.543	0.519	0.497	0.476	0.456	0.437	0.419	0.402
6	0.535	0.507	0.480	0.456	0.432	0.410	0.390	0.370	0.352	0.335
7	0.482	0.452	0.425	0.400	0.376	0.354	0.333	0.314	0.296	0.279
8	0.434	0.404	0.376	0.351	0.327	0.305	0.285	0.266	0.249	0.233
9	0.391	0.361	0.333	0.308	0.284	0.263	0.243	0.225	0.209	0.194
10	0.352	0.322	0.295	0.270	0.247	0.227	0.208	0.191	0.176	0.162
11	0.317	0.287	0.261	0.237	0.215	0.195	0.178	0.162	0.148	0.135
12	0.286	0.257	0.231	0.208	0.187	0.168	0.152	0.137	0.124	0.112
13	0.258	0.229	0.204	0.182	0.163	0.145	0.130	0.116	0.104	0.093
14	0.232	0.205	0.181	0.160	0.141	0.125	0.111	0.099	0.088	0.078
15	0.209	0.183	0.160	0.140	0.123	0.108	0.095	0.084	0.074	0.065
16	0.188	0.163	0.141	0.123	0.107	0.093	0.081	0.071	0.062	0.054
17	0.170	0.146	0.125	0.108	0.093	0.080	0.069	0.060	0.052	0.045
18	0.153	0.130	0.111	0.095	0.081	0.069	0.059	0.051	0.044	0.038
19	0.138	0.116	0.098	0.083	0.070	0.060	0.051	0.043	0.037	0.031
20	0.124	0.104	0.087	0.073	0.061	0.051	0.043	0.037	0.031	0.026

Cumulative present value table

This table shows the present value of £1 per annum, receivable or payable at the end of each year for *n* years.

Periods	Discount rates (r)									
(n)	1%	2%	3%	4%	5%	6%	7%	8%	9%	10%
1	0.990	0.980	0.971	0.962	0.952	0.943	0.935	0.926	0.917	0.909
2	1.970	1.942	1.913	1.886	1.859	1.833	1.808	1.783	1.759	1.736
3	2.941	2.884	2.829	2.775	2.723	2.673	2.624	2.577	2.531	2.487
4	3.902	3.808	3.717	3.630	3.546	3.465	3.387	3.312	3.240	3.170
5	4.853	4.713	4.580	4.452	4.329	4.212	4.100	3.993	3.890	3.791
6	5.795	5.601	5.417	5.242	5.076	4.917	4.767	4.623	4.486	4.355
7	6.728	6.472	6.230	6.002	5.786	5.582	5.389	5.206	5.033	4.868
8	7.652	7.325	7.020	6.733	6.463	6.210	5.971	5.747	5.535	5.335
9	8.566	8.162	7.786	7.435	7.108	6.802	6.515	6.247	5.995	5.759
10	9.471	8.983	8.530	8.111	7.722	7.360	7.024	6.710	6.418	6.145
11	10.37	9.787	9.253	8.760	8.306	7.887	7.499	7.139	6.805	6.495
12	11.26	10.58	9.954	9.385	8.863	8.384	7.943	7.536	7.161	6.814
13	12.13	11.35	10.63	9.986	9.394	8.853	8.358	7.904	7.487	7.103
14	13.00	12.11	11.30	10.56	9.899	9.295	8.745	8.244	7.786	7.367
15	13.87	12.85	11.94	11.12	10.38	9.712	9.108	8.559	8.061	7.606
16	14.718	13.578	12.561	11.652	10.838	10.106	9.447	8.851	8.313	7.824
17	15.562	14.292	13.166	12.166	11.274	10.477	9.763	9.122	8.544	8.022
18	16.398	14.992	13.754	12.659	11.690	10.828	10.059	9.372	8.756	8.201
19	17.226	15.678	14.324	13.134	12.085	11.158	10.336	9.604	8.950	8.365
20	18.046	16.351	14.877	13.590	12.462	11.470	10.594	9.818	9.129	8.514

Periods	Discount rates (r)									
(n)	11%	12%	13%	14%	15%	16%	17%	18%	19%	20%
1	0.901	0.893	0.885	0.877	0.870	0.862	0.855	0.847	0.840	0.833
2	1.713	1.690	1.668	1.647	1.626	1.605	1.585	1.566	1.547	1.528
3	2.444	2.402	2.361	2.322	2.283	2.246	2.210	2.174	2.140	2.106
4	3.102	3.037	2.974	2.914	2.855	2.798	2.743	2.690	2.639	2.589
5	3.696	3.605	3.517	3.433	3.352	3.274	3.199	3.127	3.058	2.991
6	4.231	4.111	3.998	3.889	3.784	3.685	3.589	3.498	3.410	3.326
7	4.712	4.564	4.423	4.288	4.160	4.039	3.922	3.812	3.706	3.605
8	5.146	4.968	4.799	4.639	4.487	4.344	4.207	4.078	3.954	3.837
9	5.537	5.328	5.132	4.946	4.772	4.607	4.451	4.303	4.163	4.031
10	5.889	5.650	5.426	5.216	5.019	4.833	4.659	4.494	4.339	4.192
11	6.207	5.938	5.687	5.453	5.234	5.029	4.836	4.656	4.486	4.327
12	6.492	6.194	5.918	5.660	5.421	5.197	4.988	4.793	4.611	4.439
13	6.750	6.424	6.122	5.842	5.583	5.342	5.118	4.910	4.715	4.533
14	6.982	6.628	6.302	6.002	5.724	5.468	5.229	5.008	4.802	4.611
15	7.191	6.811	6.462	6.142	5.847	5.575	5.324	5.092	4.876	4.675
16	7.379	6.974	6.604	6.265	5.954	5.668	5.405	5.162	4.938	4.730
17	7.549	7.120	6.729	6.373	6.047	5.749	5.475	5.222	4.990	4.775
18	7.702	7.250	6.840	6.467	6.128	5.818	5.534	5.273	5.033	4.812
19	7.839	7.366	6.938	6.550	6.198	5.877	5.584	5.316	5.070	4.843
20	7.963	7.469	7.025	6.623	6.259	5.929	5.628	5.353	5.101	4.870

All original review forms from the entire BPP range, completed with genuine comments, will be entered into one of two draws on 31 July 2010 and 31 January 2011. The names on the first four forms picked out on each occasion will be sent a cheque for £50.

Name: _____   Address: _____

_____

_____

How have you used this Kit?
(Tick one box only)

☐ Home study (book only)

☐ On a course: college _____

☐ With 'correspondence' package

☐ Other _____

Why did you decide to purchase this Kit?
(Tick one box only)

☐ Have used the complementary Study text

☐ Have used other BPP products in the past

☐ Recommendation by friend/colleague

☐ Recommendation by a lecturer at college

☐ Saw advertising

☐ Other _____

During the past six months do you recall seeing/receiving any of the following?
(Tick as many boxes as are relevant)

☐ Our advertisement in *Student Accountant*

☐ Our advertisement in *Pass*

☐ Our advertisement in *PQ*

☐ Our brochure with a letter through the post

☐ Our website www.bpp.com

Which (if any) aspects of our advertising do you find useful?
(Tick as many boxes as are relevant)

☐ Prices and publication dates of new editions

☐ Information on product content

☐ Facility to order books off-the-page

☐ None of the above

Which BPP products have you used?

Text	☐	Success CD	☐	Learn Online	☐
Kit	☑	i-Learn	☐	Home Study Package	☐
Passcard	☐	i-Pass	☐	Home Study PLUS	☐

Your ratings, comments and suggestions would be appreciated on the following areas.

	Very useful	Useful	Not useful
Passing ACCA exams	☐	☐	☐
Passing P2	☐	☐	☐
Planning your question practice	☐	☐	☐
Questions	☐	☐	☐
Top Tips etc in answers	☐	☐	☐
Content and structure of answers	☐	☐	☐
'Plan of attack' in mock exams	☐	☐	☐
Mock exam answers	☐	☐	☐

Overall opinion of this Kit	Excellent ☐		Good ☐		Adequate ☐		Poor ☐

Do you intend to continue using BPP products?   Yes ☐   No ☐

The BPP author of this edition can be e-mailed at: katyhibbert@bpp.com

Please return this form to: Lesley Buick, ACCA Publishing Manager, BPP Learning Media Ltd, FREEPOST, London, W12 8BR

Review Form & Free Prize Draw (continued)

TELL US WHAT YOU THINK

Please note any further comments and suggestions/errors below.

Free Prize Draw Rules

1 Closing date for 31 July 2010 draw is 30 June 2010. Closing date for 31 January 2011 draw is 31 December 2010.

2 Restricted to entries with UK and Eire addresses only. BPP employees, their families and business associates are excluded.

3 No purchase necessary. Entry forms are available upon request from BPP Learning Media Ltd. No more than one entry per title, per person. Draw restricted to persons aged 16 and over.

4 Winners will be notified by post and receive their cheques not later than 6 weeks after the relevant draw date.

5 The decision of the promoter in all matters is final and binding. No correspondence will be entered into.